The Unity of Consciousness

The Unity of Consciousness

Tim Bayne

OXFORD
UNIVERSITY PRESS

OXFORD

UNIVERSITY PRESS

Great Clarendon Street, Oxford OX2 6DP

Oxford University Press is a department of the University of Oxford.
It furthers the University's objective of excellence in research, scholarship,
and education by publishing worldwide in

Oxford New York

Auckland Cape Town Dar es Salaam Hong Kong Karachi
Kuala Lumpur Madrid Melbourne Mexico City Nairobi
New Delhi Shanghai Taipei Toronto

With offices in

Argentina Austria Brazil Chile Czech Republic France Greece
Guatemala Hungary Italy Japan Poland Portugal Singapore
South Korea Switzerland Thailand Turkey Ukraine Vietnam

Oxford is a registered trade mark of Oxford University Press
in the UK and in certain other countries

Published in the United States
by Oxford University Press Inc., New York

© Tim Bayne 2010

British Library Cataloguing in Publication Data

Data available

Library of Congress Cataloging in Publication Data

Data available

Typeset by SPI Publisher Services, Pondicherry, India
Printed in Great Britain
on acid-free paper by
MPG Books Group, Bodmin and King's Lynn

ISBN 978–0–19–921538–6

1 3 5 7 9 10 8 6 4 2

For Nishat

Contents

Preface

One incurs a great number of debts in writing a book. Each of the following individuals provided me with crucial assistance at some point, and I am extremely grateful to them all: Ned Block, Stephen Braude, Alex Byrne, Stephanie Carlson, Philippe Chuard, Andy Clark, Axel Cleeremans, Mike Corballis, Jillian Craigie, Martin Davies, Jérôme Dokic, Christof Koch, Uriah Kriegel, Daniel Farnham, Daniel Friedrich, Rami Gabriel, Alvin Goldman, Jakob Hohwy, Susan Hurley, Graham Jamieson, Joseph Jedwab, Mark Johnston, Sid Kouider, Tim Lane, Neil Levy, Caleb Liang, Fiona Macpherson, Chris Maloney, Farid Masrour, Peter Menzies, David Milner, Elisabeth Pacherie, Joseph Perner, Hanna Pickard, David Rosenthal, Gaia Scerif, Tobias Schlicht, Nicholas Shea, Christopher Shields, Henry Shevlin, Jeroen Smeets, Houstin Smit, Charles Spence, Maja Spener, John Sutton, Frédérique de Vignemont, Patrick Wilken, Ernan Zaidel and Adam Zeman.

I am also grateful to a number of institutions for their support. The *Centre for Consciousness Studies* at the *Australian National University* and the *Institut Jean Nicod, CNRS* (Paris) provided financial assistance for the research that forms the basis of Chapters 8 and 9 respectively. Support of another kind was provided by *C1, Café Boréal, Café Cubana, The Cup, Ecabur, Hernandez, The Lemon & Onion Café, The Missing Bean, Pablo's Vice, Raging Sage* and *Toby's Estate*. Thanks for the coffee.

There are a number of people to whom I owe a special debt of gratitude. Andrew Brook, Barry Dainton, Ian Phillips, and Lizzie Schechter each provided me with a very useful set of comments on the entire manuscript, in some cases at very short notice. Jerry Levy and Colwyn Trevarthen answered numerous questions about their split-brain research and provided the figures for Chapter 9. Stuart Crutchfield and Oliver Rashbrook provided invaluable assistance as I was preparing the volume for publication. My editor, Peter Momtchiloff, nudged me just when I needed it, and Elmandi Du Toit shepherded me through the production process. My parents, Andrew and Bridget Bayne, taught me to read and write, and—many years later—dissuaded me from opening a bagel shop. Harvey Brown invited me to lunch at Wolfson and reminded me that books are never finished but only abandoned; without that remark, this book would indeed have been abandoned. David Chalmers supervised the dissertation out of which this book developed and has been a tremendous source of encouragement and inspiration ever since. His influence on my thinking has been immeasurable.

But my deepest thanks go to Nishat, who not only took the photograph that graces the cover but also put up with me whilst I was struggling to write the pages that lie behind it. I dedicate this volume to her with all my love.

Some of the material that appears in this book has appeared in publication elsewhere:

Bayne, T. 2000. The Unity of Consciousness: Clarification and Defense, *Australasian Journal of Philosophy*, 78: 248–54.

Bayne, T. 2004. Self-Consciousness and the Unity of Consciousness, *The Monist*, 87/2: 224–41.

Bayne, T. 2005. Divided Brains & Unified Phenomenology: A Review Essay on Michael Tye's 'Consciousness and Persons', *Philosophical Psychology*, 18/4: 495–512.

Bayne, T. and Chalmers, D. 2003. What is the Unity of Consciousness?, in A. Cleeremans (ed.) *The Unity of Consciousness*. Oxford: Oxford University Press (pp. 23–58).

Bayne, T. and Dainton, B. 2005. Consciousness as a Guide to Personal Persistence, *Australasian Journal of Philosophy*, 83/4: 549–71.

Bayne, T. 2007. Hypnosis and the Unity of Consciousness, in G. Jamieson (ed.), *Hypnosis and Conscious States*. Oxford: Oxford University Press (pp. 93–109).

Bayne, T. 2007. Conscious States and Conscious Creatures: Explanation in the Scientific Study of Consciousness, *Philosophical Perspectives 21 (Philosophy of Mind)*: 1–22.

Bayne, T. 2008. The Unity of Consciousness and the Split-Brain Syndrome, *The Journal of Philosophy*, 105/6: 277–300.

Note to the Reader

No one has time to read a *whole book* these days, especially not one as long as this. Here is some advice for those looking to dip into this book. Readers interested in the analysis of the unity of consciousness would be advised to read Chapters 1 through 3, in that order. Readers interested in the question of whether consciousness remains unified in the context of particular syndromes—say, hypnosis or the split-brain syndrome—would be advised to skim Chapters 1 and 5 before turning to the chapter (or part thereof) in which the syndrome of interest is examined. Readers interested in the connection between the unity of consciousness and theories of consciousness should read Chapters 1 and 5 before turning to Chapter 10. Finally, readers with an interest in the relationship between the unity of consciousness and the self would be advised to focus on Chapters 1 and 12, but might also wish to browse Chapters 4 and 11.

. . . in so far as we have only one simple thought about a given object at any one time, there must necessarily be some place where the two images coming through the two eyes, or the two impressions coming from a single object through the double organs of any other sense, can come together in a single image or impression before reaching the soul, so that they do not present to it two objects instead of one. We can easily understand that these images or other impressions are unified in this gland by means of the spirits which fill the cavities of the brain.

René Descartes, *The Passions of the Soul*

PART I. FOUNDATIONS

1

The Phenomenal Field

'Consciousness', as William James noted, 'is of a teeming multiplicity of objects and relations' (James 1890/1950: 219). James was right: consciousness does present us with a teeming multiplicity of objects and relations. But as James also recognized, in presenting us with a teeming multiplicity of objects and relations consciousness itself remains unified. This book is about that unity—the 'unity of consciousness'.

My treatment of the unity of consciousness is a tale told in three acts. The first act unfolds over Chapters 1 to 3 and is concerned with questions of *analysis*. Some theorists assert that consciousness is unified—indeed, that it is necessarily unified. Others hold that although consciousness is typically unified there are conditions in which this unity is lost. Still others assert that consciousness is generally disunified. Without a clear conception of what it might mean to say that consciousness is unified we cannot be sure what exactly is at stake in this dispute—indeed, we cannot be sure that it is substantive rather than merely verbal. In order to articulate competing conceptions of the unity of consciousness we need to first identify the various unity relations that can be found within consciousness. That task forms the focus of this chapter. I single out *phenomenal unity* as the most fundamental of the various unity relations that permeate consciousness. With the notion of phenomenal unity in hand I go on to advance an analysis of what it might mean to say that consciousness is unified. I call this claim the *unity thesis*. Roughly speaking, the unity thesis is the claim that a human being can have only a single stream of consciousness at any one point in time. The unity thesis forms the backbone of this project.

The second act unfolds across Chapters 4 to 9, and is concerned with the question of whether the unity thesis is true. In Chapter 4 I provide some initial motivation for the unity thesis, arguing that first-person acquaintance with consciousness provides us with reason to take it seriously. But this prima facie case in favour of the unity thesis must be weighed against evidence for thinking that the unity of consciousness can break down. In order to evaluate that evidence we need a suitable framework. I develop such a framework in Chapter 5; subsequent chapters apply this framework to a variety of findings—drawn from both normal and abnormal forms of consciousness—that might be taken to show that consciousness is not always unified. Chapter 6 examines potential counter-examples to the unity thesis that are drawn from the study of perceptual experience (§6.1); behavioural control in infants and young children (§6.2); and patients in minimally responsive states (§6.3 and §6.4). Chapter 7 examines the case for thinking that the unity of consciousness might be lost in the clinical syndromes of anosognosia (§7.1), schizophrenia (§7.2), and dissociative identity disorder (§7.3). And Chapters 8 and 9 address objections to the unity thesis that derive from the study of hypnosis and the split-brain syndrome respectively. The conclusion of this section of the volume is that the unity thesis remains unrefuted by these conditions.

The final act is concerned with implications of the unity thesis and tidies up some loose ends. In Chapter 10 I suggest that the unity of consciousness has important—and widely overlooked—implications for theorizing about consciousness. If consciousness is indeed necessarily unified, then models that take specific, fine-grained states of consciousness as the fundamental units of consciousness must be rejected in favour of holistic models that begin with the subject's overall conscious state. In Chapter 11 I explore certain points of contact between the unity of consciousness and the experience of embodiment, and I argue against the claim that the unity of consciousness might be grounded in the phenomenology of bodily self-consciousness. The volume closes with Chapter 12, in which I argue that prominent approaches to the self must be rejected on the grounds that they fail to account for the essential link between the unity of consciousness and the self. In their place I sketch a view of the self that does do justice to this link.

So, that's where we are going. First, however, the central characters in our play must be introduced.

1.1 Consciousness

This is a book about the unity of consciousness rather than consciousness per se, but one's view of the unity of consciousness cannot but be informed by one's view of consciousness itself. In this section I present the framework that I adopt in thinking about consciousness. This framework is restricted to what we might think of as the 'surface' features of consciousness. Importantly, it does not make any assumptions about the 'deep' nature of consciousness, such as the relationship between consciousness and the physical world. I do assume that conscious states are grounded in neural states, but I will make few controversial assumptions about the nature of this grounding relation.

The notion of consciousness that I am interested in here is that of *phenomenal* consciousness. Phenomenal consciousness is the kind of consciousness that a creature enjoys when there is 'something that it is like' for that creature to be the creature that it is (Farrell 1950; Nagel 1974). Phenomenal consciousness—and only phenomenal consciousness—brings with it an experiential perspective or point of view. There is something that it is like for me to be me, and—I presume—there is something that it is like for you to be you. An account of consciousness is nothing more nor less than an account of what is involved in having such a point of view.

Creatures, of course, are never *merely* conscious; instead, they are conscious in particular ways. Many of these ways involve what I will call *specific conscious states*. Specific conscious states can be distinguished from each other by reference to their phenomenal character (or 'content'). Here's a description, as I remember it, of some of the specific conscious states that I enjoyed during a short episode of consciousness some years ago:

I'm sitting in the Café Cubana (47 Rue Vavin, Paris). I have auditory experiences of various kinds: I can hear the bartender making a mojito; I can hear the dog behind me chasing his tail; and there's a rumba song playing somewhere on a stereo. I am enjoying visual experiences of various kinds: I can see these words as they appear in my notebook; I can see the notebook itself; and I have a blurry visual impression of those parts of the room that lie behind the notebook. Co-mingled with these auditory and visual experiences are olfactory experiences of various kinds (I can smell something roasting in the kitchen); bodily sensations of various kinds (I am aware of my legs under my chair; I can feel my fingers on the table); and a range of cognitive and affective experiences. The bartender is talking to an old woman at the bar, and I have a vague sense of understanding what he's saying. I am soon to embark on a lengthy trip, and a sense of anticipation colours my current experiential state. Finally, I am enjoying conscious thoughts. I realize that the bar is about to close, and that I will be asked to leave if I stay for much longer.

Despite its detailed nature, this vignette barely touches on the tremendous variety of conscious state types that can be found within the stream of consciousness. There are experiences within the five familiar perceptual modalities. There are bodily sensations of various kinds, each with its distinctive phenomenal character. Staying within the sensory realm, there are conscious states associated with imagery and memory, not to mention the conscious states associated with various kinds of affect. There is the phenomenology of both directed and undirected moods and emotions. Moving from the sensory to the cognitive we can identify states of 'fringe' phenomenology, such as tip-of-the-tongue and déjà vu experiences. There are various experiential states associated with agency, such as the feeling that one is in control of one's movements. And there are conscious thoughts of familiar kinds, such as desire, intention, and judgement. There are clearly a vast number of ways in which one can be conscious.

Although few would disagree with the claim that consciousness manifests itself in many forms, many would reject the claim that all forms of consciousness are forms of *phenomenal* consciousness. According to a number of theorists, we need to distinguish those conscious states that are phenomenally conscious from those that are conscious in some other sense of the term. Theorists who hold this view typically regard bodily sensations, perceptual experiences, and affective experiences (plus or minus a bit) as modes of phenomenal consciousness, but they deny that thoughts are ever phenomenally conscious *as such*. These theorists usually allow that conscious thoughts are *accompanied* by various phenomenally conscious states—inner speech and visualization of various kinds, for example—but they deny that thoughts themselves are modes of phenomenal consciousness—that they have a distinctive or proprietary phenomenal character in the way that bodily sensations or perceptual states do. This conservative view of the reach of phenomenal consciousness can be contrasted with a *liberal* perspective. Liberals hold that conscious thoughts possess a 'what it's likeness' in precisely the same sense in which perceptual states and bodily sensations do. There is, the liberal insists, something that it is like to get a joke, to be puzzled about a problem, and to see that an argument is fallacious. According to this perspective, it is simply a mistake to restrict the domain of the phenomenal to the sensory. Sensory states may be among the most obvious and arresting examples of phenomenal consciousness, but the sensory does not exhaust the domain of the phenomenal.[1]

The contrast between these two views has a vital bearing on approaches to the unity of consciousness. From the liberal perspective it is natural to expect that there will be a single account of the unity of consciousness that might accommodate conscious states of all stripes, although liberals might allow that this account will be 'supplemented' by subsidiary analyses that apply only to restricted classes of phenomenal states (say, perceptually conscious states). Conservatives, by contrast, have no reason to expect any single approach to do the 'heavy lifting' in accounting for 'the' unity of consciousness, for the conservative denies that conscious states form a unified category. Instead, the conservative is likely to expect at least two accounts of the unity of consciousness:

---

[1] For conservatism see e.g. Carruthers (2005); Lormand (1996); Nelkin (1989); Prinz (2011); Robinson (2005); Tye & Wright (2011); for liberalism see Flanagan (1992); Horgan & Tienson (2002); Kriegel (2007); Pitt (2004); Siewert (1998); Strawson (1994).

one that applies to *phenomenally* conscious states and another that applies to *non-phenomenally* conscious states. Indeed, conservatives are likely to also need a third account of the unity of consciousness in order to accommodate the unity that holds between phenomenally conscious states and non-phenomenally conscious states.

The debate between conservatism and liberalism is a complicated one, and I will not attempt to settle it here. (That's a job for another book—see Bayne & Montague 2011.) Instead, I will simply assume that liberalism is true. In other words, I will take 'phenomenal consciousness' to be pleonastic: *all* consciousness is phenomenal consciousness. I use the terms 'conscious', 'experiential', and 'phenomenal' as synonyms, and my choice of one term over another is made on purely stylistic grounds. Conservatives are advised to take note of this fact, for some of the arguments in the following chapters—particularly those in Chapter 2—assume liberalism.

A final dimension of consciousness involves what are variously known as 'background states' or 'levels' of consciousness. The notion can perhaps be best introduced by means of examples. Consider the contrast between being conscious in the context of the normal waking state on the one hand and being conscious in the context of extreme drowsiness, delirium, hypnosis, or REM dreaming on the other. Over and above the fine-grained differences in conscious contents that might accompany this contrast, it will also be characterized by differences in the overall 'tone' of one's conscious state. One's general conscious state will be modulated in one way in the context of normal wakefulness and a very different way in the context of (say) extreme drowsiness.

Although widely recognized, the notion of a background conscious state has not received the critical attention that it deserves, and it is something of an open question how best to conceptualize it. I think that such states are best thought of as regions in a complex state-space, the parameters of which determine both the selection and functional roles of the subject's specific conscious states (or 'contents'). Consider first the role that background states play in the selection of specific conscious states. Although some types of conscious states can occur within the context of various background states—for example, one can have a pinprick experience whilst normally awake, dreaming, or hypnotized—others are restricted to particular background states. The kinds of conscious reflection and thought that are possible within the state of normal, 'clear' wakefulness are not to be found within the states of 'clouded consciousness' that occur in delirium or REM sleep. Moreover, where a specific conscious state (or 'content') can occur in the context of different background states it might play quite different functional roles. The ways in which a specific conscious state can be employed in the control of thought and action will depend on the background conscious state of the creature in question. Subjects who are in a state of normal wakefulness might be able to employ the contents of their specific conscious states in the service of multiple forms of cognitive and behavioural control, whereas subjects who are (say) delirious might be able to employ the contents of their specific conscious states in only a restricted range of cognitive and behavioural tasks.

Within the neuroscientific and clinical literatures the contrast between different background states of consciousness is often referred to as a contrast between different 'levels' of consciousness. In my view the term 'levels' should be avoided, for it suggests that differences between background states of consciousness can be mapped onto differences in *degrees* of consciousness. This assumption is problematic. Someone who has made the transition from the state of delirium to the normal waking state might be conscious *of* more than they were before, but they are not thereby *more conscious* than they were before. In this respect being conscious resembles being alive. In the same way that it is not possible for one creature to be more alive than another, so too it is not possible for one creature to be more conscious than another. (This is so even if there are cases in which there is no fact of the matter as to whether or not a creature is conscious.) That being said, talk of levels does point to the fact that background states can be ordered in some kind of rough hierarchy according to the kinds of specific conscious states that they admit and the functional roles that they support. Ordinary waking consciousness involves a 'higher' level of consciousness than that which is seen in (say) delirium, for not only does ordinary wakefulness admit forms of consciousness that do not occur within the context of delirium (such as self-conscious thought), it also involves forms of cognitive and behavioural control that are not to be found within delirium. However, in recognizing that these background states can be ordered in this way we should avoid the temptation to think that those in the state of ordinary wakefulness are more conscious than those who are delirious.

Let us recap. I have distinguished three broad 'aspects' of phenomenal consciousness. We might call the first of these three aspects 'creature consciousness'. As I use it, this term does not pick out a particular *kind* of consciousness that might be contrasted with phenomenal consciousness, but merely refers to the most general (or 'determinable') property associated with consciousness: the property of being phenomenally conscious. Creature consciousness takes two kinds of determinates: background conscious states and specific conscious states. Background states of consciousness can be contrasted with each other in terms of the kinds of conscious states that they admit and the functional roles that those states play within the subject's cognitive economy. Specific states of consciousness can be contrasted with each other in terms of their phenomenal character (or 'content')—that is, what it is like to be in them. As we will see, in accounting for the unity of consciousness we will need to take all three aspects of consciousness into consideration.

1.2 Unity relations

I turn now from consciousness per se to the various unities that structure consciousness. This section provides an introduction to the central unity relations with which I will be concerned in this book. I will return to each of these notions at various points in later chapters.

Subject unity

The self or subject of experience provides one form of unity to be found within consciousness. My conscious states possess a certain kind of unity insofar as they are all mine; likewise, your conscious states possess that same kind of unity insofar as they are all yours. We can describe conscious states that are had by or belong to the same subject of experience as *subject unified*. Within subject unity we need to distinguish the unity provided by the subject of experience across time (diachronic unity) from that provided by the subject at a time (synchronic unity). In keeping with my focus on the unity of consciousness at a time, references to subject unity should be taken as picking out synchronic subject unity unless otherwise specified.

The notion of subject unity is a formal one, and just what the notion amounts to materially will depend in no small part on how the subject of experience (or self) is understood. We need to ask what role the notion of a subject of experience might play within our conceptual scheme, and what kind of thing might actually play that role. There is famously little agreement with respect to these questions. It would be an exaggeration to claim that there are as many conceptions of the subject of experience as there are theorists who have written on the topic, but it would not be much of an exaggeration. Some theorists regard selves as immaterial substances or souls. Other theorists regard selves as brains or some part thereof. Still others regard selves as psychological networks that are realized in or constituted by brains but are in principle distinct from them. Yet another approach conceives of the self as a kind of virtual entity, albeit one that may play an indispensable role in theoretical and practical reason. A final approach identifies selves—at least the kind of selves that we are—with organisms.

In the final chapter I will argue that we ought to think of the self in virtual terms. However, for the majority of this project I will employ an organismic (or biological) conception of the self, according to which the self is nothing other than an organism—in our case, the human animal. Adopting this conception of the self provides a particularly useful framework in which to explore questions relating to the unity of consciousness. Unlike other conceptions of the self, the biological account enables us to determine the boundaries between selves with relative ease.

Representational unity

A second kind of unity to be found within consciousness concerns not the subject of conscious states but their 'objects' or 'intentional contents'. Let us say that conscious states are *representationally unified* to the degree that their contents are integrated with each other. Representational unity comes in a variety of forms. A particularly important form of representational unity concerns the integration of the contents of consciousness around perceptual objects—what we might call 'object unity'. Perceptual features are not normally represented by isolated states of consciousness but are bound together in the form of integrated perceptual objects. This process is known as *feature-binding*. Feature-binding occurs not only within modalities but also between them, for we enjoy multimodal representations of perceptual objects. Representational unity extends beyond perceptual objects to include the perceptual fields in which those objects are located. As Kant emphasized, one experiences the objects of perception as bearing determinate spatial relations, both to each other and to oneself. So, representational unity involves multiple layers of structure: features are bound together into objects, and objects are bound together into scenes.

Representational unity isn't restricted to the contents of perceptual states but can also be found within conscious thought. A set of thoughts that is consistent with each other is more representationally unified than a set of thoughts that is not; and a set of thoughts that is both consistent and structured around a common theme is even more representationally unified than a set of thoughts that is merely consistent. Self-consciousness and various forms of metacognitive monitoring bring with them additional opportunities for representational unity and disunity. We might say that a creature enjoys representationally unified states to the extent that it has an accurate awareness of its own first-order states of consciousness, and that it enjoys representationally disunified experiences to the extent that it misrepresents its own first-order states of consciousness.

Phenomenal unity

Subject unity and representational unity capture important aspects of the unity of consciousness, but they don't get to the heart of the matter. Consider again what it's like to hear a rumba playing on the stereo whilst seeing a bartender mix a mojito. These two experiences might be subject unified insofar as they are both yours. They might also be representationally unified, for one might hear the rumba as coming from behind the bartender. But over and above these unities is a deeper and more primitive unity: the fact that these two experiences possess a *conjoint experiential character*. There is something it is like to hear the rumba, there is something it is like to see the bartender work, and there is something it is like to hear the rumba *while* seeing the bartender work. Any description of one's overall state of consciousness that omitted the fact that these experiences are had together as components, parts, or elements of a single conscious state would be incomplete. Let us call this kind of unity—sometimes dubbed 'co-consciousness'—*phenomenal unity.*

Phenomenal unity is often in the background in discussions of the 'stream' or 'field' of consciousness. The stream metaphor is perhaps most naturally associated with the flow of consciousness—its unity through time—whereas the field metaphor more accurately captures the structure of consciousness at a time. We can say that what it is for a pair of experiences to occur within a single phenomenal field *just is* for them to enjoy a conjoint phenomenality—for there to be something it is like for the subject in question not only to have both experiences but to have them *together.* By contrast, simultaneous experiences that occur within distinct phenomenal fields do not share a conjoint phenomenal character. This claim is stipulative. It is not to be taken as a substantive thesis about the relationship between phenomenal unity and the phenomenal field, but as a way of fleshing out the notion of phenomenal unity.

Although there is no denying that phenomenal unity is a puzzling feature of consciousness, I take the existence of some such relation to be beyond doubt. The multiplicity of objects and relations that we experience at any one point in time are not experienced in isolation from each other; instead, our experiences of them occur as components, aspects, or elements of more inclusive states of consciousness. It is this fact—however exactly it is to be understood—that the notion of phenomenal unity attempts to capture. I will say much more about phenomenal unity in the following chapters, but I trust that the foregoing suffices to provide readers with an initial grip on the notion.

1.3 Conceptions of the unity of consciousness

Although it is common to speak of *the* unity of consciousness, this locution can be misleading. As we have noted, multiple unity relations can be discerned within consciousness, and it is possible to draw on each of these relations to construct a conception of what it would be for consciousness to be unified. Indeed, various conceptions of the unity of consciousness *have* been constructed from these relations. We will get to these conceptions of the unity of consciousness shortly, but let us first reflect on what we might want from a conception of the unity of consciousness.

What we want—or at least, what *I* want—is a thesis that might capture the thought that the simultaneous experiences of a single subject must bear some kind of unity relation to each other. We might call such a thesis 'the unity thesis'. Ideally, we want our unity thesis to have three properties. First, it must be substantive. If true it must not be a trivial truth. Secondly, it must be plausible. There is no point in exploring the viability of a unity thesis that has little chance of being true. Thirdly, it must be interesting—it must have the potential to significantly inform our understanding of consciousness. Let us examine some candidate unity theses with these desiderata in mind.

Some theorists conceive of the unity of consciousness in terms of the representational integration of its contents. Baars adopts a somewhat defla- tionary version of this approach, claiming that the unity of consciousness is the thesis that 'the flow of conscious experience ... is limited to a single internally consistent content at any given moment' (Baars 1993: 285). Drawing on a more expansive conception of the representational structure of consciousness, Shoemaker suggests that the 'unity of consciousness is in part a matter of one's various beliefs forming, collectively, a unified conception of the world' (Shoemaker 1996: 184). He goes on to say that 'perfect' unity of consciousness 'would consist of a unified representation of the world accompanied by a unified representation of that representation' (1996: 186).

What should we make of these conceptions of the unity of consciousness? It is pretty clear that Baars' conception of the unity of consciousness does not provide us with a plausible unity thesis. Although perceptual experience does exhibit some kind of drive towards consistency, there is good reason to think that a single subject of experience can enjoy conscious states that are inconsis- tent with each other (see §3.2). For example, the visual experiences that one enjoys on looking at the two lines of a Müller-Lyer illusion might be at odds with one's judgements about their relative lengths. And even if it were true that the contents of a creature's simultaneous conscious states must be consistent with each other, this conception of the unity of consciousness would lack the scope that we might want from a robust conception of the unity of conscious- ness, for at best consistency is only a necessary condition on unity.

What about Shoemaker's suggestion that the unity of consciousness can be thought of in terms of representational integration? This certainly captures *a* viable notion of the unity of consciousness. The conscious states of some subjects of experience will exhibit more representational integration than others, and it would be natural to describe a subject whose conscious states exhibited a high degree of representational unity as having a more unified consciousness than a subject whose conscious states exhibited a low degree of representational unity. But although Shoemaker's conception of the unity of consciousness might be suitable for some purposes, it does not suit our purposes for it does not capture a conception of the unity of consciousness according to which it is plausible to suppose that the simultaneous experiences of a single subject are necessarily unified. This is because it is possible for a subject to have conscious states that exhibit very little in the way of representational integration (see §6.3). Suitably qualified, representational unity might provide us with some kind of regulative ideal on consciousness, but it does not provide us with a constraint on unity that every subject of experience must meet.

Another version of the representational approach to the unity of consciousness appeals to self-consciousness. Rosenthal holds that the 'so-called unity of consciousness consists in the compelling sense we have that all our conscious mental states belong to a single conscious subject' (2003: 325). This claim suggests a certain conception of what it is for consciousness to be unified, according to which it is a necessary truth that any subject of experience will be aware of their conscious states *as* their own conscious states. As his use of the term 'so-called' suggests, Rosenthal himself does not think that consciousness is unified in this sense, but his approach might nonetheless provide us with a viable analysis of what it would be for consciousness to be unified.

This conception of the unity of consciousness certainly captures an important aspect of the unity of consciousness. It gives us a substantive conception of the unity of consciousness, for it is no trivial truth that subjects will always experience each of their conscious states as their own states. It also provides us with an interesting conception of the unity of consciousness, for if consciousness were unified in this sense then we would have an important constraint on theories of consciousness. But does it also provide us with a conception of the unity of consciousness according to which it might be plausible to suppose that consciousness is necessarily unified?

Opinions will differ on this point. Those theorists who hold that all conscious states involve some kind of self-consciousness may be inclined to think that it captures a sense in which consciousness might be necessarily unified. But those theorists who doubt whether consciousness necessarily involves any form of self-consciousness—even one that might be 'implicit' or 'pre-reflective'—are very unlikely to think that this captures a sense of the unity of consciousness that might hold necessarily. This suggests that Rosenthal's conception of the unity of consciousness does not capture the basal phenomenon that we are after. We want a conception of the unity of consciousness that might be endorsed even by those who deny that subjects of experiences are invariably aware of their conscious states as their conscious states.

It might be suggested that a plausible modification of Rosenthal's conception of the unity of consciousness can be found by drawing on Kant's famous claim that 'it must be possible for the "I think" to accompany all my representations' (1781/1787/1999: B131-2). Just what Kant really meant by 'the unity of consciousness' is notoriously obscure, but we might take him to have held that the members of a set of conscious states are unified with each other exactly when the subject of those states is *able* to self-ascribe them.[2] Might *this* conception of the unity of consciousness be the one that we are after?

The first question to ask is just what this Kantian conception of the unity involves. Does it require that the subject in question be able to self-ascribe its conscious states right *here and now*, or does it require only that the subject be able to self-ascribe its conscious states under certain *idealized* conditions? Does it require that those conscious states must be *conjointly* self-ascribable, or does it require only that they be *individually* self-ascribable? Whatever the answers to these questions, it seems unlikely that this conception of the unity of consciousness will do a better job of meeting our desiderata than Rosenthal's conception did. Although the Kantian conception of the unity of consciousness is both substantive and interesting, it too fails to capture a thesis that might be generally regarded as plausible. Those who deny that conscious states are always experienced as the subject's own states will often also deny that subjects are invariably in a position to self-ascribe their conscious states. Awake adults will typically be able to self-ascribe their conscious states but they might lose this capacity in the context of certain pathologies of consciousness. Moreover, young children and non-linguistic animals might not have ever had this capacity to begin with. The potential for self-ascription undoubtedly contributes to the rich sense of conscious unity that we enjoy, but it does not provide us with the basis for a conception of the unity of consciousness that meets the constraints that I have set out.

1.4 The unity thesis

The conception of the unity of consciousness that I am after has at its heart the notion of phenomenal unity. Consider again the vignette of my experience in the Parisian cafe (see p.5). Although it is something of an open question just how rich the stream of consciousness can be at any one point in time (see §4.1), let us suppose

---

[2] For discussion of Kant's conception of the unity of (self)-consciousness see Blackburn (1997), Brook (1994), Keller (1998), Powell (1990), and van Cleve (1999).

that there was a period during which I simultaneously enjoyed a visual experience of the bartender in front of me, an auditory experience of a rumba, a vague sense of embodiment, and a background experience of dull anxiety. Each of these experiential elements were, I suggest, phenomenally unified with each other within my overall phenomenal field. This unity was not something that I reflected on in enjoying this stream of experience—it was not itself an *object* of experience—but it was nonetheless a feature of my experience. Irrespective of their modality, each of the experiences that I was enjoying at a particular time were phenomenally unified with each other.

Let us say that a subject has a unified consciousness if, and only if, every one of their conscious states at the time in question is phenomenally unified with every other conscious state. We can think of such subjects as *fully unified*. Where a subject is fully unified, we can say that they enjoy a single *total conscious state*. A total conscious state is a state that is subsumed by nothing but itself, where one conscious state subsumes another if the former includes the latter as a 'part' or 'component'. This total state will capture what it is like to be the subject at the time in question. In specifying the subject's total conscious state one thereby provides a full specification of the subject's specific conscious states. By contrast, if we are dealing with a creature whose consciousness is disunified, then there will be no single conscious state that 'subsumes' each of their specific conscious states.

How common is it for human beings to have a unified consciousness in this sense of the term? Quite common, it seems to me. Take any set of conscious states that you are currently enjoying—visual experiences, auditory experiences, emotional experiences, bodily sensations, conscious thoughts, or whatever. Irrespective of the degree to which these states might be representationally unified with each other, they will—I wager—be mutually phenomenally unified with each other. You might not have been aware of this unity until I drew your attention to it, but having drawn your attention to it I trust that you recognize it in your own experience.

Generalizing somewhat, we might hazard the guess that unity in this sense is a deep feature of normal waking experience. Indeed, we might even go further, and suggest that this kind of unity is not just a feature of normal waking experience but also characterizes other kinds of background states of consciousness, such as those that are present in REM dreaming, hypnosis, and various pathologies of consciousness. One might even hazard the thought that this kind of unity is an *essential* feature of consciousness—one that it cannot lose (at least when it comes to creatures like us). As Searle puts it, 'all of the conscious experiences at any given point in an agent's life come as part of one unified conscious field' (Searle 2000: 562). Indeed, Kant himself gestures at this idea in referring to the 'one single experience in which all perceptions are represented' (1781/ 1787/1999: A110).

All of this leads directly to a conception of the unity of consciousness that can be captured by appeal to the following thesis (Bayne & Chalmers 2003).

> *Unity Thesis*: Necessarily, for any conscious subject of experience (*S*) and any time (*t*), the simultaneous conscious states that *S* has at *t* will be subsumed by a single conscious state—the subject's total conscious state.

Here, I think, we have found an acceptable characterization of the unity of consciousness. First, this thesis is substantive: if true, it is not trivially true. Secondly, this thesis is interesting, for it offers us an exacting constraint on theories of consciousness. Thirdly, it is plausible: although it faces plenty of hard cases (as we shall see), there are no obviously decisive counter-examples to it. All up, the unity thesis provides us with just what we have been looking for.

This analysis of the unity of consciousness provides us with a deeper analysis of the unity of consciousness than that which is provided by the representationally based approaches that we examined in the previous section. As we will see in the following chapters, there are many ways in which the representational unity of consciousness can break down. Patients who suffer from integrative agnosia no longer experience objects as unified and coherent wholes (see also §3.3). Patients who suffer from anosognosia have difficulty tracking the contents of their own conscious states (§7.1). And patients who suffer from certain dissociative disorders seem to have lost the sense that their conscious states are their own (§7.3). But despite the breakdowns in representational unity that characterize these conditions, there is every reason to suspect that patients might nonetheless retain a more primitive form of conscious unity. It is this kind of unity—the unity of the phenomenal field—that the unity thesis is concerned with.

Although we have located a viable conception of the unity of consciousness, we cannot bring this chapter to a close just yet, for the unity thesis raises three issues that require comment. The first of these issues concerns the notion of the subject of experience. It is clear that the plausibility of the unity thesis will depend in no small part on just how we conceive of subjects of experience. As I indicated earlier, I will work with an organismic conception of the subject, according to which subjects of experience are animals of a certain kind—in our case, human beings. We could of course employ some other conception of the subject of experience (see Chapter 12), but any other view would enormously complicate the task of assessing the unity thesis. So, in the interests of keeping the discussion manageable I will assume that we can count subjects of experience by counting human beings.

The second of the three issues that needs to be addressed concerns the kind of necessity that governs the unity thesis. In what sense is the unity of consciousness a necessary feature of human experience? I will argue that we *never* have disunified experiences. Not only do we retain a unified consciousness within normal everyday contexts, we retain this kind of unity even in the context of the most severe impairments of consciousness. The mechanisms underpinning consciousness function in such a way that the conscious states they generate always occur as the unified components of a single phenomenal field. However, I do not claim that it is a conceptual or metaphysical truth that our conscious states are always unified; indeed, I do not even claim that the unity of consciousness is grounded in the laws of nature. Perhaps there are surgical innovations or evolutionary developments that could bring about a division in the stream of consciousness; perhaps there are other species in which the unity of consciousness can be lost. My only claim is that we have no good reason to think that any such division has actually occurred in the members of our own species.

The third of the three outstanding issues concerns the temporal structure of consciousness. The unity thesis asserts that the simultaneous conscious states of a single subject will be phenomenally unified with each other. The idea, roughly, is that any 'instantaneous snapshot' of a subject's experience will reveal it to be fully unified (in the sense identified). Some will object to the idea that we might be able to take snapshots of the stream of consciousness, for—they might say— to do this would be to impose a static structure on something that is fundamentally dynamic and temporally extended. I think that this objection misses its target. Even if consciousness is essentially temporally extended, we can nonetheless take a slice of the stream of consciousness and investigate its internal structure. (What we cannot assume if consciousness is essentially dynamic is that the content and structure of the slice that we select is independent of the content and structure of the stream from which it is taken.) Taking the unity thesis seriously doesn't presuppose a naïvely static metaphysics of experience.

But what sort of time-slice should we take? The temporal structure of consciousness has two aspects. On the one hand, conscious events themselves (or their neural realizers) have locations in objective time. We can ask of any particular conscious event when it happened. This is the temporal structure of the *vehicles* of consciousness. On the other hand, conscious events also *represent* events as occurring at particular times. This is the temporal structure of the *contents* of consciousness. As Dennett and Kinsbourne (1992) pointed out, in principle the temporal relations between the vehicles of conscious events can dissociate from the temporal relations between their contents. The possibility of this kind of dissociation is most evident in the context of conscious thought, for it is obvious that the temporal content of a thought can come apart from the temporal location of the thought itself. But it is no less important to distinguish content from vehicle when it comes to perceptual experience. Consider two perceptual events, e_1 and e_2. In principle, e_1 might occur before e_2 even if the intentional object of e_1 is represented as happening after the intentional object of e_2 is represented as happening. Just as there is no *a priori* requirement that the brain use space to represent space, so too there is no *a priori* requirement that it use time to represent time. So, we need to ask whether the unity thesis is best understood in terms of the temporal structure of the vehicles of consciousness or in terms of the temporal structure of its content.

It is clear that the motivation behind the unity thesis is not captured by an appeal to the contents of conscious thought. Suppose that at 9 a.m. this morning I formed the intention to book some airline tickets at noon today, and that when noon arrived I remembered this intention and as a result booked some tickets. Now, the intention to book the tickets and the actual booking of the tickets all involved a reference to the same time (namely, noon), but it is clear that the conscious states involved in these processes were not phenomenally unified with each other. Furthermore, I might now remember that I booked the tickets at noon, and this memory would not be phenomenally unified with either the conscious intention to book them or the actual act of booking them. These states might (or might not) have occurred within the same temporally extended stream of consciousness, but there was no single phenomenal state that subsumed them all. This suggests that when it comes to conscious thought, the frame of reference that concerns us must be that of the states themselves rather than their contents. And indeed that is precisely how the unity thesis is formulated: the temporal framework in question is that of clock–time, not that of the contents of experience.

Although the distinction between the temporal structure of consciousness itself and that of its content is of deep theoretical interest, it will be of little direct concern to us here. There may be no *a priori* requirement that the brain use neural time to represent time, but in practice the experience of temporal relations is tightly constrained by the temporal relations between experiences themselves. In light of this, in the pages that follow I will frequently move back and forth between claims about simultaneous experiences on the one hand and claims about the experience of simultaneous events on the other.

1.5 Conclusion

There are many ways in which consciousness might be said to be unified—or, as the case may be, disunified. In some senses of 'unity' the claim that con-sciousness is necessarily unified is clearly implausible; in other senses of 'unity' it is well-nigh trivial. The main business of this chapter has been to identify a conception of the unity of consciousness according to which the claim that consciousness is unified is substantive, plausible, and of some interest.

I began the search for such a conception by first considering the central unity relations that structure consciousness: subject unity, representational unity, and phenomenal unity. Subject unity does not itself provide us with a conception of the unity of consciousness that we are after, for it is trivial that each of a subject's simultaneous conscious states will be subject unified with each other. Various forms of representational unity appeared to be more promising, and certainly many theorists have taken some form or another of representational unity to capture what it is for consciousness to be unified. However, I suggested that representational analyses of the unity of consciousness fail to provide us with what we are after. Instead, we were able to find a viable conception of the unity of consciousness by putting together the notions of subject unity and phenom-enal unity: what it is for a subject's consciousness to be unified is for each of their simultaneous conscious states to be phenomenally unified with each other. Putting the same point in different terminology, it is for the subject to have a single conscious state—a total conscious state—that subsumes each and every one of the conscious states that they enjoy at the time in question. We might identify this total conscious state with a phenomenal field. And what it is for 'consciousness itself' to be unified is, I suggested, for it to be the case that no human subject can have a disunified consciousness. This claim is encapsulated in the unity thesis.

The unity thesis is the gravitational centre around which the following chapters orbit, although some chapters are more tightly bound to that centre than others. Chapters 2 and 3 focus on the notion of phenomenal unity, and are somewhat independent of the unity thesis. Chapters 4 and 5 examine the unity thesis in the abstract: the former provides a first-person based case for taking the unity thesis seriously, while the latter provides a third-person framework for evaluating potential counter-examples to it. Chapters 6 through 9 apply this framework to a variety of phenomena drawn from the study of both normal and abnormal forms of experience. The remaining three chapters explore some of the implications of the unity thesis: for theories of consciousness (Chapter 10), treat-ments of embodiment (Chapter 11), and accounts of the self (Chapter 12).

2

Phenomenal Unity: Mereology

In the previous chapter I introduced the term 'phenomenal unity' for the relation of conjoint phenomenality—the unity relation that permeates experience and provides us with a plausible conception of what it is for consciousness to be unified. Discussions of the unity of consciousness often treat phenomenal unity (or 'co-consciousness', as it is sometimes called) as a primitive. That is perfectly fine for some purposes, but a thorough treatment of the unity of consciousness needs to give an account of phenomenal unity. My treatment of phenomenal unity comes in two instalments. This chapter develops and defends a mereological account of phenomenal unity, according to which conscious states are phenomenally unified in virtue of the fact that they occur as the parts of a single conscious state. The following chapter examines the question of whether phenomenal unity can (also) be understood in terms of relations between the representational contents of consciousness.

2.1 The mereological model

In seeking to account for phenomenal unity it is natural to invoke the notion of subsumption (Bayne & Chalmers 2003). We might say that two conscious states are phenomenally unified when, and only when, they are co-subsumed. What it is to experience a headache and the sound of a trumpet together—what it is for these two experiences to possess a 'conjoint phenomenal character'—is for there to be a single experience that in some way includes both the experience of the headache and that of the trumpet. Whereas treating phenomenal unity as a primitive provides us with a 'bottom-up' approach to the unity of consciousness, one that starts with the multiplicity in consciousness, taking subsumption as our primitive is to adopt a 'top-down' approach to the unity of consciousness and begin with the unity that subsumes this multiplicity.

How should we think of subsumption? It is tempting to think of it in mereological terms—that is, in terms of parts and wholes. What it is for one experience to subsume another is for the former to contain the latter as a part. My total experiential state is a whole that includes within itself various experiential parts, such as my overall perceptual experience, my overall auditory experience, and my experience of the diesel trucks outside my window. One's overall phenomenal field is an experience that contains within itself other experiences, nestled like Russian dolls within each other. Indeed, we might venture the thought that total phenomenal states are homoeomerous: all the parts of which they are composed share their experiential nature.

Mereological language is often used in connection with the unity of consciousness. To take just a couple of examples, Lockwood says that experiences are co-conscious 'when they are parts of a complex experience' (Lockwood 1989: 88); Siewert suggests that phenomenal unity 'normally relates the constituent experiences of a single "visual" field to one another, as well as those making up a single temporal "stream" of thought and imagery' (Siewert 2001: 548); while Shoemaker holds that 'conscious states are co-conscious when they are parts of a unified state of consciousness' (Shoemaker 2003: 59). But although the mereological approach has some claim to be regarded as the standard conception of phenomenal unity it has rarely been developed in any detail. The aim of this chapter is to do precisely that.

2.2 Experience: the tripartite account

The mereological view treats phenomenal unity as a relation between token experiences—that is, between particular mental states or events.[1] Some token experiences—such as my headache experience and my auditory experience of the trumpet—are parts of a single composite experience and hence phenomenally unified with each other; other token experiences—such as my experience of the trumpet and *your* experience of it—are not phenomenally unified with each other, for there is no experience that contains both of these experiences as parts.

This account is at odds with certain conceptions of experiences, such as that which Tye develops under the 'one-experience' label. According to Tye, the only experiences that human beings have are entire streams of consciousness, where a stream of consciousness is 'a period of consciousness between one state of unconsciousness and the next' (2003: 97). The mereological model would be untenable if Tye's conception of experience were right; in fact, Tye's account *entails* that no two experiences can be phenomenally unified with each other. Tye provides

---

[1] I do not invest anything in the distinction between states and events, and use one term rather than the other only on grounds of stylistic convenience.

both 'positive' and 'negative' arguments for his view. His negative arguments are intended to undermine the appeal of 'subsumptive' approaches to phenomenal unity. I examine those arguments in §2.3. Here, I focus on the positive motivation that he provides for identifying experiences with entire streams of consciousness.[2]

Tye's conception of experience is *revisionary*. It is not an analysis of our pre-theoretical notion of experience, for ordinary thought has no difficulty in taking a stream of consciousness to contain multiple experiences, both at a time and through time. This fact doesn't mean that it should be rejected—after all, revisionary analyses can be well motivated—but it does mean that his proposal starts off on the back foot: we should identify experiences with streams of consciousness only if there are good reasons to do so.

Central to Tye's case for the one-experience view is a supposed parallel between experiences on the one hand and clouds and statues on the other (2003: 30, 99). Clouds contain undetached collections of water molecules as proper parts, but such collections are not (typically) themselves clouds. Similarly, statues of clay may contain as proper parts undetached chunks of clay, but such chunks don't (typically) constitute statues in their own right. Tye grants that experiences can have experiential 'stages', but he claims that experiential stages are no more bona fide experiences than undetached cloud parts are bona fide clouds or undetached parts of statues are bona fide statues.

I don't find this proposal persuasive. First, a picky point: although clouds (statues) don't typically contain clouds (statues) as proper parts, there is no principled reason to deny that they *could*. One can build a statue that contains other statues as parts. But Tye is certainly right to point out that we don't typically regard undetached regions of water molecules contained within clouds as clouds in their own right, nor do we regard undetached regions of clay contained within statues as statues in their own right. So why should we regard arbitrary components of a stream of consciousness as experiences in their own right?

Well, I'm not sure that we *should* regard every undetached component of a stream of consciousness as an experience in its own right. Consider the stream of consciousness that began when you woke up this morning and that will conclude when you fall into a dreamless sleep tonight. The component of this stream that occupied the first waking hour of your day is not itself an experience—at least not in the sense that I am considering here. I don't deny that there is *a* use of the term 'experience' that can be used to pick out arbitrarily large stretches of consciousness. ('Tell me about your time in the Gobi desert.' 'It was

---

[2] For further discussion of Tye's position see Bayne (2005) and Dainton (2004).

great—a really fantastic experience.') In this very broad sense of 'experience' the chunk of my stream of consciousness that occupied the first waking hour of today might indeed qualify as an experience in its own right. But this is not the notion of experience that I am after here. Experiences, as I am interested in them here, are states that can be enjoyed 'all at once'.

Nonetheless, although I would resist the claim that *every* part of a stream of experience is an experience in its own right, it does seem to me that *many* parts of a stream of experience qualify as experiences in their own right. My current conscious state is an experience in its own right, as are the various fine-grained conscious states—the pain in my left leg; my olfactory experience of the coffee; my auditory experience of the dog barking in the alley—that are contained within it.

We should not be misled by Tye's discussion of clouds and statues, for there are important differences between clouds and statues on the one hand and experiences on the other. For one thing, clouds and statues are physical objects, whereas experiences are events. Even if it is generally true that the proper parts of an *object* of kind K do not constitute objects of kind K in their own right (and there are exceptions to this generalization—consider computers), *events* often contain as proper parts events of the same kind. Arguments contain as proper parts other arguments, battles contain as proper parts other battles, traffic jams contain as proper parts other traffic jams, and stories can contain as proper parts other stories. (Consider *Hamlet*.)

Furthermore, there is usually little need to distinguish the parts of a cloud from each other or the parts of a statue from each other, but there is indeed some point in distinguishing the parts of a stream of consciousness from each other. For one thing, we need some way of referring to the distinct instances of a particular experiential type that occur within a single stream of consciousness. Consider again the stream of consciousness that began when you woke up this morning and will conclude when you fall into a dreamless sleep tonight. Now, suppose that this stream contains one instance of headache phenomenology at its beginning and another towards its end. It is natural to say that this stream of consciousness contains two headache experiences. Indeed, it becomes very difficult to describe the internal structure of a stream of consciousness if we insist on identifying experiences with entire streams of consciousness. Tye, of course, could say that such a stream of consciousness contains two stages that include headache phenomenology, but at this point his 'experiences stages' would appear to be experiences in all but name. I suppose that one could insist on distinguishing experiences from experiences stages, but I don't see anything to be gained from doing so. All in all, I see no reason to follow Tye in reserving the term 'experience' for entire streams of consciousness. In fact, on the conception of experiences that I will embrace, the typical stream of consciousness does *not* constitute an experience in its own right.

Tye's one-experience conception of consciousness can be set to one side, but it does raise the important question of how we should think of token experiences. I am not convinced that there is any single way in which experiences should be individuated. Counting experiences is arguably more like counting the number of objects in a room or the number of events that took place during a meeting than it is like counting the number of beans in a dish: one has some idea of how to go about one's business, but the idea that there is only one way in which to proceed is somewhat farcical. The notion of a token experience is elastic, and different approaches to the individuation of experiences might be appropriate in different contexts.

That said, I do think that there is one conception of experiences that is particularly well-suited for addressing the questions raised by the unity of consciousness: the *tripartite conception*. According to the tripartite conception of experience, experiences are to be individuated in terms of subjects of experience, times, and phenomenal properties.[3] In other words, token experiences must differ from each other in terms of whose experiences they are, when they occur, or the kinds of phenomenal properties that they involve. Although I have introduced the tripartite analysis by reference to phenomenal properties, we can also think of it in terms of phenomenal events, for events can be understood in terms of the instantiation of properties (Kim 1976).

There is a natural fit between the tripartite conception of experience and the mereological conception of phenomenal unity, for within the stream of consciousness we can identify both more and less complex experiences. An experience produced by tasting a strawberry will involve a range of distinct phenomenal properties, such as 'tanginess', 'sweetness', and—dare one say it—'strawberryness'. We can think of each of these phenomenal properties as involving distinct experiences that are parts of the more complex experience of tasting the strawberry. That experience, in turn, will be a part of even more complex experiences. Some of these more complex experiences will be modality-specific, others—such as the experience that corresponds to one's overall perceptual phenomenology—might include content drawn from multiple modalities. Indeed, one's overall phenomenal field—what it is like to be you right now—is, in

---

[3] The notion of temporal location that I am working with here allows both temporal points and brief periods of time. I suspect that there are no instantaneous experiences, but I see no reason to assume that here. By a brief period I mean something that is no longer than a specious present (however long that is).

my view, a very complex phenomenal event that contains within it the rest of one's experiential states.

According to this conception of experiences, not everything that has experiences as parts is itself an experience. The typical stream of consciousness—'a period of consciousness between one state of unconsciousness and the next'—is not best thought of as a phenomenal event, for there is no single phenomenal property that corresponds to a typical stream of consciousness. There is something it is like to enjoy a typical stream of consciousness, but this 'what it's likeness' is spread out—distributed across a number of distinct conscious states. It lacks the kind of unity that the phenomenal field possesses. (The only stream of consciousness that might qualify as a phenomenal event would be a very short stream—a stream whose duration was no longer than a single specious present.)

It might be objected that the tripartite account of experiences has counter-intuitive consequences—that it individuates experiences in ways that are significantly at odds with our ordinary ways of counting experiences. Of course, one might wonder just how much weight our pre-theoretical practices ought to be afforded here, but waiving that concern let us examine just what kind of friction there might be between the tripartite approach and 'common sense'.

Consider first colour experience. Suppose that you are experiencing a certain shade of blue. According to the tripartite account, there will be an experience corresponding to the event of your instantiating this phenomenal property. But, intuitively, one could have multiple experiences of blue at a single point in time, for one can see multiple objects and regions of space as being blue. Here, the tripartite account appears to entail that one would have only a single experience whereas there is some pre-theoretical force to the thought that one actually has multiple experiences of blue.

There are various ways in which we might respond to this objection, but perhaps the best response is to restrict the tripartite account to maximally specific or fine-grained phenomenal properties, where a phenomenal property is maximally specific if it has no determinates (Bayne & Chalmers 2003). The phenomenal property of blue is a determinable that has as determinates the phenomenal property of blue occurring in a certain location of space, but arguably this phenomenal property has no determinates. And there is an intuitive sense in which one couldn't have multiple instantiations of *that* phenomenal property. Once restricted to fine-grained, maximally determinate phenomenal properties the tripartite account faces no objection from this quarter.

Another objection to the tripartite account derives from considerations concerning the 'common sensibles'—that is, properties that can be detected via more than one modality. Consider a fundamental common sensible:

motion. Suppose that you are watching an ant crawl across your skin. You are aware of the ant's movement in two ways: via vision and via touch. Yet—the objection runs—although there are intuitively two experiences of motion here, the tripartite account entails that there is only a single experience, for there is only one phenomenal property in question: a representation of motion. It looks as though we will need to appeal to some further element over and above the three components of the tripartite model in order to account for the contrast between visual experiences of motion and tactile experiences of motion.

One line of response to this objection would be to argue that the visual experience of motion involves one phenomenal property while the tactile experience of motion involves another. Generalizing this response, we might say that when different senses represent the same property they will often do so via distinct ways—that phenomenal properties are more fine-grained than the worldly properties that they represent. This 'Fregean' conception of phenomenal properties will allow that experiences can be grouped into modality-specific clusters without putting any pressure on the tripartite account.[4]

Although the approach just outlined will have its advocates, I prefer a rather different response to it. I think the objection is best met by biting the bullet: in the situation outlined one *would* have only a single experience of the ant's motion. I'm inclined to think of phenomenal properties in 'Russellian' terms—that is, in terms of 'external world' properties such as motion itself.[5] On this view, what it is like to see the ant as moving at such-and-such a speed is identical to what it's like to feel it as moving at such-and-such a speed, for the two cases involve the representation of one and the same property—namely, movement at such-and-such a speed. On this view, the experience of the ant's motion is 'amodal' when considered in and of itself. Situations in which one is both visually and tactually aware of the ant's motion are not best described as situations in which one has two experiences of the ant's motion, but as situations in which one has a single experience of the ant's motion that is supported by two streams of perceptual processing (each of which is redundant given the presence of the other).

Of course, there *are* differences between seeing an ant move and feeling it move. For one thing, sight and touch will rarely have the same degree of resolution. Moreover, even if these two senses were to represent exactly the same speed of the ant, they would do so in the context of other modality-specific representations. For example, the visual representation of the ant's motion will occur in the context of a visual representation of its colour, whereas

---

[4] See e.g. Chalmers (2004), Thompson (2009), Kulvicki (2007).
[5] See e.g. Dretske (1995); Harman (1990); Tye (2003).

the tactile representation of the ant's motion will occur in the context of a representation of one's own body. In this way the Russellian can account for our ability to say whether an experience of an ant's motion is visual, tactile, or both visual and tactile. The upshot of the foregoing is that the tension between the tripartite analysis and our ordinary ways of counting experiences is more apparent than real.

Before concluding this section, let me contrast the tripartite approach with another approach to the individuation of experiences, an approach that is perhaps its natural rival. The approach in question appeals to the physical-functional basis of experience in order to segment the stream of consciousness into parts. To invoke a term that has some currency in the current literature, we might try to individuate experiences in terms of their *vehicles*.

Although there may be perspectives which demand a vehicular approach to the individuation of experience, I think we have reason to prefer the tripartite approach when it comes to questions concerned with the unity of consciousness. Experiential states are states of organisms—they are not states of hemispheres or parts of brains. There is, of course, a sub-personal account to be given of why a particular organism might enjoy experiential states at any one point in time, and of why it might enjoy the particular experiential states that it does, but we ought to be wary of the suggestion that the sub-personal features of consciousness might enter into their identity conditions. The unity of consciousness is an *experiential* aspect of consciousness, and our approach to it must take this fact seriously.

A second concern with vehicular approaches to consciousness is somewhat pragmatic in nature. Although there is much talk of the vehicular nature of consciousness, there are rather few worked-out accounts of just what the vehicles of experience are supposed to be or how one might go about pinning them down. The problem here is not (just) that we know so little about the neuro-functional basis of consciousness—although that certainly doesn't help—but that the very notion of a vehicle of consciousness remains obscure. On some accounts the vehicles of consciousness are identical to conscious states, and phenomenal properties are simply entities that those states 'carry'. On other accounts the vehicles of consciousness are not identical to experiences but they do constitute them or form their supervenience base. On still other accounts, vehicles are neuro-functional states that underwrite a certain kind of explanation of consciousness. Even within the explanatory conception of vehicles there are various positions that might be adopted, depending on the kind of explanation that one is looking for (Hurley 2010). Given this confusing welter of conceptions, it is very difficult to say just what a vehicular approach to the individuation of experiences might look like. Would it individuate experiences in fine-grained terms, say, according to perceptual qualities such as colour, shape, motion, timbre, and so on, or would it individuate experiences in coarse-grained terms, according to (say) perceptual objects, particular modalities, or indeed entire phenomenal fields? Not only do we lack good answers to these questions, it is rather unclear how we ought to go about determining the answers to them.

Certain readers might be inclined to respond that cognitive neuroscience has already identified the vehicles of consciousness. Don't we know—some may say—that V4 functions as the vehicle for the visual experience of shape (Pasupathy & Connor 1999, 2001); V4/V8 functions as the vehicle for the experience of colour (Bartels & Zeki 2000; Hadjikhani et al. 1998); and V4 (MT/MST) functions as the vehicle for the experience of motion (Tootell, Reppas, Dale, et al. 1995; Tootell, Reppas, Kwong, et al., 1995)? But whether indeed this is something that is known depends very much on just what vehicles are supposed to be. These regions may indeed play a particularly important role in the generation of states with the appropriate contents—for example, activation in V4 might explain why the creature in question is enjoying experiences of shape rather than some other type of experience—but we should not *identify* such experiences with activity in V4 (see also §10.5). Indeed, it is implausible to suppose that V4 activity is even sufficient for visual experiences (as) of shape. A slice of V4 that has been placed in a test tube won't generate visual experiences no matter how much current is run through it. I suspect that even with a completed cognitive neuroscience of consciousness, we will still be left with competing ways of carving up the stream of consciousness into distinct experiential vehicles.

Let us recap. The business of counting experiences is a messy one, and there is more than one respectable way of going about it. That being said, I suggested that experiences should be thought of in tripartite terms: an experience is to be understood in terms of the instantiation of a phenomenal property by a subject at a time. We can think of these instantiations as phenomenal events. And in light of this, phenomenal unity can be understood in terms of mereological relations between phenomenal events. At any one point in time one's stream of consciousness takes the form of a single highly complex phenomenal event that subsumes a number of less complex phenomenal events. It is the fact that these less complex events are proper parts of more complex events that accounts for their unity. The mereological relations between phenomenal events might be reflected in mereological relations between their vehicles but they need not be.

2.3 Objections and replies

Let us consider now some objections to the mereological account. I begin with Tye's objections to the view, before turning to criticisms from Brook and Raymont on the one hand and from Searle on the other.

The self-undermining objection

A first objection to the mereological account holds that it is in some way self-undermining:

> Consider a maximal phenomenal state (e_m); that is, a phenomenal state that is not subsumed by any other phenomenal state. e_m includes as two of its elements a visual experience (e_1) and an auditory experience (e_2). Not only are these two experiences unified with each other, but each is unified with e_m. Now, if the unity of each of these two experiences requires that there be a unifying experience that subsumes them, then the unity of e_1 (e_2) and e_m seems to demand that the subject have a further experience, 'bigger' than e_m, that subsumes both e_m and e_1 (e_2). But we stipulated that e_m was a maximal phenomenal state, a state not subsumed by any other phenomenal state. So if phenomenal unity is a relation between experiences, then the notion of a maximal phenomenal state is incoherent. But the notion of a maximal phenomenal state clearly *is* coherent, so phenomenal unity cannot be a relation between experiences. (Tye 2003: 22)[6]

The notion of a maximal (or 'total') phenomenal state is indeed coherent, but why exactly must the proponent of the mereological account deny this? The crucial move in the argument is the claim that, on the subsumptive view, the unity of e_1 and e_m requires that there be an experience that is 'bigger' (that is, contains more phenomenal content) than e_m itself. But we are under no obligation to accept this claim, for parthood is a reflexive relation—any event is an (improper) part of itself. The state that unifies e_m and e_1 need be none other than e_m itself.

As an analogy, think of what it is for two actions to be 'unified'. We might regard writing a book as an act that subsumes the act of writing the book's first sentence. What it is for these two actions to be unified is for the latter to be included as a component or proper part of the former. Nonetheless, we can still think of writing a book as a maximal action that is not—or at least need not be—subsumed by any more complex action. Similarly, we can think of a total phenomenal state as a state that subsumes each of the phenomenal states that the subject has at the time in question without being subsumed by any state other than itself.

---

[6] I have substituted Tye's nomenclature for my own.

The 'phenomenal bloat' objection

A second objection holds that the mereological account is faced with the problem of what we might call *phenomenal bloat*. Various versions of this objection have been circulating in the literature (see Hurley 1998; Bayne 2001), but I will focus on Tye's version of it.

(1) Suppose that phenomenal unity is a relation between experiences e_1–e_5 (assumption for *reductio ad absurdum*).

(2) This unity relation (R_1) between experiences must itself be experienced, for if there were no experience of the unifying relation, then there would be nothing it is like for e_1–e_5 to be unified. (Alternatively, there would be no phenomenal difference between a situation in which e_1–e_5 were phenomenally unified and a situation in which they are not unified.)

(3) If R is itself experienced, it must have its own phenomenology.

(4) If R has its own phenomenology, its phenomenology must be unified with that of e_1–e_5.

(5) In order to account for the fact that R_1 is unified with e_1–e_5 we need to posit another unity relation (R_2).

(6) But of course R_2 must itself be experienced, for if there were no experience of the unifying relation, then there would be nothing it is like for e_1–e_5 to be unified with R_1.

(7) But now we have embarked on a vicious infinite regress.

(8) So (1) must be false: phenomenal unity is not a relation between experiences. (Tye 2003: 22)

The first thing to say about this argument is that if it is any good it seems to be too good, for variants of it threaten to undermine *any* account of phenomenal unity. If phenomenal unity is not a relation between experiences, it looks like it must be a relation between the contents of experience, as Tye has claimed (see §3.1). And what could make it the case that simultaneously experienced perceptual qualities—the loudness of a sound, the smoothness of a surface, and the sweetness of a taste—enter into the same phenomenal content? Arguably, these qualities could enter into a single content only if there were an experiential difference between experiencing the loudness of a sound, the smoothness of a surface, and the sweetness of a taste together as opposed to experiencing these properties separately. But—the objection continues—this surely entails that the subject must be conscious *that* they are conscious of the sound, the surface, and the taste, and if that's right then we face the task of explaining how *that* experiential content is unified with the rest of the subject's phenomenology. We appear to have embarked on an apparently vicious regress, not unlike the one outlined above. It is no accident that Hurley's (1998) version of the phenomenal bloat objection—which she dubbed the 'just more content' objection—targeted content-based accounts of the unity of consciousness.

Leaving aside the question of whether content-based conceptions of phenomenal unity might face their own problem of phenomenal bloat, how is the mereological account to respond to it?

One line of response to the argument is to reject premiss (5). We might suppose that although phenomenal unity is an experience it is a peculiar sort of experience: it is a *self-binding* experience. Unique amongst experiences, perhaps phenomenal unity binds experiences together to form unified phenomenal wholes without itself needing to be so bound. However, I am not much attracted to this objection, for why should some experiences be self-binding and others not?

Another line of response would be to reject (3). One might hold that although relations of phenomenal unity are experienced, the experience of them does not possess a distinctive phenomenal character of its own. Christopher Hill may have had something like this view in mind when he suggested that there is a kind of 'pure' or 'ghostly' element in consciousness, an element that 'has no distinguishing characteristics other than its ability to unite sensations' (Hill 1991: 239). However, Hill came to reject this view, and I think he was right to do so. For one thing, phenomenal unity lacks the kind of positive character that would allow it to be singled out via introspection. We seem unable to attend to phenomenal unity as such. One can attend to phenomenally unified experiences, and one can attend to the conjoint experience that subsumes them, but one cannot attend to relations of phenomenal unity or subsumption themselves. Here is another way to appreciate the difference between phenomenal unity and experiences. Unlike experiences, relations of phenomenal unity cannot themselves be phenomenally unified. But, since any experience is the sort of thing that could be phenomenally unified, it follows that relations of phenomenal unity are not experiences. (Judgements about relations of phenomenal unity might have their own phenomenology, but that's a different matter.)

In my view, the argument's flaw lies with premiss (2)—the claim that in order to make a phenomenal difference phenomenal unity must itself be experienced. Tye provides the following argument for (2): 'If there were no experience of the unifying relation, then there would be nothing it is like to have the sense specific experiences unified' (2003: 22). I think this inference should be resisted. Why could there not be something it is like to have a set of unified experiences, without that 'what it's like' subsuming or involving an experience *of* the unity relation that binds the experiences in question together? Phenomenal unity is a phenomenal relation in the sense that it makes a phenomenal difference, but not in the sense that it has its own phenomenal character that makes an *additional* contribution to what it is like to be the subject in question. We can think of this in terms of the different *ways* of undergoing experiences e_1-e_5. In principle, one can have these experiences separately or one can have them together, as parts of a subsuming experience. Unity then is not an *object* of experience but a *manner* of experiencing.[7] The lesson to be learnt from the phenomenal bloat objection is that phenomenal relations can make a phenomenal difference without themselves being either experiences or experienced.

The transparency objection

Rather than attack the mereological account head-on, one might attempt to undermine its epistemic basis. In fact, Tye has done precisely that by appealing to the so-called transparency (or diaphanousness) of consciousness. Introspection, says Tye, gives one access only to the contents of experience. And this fact, says Tye, undercuts any account of phenomenal unity that treats it as a relation between token experiences:

Visual experiences are transparent to their subjects. We are not introspectively aware of our visual experiences any more than we are perceptually aware of transparent sheets of glass. If we try to focus on our experiences, we 'see' right through them to the world outside ... If we are not aware of our experiences via introspection, we are not aware of them as unified. The unity relation is not given to us introspectively as a relation connecting experiences. Why, then, suppose that there is such a relation at all? (Tye 2003: 24 f.)[8]

The so-called transparency of consciousness is a rather complex matter, and appeals to it must be handled with care.[9] Consider first the bold claim that we are not aware of *any* of our conscious states via introspection but only of their contents. If the notion of a 'conscious state' is understood to include thoughts then this claim is surely implausible, for there is an introspectible difference between consciously judging that it is sunny and consciously hoping that it is sunny. And if introspection can distinguish thoughts that differ only with respect to their mode or attitude, then it must have access to more than the contents of thoughts. Of course, Tye's claim here is only that *visual* experiences are transparent to their subjects, but once we have allowed that introspection can distinguish between thoughts with the same content we have some reason to wonder whether it mightn't also allow us to distinguish between perceptual experiences with the

---

[7] I am indebted to Ian Phillips here.

[8] Tye's one-experience view of course entails that there are no purely visual experiences, so presumably he means 'visual experiential stages' or some-such.

[9] The contemporary discussion of transparency begins with Harman (1990). For critical discussion see Kind (2003), Stoljar (2004) and (2007), and Thompson (2008).

same content—indeed, whether we can't even introspectively distinguish between *visual* experiences with exactly the same content. Contrast visual *perception* (as) of an apple with visual *imagery* (as) of an apple. One might argue that it is possible to distinguish these two states from each other on the basis of introspection even though they have exactly the same contents. Advocates of transparency do have responses to this objection—for example, they can argue that there must be subtle content-based differences between the perceptual state and the imagery state if indeed they are introspectively distinguishable—but the plausibility of such responses is something of an open question.

Despite these reservations, I do think that there is something to claims of transparency. We certainly do not have introspective access to the sub-personal basis of conscious states—their nature as neuro-functional states. However, whether this implies that we are not introspectively aware of our experiences depends on just how we conceive of experiences. Suppose, as I have suggested, that we identify experiences with the instantiation of phenomenal properties. On this conception of experiences, we *are* aware of our experiences as such in being aware of which phenomenal properties we instantiate. I am currently aware that I instantiate the phenomenal property distinctive of tasting coffee, and in being aware of this fact I am also aware of the corresponding experience. On the tripartite conception of experience, the contrast between 'access to experiences' and 'access to the contents of experience' is a false one, for in having access to the contents of experience one also has access to experiences themselves.

Of course, advocates of transparency will be likely to reject this conception of experiences in favour of a vehicular conception. On their view, experiences themselves are (say) neural events that 'carry' contents (whatever that means). From this perspective, introspective access to experience itself would require that one be aware of neural events as such, and it is clear that introspection involves no such awareness. But even from within this framework we have the resources to motivate the view that phenomenal unity is a relation between experiences.

Distinguish between introspective access to a *state* and introspective access to a *fact*. The vehicular conception of experience may imply that we lack introspective access to our experiential states, but it must surely allow that we have introspective access to certain facts about our experiences. For example, one might have introspective access to the fact that one is conscious, to the fact that one is visually conscious, and to the fact that one has a visual experience (as) of there being an apple in front of one. Furthermore, some of the facts that introspection provides access to concern the relations between one's experiences. The reason for this is that one has introspective access to facts about the contents of one's consciousness, and such facts constrain the relations between one's experiences themselves. One doesn't merely have (say) an experience of an apple, a trumpet, and an itch; instead one experiences the apple, the trumpet, and the itch 'together' within a single phenomenal field. In order for these contents to be unified the experiences that underlie them must also be unified: no unity in content (or phenomenal character) without unity between the experiences that carry those contents. In short, we can have introspective reasons for thinking that there is a unity relation connecting experiences even if that relation is not directly 'given to us' in introspection.

The 'Jamesian' objection

Tye is not the only critic of the mereological approach to phenomenal unity. Joining him are Brook and Raymont, who argue that the account fails for reasons that can be found in the work of William James (and which in fact have their roots in Kant). Merely putting conscious experiences together, Brook and Raymont claim, will fail to generate a unified state of consciousness, for a 'mere combination of experiences is not the experience of a combination' (Raymont & Brook2009: 575). Here is how James put the point:

Take a hundred [feelings], shuffle them and pack them as close together as you can (whatever that may mean); still each remains the same feeling as it always was, shut in its own skin, windowless, ignorant of what the other feelings are and mean . . . Take a sentence of a dozen words, take twelve men, and to each one word. Then stand the men in a row or jam them in a bunch, and let each one think of his word as intently as he will; nowhere will there be a consciousness of the whole sentence. (James 1890/1950: 160)

We can—indeed, we *should*—accept that the mere combination of experiences is not identical to the experience of combination. Simply packing together experiences of a number of words—'jamming them together in a bunch'—does not suffice to generate an experience of the sentence as a whole. But the mereological account does not claim that it does. The mereological account is intended only as an account of what it is for experiences to be phenomenally unified, it is *not* intended as an account of what it is for consciousness to be representationally integrated. It is not an account of what it is for experiences of (say) the parts of a face to give rise to an experience of the face to which those parts belong, for the experience of individual notes to give rise to an experience of the melody those notes realize, or for the experience of individual words to give rise to an experience of the sentence that those words compose. We obviously *do* need an account of how the experience of parts generates an experience of the whole of which those parts are parts, and it is plausible to suppose that phenomenal unity will play an important role in such an account, but we should not conflate representational unity with phenomenal unity. Experiencing the parts of an object (scene, event) might be *necessary* in order to experience the object (scene, event) as such, but it typically isn't *sufficient* for it, and the two forms of experience should certainly not be identified.

One of the upshots of the foregoing is that we must distinguish between two kinds of binding problems (Revonsuo 1999). The binding problem is typically thought of in representational terms—that is, as the problem of ensuring that perceptual features are integrated into unified percepts of objects. Consider vision. Given that we typically experience multiple visual objects at a time, the brain needs to work out which perceptual features (colour, shape, texture, etc.) belong to which objects. Suppose that one is looking at a red berry nestled in green leaves. It is important that one represents the berry as red and the leaves as green rather than vice versa. This binding problem must be distinguished from the phenomenal binding problem—the problem of ensuring that each of the phenomenal features that one enjoys at a certain point in time occurs within a single conscious state. Even when features are not bound together as the features of a single object (as in visual agnosia), they are nonetheless experienced together within a single conscious state. James was surely right to note that merely sticking features together in a single representation—'jamming them as close together as one can'—does not ensure that they will be experienced as the features of a single object, but it arguably does ensure that they will enjoy a conjoint phenomenal character. Here, as elsewhere, it is vital that we distinguish phenomenal unity from representational unity.

The building block objection

A final objection to the mereological view comes from Searle. Searle contrasts mereological conceptions of consciousness—which he dubs 'building block models'—with unified field models, according to which the multiplicity to be found within consciousness ought to be understood in terms of modifications to an overall field of consciousness:

The urge to think of consciousness . . . as made up of smaller building blocks is over-whelming. But I think it may be wrong for consciousness . . . Indeed, maybe it is wrong to think of consciousness as made up of parts at all . . . Instead of thinking of my current state of consciousness as made up of the various bits—the perception of the computer screen, the sound of the brook outside, the shadows cast by the evening sun falling on the wall—we should think of all these as modifications, forms that the underlying basal conscious field takes after my peripheral nerve endings have been assaulted by the various external stimuli. (2000: 575)

I share Searle's suspicion of building block approaches to consciousness. I also share his attraction to the thought that the multiplicity in consciousness might involve the modification of an underlying basal field (see Chapter 10). But—unlike Searle—I want to distinguish the mereological conception of consciousness from the building block conception. Searle's 'building block' terminology suggests a particular conception of the relationship between the overall phenomenal field and the parts of consciousness—namely, a view on which those parts are autonomous units of consciousness, states whose status as conscious states is independent of their location in the particular phenomenal field in which they occur. No such assumption is implicit in the mereological account of phenomenal unity. To say that the phenomenal field contains experiential parts is to make no claim whatsoever about the relationship between those parts and the whole of which they are parts. We could take the experiential parts of a phenomenal field as more fundamental than the phenomenal field itself, but we could also hold that there is a sense in which the overall phenomenal field is more fundamental than its parts. Indeed, my own view—for which I argue at length in Chapter 10—is that the total phenomenal state is prior to and more fundamental than the experiential parts that it subsumes. But that claim is independent of the mereological account, which is strictly neutral on the question of whether in seeking to understand the structure of consciousness we should assign explanatory priority to the parts (Searle's 'building block' model) or to the whole (his 'unified field' model).

This completes my defence of the mereological account of phenomenal unity. I turn now to consider one of the central questions that it raises.

2.4 Partial unity

Phenomenal unity is clearly both reflexive (every state is unified with itself) and symmetrical (if e_1 is phenomenally unified with e_2 then e_2 must be phenomenally unified with e_1). But is it also transitive? If e_1 and e_2 are each phenomenally unified with e_3 does it follow that they must also be unified with each other? The mereological account as such leaves this question open, but it is a question that a full analysis of the unity of consciousness must address.

Arguably phenomenal unity need not be transitive when the states involved are not simultaneous. Consider what it's like to hear three successive notes (*Do*, *Re*, and *Me*) where these notes are played such that one's experiences of *Do* and *Re* occur together within a single specious present, one's experiences of Re and Me also occur within a single specious present, but one's experiences of Do and Me do *not* occur within a single specious present. Such episodes appear to involve a failure of transitivity in phenomenal unity, for one's experiences of Do and Me both appear to be unified with an experience of Re but not with each other (Dainton 2006). But it is far less plausible to suppose that transitivity can fail for sets of *simultaneous* experiences. In fact, it is tempting to suppose that the phenomenal field *cannot* fragment in the way that a failure of transitivity would require. In other words, it is tempting to suppose that for any three simultaneous experiences, e_1, e_2 and e_3, if both e_1 and e_2 are phenomenally unified with $e3$ then they must also be unified with each other. Let us call the assumption that phenomenal unity is transitive with respect to simultaneous states *the transitivity thesis*.

Although the transitivity thesis has a great deal of intuitive plausibility, it has not gone unquestioned. In *Mind, Brain and the Quantum*, Michael Lockwood suggested that it might be possible for a subject's consciousness to fragment into a single partially unified stream of experience in which transitivity fails. (In fact, Lockwood suggested that the partial unity model of consciousness might even capture the structure of consciousness in certain split-brain patients (see §9.4)). Lockwood's proposal has met with a mixed response. Tye claims that there is no difficulty with partial unity, although it is far from clear that his conception of partial unity is the same as Lockwood's (as we shall see). Dainton allows that transitivity might fail in the context of successive experiences, but he denies that such failures are possible when it comes to simultaneous experiences (Dainton 2006). Hurley neither accepts nor rejects the transitivity thesis, but she does provide an account of the split-brain syndrome that is designed to remove the attractions of the partial unity model and in so doing implies that we should be at least sceptical of partial unity. Indeed, even Lockwood himself came to harbour reservations about the possibility of partial unity (Lockwood 1994).

The possibility of partial unity is a matter of no little importance. As we shall see in later chapters, apparent breakdowns in the unity of consciousness are rarely clean, and there is some temptation to think that if and when the unity of consciousness is lost it is lost because consciousness takes the form of a single, partially unified stream of consciousness rather than two streams of consciousness, each of which is fully internally unified. So, is partial unity possible?

Let us begin by considering in more detail just what it would take to have a case of partial unity. Tye offers the following as an example of such a scenario:

S has two multimodal experiences, e_1 and e_2. e_1 represents the pinprick in S's neck, his left arm, fingers and the surface his left forefinger is touching. e_2 represents the pinprick in S's neck, his right arm, fingers, and the surface the right forefinger is touching. The pricking is phenomenally unified with redness by entering into the same phenomenal content—the phenomenal content of e_1. The pricking is phenomenally unified with greenness in like manner, but this time the common content is the phenomenal content of e_2. Since S has no experience whose phenomenal content has entering into it both greenness and redness, the two colours are not phenomenally unified. (2003: 130 f.)[10]

Strictly speaking, Tye's one-experience view requires that e_1 and e_2 must be experience stages rather than experiences, for neither e_1 nor e_2 is an entire stream of consciousness, but let us waive that concern here. The central question is whether this scenario does indeed involve a failure of transitivity. In my view it does not. Lockwood introduced the notion of non-transitivity in order to describe a split within the structure of consciousness itself, but—as befits his conception of phenomenal unity (see §3.1)—Tye conceives of partial unity in terms of relations between the *contents* of consciousness. Tye denies that e_1 and e_2 share a common experiential part. Instead, on his view they 'overlap' only in the sense that both experiences have a common content—namely pricking. But this is a very different conception of partial unity from that which I, following Lockwood, am considering. Partial unity, as I am thinking of it here, would occur when—and only when—the experience of pricking that occurs in e_1 is *numerically identical* to that which occurs in e_2. On this view, e_1 and e_2 must share an experiential part—namely, an experience of pricking.

Having clarified the notion of partial unity let us return to the question of whether it is possible. In asking about the coherence of partial unity it is vital that we take into account the fact that we are addressing relations between *conscious* states. It is not difficult to make sense of the idea that there might be a kind of 'partial unity' between unconscious mental states. Consider beliefs, understood as dispositional states that play a distinctive functional role. It is clear that partial unity can obtain between beliefs thus understood. We can easily conceive of a scenario in which beliefs m_1 and m_2 are both disposed to exert control over thought and behaviour in conjunction with m_3 but not in conjunction with each other. Indeed, beliefs m_1 and m_2 might be at odds with each other, in the sense that the activation of the one belief tends to inhibit the activation of the other. (Something like this might occur in the context of self-deception.) But conscious states are not dispositional states, and the fact that we can make sense of 'partial unity' when considering dispositional states has little bearing on whether *phenomenal* states can be partially unified.

One might argue that partial unity is incoherent on the grounds that there is no consistent assignment of partially unified states to subjects of experience. Suppose that e_1 and e_2 are both unified with e_3 but not with each other. One might reason as follows. Both e_1 and e_3 must be assigned to the same subject for

---

[10]   Here too I have substituted Tye's nomenclature for my own.

they are phenomenally unified, and as phenomenally unified states they are subsumed by a single experiential state. Precisely the same considerations suggest that e_2 and e_3 must also belong to the same subject. But, so the argument goes, e_1 and e_2 *cannot* belong to the same subject of experience, for they are not phenomenally unified with each other. In short, the objection is that there is no consistent way of assigning partially unified experiences to subjects of experience.

The key move in the argument is obviously the final one: the assumption that simultaneous experiences that belong to the same subject must be phenomenally unified. There is some plausibility to this claim—in fact, it follows from the unity thesis—but we cannot assume that it is true at this stage of proceedings. The unity thesis might be true but it is not a conceptual truth, at least not if we are thinking of subjects of experience in biological terms. In fact, the unity thesis is unlikely to be a conceptual truth even on certain *psychological* conceptions of the subject of experience. For example, views that identify subjects with networks of functionally defined mental states appear to allow that there might be occasions on which a single subject has experiences that are not phenomenally unified with each other (see e.g. Shoemaker 1996). So, although there is something to the thought that a single subject could not have disunified experiences, let us assume that there is at least a viable notion of subjecthood according to which simultaneous but disunified experiences can be assigned to the same subject.

The most tempting reason to reject partial unity is simply that it is difficult if not outright impossible to project oneself into the perspective of a partially unified subject (Lockwood 1994: 95). We can convert this thought into the following argument:

(1) If partial unity were possible then there would be something distinctive it is like to be a partially unified subject—there would be such a thing as a partially unified phenomenal perspective.

(2) We are unable to project ourselves into a partially unified phenomenal perspective.

(3) If there were such a thing as a partially unified phenomenal perspective then we should be able to project ourselves into it.

(C) Thus, partial unity is impossible.

Let us call this *the projectability argument*. On the face of things the first premise of the argument seems secure. Although there are those who might reject it—Paul Snowdon describes the assumption that for each subject of experience there is a way that it's like to be them as 'hazy' (1995: 78)—I see no *prima facie* reason to doubt it. But in a very provocative discussion of the projectability argument Hurley suggests that premise (1) might be rather more problematic than it appears.[11]

Hurley argues that it is a mistake to conceive of the difference between full unity and partial unity in subjective terms.[12] Her objection centres on the claim that the contrast between partial unity and full unity is a matter of the relations between token experiences, whereas the subjective perspective has access only to the content (better: phenomenal character) of consciousness. Hurley develops this objection by contrasting two subjects of experience, S_1 and S_2. S_1 has two unified experiences, an experience of red at a particular location in her visual field (v_1) and an experience of hearing a violin (a_1). S_2, however, has a partially unified consciousness. She has three experiences: an experience of red (v_1) and *two* experiences of hearing a violin (a_1 and a_2). Each of S_2's auditory experiences are unified with her visual experience but they are not unified with each other. Importantly, a_1 and a_2 are what I call *phenomenal duplicates*: they have exactly the same phenomenal character. Hurley suggests, plausibly enough, that there would be no subjective contrast between S_1 and S_2, and hence that there is no such thing as a distinctive partially unified phenomenal perspective. The upshot, she argues, is that objections to partial unity based on projectability cannot succeed. 'Suppositions about the structure of consciousness . . . are not necessarily captured by or subject to the "what it is like" test' (Hurley 1998: 166).

The first thing to note is that the objection requires S_2 to have phenomenal duplicates. We can see this by contrasting the two other subjects of experience—S_3 and S_4. These two subjects enjoy tokens of the same experiential types: an experience of red at a particular location in the visual field, an experience of hearing a violin, and an experience of a trumpet. In S_3's case these three experiences are fully unified with each other, but in S_4's case the two auditory experiences are unified with the visual experience but not with each other. In this scenario, there would clearly be a subjective, introspectable difference between what it's like to be S_3 and what it's like to be S_4. Whereas S_3

---

[11] There are deep connections between Hurley's objection and Tye's treatment of the unity of consciousness (see in particular his transparency objection to the mereological account of phenomenal unity). Both Hurley and Tye take there to be a tension between the claim that the unity of consciousness is subjectively accessible and the claim that it is a relation between token experiences. However, they respond to this tension in very different ways. Hurley retains the token experience conception of unity but rejects subjective accessibility, whereas Tye retains subjective accessibility but rejects the token experience conception of unity. The tripartite conception of experiences shows how these two claims can be reconciled with each other: the unity of consciousness is a relation between token experiences that is also subjectively accessible.

[12] I have changed the details of Hurley's case, but the changes do not alter the essential structure of her argument.

has a conjoint experience of the violin and the trumpet, S_4 has no such experience. So, Hurley's objection to the projectability argument poses a threat only if phenomenal duplicates are possible. Are they?

In §2.2 I suggested that we should individuate experiences in tripartite terms. This conception of experiences leaves no room for phenomenal duplicates, for by definition phenomenal duplicates are experiential states with the same phenomenal character that are had by the same subject at the same time. Of course, there are other accounts of how to individuate experiences, and some of those accounts might recognize the coherence of phenomenal duplication. But although there may be views of consciousness that provide Hurley's objection with a toehold, they are not views that I regard as particularly attractive. I conclude that premise (1) is secure: if partial unity were possible, then there would be such a thing as a distinctive partially unified subjective perspective.[13]

What about the second premiss—the claim that we are unable to project ourselves into a partially unified perspective? On the face of things, one might have thought that the task of projecting oneself into a partially unified phenomenal perspective poses no difficulty whatsoever. Lockwood has suggested that one could project oneself into a partially unified perspective simply by imagining each of the subject's overlapping experiences ($e_1\&e_3$ and $e_2\&e_3$) in turn (1989: 92). Since these two acts of imagination are successive they need not bring with them an experience of $e_1\&e_2$ in the way that attempting to imagine $e_1\&e_3$ and $e_2\&e_3$ *all at once* would.

Lockwood's proposal has not enjoyed a warm reception. Peacocke worries that successive acts of imagination would fail to capture the fact that one is imagining the simultaneous experiences of a single subject (Peacocke 1994: xx), while Dainton objects that successive acts of imagination would fail to ensure that the e_3-type experience in $e_1\&e_3$ was numerically identical to the e_3-type experience that occurs in $e_2\&e_3$ (Dainton 2006: 98). At first sight these objections are puzzling. Can't one simply *stipulate* that one is imagining the simultaneous experiences of a single subject, or that the e_3-type experience in $e_1\&e_3$ is identical to that in the $e_2\&e_3$ experience? Aren't the objects of our imagination up to us? As Wittgenstein pointed out, 'if a man says "I am

---

[13] As an aside, note that Hurley's objection raises questions about just how to understand her notion of phenomenal unity ('co-consciousness', in her terminology). Despite claiming that the objection shows that we cannot think of the unity of consciousness in 'what it's like' terms, Hurley herself appeals to just such a view in introducing the very notion of co-consciousness. 'There is unity of consciousness when various states and their contents are co-conscious: are together within one consciousness, rather than featuring in separate conscious points of view' (1998: 88). What might it mean for conscious states to be 'together within one consciousness' if not that the states share a conjoint phenomenal character? Given Hurley's rejection of 'what it's like' accounts of the unity of consciousness it's not entirely clear what she means by 'co-consciousness'.

imagining King's College on fire", it seems absurd for his friend to respond, "How do you know it is King's College you are imagining? Are you aware that there is a precise replica of it on a film set in Los Angeles? May you not be imagining *it*?"' (Wittgenstein 1965: 39). In short, it is unclear why we can't imagine what it would be like to be a partially unified subject merely by engaging in successive acts of imagination.

In order to get a better fix on this issue we need to examine the notion of projective imagination in more depth. As I am conceiving of it here, projection involves imagining something 'from the inside'. Nagel has called this state 'sympathetic imagination'. To imagine something sympathetically one 'puts oneself in a conscious state resembling the thing itself' (Nagel 1974: fn 11). It follows from this that one can sympathetically imagine only conscious states— more accurately, that one can sympathetically imagine only what it is like to *be* in a certain type of conscious state. In this respect sympathetic imagination must be strictly distinguished from perceptual and propositional imagination. Unlike acts of perceptual or propositional imagination, acts of sympathetic imagination must have the same structure as their targets, for sympathetic imagination involves *replicating* the state being imagined. One cannot sympathetically imagine an atemporal phenomenal perspective without one's own conscious state taking on an atemporal character. Nor, to use Nagel's own example, can one sympathetically imagine what it would be like to echolocate without actually having that ability (or at least something very much like it) oneself. We can now see why it is not possible to stipulate either that one is imagining the simultaneous experiences of a single subject, or that the e_3-type experience in $e_1 \& e_3$ is identical to that in the $e_2 \& e_3$ experience, for such stipulation doesn't extend to sympathetic imagination. Engaging in successive acts of projection would only enable one to imagine being a subject with one kind of phenomenal state that was followed by another. In order to project oneself into the phenomenal perspective of a subject at a particular time one would need to engage in a *single* act of imaginative projection. In short, premiss (2) of the projectability argument appears to be secure when suitably understood.

But although both premisses (1) and (2) are plausible when suitably understood premise (3) is not, for neither unimaginability in general nor sympathetic unimaginability in particular is a reliable guide to impossibility. The fact that we are unable to imagine what it is like to be a bat provides no reason at all for thinking that there is nothing it is like to be a bat. Nor, to take another well-worn example, does the fact that Mary in her black and white room cannot imagine what it is like to experience red give her any reason to doubt the possibility of such experiences (Jackson 1982). Premise (3) could be defended only if there were reason to think that our projective abilities limn the space of phenomenal possibility, and there isn't. (In fact, there is good reason to think that our projective capacities extend to only a very small region of that space.) Being *able* to project oneself into the perspective of a disunified subject would be relevant to the current debate—it would be an existence proof that disunified subjects are possible, for only a disunified subject would be able to project itself into the perspective of a disunified subject—but being *un*able to project oneself into such a perspective doesn't go any way towards showing that such subjects are impossible.

The projectability argument fails, but perhaps something can be salvaged from its wreckage. Why is it so plausible to suppose that there are possible phenomenal perspectives that are imaginatively inaccessible to us? Surely our basis for thinking that such perspectives are possible is grounded in the fact that we can *conceive* of them. This, in turn, suggests that it might be useful to consider whether there might be something *incoherent* in the notion of partial unity. Perhaps we can construct a conceivability-based argument against partial unity.

Following van Cleve (1983), let us distinguish two types of inconceivability: *strong inconceivability* and *weak inconceivability*. A scenario is strongly inconceivable for S when S seems to see that it is impossible, whereas a scenario is weakly inconceivable for S when S cannot see that it is possible. As the terms suggest, strong inconceivability entails weak inconceivability but not *vice versa*: that is, if a scenario is strongly inconceivable for someone then it is also weakly inconceivable for them, but the converse conditional does not hold. (Note that 'strength' here concerns the content of the inconceivability intuition rather than its epistemic status or degree of subjective certainty.)

Examples of strong inconceivability—or at least putative strong inconceivability—are not hard to find. Scratch a putative metaphysical truth and one finds a claim of strong inconceivability underneath it. Arguably, uncaused events are inconceivable; physical objects that can survive the process of being shrunk to an extensionless point are inconceivable; square circles are inconceivable; tigers that lick all and only all tigers that do not lick themselves are inconceivable, and so on. As an example of a proposition that is weakly inconceivable consider Goldbach's conjecture that every even integer greater than 3 is the sum of two prime numbers. I take it that you neither see that Goldbach's conjecture is true nor do you see that it is false.

Is partial unity *strongly* inconceivable? That seems unlikely. Transitivity may be a deep feature of synchronic unity, but I very much doubt whether it reveals itself to us as such. Indeed, I am not convinced that first-person acquaintance with consciousness reveals *any* substantive features of it to be necessary. How could first-person reflection on experience provide one with grounds for thinking that certain features of one's own consciousness derive from the essential nature of consciousness itself as opposed to contingent aspects of one's own cognitive architecture? There may be some sense in which partial unity is inconceivable, but it is not, I think, strongly inconceivable.

That leaves weak inconceivability. Is partial unity weakly inconceivable? I am inclined to think that it is. At any rate, I cannot 'see' that partial unity is possible, and as far as I can tell I am not alone in this. Of course, to claim that partial unity is weakly inconceivable is not to claim a great deal, for an inability to see that P is impossible may be due to nothing more than a cognitive limitation on the part of the cognizer. (Consider again Goldbach's conjecture.) The prudent position, it seems to me, is to retain partial unity as a potential model of consciousness, albeit one that is surrounded by a significant degree of suspicion.

Some theorists might be inclined to think that I am being overly cautious here. One might argue that reflection on the phenomenal continuity of consciousness—its unity across time—gives us positive reason to think that partial unity is coherent. As we noted above, there is good reason to think that transitivity can fail with respect to successive experiences. In hearing the notes Do, Re, and Me, one's experiences of Do might be unified with one's experience of Re, and one's experience of Re might in turn be with one's experience of Me without one's experience of Do being unified with one's experience of Me. But—a critic might press—if transitivity can fail when it comes to conscious states that are spread out across time, why can't it also fail when it comes to simultaneous states?

Here is not the place to enter into a protracted discussion of the mysteries of temporal experience, but I do want to briefly present two possible lines of response to the objection. First, there is at least one model of phenomenal continuity on which transitivity holds. Suppose that hearing the notes Do, Re, and Me involves successive punctate experiences, e_1 and e_2, which have as their contents <Do at t_1; Re at t_2> and <Re at t_2; Me at t_3>. Moreover, suppose that these experiences are not phenomenally unified with each other: although both e_1 and e_2 represent <Re at t_2>, the representation of Re that occurs in the context of e_1 is completely distinct from that which occurs in the context of e_2. (As an aid to intuition, we might suppose that visual experience is pulse-like, and there is a very short temporal gap between e_1 and e_2.) This view appears to account for temporal experience without supposing that there is any failure of transitivity for phenomenal unity across time. This account of phenomenal continuity may not be particularly plausible, but it does undermine the thought that we *must* give up on transitivity in order to account for phenomenal continuity.

A second—and perhaps more compelling—response to the objection is that there may be constraints on the unity of consciousness that don't apply to its continuity. In fact, one might venture the thought that the unity of consciousness is in part distinguished from its continuity by virtue of the fact that transitivity must hold with respect to simultaneous experiences but not with respect to successive experiences. We can see how experiences of *Do* and *Me* might each be unified with an experience of *Re* without being unified with each other, for the temporal locations of these experiences generates a gap between the experiences of *Do* and *Me* that is not matched by a corresponding gap between the experiences of *Do* and *Re* or between the experiences of *Re* and *Me*. There are, of course, no temporal gaps between simultaneous experiences, and so any failure of transitivity here would need to derive from another source. There may be such sources—for example, there might be something in the structure of the neuro-functional relations underlying consciousness which allow for partial unity—but the central point is that there is no inconsistency in allowing that transitivity can fail for successive experiences but at the same time asserting that it must hold for simultaneous experiences.

2.5 Conclusion

Although the unity of consciousness could hardly be a more familiar phenomenon we are still some way from having an adequate theoretical grasp of what it is for consciousness to be unified. The focus of this chapter has been to develop and defend a mereological account of phenomenal unity, according to which experiences are phenomenally unified with each other exactly when they occur as parts of a single experience. Section §2.2 focused on the notion of experience that lies at the bottom of the mereological account. I began by noting that the mereological account is inconsistent with Tye's one-experience view, according to which experiences are to be identified with entire streams of consciousness. However, I suggested that there is little reason to embrace this revisionary conception of experience, and that we can quite happily think of certain components of a stream of consciousness—what Tye calls 'experience stages'—as experiences in their own right. But not every stretch of a stream of consciousness is an experience. I suggested that we should think of experiences in terms of the instantiation of phenomenal properties, where a phenomenal property is a property that there is 'something it is like' to enjoy. More precisely, I advanced a tripartite conception of experiences: a token experience can be equated with the instantiation of a phenomenal property by a subject at a time.

In §2.3 I addressed a number of objections to the mereological account of phenomenal unity. Some of these objections were well targeted but could be answered from within the mereological framework (the self-undermining objection; the phenomenal bloat objection; the transparency objection); others missed their target, either because they assumed that the mereological account has commitments that it doesn't (the building block objection), or because they assumed that it is trying to capture a kind of unity that it isn't (the Jamesian objection).

In the final section of this chapter I turned from the mereological analysis of phenomenal unity as such to a question that it raises: is it possible for a set of simultaneous experiences to be merely partially unified? The central objection to the coherence of partial unity took the form of the projectability argument. Although influential criticisms of the projectability argument turned out to be uncompelling, I argued that the objection nonetheless fails because it pre-supposes an overly tight connection between projectability and possibility. We saw however that there is something to be salvaged from the demise of the projectability argument: an inconceivability argument. We may not be able to see that partial unity is impossible, but we cannot—I suggest—see that it is possible. The upshot of these reflections, I suggest, is that an air of suspicion ought to accompany any talk of partial unity. As with many of the other issues examined in this chapter, we will return to the question of partial unity in later chapters.

3

Phenomenal Unity: Closure

The previous chapter defended a mereological account of phenomenal unity, according to which phenomenal unity is to be understood in terms of part–whole relations between token experiences. In this chapter I turn my attention to a rather different approach to phenomenal unity, one that attempts to capture phenomenal unity by appealing only to the representational content of phenomenal states. Our focus will be on the claim that phenomenal unity can be understood in terms of the conjunctive closure of phenomenal content—'closure' for short. As we will see, taking the measure of closure will run us up against some of the thorniest issues in the philosophy of mind.

The chapter will unfold as follows. The following section explicates and provides some motivation for closure; subsequent sections subject closure to critical scrutiny. §3.2 examines a challenge to closure that derives from inconsistency within experience; §3.3 examines a pair of objections that concern the complexity of visual experience; §3.4 examines whether closure might accommodate inter-modal unity; and §3.5 examines the claim that closure cannot accommodate unity between conscious states of different kinds. There are plausible responses to the first three objections, but closure succumbs to the last. At least, so I will argue.

3.1 Closure introduced

Let us begin by reminding ourselves of what an account of phenomenal unity is an account of. Irrespective of their phenomenal character, one's experiences don't occur as independent units of consciousness but are invariably subsumed by a single phenomenal state. They occur within the context of a single phenomenal field—a time-slice of a stream of consciousness. Suppose that you are listening to Mingus, enjoying some olives, and have a slight ache in your shoulders from yesterday's labour. These experiences won't be autonomous states but will have a conjoint phenomenal character—they will be had 'together'. An account of phenomenal unity ought to shed some light on what it is for experiences to be had together in this way.

The mereological account developed in the previous chapter holds that phenomenal unity can be understood in terms of part–whole relations between phenomenal states. Take two phenomenally unified states—for example, two visual experiences (v_1 and v_2). These experiences are phenomenally unified with each other in virtue of the fact that they occur as the parts of a more complex visual state (v_3). But experiential states don't merely have a phenomenal character or 'what it's likeness', they also possess representational content. Indeed, it is plausible to hold that the phenomenal character of conscious states is intimately related to their representational content. And this suggests that it might be possible to analyse phenomenal unity in terms of relations between the representational contents of unified states. It suggests that there might be something to be said about the relationship between the content of v_3 on the one hand and that of v_1 and v_2 on the other in virtue of which these three states are phenomenally unified with each other.

That 'something' is most naturally understood in terms of the closure of phenomenal content under conjunction. If closure holds, then v_1 and v_2 will be phenomenally unified if, and only if, the subject in question has a state (v_3) that has as its content the conjunction of the contents of v_1 and v_2. So, if v_1 has the content <p> and v_2 has the content <q>, then v_3 will have the content <p&q>. And if the subject in question doesn't have an experience with the content <p&q>, then it follows that v_1 and v_2 cannot be phenomenally unified with each other.

Closure entails that subjects with a fully unified consciousness will have a single phenomenal state—the subject's total phenomenal state—whose content corresponds to that of the conjunction of each of their phenomenal states. If closure is right, then the components of a single phenomenal field—the representation of the music of Mingus, the taste of olives, the ache in one's shoulders—will be unified with each other in virtue of the fact that their contents are included within the content of the subject's total state. Note, however, that closure does not itself entail that a subject's consciousness will be unified. Closure is an account of *what it is* for consciousness to be unified and does not as such entail any particular view about the degree to which consciousness is in fact unified.

What motivates closure? I think there are three reasons for taking it seriously. First, closure seems to follow quite naturally from the mereological conception of phenomenal unity defended in the previous chapter. If the content of v_3 did entail the contents of v_1 and v_2, then we could see why any subject that enjoyed a v_3-type experience must also enjoy v_1-type and v_2-type experiences, as is implied by the mereological account. So those attracted to the mereological treatment of phenomenal unity have reason to be sympathetic to closure as well.

A second reason for taking closure seriously is that it seems to follow from a representational conception of experience. If phenomenal character is fixed by representational content, as representationalist accounts of phenomenal character hold, then it looks as though the notion of conjoint phenomenal character must be cashed out in terms of conjunctive content. We will return to the relationship between closure and representationalism (see 3.6).

A third reason for taking closure seriously is that it can capture the intuitive contrast between the unity of consciousness and other forms of mental unity. Consider belief, understood not as an occurrent state but as a dispositional state. Thus understood, it is possible to believe both <p> and <q> without also believing <p&q>. Indeed, something similar holds of desire: one can desire <p> and <q> without desiring <p&q>. But contrast belief and desire with conscious judgement. Could one consciously judge <p> and <q> without also judging <p&q>? Such a feat might be possible for a subject with a disunified consciousness, but it is far less obvious that it could be carried out by a creature with a single stream of consciousness in which each of its conscious states are phenomenally unified with each other. Perhaps, the suggestion runs, what it is for the thoughts <p> and <q> to be 'together in a single state of consciousness' *just is* for the subject in question to have a conscious thought <p&q>. All up, we have good reason to suppose that closure might capture the intuitive conception of the unity of consciousness that we are after.

I am not the first person to have suggested that the unity of consciousness might be cashed out in terms of the closure of representational content. In fact, the notion can be found in the work of both Hurley and Tye, although in two quite different forms. Exploring the contrast between their two treatments will provide us with further insight into just what the view might or might not involve.[1]

Hurley (1994) presents closure under the label of 'the agglomeration principle':

What determines whether two conscious states are unified, together, co-conscious, or whether they are separate? Whatever this is, let's make a placeholder index for it, 'I', so we can say:

---

[1] Sympathy with closure is not limited to Hurley and Tye. Arguably, Shoemaker's (1996), (2003) account of co-consciousness also entails closure, and although Brook & Raymont (2009) do not explicitly endorse closure they do seem to be quite sympathetic to it. For example, they characterize the unity of consciousness as involving 'the consciousness not of A and, separately, of B and, separately, of C, but of A-and-B-and-C together, the contents of a single conscious state' (2009: 1). This characterization sounds very much like a commitment to some form of closure.

> if it is thought that p in i at t and thought that q in i at t, then it is thought that p and q in i at t.

We can call this the *agglomeration principle*. Contents of consciousness agglomerate just when the indices of agglomeration, the 'i's, match. (Hurley 1994: 57 f.; see also Hurley 1998: 117–18)[2]

Here is how Tye puts the core idea:

> phenomenological unity is a matter of simultaneously experienced perceptual qualities entering into the same phenomenal content...A consequence of the above position is that phenomenal unity goes with the closure of perceptual experience under conjunction with respect to the unified properties. Thus, in the case mentioned [above] in which the loudness of a sound is phenomenally unified for person P with the brightness of a flash of light, the statements
>
>> P has an experience of a loud sound
>
> and
>
>> P has an experience of a bright flash
>
> jointly entail
>
>> P has an experience of a loud sound and a bright flash. (Tye 2003: 36–37)

There are three noteworthy differences between Hurley's and Tye's treatments of closure. A first contrast concerns the intended *scope* of the two accounts. Whereas Hurley advances closure as a quite general account of what it is for conscious states to be unified, Tye focuses only on perceptual experiences. Tye does not explicitly deny that closure might provide an account of the unity between conscious thoughts, but the tenor of his discussion certainly points in that direction. I will follow Hurley in treating closure as an unrestricted account of the unity of consciousness—an account that attempts to capture the unity within and between bodily sensation, perceptual experience, and conscious thought. In taking this approach I am assuming a liberal account of the reach of phenomenal consciousness, according to which thoughts themselves, and not just their sensory accompaniments, posses phenomenal character (see Chapter 1).

A second point of contrast between Hurley and Tye concerns their conception of the relationship between closure on the one hand and accounts that treat phenomenal unity as a relation between token experiences, such as the mereological model, on the other. Hurley regards these two approaches as

---

[2] It should be noted that the agglomeration principle plays only a minor role in Hurley's developed treatment of the unity of consciousness (Hurley (1998) and (2003)). She seems to have taken Lockwood's (1994) criticisms of it to heart.

complementary, whereas Tye assumes that they are inconsistent. Again, I am inclined to take Hurley's side here. In fact, as I suggested above, it is tempting to think that closure might be *entailed by* views of phenomenal unity that conceive of it as a relation between token experiences (as the mereological account does). Whether or not that entailment goes through, we should keep open the possibility that phenomenal unity might be a relation between token experiences that brings closure with it.

A third contrast between Hurley and Tye concerns the nature of the entities that they take to be 'conjoined' within the contents of consciousness. Hurley takes closure to be defined over propositional contents, whereas Tye refers to 'perceptual qualities' as entering into the same phenomenal content. It is, of course, something of an open question just how perceptual qualities are related to propositions. On the face of things, they appear to be quite different kinds of beasts; for one thing, propositions have truth-values but perceptual qualities do not. However, I suspect that Tye intends for his reference to perceptual qualities to be glossed in propositional terms—as shorthand for something like 'the representation of a certain perceptual quality as instantiated in such-and-such an object or at such-and-such a location'. At any rate, I will assume here that closure is to be understood in propositional terms.

This is a far from insignificant point, for although propositional analyses of the contents of consciousness are popular they do not meet with universal approval.[3] One challenge to the view involves the allegation that there are conscious states—such as moods, pains, and orgasms—that either lack representational content altogether or are such that their phenomenal character is not fully captured by their representational content (see e.g. Searle 1992; Block 2003). I have some sympathy with this challenge, particularly insofar as it concerns the phenomenology of undirected moods. It is far from clear to me what the phenomenology of a state of (say) boredom might represent. At the very least, if the experience of boredom has intentional objects then its objects are not 'open to view' in the way that those of perception, imagery, or bodily sensations are. No doubt the experience of boredom depends on the state of one's 'internal milieu', such as the levels of particular neurotransmitters, but there is little reason to think that this is what it represents. Nor, for that matter, does it seem likely that boredom represents the overall state of the world or one's relation to the world. In short, there is something to be said for the view that experiences associated with boredom and other undirected mood states are 'phenomenological danglers'—states whose phenomenal character outruns

---

[3] For discussion of representationalist (or intentionalist) accounts of phenomenal consciousness see Byrne (2001); Chalmers (2004); Dretske (1995); Harman (1990); McGinn (1989); and Tye (1995).

whatever representational content they might possess. Even where conscious states do have representational content, it is a further question whether that content must always be propositional. Consider conscious emotions, such as Anna's love of Vronsky or Raskolnikov's hatred of Alëna. These states seem to take people as their respective objects rather than any propositions that might describe them (see Crane 2001; Montague 2007).

These challenges to representationalism 'problematize' closure. It is hard to see how we might capture phenomenological danglers by appeal to an analysis of phenomenal unity that appeals only to representational content; at best any such account could hope to capture only certain aspects of the phenomenal character of the states whose unity is in question. It is also hard to see how we might capture the phenomenal unity between emotions and other conscious states if the contents of emotions cannot be fully captured in propositional terms.

Although these challenges are important ones, I will set them to one side here and assume that there are plausible responses to them. In other words, I will adopt what we might call 'weak representationalism'—the claim that the phenomenal character of consciousness can be fully captured by appeal to the propositional contents of representational states. Weak representationalism must be distinguished from strong representationalism, according to which phenomenal states *just are* representational states of a certain kind. Closure does not require strong representationalism but it does require commitment to weak representationalism, for if phenomenal character is not fixed by propositional content then phenomenal unity will not be fixed by propositional content. Those who have doubts about the plausibility of weak representationalism should read the remainder of this chapter in terms of the following conditional: could closure provide us with an acceptable account of phenomenal unity if phenomenal character were to be captured by appeals to representational content?

3.2 Inconsistency

In principle, there are two ways in which closure could fail as an account of phenomenal unity. On the one hand, it would fail if it were possible for a creature's conscious states to be conjunctively unified without being phenomenally unified. On the other hand, it would also fail if it were possible for phenomenal unity to obtain even in the absence of conjunctive unity.

Consider first the inference from conjunctive unity to phenomenal unity. What might it take for conjunctive unity to hold but phenomenal unity to fail?

We would need a situation in which a subject has conscious states with contents <p>, <q>, and <p&q>, but where these states are not phenomenally unified with each other. Although it may be difficult to see how such a situation might arise, we have in fact already seen how such a case might be constructed. Suppose that it is possible for a subject to have phenomenal duplicates (that is, simultaneous states with the same phenomenal character). If so, then we might imagine that our subject has two token <p> experiences. One of these experiences is phenomenally unified with an experience of <q>, and both of these experiences are themselves unified with an experience of <p&q>. But the other <p> experience exists all on its lonesome; it is not phenomenally unified with either the subject's experience of <q> or its experience of <p&q>. Of course, it is far from clear that phenomenal duplicates are possible. Indeed, the tripartite conception of experiences that I have adopted rules out the possibility of phenomenal duplication (§2.4). And if duplicate experiences are not possible, then it very much looks as though states that are conjunctively unified must also be phenomenally unified. In light of this, I will focus on objections to closure that target the inference from phenomenal unity to conjunctive unity.

The first objection in this vein takes as its point of departure the idea that conscious states with inconsistent contents might be phenomenally unified. The idea is this. Consider a subject of experience with conscious states with contents <p> and <not-p> respectively, where these two states are phenomenally unified with each other. If closure holds, then such a subject would have a single conscious state with the content <p> and <not-p>. But—the argument continues—no state could have inconsistent content. So, either there is a consistency constraint on consciousness that prevents states with inconsistent contents from being unified or closure is false.

It is widely held that there is indeed a consistency constraint on phenomenal unity—that consciousness is deeply resistant to disunity. For example, Hurley says that 'consciousness is partitioned in a way that avoids incoherence within units' (Hurley 1998: 115, 118; but see also Hurley 2000). Are such claims plausible, or is it possible for inconsistent states to be phenomenally unified with each other?

There are a number of places in which we might look for inconsistency within consciousness. Let us begin with the waterfall illusion. First described by Aristotle, this illusion can be produced by looking at a waterfall for a period of time and then directing one's gaze to a stationary object. Here is a description of the experience that this is said to generate:

Although the after-effect gives a very clear illusion of movement, the apparently moving features nevertheless seem to stay still! That is, we are still aware of features

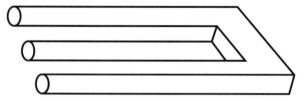

Figure 3.1 The Devil's pitchfork

remaining in their 'proper' locations even though they are seen as moving. What we see is logically impossible! (Frisby 1979: 101)[4]

Frisby seems to think that we are simultaneously conscious of the target object as both moving *and* not-moving, and a number of authors have followed him in this regard (Crane 1988; Tye 2003). Pictures of so-called impossible objects, such as the Devil's pitchfork (see Figure 3.1), provide further cases in which one might think visual experience contains inconsistent content (Priest 1999; Tye 2003). In looking at such pictures one seems to enjoy visual experiences whose contents are mutually inconsistent.

Another putative example of inconsistency within vision is provided by illusions (Smeets & Brenner 2008). Consider, for example, the Brentano version of the Müller-Lyer illusion (see Figure 3.2). Here, the vertical lines and the points of the arrows appear to be perfectly aligned (which they are). The vertical line in (b) also appears to bisect the horizontal line into two equal parts (which it does). Yet, at the same time, the central arrow in (a) appears to bisect the horizontal line into two unequal parts. On the face of it, one's visual experience when looking at Brentano's version of the Müller-Lyer illusion has inconsistent content.[5]

What should we say about these cases? They certainly put *some* pressure on the consistency constraint, but I'm not convinced that they falsify it, for it is not clear to me that the inconsistent experiences evoked by these stimuli are ever simultaneous with each other. With respect to the waterfall illusion, it seems to me not implausible to suppose that one experiences the target object as moving or as stationary but never as both moving and as stationary at one and the same time. (At any rate, I am not sure that *I* ever experience the object as moving and as stationary at one and the same time). The same worry applies to the Devil's Pitchfork. When I focus on the prongs I experience them as straight, and when I focus on the 'handle' I experience the middle prong as lying behind the upper

---

[4] See Frisby (1979: 100–1) for a description of how to produce the waterfall illusion using a record player. Those readers born after 1980 might have to borrow their parents' record player.

[5] We perceive the stimulus in this way because the alignment of the points of the arrows in (a) with the vertical lines in (b) is based on the perceived positions of the line intersections, whereas the bisection of the horizontal lines is based on the perceived extent of the line segments (Smeets & Brenner (2001)).

(a)

(b)

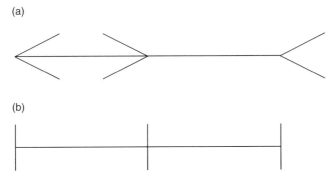

Figure 3.2 The Brentano version of the Müller-Lyer illusion

and lower prongs, but at no point do I experience all three prongs at once. (More carefully, at no point do I experience any one prong as having incompossible properties). A similar concern applies also to Brentano's version of the Müller-Lyer illusion. When I attend to (a) I experience the horizontal line as bisected into two unequal sections but I do not also experience the middle arrow in (a) as aligned with the vertical line in (b)—at least, if I do then I don't also experience the vertical line in (b) as bisecting the horizontal line into two equal segments. And when I *do* experience the middle arrow in (a) as aligned with the middle arrow in (b) I don't experience it as bisecting the horizontal line in (a) into unequal segments—at least, not when I also experience the vertical line in (b) as bisecting it into two equal segments.

In short, I am inclined to think that the inconsistency present in these phenomena is not contained within a single experiential state but occurs only as one attempts to integrate a series of distinct visual experiences that are not phenomenally unified with each other. There may be a legitimate sense in which one's overall representation of these objects has impossible content, but this representation is perhaps best thought of as a judgement about the kind of object that would have to exist in order for each of one's experiences of its parts to be veridical rather than an experience as such. I do not think we should rule out the possibility that there could be inconsistency within the context of a single experiential modality, but I am not convinced that any of these phenomena provide us with genuine examples of such a case.[6]

---

[6] I think that a similar diagnosis applies to putative instances of intra-modal inconsistency drawn from other modalities. For example, it is sometimes said that the Shepard-tone illusion involves inconsistent auditory content (Shepard (1964)). The composer James Tenney exploited this illusion in his composition *For Ann*, a piece in which a series of notes seems to rise endlessly in a way that critics have likened to the staircase of an Escher print. Listeners describe what they are hearing as 'not logically possible'. I suspect, however, that the inconsistency in question is not contained within any auditory experience but involves only a thought to the effect that it is not possible to reconcile the contents of each of a series of auditory experiences. Thanks to Jérôme Dokic for drawing my attention to the Shepard-tone illusion.

What about experiences that are drawn from different modalities? There is clearly a strong drive for perceptual coherence between modalities (see chapter 10), but perhaps it is possible to find examples of inter-modal inconsistency nonetheless. Consider first the effects of wearing inverting goggles. Although the use of inverting goggles does usually lead to a realignment of the spatial content of the visual field with that of the subject's other perceptual fields, no study reports instantaneous adaptation and some studies report little to no adaptation (Kohler 1951/1964; Taylor 1962). Here is an extract from a recent paper:

> The subjects reported that at times they had the impression that they themselves had been turned upside down, but that they knew that this was not the case. But no subject claimed that he had regained upright vision or that his visual image matched his body sense at any point during the experiment, not even when the subjects were exploring the visual scene by touch. (Linden et al. 1999: 475)

On the face of things, such reports indicate that the contents of vision can be inconsistent with the contents of proprioception.

There are, however, ways in which the advocate of the inter-modal consistency constraint might attempt to challenge such claims. With respect to this particular example, they might argue that although vision represents object O_1 as having a certain property and touch represents object O_2 as not having that property, there is nothing internal to the subject's perceptual experience that identifies O_1 with O_2. On this view, identifying the objects or events represented by one perceptual modality with those represented by another involves an inference that goes beyond the contents of the experiential states themselves. Building on this theme, the advocate of the consistency constraint might attempt to defuse the threat of inter-modal inconsistency by arguing that perceptual experiences ascribe only 'appearance properties' to their objects (Glüer 2009). Rather than supposing that vision (say) represents an object as having one spatial orientation and touch represents it as having another, we might suppose only that vision represents an object as *looking* to have one spatial orientation whereas touch represents it as *feeling* to have another. If this analysis of perceptual content were right then there would be no threat of inter-modal inconsisteny (or, indeed, intra-modal inconsistency), for although it is inconsistent to suppose that an object might be both p and not-p, there is no inconsistency in supposing that an object visually appears to be p but tactually appears to be not-p.

I remain unpersuaded. As Bedford (2004) has pointed out, in order to explain why perceptual adaptation occurs we need to assume that perceptual experiences across different modalities can represent a common fund of objects and properties (see also §10.1). Putting the perceptual modality into the contents of perceptual experience as Glüer's analysis would have us do introduces a needless level of complexity into explanations of perceptual adaptation. Better, I think, to suppose that perceptual content can represent the actual properties of objects and is not limited to the representation of appearance properties.

But we are not yet done with putative examples of inconsistency within consciousness. In fact, we have yet to consider what are perhaps the most persuasive examples of conscious inconsistency: situations in which the contents of judgement are at odds with those of perception. The Zöllner illusion presents us with one such scenario (see Figure 3.3). Judging that the diagonal lines of this illusion are parallel does not ensure that they *look* to be parallel. Perceptual content takes the form of an invitation to judge that the world is thus-and-so, but one need not accept the invitation. And when, as in this case, one refuses to accept the invitation, one is left with an inconsistency between the contents of perception and those of conscious thought.

Where does this leave the consistency constraint? Not in good shape, it would seem. Although the question of intra-modal inconsistency is an open one, there is very good reason to think that inconsistency can occur both between simultaneous experiences in different perceptual modalities and between perceptual states on the one hand and conscious judgements on the other.

Let us return to the inconsistency objection to closure. The objection, you will recall, proceeded on the basis of the assumption that no conscious state can have inconsistent content. With this assumption in hand the proponent of closure is faced with the unpalatable choice between rejecting closure on the one hand and clinging to the consistency thesis on the other. But perhaps

Figure 3.3 The Zöllner illusion

we should reconsider the assumption that no conscious state can have inconsistent content. Why exactly might one insist that no conscious state could have inconsistent content?

The main motivation for this assumption derives from possible worlds treatments of intentional content. According to such accounts, the content of a mental state is given by the set of possible worlds that it satisfies (Stalnaker 1984; Lewis 1986). On the plausible assumption that there are no impossible worlds, the set of worlds that would satisfy states with inconsistent content is the null set. The upshot of this is that we have a choice between endorsing closure and rejecting possible worlds treatments of content. No doubt opinions will differ as to what the best option is here, but my own inclination is to retain closure but reject the possible worlds approach to the contents of consciousness in favour of structured approaches. And in fact there are plenty of reasons for adopting a structured conception of the contents of consciousness that are independent of any desire to save closure. As Mellor (1988) points out, if I believe that all even numbers are the sum of two primes and you do not, then one of us must have a belief that is necessarily false (see also Brown 1990, 1991). And even if one were to insist that necessary falsehoods cannot be believed they can surely be *entertained*, for every logic student is familiar with the experience of realizing that a certain claim must be false because it entails a contradiction (Sorensen 1996). There may be good objections to closure, but the argument from inconsistency is not among them.

3.3 Visual experience

A second objection to closure takes its point of departure from everyday visual experience. Suppose that you are looking at a speckled hen in broad daylight. You see it as speckled; indeed, you see it as having numerous speckles. Allowing for the fact that visual acuity rapidly deteriorates outside of one's attentional focus, let us assume that the hen has twelve visible speckles, and let us label these speckles '1', '2', '3' ... '12'. You see 1, 2, 3, and so on for each of the 12 visible speckles. In other words, your visual experience represents the hen as having one speckle *there*, another speckle *there*, a third speckle *there*, and so on. But do you have a visual experience that conjunctively represents all 12 speckles? Arguably not. At the very least, your ability to say whether the hen had 12 speckles as opposed to 11 speckles or 13 speckles would be near chance. But if you do not experience the hen as having 12 speckles then the contents of your visual experience would appear not to be closed under conjunction, despite the fact that they are unified with each other. In short, the speckled hen appears to present us with a case in which phenomenal unity holds in the absence of conjunctive content. Call this the *speckled hen objection*.

In response to the objection some might be tempted to deny that one's visual experience when looking at a specked hen *would* exhibit phenomenal unity, and thus that we should expect closure to fail in this context. But this response is not compelling, for it is highly implausible to suppose that the unity of consciousness—that is, the *phenomenal* unity of consciousness—breaks down when looking at a speckled hen. Representational unity might fail in such cases, but there is no reason at all to think that phenomenal unity might fail.

A rather more plausible response is to deny that one visually experiences *each* of the hen's speckles. One of the lessons to be learnt from recent vision science is that the visual system is very good at encoding the high-level properties (or 'gist') of a scene but rather poor at encoding its low-level details.[7] A brief visual fixation might suffice to provide us with an awareness of whether a presented scene involves an urban setting or a natural setting, but leave us in the dark about (say) the number or distribution of people that it contains. Drawing on this research, one might be tempted to suggest that seeing a speckled hen involves nothing more than 'speckled hen gist'. Perhaps visual experience represents only that the target hen is speckled—or, perhaps, 'specked to some degree'—without representing *each* of the hens' visible speckles as such.[8]

This response has much to be said for it. I have little doubt that visual experience can contain 'speckled gist', and I am inclined to think that there are contexts in which one's experience of a speckled hen might be purely gisty. But I am not sure that this approach does justice to the phenomenal character of *all* speckled hen experiences. Suppose that one is looking at a speckled hen in broad daylight. The hen is not far away, and each of its 12 visible speckles seems to be present in a single visual experience. One has the impression that one could have attended to each of the hen's speckles had one chosen to do so. This speckled hen experiences may be gisty but I'm not convinced that it would be *merely* gisty. Instead, it seems to me very plausible to suppose that *each* speckle would be individually represented in visual experience.

Does that mean that the speckled hen objection succeeds? I don't think so. Let us return to the assumption that one would lack a conjunctive experience of all 12 speckles. Why exactly might one endorse this thought? Well, according

---

[7] See Henderson & Hollingworth (1999); Oliva (2005); Potter (1976).

[8] Tye (2009) develops an account of the speckled hen along roughly these lines, although he doesn't put it in terms of gist. In his terms, one sees the speckles collectively without seeing them individually.

to certain accounts of perceptual content, experience can represent <p> only if any subject with the requisite concepts is 'positioned' to judge <p> on the basis of that experience (see e.g. McGinn 1982; Peacocke 1983). This constraint on perceptual content would, it seems, entail that one would not have an experience of the hen as having 12 speckles, for even someone with the appropriate concepts would not be in a position to say how many speckles the hen had, nor would they be in a position to sort the hen on the basis of its speckles.

But should we accept this constraint on perceptual content? I am prepared to grant that there may be *a* notion of 'seeing' that is constitutively tied to 'saying' and 'sorting', but I would resist the thought that this notion is the one that we are after in attempting to capture the phenomenal content of vision. It is an open question whether visual experience might 'outrun' what is available to the mechanisms of saying and sorting. In order for such content to be available for judgement its non-conceptual content must be brought under concepts, and processing bottlenecks might restrict the degree to which that can be done. And if that is right, then the contents of a subject's visual experience might outrun what they are in a position to judge even under ideal conditions. In sum, I suggest we should allow that subjects might have visual experiences that conjunctively represent the hen as having 12 speckles, despite there being a legitimate sense in which they fail to see the hen as having 12 speckles (Fantl & Howell 2003).

Speckled hen experiences are not the only visual phenomenon to put pressure on closure. Another such phenomenon is apperceptive (integrative) agnosia, a condition in which patients can see the parts of objects but have difficulty in seeing objects as unified wholes.[9] A patient might see the wheels, bonnet, and body of a car, but be unable to form a visual experience of the car as a unitary object. Here too one might think that we have an example of visual experiences whose contents are not conjoined: the patient has visual experiences with contents <p> and <q> respectively but no visual experience with the content <p&q>.

Some proponents of closure might be tempted to argue that because apperceptive agnosia involves a breakdown in the unity of consciousness we should expect closure to fail. But this is too quick. It is undoubtedly true that apperceptive agnosia involves *some* kind of breakdown in the unity of consciousness, but there is little reason to suppose that it involves a breakdown of phenomenal unity. Although the contents of the agnosic's experiences of the car are not representationally integrated in the way that they ought to be,

---

[9]   See Benson & Greenberg (1969); Farah (2004); Humphreys (1999); Riddoch & Humphreys (1987).

we have no reason to deny that they are phenomenally unified with each other within the context of a single overall visual state.

I think that the objection from apperceptive agnosia fails for the same fundamental reason that the speckled hen objection fails: despite appearances to the contrary, the contents of the agnosic's visual experiences *are* closed under conjunction. The agnosic may not perceive objects as unified wholes, but she does have visual experiences whose contents conjunctively represent their parts. What fails in agnosia is not closure but a certain kind of representational integration that we might call *representational holism*. There is a difference between seeing the parts of an object conjunctively and seeing the parts of an object *as* the parts of a single object. Closure demands only that when conscious states are unified their contents are embedded in a representation with conjunctive content; it does *not* require that the representation of local features be integrated into perceptual gestalts. The conjoint representation of local and low-level features might be necessary for the representation of global or high-level features, but it is clearly not sufficient for it.

Where does this leave us? I have argued that the advocate of closure may have nothing to fear from either the speckled hen or visual agnosia. With respect to the former, I suggested that there may well be a layer of experiential content that outruns that which is available for 'sorting' and 'saying'. And if that's right, then the phenomenal contents of someone looking at a speckled hen may well be closed under conjunction. The lesson to be learned from apperceptive agnosia is that we must distinguish representational closure from representational holism: it is one thing to enjoy a conjunctive representation of the parts or features of an object and quite another thing to represent those parts or features *as* the parts or features of a single object. Thus far, closure remains a viable account of phenomenal unity.

3.4 Inter-sensory unity

Let us consider now the question of whether closure can account for the unity that holds between perceptual experiences drawn from different modalities. Take a visual experience (V) and a tactile experience (T) that are phenomenally unified with each other. Closure entails that there will be a conscious mental state whose content corresponds to the conjunction of the contents of V and T. Call this state 'P'. What kind of state could p be? Clearly it could not be visual, for were it visual it would not be able to capture T's tactile content; nor, for parallel reasons, could it be tactile. So how are we to think of P?

The obvious response is that P is an amodal—or, if you like, 'multimodal'—state: it is neither visual nor tactile but visuo-tactile. This response generalizes to situations in which experiences drawn from multiple modalities are unified with each other. What it is for auditory, visual, and tactile experiences with contents <a>, <v>, and <t> to be phenomenally unified with each other is for the subject in question to enjoy an amodal perceptual state with content <a&v&t>. According to this proposal, the unity between experiences drawn from different modalities will take the form of 'amodal' experiences that straddle the boundaries between modalities.

In implying that the distinction between sensory modalities is a fairly superficial one it might be thought that this response fails to do justice to the phenomenal differences between the perceptual modalities. This thought can be developed by considering the 'common sensibles'—properties such as shape and motion that are detectible via more than one sensory modality (see p. 25). Consider two scenarios, A and B, in each of which you experience one of two coins as larger than the other. In scenario A you are aware of the large coin by sight and the small coin by touch, whereas in scenario B you are aware of the large coin by touch and the small coin by sight. It is clear that the overall phenomenology of A and B differ. What it is like to enjoy visual awareness of a large coin and tactile awareness of a small coin differs in familiar ways from what it is like to enjoy visual awareness of a small coin and tactile awareness of a large coin. But—so the objection goes—if our account of these two scenarios involves a multimodal representation of the one coin as larger than the other, then we seem to have lost the phenomenal contrast between them.[10] How might we recover the phenomenal contrast between A and B without giving up on the idea that the unity between one's visual and tactile experiences can be fully captured by appealing to the contents of an amodal perception?

There are two options available to us here. On the one hand, we could think of the experiences of the coins in Fregean terms (see p. 26). According to this approach, even when vision and touch represent the same properties—say, the size of a coin—they do so via different phenomenal characters. Vision represents the property in question in a 'visual manner' whereas touch represents it in a 'tactile manner'. In the same way that the thought 'The evening star is bright' and the thought 'The morning star is bright' involve different modes of presentation of the same state of affairs, so too Fregean treatments of phenomenal content claim that visual and tactile experiences involve distinct modes of presentation of the same property or event. The Fregean will deny that tactile

---

[10] I am indebted here to O'Dea (2008), who is in turn indebted to Grice (1962).

and visual experiences of shape (considered as such) have the same phenomenal content, for although the two experiences may represent exactly the same properties they will differ in the ways in which those properties are manifest to the subject.

The Fregean treatment of perceptual content is controversial, and many representationalists reject it in favour of a Russellian (or Millian) view. Russellians reject modality-specific 'modes of presentation', and will deny that there could be any phenomenal difference between the visual and tactile representation of a particular property. There may of course be neurophysiological differences between these representations, but such differences will have no impact on what it is like to have these perceptual experiences. Because the Russellian identifies phenomenal content with those properties (or states of affairs) represented by perceptual experience he cannot account for the difference between scenarios A and B by appealing to modality-specific modes of representation. Nonetheless, Russellians do have the resources to account for the phenomenal contrast between A and B.

First, perceptual awareness will provide the subject with access to many features of the coins over and above their size. For example, touch will convey representations of texture and temperature, while vision will mediate experiences of colour. These differences will themselves go a long way towards accounting for the contrast between A and B. Secondly, even when vision and touch do represent the same spatial properties they do so with varying degrees of specificity; for example, vision might contain a more determinate representation of a coin's size and shape than touch does. Thirdly, the various perceptual modalities may contain self-representational content that distinguishes them from their neighbours. Arguably, it is part and parcel of one's overall visual experience that it is mediated by movements of the eyes and head, whereas it is part and parcel of one's overall tactile experience that it is mediated by movements of the hand (O'Dea 2010). In this way, even perceptual experiences that attribute exactly the same property to a represented object will have relational content that marks them as visual or tactile. This too will contribute to the phenomenal contrast between scenarios A and B: in the former one will be implicitly aware that one's experience of the larger coin is mediated by visual exploration and one's experience of the smaller coin is mediated by tactile exploration, whereas the converse will be the case in the latter scenario. We might think of the visual representation of a coin's size as 'embedded' in a larger experience with uniquely visual content, and the tactile representation of the coin's size as 'embedded' in a larger experience with exclusively tactile content.

So, the advocate of closure has two ways in which they can 'recover' the phenomenal contrast between these two scenarios: a 'Fregean' response and a 'Russellian' response. Each of the two responses suffices to block the two-coins objection, and we need not choose between them here. And if the objection can be met, then there is no obstacle to the suggestion that the phenomenal unity between experiences drawn from different modalities can be captured by appealing to the conjunctive contents of amodal perceptual experiences.

3.5 The distinct kinds objection

We might have found an adequate response to the two-coins objection, but that objection turns out to be the tip of a very large iceberg. In addition to perceptual states of various kinds, any catalogue of phenomenally conscious states must include bodily sensations, emotional and mood states, states of imagination and imagery, memories, and experiences of agency. Theorists of a liberal persuasion would also include cognitive states of various kinds—judgements, intentions, and desires—on this list (see p. 6). Further, states drawn from any two of these categories can co-occur within consciousness, and as co-occurrent will typically if not invariably be phenomenally unified with each other. Bodily sensations can be unified with imagery experiences; imagery experiences can be unified with conscious judgements; and both bodily sensations and imagery experiences can be unified with affective experiences.

This poses what is clearly the most serious challenge to closure. Suppose that a subject (S) has a conscious judgement with content $<p>$ and a conscious desire with content $<q>$. Given closure, S must have a conscious state with content $<p\&q>$. But what kind of state could this state be? It couldn't be a judgement, for then it wouldn't capture the fact that the subject *desires* $<q>$. Nor could it be a desire, for then it couldn't capture the fact that the subject *judges* $<p>$. But if it is neither a judgement nor a desire then it would be unable to capture the fact that the subject desires $<q>$ *nor* the fact that it judges $<p>$. There seems to be no plausible account of the nature of the state with content $<p\&q>$. Although I have developed the objection with reference to the unity between a judgement and a desire nothing turns on the choice of those two particular mental state types, and equally potent versions of the objection could be developed with reference to any pair of distinct kinds of conscious states. Call this the *distinct kinds objection*.

The problem posed by accounting for the unity between different kinds of states is importantly different from that posed by accounting for the unity between different kinds of perceptual states which we examined in the previous section. There, we noted that intermodal unity can be accounted for by positing amodal (or 'multimodal') states. However, that move was plausible only because all perceptual states have the same fundamental structure—namely, they are all perceptual. By contrast, the distinct kinds objection concerns states that appear to have no underlying intentional structure in common.

It is clear that the distinct kinds objection cannot be met by denying that phenomenal unity holds between states of different kinds. That would be a response of absolutely last resort—a tactic to be adopted only if closure constituted the only viable account of the unity of consciousness (which it clearly doesn't). And even if someone were somehow able to show that the architecture of *human* cognition prevents conscious states of different kinds from being unified with each other in our experience, it stretches credulity to suppose that such a constraint might capture a deep feature of phenomenal unity. The fundamental challenge posed by the distinct kinds objection is to explain within a closure-based framework *what it would be* for different kinds of mental states to be unified with each other, and that challenge would not be met by simply denying that states belonging to different mental state kinds are unified with each other.

As far as I can see, the only viable strategy for blocking this objection involves showing that the different kinds to which conscious states can belong are only superficially distinct, and that despite appearances any two phenomenally unified conscious states can be assigned to a single *fundamental* kind. The goal, in other words, would be to appropriate the response made to the objection from inter-sensory unity and look to capture the experiential contrast between different kinds of conscious states by appealing only to the contents of a single mental state kind. But what category of mental state could possibly admit bodily sensations, emotional and affective states, memories, imaginative experiences, agentive experiences, and 'cognitive feelings' as determinates?

One answer to this question worth taking seriously is that 'all consciousness is perceptual', as Prinz (2007) puts it. Might there be a notion of perceptual experience—a very broad notion of perceptual experience—according to which all forms of consciousness qualify as modes of perception? Providing a thorough answer to this question goes well beyond the parameters of this chapter, but let me provide some general reasons for pessimism concerning the prospects of 'perceptualism'.

The perceptualist certainly starts off on the right foot, for there are plausible perceptual accounts of certain kinds of conscious states that are not ordinarily regarded as species of perception. Representationalists have long argued for perceptual treatments of bodily sensations: pains are perceptions of bodily damage of some kind; itches are perceptions of mild skin irritation; and experiences of orgasm are perceptions of certain distinctive changes taking place in particular parts of one's body.[11] Drawing on the James-Lange theory of emotions, Prinz (2004) argues that emotional and affective experience can also be understood in terms of the perceptions of patterned changes in the body. Further, it is not implausible to suppose that 'cognitive feelings' might be regarded as broadly perceptual. For example, one might take the tip-of-the-tongue experience to represent in a quasi-perceptual format that the sought-for word is (say) poised for cognitive deployment. It may also be possible to provide a plausible perceptual treatment of recollective ('episodic') memory. Of course, any such account will need to capture the phenomeno-logical differences between recollective memory and perception strictly speaking, but there are a number of ways in which this can be done without giving up on the thought that conscious memory is broadly perceptual. For example, one might argue that the contents of perceptual phenomenology are more fine-grained than are the contents of memory phenomenology, or that memory phenomenology contains a certain type of meta-representational con-tent that is not present in ordinary perceptual phenomenology.

So far, perhaps, so good. But there are further challenges for the perceptu-alist treatment of consciousness. The first of these challenges derives from agentive experiences—'experiences of acting'. Consider what it's like to experience oneself as (say) reaching for a glass of water. Such an action will typically be accompanied by a 'feeling of doing', an experience whose content represents oneself as an agent, one's goals, and the means by which one is attempting to realize those goals. What is the *structure* of agentive experiences? According to an influential view, experiences of acting are to be identified with actions (or willings) themselves rather than representations of actions (or willings) (see e.g. O'Shaughnessy 1980; 2003). In developing this approach Searle (1983) explicitly contrasts the structure of experiences of acting with that of perceptual experiences: whereas the latter are in the business of saying how the world is (in his terms, they have a mind-to-world direction of fit), the former are in the business of making it the case that the world is a certain way (they have a world-to-mind direction of fit). It should be noted that there are 'perceptual' treatments of agentive experience—indeed, I myself have defended a version of the view in places (Bayne 2008a, 2010)—but it is far from certain that the perceptual approach will be able to account for *all* forms of agentive experience. At the very least, it is arguable that the experience of

---

[11] See e.g. Armstrong (1962); Bain (2003); Pitcher (1970); and Tye (1995).

trying to do something is not best thought of as a perception of trying; instead, it may simply be a kind of trying.[12]

Agentive experiences pose problems for the perceptualist because their structure seems to be directive (or 'telic') rather than descriptive (or 'thetic'). Other conscious states pose problems because they seem to be neither directive nor descriptive. Consider what it is like to idly imagine that there is a tiger in one's kitchen. This mental episode may be quasi-perceptual in the sense that it will have a sensory character, but it lacks the world-directed structure of perception. It would not be appropriate to evaluate one's states of imagination with respect to how well they represent the world. (Nor, for that matter, would it be appropriate to evaluate them with respect to how successful they are in bringing it about that the world is a certain way.) The state of imagining that there is a tiger in one's kitchen has intentional content, but—unlike the experience of seeing a tiger—it is not in the business of saying how the world is, and hence is not properly thought of as a species of perception in even the most liberal sense of the term.

But perhaps the most robust challenge facing the perceptualist concerns conscious thought. In order to have any plausibility, the perceptualist will need to embrace a conservative account of cognitive phenomenology, according to which the phenomenology of thought is exhausted by the phenomenal character of the various sensory accompaniments of thought, such as visual, auditory and motor imagery. I reject this deflationary treatment of the phenomenal character of thought in favour of a liberal view, according to which occurent thoughts possess phenomenal character in their own right. There is, I submit, something distinctive that it is like to judge that an argument is invalid, hope that the trains are running on time, and wonder what might have happened had early humans not left Africa, just as surely as there is something it is like to smell coffee, see a Ferris wheel turn, or hear the rain fall on a tin roof.

The combined force of these worries indicates that it is not the case that all consciousness is perceptual, even on the most inclusive conception of perception.

There is, however, another way in which the advocate of closure might attempt to argue that all conscious states are really forms of a single kind of state. Suppose that one were to adopt a monitoring account of consciousness, according to which mental states are conscious in virtue of being represented in a certain kind of way (Gennaro 2004; Kriegel & Williford 2006). On this view, the fact that mental states of various kinds can be phenomenally unified

---

[12] See also Klein (2007) and Hall (2008), who argue that pains and related bodily sensations have imperative rather than descriptive structure.

with each other would be neither here nor there as far as closure is concerned, for each of these states would be conscious in the same way: in virtue of being monitored by a certain type of mental state. Once the distinction between mental states that are consciously *monitored* and those that consciously *monitor* is appreciated the distinct kinds problem evaporates. The unity between a desire and a judgement is not to be found by looking for a state that might 'inherit' the contents of both states, but by finding a state that represents their contents conjunctively. And—the thought continues—such a state will not be difficult to find: it will simply be the state in virtue of which one is conscious of both the desire and the judgement. In other words, the unity between a judgement with content <p> and a desire with content <q> can be secured by supposing that the subject has a suitable monitoring thought with the content <I am judging that p and desiring that q>. From the perspective of the monitoring account, the fact that one can be conscious of (say) desires, perceptions, and imaginings together is no more puzzling than the fact that one can be conscious of ships, shoes, and sealing wax together. What matters is not the structure of the states that one is conscious *of* (first-order unity) but the structure of the states that one is conscious *with* (higher-order unity). Indeed, a monitoring theorist attracted to the unity thesis could even posit 'total' thoughts that conjunctively represent *all* of the subject's concurrent conscious states.

So far, perhaps, so good: monitoring accounts of consciousness may well have the resources to solve—or perhaps 'dissolve'—the problem of distinct kinds. But the monitoring account can save closure only if it is *true*. Is it? Although it has many advocates, I myself am not much attracted to the approach. My reservations can be captured in terms of the following dilemma. If the monitoring account of consciousness is true then it must be either a conceptual truth or an empirical truth. Is it a conceptual truth? Its proponents sometimes write as though they think that it is. A conscious mental state, it is sometimes said, is nothing other than a mental state *of* which one is conscious, and hence—the argument goes—it follows that mental states are conscious in virtue of being monitored in some way (see e.g. Lycan 2001; Rosenthal 2003). But this is a sleight of hand, for the 'of' in question need not be read as the 'of' of intentional directedness. The only uncontroversial sense in which conscious thoughts are thoughts of which one is conscious is the sense in which conscious thoughts make an impact on one's overall conscious state, but there is nothing in that claim to encourage the monitoring theorist. Is there good empirical evidence in favour of the monitoring approach? I don't know of any. Empirical arguments for monitoring treatments of consciousness often appeal to the fact that neural activity in perceptual cortex generates conscious states only when it is processed by downstream systems, often in the form of feedback from higher levels to lower levels (see e.g. Rolls 2004; 2008). But this data provides evidence in favour of monitoring approaches only if the processing in higher cortical areas is conceived of as *representing* earlier stages of neural activity and I see little reason to put that gloss on it. It seems to me that if the distinct kinds objection can be met only by adopting a monitoring approach to consciousness, then we will need to look elsewhere for an account of phenomenal unity.

Where does that leave us? I earlier suggested that there is really only one viable strategy for blocking the objection from distinct kinds: we need a way of conceiving of all forms of consciousness as manifestations of a single kind of mental state. We have seen that there are two ways in which this strategy might be executed: a 'first-order' way that appealed to the idea that all conscious states are forms of perceptual consciousness, and a 'higher-order' way, according to which the fundamental kind in question takes the form of the monitoring state in virtue of which mental states are conscious. Neither proposal proved to be viable. The upshot, I suggest, is that there are indeed fundamentally different kinds of conscious states. And if that is right, then closure must be false, for closure provides no viable account of what it is for conscious states drawn from (fundamentally) different kinds to be unified with each other.

3.6 Implication

By way of drawing this chapter to a close, let us briefly consider some of the implications that the failure of closure might have. The first potential implication concerns the prospects for representationalist treatments of phenomenal consciousness. Representationalism claims that a subject's phenomenal states supervene on its representational states. Even if this supervenience holds with respect to 'atomic' conscious states—perceptual experiences, mood experiences, and so on—the failure of closure raises questions about whether it also holds for complex phenomenal states, such as the subject's total phenomenal state. On the face of things it looks as though it might not hold, for the distinct kinds objection shows that there will often be no representational state corresponding to the subject's total phenomenal state.

There is a challenge here, but it is not decisive. In order to address it the representationalist need hold only that a subject's phenomenal states supervene on (are fixed by) their representational states *as a whole*: no phenomenal difference without a representational difference. Even when there is no representational state corresponding to a subject's total phenomenal state, the only way in which two subjects might have different total phenomenal states is by having different representational states (at least, as far as the distinct kinds objection shows). The failure of closure might be problematic for strong representationalists who *identify* phenomenal states with representational states, but weak representationalism is left unscathed by the failure of closure.

What implications might the failure of closure have for the mereological account of phenomenal unity? In §3.1 I suggested that closure might be entailed by the mereological account. If that thought is right, then the failure of closure is not good news for those who are inclined to endorse the mereological account (as I am). But is that thought right? Does closure follow from the mereological account?

Why does closure appear to follow from the mereological account? Well, one might reason as follows. The mereological account holds that if experiences e_1 and e_2 are phenomenally unified with each other, then the subject will have a conscious state e_3 that subsumes—that is, includes as proper parts—both e_1 and e_2. Now, in order for e_3 to subsume e_1 and e_2 its content must entail the contents of e_1 and e_2, for it would be mysterious why they might be related in this way if the content of e_3 didn't entail that of e_1 and e_2. This, of course, doesn't mean that the content of e_3 must correspond to the conjunction of the contents of e_1 and e_2, but it seems to point in that direction, for any other account of the content of e_3 would involve attributing to it additional (and redundant) complexity. In short, there seems to be a fairly direct route from the mereological account to closure.

To see where this argument might go wrong we need to distinguish between phenomenal states as such and phenomenally conscious intentional (or 'representational') states (Bayne & Chalmers 2003). Phenomenal states involve the instantiation of phenomenal properties—properties that are individuated in terms of what it is like to have them. Intentional states are not individuated in terms of what it's like to instantiate them, but in terms of their attitude/mode (belief, desire, perception, etc.) and content (that p, that q, etc.). Whereas intentional states can be 'factorized' into two components (attitude and content), phenomenal states cannot. Of course, intentional states can 'be' phenomenally conscious, in the sense that certain intentional states will be associated with particular phenomenal states. When this happens, the phenomenal state associated with any intentional state will be a function of that intentional state's attitude and content. What it is like to desire that <p> differs from what it is like to judge that <p>, and both of these states differ from what it's like to desire that <q>. Although there is an intimate relationship between phenomenal states and phenomenally conscious intentional states, we should not identify them. They are simply different kinds of beasts, with different kinds of structure.

We can now see why it is a mistake to think that mereological relations between phenomenal states can always be captured in terms of entailment relations between the contents of phenomenally conscious mental states. What a subject's total phenomenal state must capture is the *phenomenal character* of those states that it subsumes. Many of the subject's phenomenal states will be associated with particular intentional states, but others—particularly those with a complex phenomenology—will not be able to be paired with any intentional state in this way. This will be particularly true when it comes to the subject's total phenomenal state—the state that fully captures what it is like to be the subject at the time in question. The phenomenal character of this state might be determined by the subject's various intentional states, but there will usually be no single intentional state with which it can be paired. There is daylight between the notion of a phenomenal state and that of a phenomenally conscious intentional state, and it is this daylight that allows the mereological analysis of phenomenal unity to survive the failure of closure unscathed.

3.7 Conclusion

It is time to recap. This chapter has focussed on the thought that the unity of consciousness might be understood in terms of the closure of conscious content under co-instantiated conjunction—'closure', for short. I began with the observation that closure can provide us with a plausible analysis of phenomenal unity only if phenomenal content can be fully captured in propositional terms. Having noted concerns about 'phenomenological danglers' and object-directed (rather than proposition-directed) states, I granted that (weak) representionalism has sufficient plausibility to be taken seriously. I then turned to four objections to closure. The first of the four objections was an objection from inconsistency. Closure entails that a subject with inconsistent conscious states must also have a conscious state with inconsistent content, and that result looks to be problematic. I suggested that the appropriate response to this objection is to neither reject closure nor deny that inconsistent states can be unified, but to insist that any account of phenomenal content must be able to accommodate states with inconsistent contents. A second objection focused on visual experiences with contents that appear not to be closed under conjunction. I examined two kinds of visual experiences that might be thought to meet this description—the kind of experience one might have in looking at a speckled hen in good light, and the kind of experience that characterizes apperceptive agnosia—and argued that in each case there is much to be said for the thought that visual content is indeed conjunctively closed despite appearances to the contrary. A third objection to closure turned on the question of how the account might capture the unity between experiences drawn from different modalities. I argued that this challenge can be met by positing perceptually amodal states—states that do not themselves fall squarely within any single modality, but whose contents belong to multiple modalities. A fourth and final objection generalized the challenge implicit in the inter-sensory objection and asked how closure might account for the unity between different kinds of conscious states. I outlined two responses to this objection, a 'perceptual' response and a 'monitoring' response, and argued that neither is successful.

Although closure fails as an analysis of phenomenal unity, our investigation of it has not been in vain. There are two lessons in particular that we might take from it. Firstly, the failure of closure suggests that there is a certain 'slippage' between phenomenal states on the one hand and intentional ('representational') states on the other. This slippage shows that strong versions of representationalism—versions that identify all phenomenal states with representational states—are false. Even if the components of a subject's total phenomenal state are representational states, that total state itself will not (in general) be a representational state. Secondly, even though phenomenal unity cannot be identified with the closure of phenomenal content under conjunction, there is still reason to think that phenomenal unity will often go together with closure. With that in mind, we might take failures of closure to be diagnostic of failures of phenomenal unity. I return to this theme in chapter 5.

PART II. IS CONSCIOUS UNIFIED?

4

Motivating the Unity Thesis

In the first chapter I surveyed a number of things that might be meant by the claim that consciousness is unified. Of these, I singled out the unity thesis for special consideration. According to the unity thesis, the conscious states that any subject of experience enjoys at any one point in time will occur as the components of a single total phenomenal state—a unitary 'phenomenal field.' The unity thesis, I suggest, provides us with a conception of the unity of consciousness that is substantive, interesting, and plausible. But what exactly is the source of its appeal?

The plausibility of the unity thesis derives largely from introspection. Consider the structure of your overall conscious state. I suspect that you will be inclined to the view that all your current experiences are phenomenally unified with each other—that they occur as the components of a single phenomenal field; to put the same point in different terminology, that you enjoy a single phenomenal state that subsumes them all. Call this claim *the unity judgement*. Although the unity judgement doesn't entail the unity thesis, there is a line of argument from the unity judgement to the unity thesis. According to this argument, the unity of consciousness that is revealed to introspection is not a feature that consciousness possesses only when one attends to its structure but is a feature that it enjoys all the time—even when one doesn't (and perhaps cannot) introspect. Moreover, the fact that one's own experiences are unified gives one reason to think that other subjects of experience also enjoy conscious unity. That, in a nutshell, is the introspection-based argument for the unity thesis.

This chapter explores the tenability of this argument. My examination will proceed in two stages. The first stage (§4.1–§4.3) focuses on 'the unity judgement'—the introspective judgement to the effect that each of one's current experiences is unified with each other; the second stage (§4.4–§4.5) examines whether the route from the unity judgement to the unity thesis is a legitimate one. We will see that although the argument from introspection is far from decisive, it does provide us with a respectable case for the unity thesis.

4.1 The unity judgement

Perhaps the most general objection to the unity judgement concerns the fact that it relies on introspection. Worries about the trustworthiness of introspection are nothing new but date back to the earliest days of the science of consciousness. Indeed, the demise of the study of consciousness in the early years of the twentieth century was due in no small part to introspectively based disputes (Boring 1950; Lyons 1986). A century later, the science of consciousness is still grappling with introspective disputes and the sceptical challenges that they engender (Schwitzgebel 2008; Bayne & Spener 2010).

This is not the place to engage in a comprehensive examination of introspection's credentials, but in fact no such examination is needed. The question 'Is introspection reliable?' is not a good one to ask, for epistemic faculties are reliable only with respect to certain questions and under certain conditions. Vision is typically a good way of determining the colour of a nearby British telephone box on a bright summer's day, but a rather poor way of determining the identity of a small, rapidly moving animal on a dark winter's night. The question we need to ask is whether introspection is likely to be reliable *with respect to the unity judgement*.

Evidence that might directly bear on this question is hard to come by, for in order to have such evidence we would already need to know whether or not consciousness is unified, but if we knew that then we wouldn't need to invest any faith in the unity judgement. However, there might be less direct ways of putting pressure on the unity judgement. According to many, introspection is not to be trusted when it comes to determining the *capacity* of consciousness. Such claims might be taken to have an indirect bearing on the unity judgement, for if introspection is an unreliable witness with respect to the capacity of consciousness then we may have reasons to think that it is also unreliable with respect to its structure. Let us consider this line of thought in some detail.

Introspection, it is commonly said, suggests that we enjoy a 'rich' or 'lavish' stream of consciousness, according to which a single moment of consciousness will typically contain a rich, detailed, and multimodal representation of the world. There is, however, reason to doubt whether this introspective picture is accurate. Research on 'the span of apprehension' dating back to the earliest days of empirical psychology is often taken to show that this introspective judgement is radically wrong, and that the bandwidth of consciousness is vastly more 'austere' or 'sparse' than introspection suggests.

Let us begin with a selective overview of the evidence in favour of the sparse view of the capacity of consciousness.[1] One line of evidence involves research on numerosity judgements, in which subjects are required to determine the number of items presented in a display. A much-replicated finding is that subjects are able to identify the number of items in displays with four items or fewer with high degrees of confidence, rapidly, and with very low error rates, whereas levels of confidence, reaction times, and error rates worsen for displays containing five or more items (Atkinson et al. 1976). This is true not just for visual items but applies also to other modalities: within olfaction subjects are able to discriminate and identify only four items in mixtures containing multiple odours (Livermore & Laing 1996, 1998); within audition subjects are able to discriminate one speaker from two speakers but have great difficulty in segmenting an auditory stream that contains the voices of three or more speakers (Kashino & Hirahara 1996); and within touch subjects can reliably discriminate one tactile stimulus from two, but with three or more stimuli error rates exceed 30 per cent (Gallace et al. 2006). Small numbers of perceptual items can be subitized but larger groups of items need to be counted. Counting requires the deployment of attention, which in turn suggests that subjects can no longer draw on the contents of a single conscious state but must integrate the contents of successive experiences.

A second line of evidence for the sparse model derives from the work of Pylyshyn and colleagues on the ability of subjects to track visual objects in the context of distractors (Pylyshyn & Storm 1988; Sears & Pylyshyn 2000; Yantis 1992). In a typical experiment, a subset of items within a larger display set is cued, and subjects are required to track the cued objects whilst all the items—both targets and distractors—move randomly through the display. The items are then made stationary, and subjects are required to identify whether a randomly selected object is a target or a distractor. Results suggest that subjects are able to track only four items with any degree of reliability.

Change blindness provides a third motivation for the sparse conception of consciousness. This label refers to the surprising inability of subjects to detect large changes in naturalistic scenes across successive presentations.[2] In a representative experiment (Grimes 1996), subjects were shown an image of two cowboys sitting on a bench. Over 50 per cent of the subjects failed to notice when the heads of the cowboys were swapped during a saccade, despite the fact that they had been told to expect such changes. Kevin O'Regan (1992), amongst

---

[1] See also Cowan (2001); Huang et al. (2007); Irwin (1996); Luck & Vogel (1997).
[2] Nakayama (1990); McConkie & Rayner (1975); McConkie & Zola (1979); Rensink et al. (1997); Simons & Levin (1997).

others, has argued that subjects are unaware of such changes because visual experience fails to encode the information required for their detection. We have here the roots of the 'grand illusion' conception of visual experience, according to which the apparent richness of perceptual consciousness is an illusion generated by the fact that much of the world is immediately and effortlessly *available* to awareness.

Taken as a whole this research certainly provides *some* support for the sparse conception of consciousness. After all, the very fact that these results are surprising suggests that they are at odds with our naïve conception of the capacity of consciousness (Dennett 2001). However, some degree of caution would not be inappropriate here. First, each of these experimental paradigms requires the exercise of capacities that go beyond those required for consciousness as such. This is perhaps most obvious with respect to change blindness. It is one thing to be aware *of* features in a scene that have changed, and it is another to be aware *that* they have changed. Detecting a change requires not only that one represent the features that have changed but also that one integrate the representations of those features, and it is possible that the failure to detect changes often arises not because the features themselves haven't been consciously represented but because the representations of those features haven't been appropriately integrated (Dretske 2004; Henderson & Hollingworth 2003; Hollingworth et al. 2001; Simons et al. 2002). Similar concerns can be raised about the numerosity and multi-object tracking experiments. In each case, reliable performance requires not merely that subjects are aware of the presented items but that they also bring them under certain kinds of representations—either number categories (numerosity judgements) or temporally stable object files (multi-object tracking).

A second ground for caution is that much of this work is concerned with identifying the capacity of accurate visual *perception* rather than that of visual *experience* as such. In other words, these results may show not that visual experience is austere, but that its content owes a great deal more to top-down expectation and 'filling-in' than we tend to assume. Perhaps part of the surprise that we experience in response to these experiments is a reaction to discovering how poor we are at tracking the world rather than a reaction to discovering how impoverished the contents of consciousness are.

Finally, we should keep in mind the fact that these experiments are typically unimodal. Even if there is a four-item limit on experience within any one modality the *overall* capacity of consciousness may be somewhat larger. One could argue that although these experiments are unimodal in structure they actually tap the overall capacity limits of consciousness, for in the relevant experimental contexts the subject's experience is restricted to a single modality, but it is hard to believe that the stream of consciousness is ever restricted to a single perceptual modality, even in the context of (say) a visual-tracking experiment. These impressionistic remarks can be buttressed by research on intermodal integration, which strongly suggests that the various perceptual modalities do not function as autonomous streams of processing but are highly interdependent (see § 10.3). All in all, the evidence for the sparse conception of the capacity of consciousness is rather less compelling than it is often taken to be.

We should also note that it is not entirely obvious how much support introspection actually does provide for the 'lavish' conception of consciousness. Although introspection appears to lead some subjects to embrace a rich account of consciousness, others take introspection to support a rather more modest picture of the capacity of consciousness (Schwitzgebel 2007). I myself incline towards some degree of modesty here. As best I can tell, my typical phenomenal field involves a small band of focal experience surrounded by an experiential penumbra. This focal experience is usually dominated by at most two or three modalities at a time, with only a few objects and features represented in any detail across these two or three modalities. The penumbra surrounding this focus might include a background sense of affective tonality, an awareness of the general orientation of my body, and perhaps also various fragments of fringe and cognitive phenomenology, such as tip-of-the-tongue experiences or stray thoughts. This sketch might not qualify as an endorsement of the 'sparse' view of consciousness, but it is certainly some distance from the lavish model. Naïve introspection—or, perhaps better, our naïve theorizing about consciousness on the basis of naïve introspection—might lead us to overestimate the capacity of consciousness somewhat, but the case for thinking that it is radically unreliable has not been made.

Let us return to the unity judgement. Even if introspection *were* an unreliable witness with respect to the capacity of consciousness, it is a further question whether it is also unreliable with respect to the unity judgement. Taking their lead from the 'grand illusionists', the critic might suggest that the sense of experiential unity provided by introspection is an illusion that arises from mistaking features of the world for features of consciousness. The world itself may be unified but our experience of it is fragmentary and piecemeal, built up over successive experiences rather than contained within a single unified conscious state.

I don't find this line of thought convincing. It is certainly true that the world is unified (whatever that might mean), and it is also true that the representational contents of our experience of the world are also built up over successive experiences. But there is nothing in these platitudes that might undercut or 'explain away' the force of the unity judgement. Not only is the world itself unified, so too are our experiences of it. Perceptual *content* is often 'fragmentary' and 'piecemeal', but no matter how partial one's take on the world may be it is invariably contained within a single overarching experiential state. I submit that the unity judgement has little to fear from attacks on the reliability of introspection.

4.2 Beyond the reach of introspection

Introspection itself might be reliable when it comes to the unity judgement, but what about experiences that elude the reach of introspection? Even if each of the experiences of which one is introspectively aware were phenomenally unified with each other, those experiences might constitute only a subset of one's overall set of experiences. The possibility of introspectively inaccessible experiences casts a shadow of suspicion over the unity judgement.

In examining this objection it is useful to distinguish between two types of introspective inaccessibility. One type of inaccessibility obtains when experiences occur within parts of cognitive architecture that are sealed off from the mechanisms of introspection. We might call such states 'deeply inaccessible'. Experiences immured within Fodorian modules (Block 2007) or sub-personal homunculi (White 1987)—if such there be—would be deeply inaccessible. I am going to set the question of deeply inaccessible states to one side here. I do this not because I regard deeply inaccessible experiences as conceptually or metaphysically impossible, but because we have no evidence of such states. It seems to me that deeply inaccessible experiences ought to be treated in the way that we treat radically sceptical scenarios: although they may be of interest to certain philosophical projects, they ought not constrain sober exercises in theory-building.

Another class of inaccessible experiences cannot be dismissed quite so easily. If introspection has a more restricted 'bandwidth' than consciousness itself, then we might expect that complex experiences would not be introspectively accessible (as such). Let us call such states 'superficially inaccessible'.

Unlike deeply inaccessible experiences, there may be reason to think that superficially inaccessible experiences occur. The data in question involves Sperling's well-known experiments on the reportability of briefly presented visual stimuli (Sperling 1960; Averbach & Sperling 1961). In these experiments, subjects are presented with a matrix containing twelve or so alphanumeric figures for a brief period (say, 250 milliseconds). There are two kinds of conditions, a *full report* condition and a *partial report* condition. In the full report condition subjects are required to report the contents of the entire matrix.

Typically, subjects are able to correctly report only 4.3 of the twelve figures (on average). In the partial report condition, a tone is sounded immediately after the presentation of the matrix indicating which of the three rows the subject is to report; for example, a high tone indicates that subjects are to report only the four figures in the top row. On such trials, trained subjects are able to report three of the four figures in the cued row (on average). In other words, subjects are able to report more figures with respect to a row that has been cued (after display offset) than they are with respect to any arbitrary uncued row. This is known as the *partial report superiority effect*.

Arguably, the most natural explanation of this effect is that there is a bottleneck on reportability—and, perhaps more fundamentally, on introspection—that prevents subjects from gaining access to the full sweep of their experiential content (Block 2007). Subjects in the experiment enjoy a rich visual experience whose content 'outstrips' that to which they have introspective access. According-ing to this interpretation, the visual phenomenology of subjects is not limited to a generic representation of the matrix as (say) containing twelve alphanu-meric figures, but includes a detailed representation of the specific identity of each—or at least most—of the figures in the matrix. There are other inter-pretations of the Sperling data (see the commentaries on Block 2007; Phillips forthcoming), but this is perhaps the most plausible one.

What implications might this picture have for the unity judgement? Well, if subjects have a detailed, fine-grained experience of the matrix as a whole to which they lack introspective access, then they are hardly in a position to have introspective warrant for thinking that each of their current experiences is unified with each other. Subjects might be able to tell whether or not their experiences of each of the *rows* and/or *columns* of the matrix are unified with each other, but they will not be able to tell whether those experiences are unified with their experience of the entire matrix. And, the objection con-tinues, there is no reason why it shouldn't be possible for experiences of the parts of the matrix to be unified with each other without also being unified with a non-generic experience of the matrix as a whole. (As an aid to intuition imagine a subject with one stream of consciousness in its right hemisphere and another in its left hemisphere: its experiences of the parts of the matrix might be located in one hemisphere and its experience of the matrix as a whole might be located in the other hemisphere.) What should we make of this objection?

It is, I think, an open question whether the scenario just outlined is possible, for one might argue that there are deep constraints between phenomenal unity on the one hand and representational unity on the other, such that experiences of the parts of an object cannot be phenomenally unified with each other without also being unified with an experience of the whole of that object at least for subjects who do have an experience of the whole of the object (although see §3.3). But even if it is *possible* for a subject to have an experience of the matrix as a whole that is not itself phenomenally unified with experiences of the various parts of that matrix, this would surely be a highly unusual state of affairs. If there is one place where we should expect relations between the contents of experience to constrain relations between the experiences that carry those contents it is here. A cognitive architecture in which experiences of a matrix as a whole were not phenomenally unified with experiences of its various parts would surely have little to recommend it. In sum, it seems reasonable to assume that if the experiences of the parts of an object are phenomenally unified with each other then they will also be unified with an experience of the object as a whole, at least when that object is indeed experienced as a whole.

But the critic is not yet done. Consider experiences e_1 and e_2, which are such that each represents a single column of the Sperling matrix. Although the contents of e_1 and e_2 are *individually* accessible to introspection, they are not *conjointly* accessible. And, the critic might continue, the fact that a pair of experiences is not conjointly introspectable suggests that they are not phenomenally unified with each other. Indeed, it is not implausible to suppose that it is part of the functional role of phenomenal unity that phenomenally unified experiences are conjointly available to introspection.

Although this argument has some force, there is another line of argument that must also be taken into account. The fact that e_1 and e_2 are individually introspectible surely gives us some reason to think that they are phenomenally unified with each other, for experiences that are not phenomenally unified are unlikely to be available to the same consuming systems. So we have two competing considerations: the fact that e_1 and e_2 are not conjointly introspectable suggests that they are *not* unified, but the fact that each is introspectable suggests that they *are* unified. Which of these lines of argument has most weight?

It seems to me that the case for unity trumps the case for disunity. The reason for this is that we have an account of why e_1 and e_2 are not conjointly introspectible—namely, that any experience that subsumes both e_1 and e_2 would be 'too large' to make it through the bottleneck of introspection. Just as the experience of the entire matrix is too complex to make it from the visual buffer to working memory 'in one piece', so too the experience of any two columns is also too complex to make it through this channel. If, however, it turned out that the content of the conjunction of e_1 and e_2 was 'smaller' than that of an experience that could be introspected, then we would have reason to think that e_1 and e_2 are not phenomenally unified. But, to the best of my knowledge, it doesn't and so we don't.

Let us take stock. I began this section by distinguishing two forms of introspective inaccessibility: deep inaccessibility and superficial inaccessibility. I then set to one side the potential threat from deeply inaccessible experiences in order to focus on the more pressing—not to mention more tractable—challenge posed by superficially inaccessible experiences. Although it is contested, we noted that Sperling's data provides us with some evidence of superficially inaccessible experiences. Do such states call the unity judgement into question? In principle they might, for the fact that experiences are not conjointly available for introspection gives us some reason to deny that they are phenomenally unified. But such reasons must be weighed against the fact that such states are individually introspectible. Introspective support for the unity judgement derives not only from the fact that one is aware of one's experience *as* unified, but also from the fact that experiences that are available to introspection—whether conjunctively or individually—are likely to be unified with each other.

4.3 Hurley's objection

Hurley's treatment of the unity of consciousness provides us with the materials for a quite different objection to the argument from introspection. According to this objection, thinking that introspection might provide support for the unity thesis would involve something akin to a category mistake, for introspection provides us with access only to the *contents* of consciousness and not to its *structure*. This objection should be familiar, for we examined a version of it in Chapter 2 in connection with the question of partial unity. Let us begin by briefly revisiting that discussion.

One of the main objections to partial unity concerns the challenges one confronts in projecting oneself into a partially unified perspective. As we noted, Hurley argues that it would be wrong to think that such difficulties show that the notion of a partially unified perspective is incoherent, for the subjective perspective has access only to the contents of experiences. There are, she suggests, partially unified perspectives that would be subjectively indistinguishable from certain fully unified perspectives.

To appreciate the force of Hurley's argument consider *Fully Unified* and *Partially Unified* (see Figure 4.1).[3] Despite the fact that *Fully Unified* has a fully unified consciousness and *Partially Unified* has only a partially unified conscious-

---

[3] Because Hurley's cases involve unnecessary complications I have changed their details whilst preserving their spirit (1998: 108–12; see also Hurley (2003)).

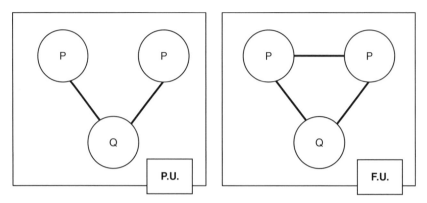

Figure 4.1 A partially unified perspective (P.U.) and a fully unified perspective (F.U.)

ness, there will be no subjective ('what it's like') difference between them. Both subjects will be aware of experiencing <p> and <q> together, in the context of a single experiential state. Introspection might lead both subjects to endorse the unity judgement ('I have a unified consciousness'), but only in *Fully Unified's* case would that unity judgement be correct.

Although Hurley's point focuses on the question of partial unity, parallel considerations apply to the question of disunity more generally. Contrast *Fully Unified* not with *Partially Unified* but with *Disunified* (Hurley 1998: 110; see Figure 4.2). *Disunified* and *Fully Unified* have experiences with the same contents, but whereas *Disunified* has two streams of consciousness *Fully Unified* has only a single stream of consciousness. Again, the thought is that there would be

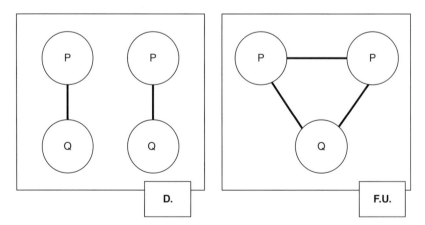

Figure 4.2 A disunified perspective (D.) and a fully unified perspective (F.U.)

no subjective—and hence no introspectively accessible—difference between these two perspectives. *Disunified* would have as much reason to endorse the unity judgement as *Fully Unified* has, but in her case it would be false. Call this *Hurley's objection*.

In response to Hurley's objection one might argue that because consciousness is necessarily unified then neither *Disunified* nor *Partially Unified* is possible, and as a result we needn't worry that our treatment of the unity of consciousness cannot distinguish their phenomenal perspectives from each other. Although tempting, this response is dialectically problematic. Perhaps it is true that neither *Disunified* nor *Partially Unified* is possible, but it would be illegitimate to dismiss Hurley's objection on that basis given that the very point of the objection is to undermine the main argument for the unity thesis. To appeal to the unity thesis here would be placing the cart before the horse, to put it mildly.

But there are responses to Hurley's objection that do have some force. Hurley's cases make essential appeal to the notion of *phenomenal duplication*, the idea that a subject can have multiple tokens of a single experiential type at one and the same time. If phenomenal duplication is not coherent then neither is her objection. And we have seen that the coherence of phenomenal duplication is very much up for grabs (see §2.4). Phenomenal duplication might be possible if we were to individuate experiences in sub-personal or vehicular terms, but I argued that experiences should be individuated in tripartite terms— that is, by appeal only to their subject, time, and phenomenal character. And the tripartite account rules out the possibility of phenomenal duplication, for it requires that numerically distinct experiences differ from each other in terms of either their subject of experience, time, or phenomenal character, and—by definition—phenomenal duplicates differ from each other in none of these three ways.

Might we be able to reformulate Hurley's objection without appealing to phenomenal duplicates? No, for were the subjects in question to have experiences with different contents then there would also be subjective (and hence introspectable) differences between their perspectives. Suppose that we replace one of *Disunified*'s <p> experiences with (say) an experience with the content <r>. In that case, *Disunified* would have conjoint experiences with contents <p&q> and <p&r> respectively, but no experience that subsumes both of those experiences. As a result, *Disunified* would have introspective reason to reject the unity judgement. In short, Hurley's objection cannot be formulated without appealing to phenomenal duplication.

What if we were to individuate experiences in vehicular terms, and thus allow for the possibility of phenomenal duplication? Even then, I doubt that we should be overly worried by Hurley's objection. The unity judgement would be under real threat only if it were to turn out that we are subject to phenomenal duplication on a widespread scale. Do we have reason to believe that that is the case? Some theorists have suggested that we do. Puccetti (1981) and Bogen (1977) argue that since split-brain patients have two streams of consciousness with duplicate contents, we have reason to suppose that we too enjoy two streams of consciousness with duplicate contents. On their view, the left and right hemispheres of a normal human brain sustain distinct streams of consciousness—with essentially the same contents—that operate in parallel. The split-brain procedure doesn't create two streams of consciousness but merely reveals the presence of the two streams of consciousness that were already in place prior to the operation.

This proposal is best rejected. For one thing, the two-streams interpretation of the split-brain data is far from irresistible, as I will argue in Chapter 9. But even if we had good reason to suppose that *split-brain* patients have two streams of consciousness, we should not read the phenomenal structure of the split-brain syndrome back into that of normal cognition. The two-stream model of the split-brain is motivated by the striking cognitive disunities that split-brain patients manifest, but these disunities are striking only against the backdrop of the unity exhibited by normal human subjects.

In attempting to motivate the claim that normal human beings are subject to phenomenal duplication Puccetti and Bogen don't just appeal to the supposed parallels between normal subjects and split-brain subjects, they also appeal to the bilateral structure of human consciousness.[4] They argue that because each hemisphere has areas devoted to processing the same kinds of stimuli, we should think of consciousness as taking the form of two streams, one of which is located in the subject's left hemisphere and the other in the right hemisphere. What should we make of this argument?

The first point to note is that this argument could undermine the unity judgement only if a great deal of neural processing were bilaterally duplicated. If bilaterality held only occasionally—say, for only a few select types of conscious states—then it would leave the unity judgment unscathed even if there were a direct inference from bilaterality to phenomenal duplication. How much bilaterality is there within consciousness? We don't really know. We do know that although a good deal of neural processing is lateralized to one or other hemisphere—for example, early visual processing of events in each visual hemifield is carried out in the contralateral visual cortex—some neural processing seems to be bilaterally duplicated. Perceptual processing of certain high-level categories

---

[4] Arguments against the unity of consciousness based on the bilateral structure of the brain have a long history. See Harrington (1987) for a fascinating account of their 19th-century roots.

appears to be carried out by each hemisphere in parallel (see e.g. Marsolek et al. 2002; Andresen & Marsolek 2005; and Rousselet et al. 2002), as does the representation of objects that are located near the centre of the visual field (where the two visual fields overlap). However, we do not yet have a clear conception of the degree to which consciousness involves neural processing that is inter-hemispherically duplicated.

Even where bilaterality does obtain it may not support claims of phenomenal duplication. In order to move from bilaterality to phenomenal duplication we need to consider how the homologous areas in each hemisphere are related to each other. Do they function as a single unit or as autonomous causal nodes? Does the left-hemisphere neural state subserve (say) verbal behaviour and the right-hemisphere state subserve (say) non-verbal grasping behaviour, or do both right- and left-hemisphere states conspire together to subserve all forms of behavioural control that are based on this experiential state? Homologous neural events might underpin or realize distinct experiential tokens if they operate autonomously, but if they operate as an integrated unit then it might be best to think of them as jointly underpinning or realizing a single experiential token—a token whose realizer is distributed between the two hemispheres (Marks 1981; Tye 2003)—rather than two tokens of the same experiential type. So even on a vehicular conception of experiences the route from bilaterality to phenomenal duplication is not straightforward, and may turn on questions about the architecture of consciousness to which we do not yet have the answers. In sum, the bilaterality-based case for thinking that normal subjects of experience have two streams of consciousness has not yet been made.

At this point it might be useful to review the various steps that we have taken in our examination of the unity judgement thus far. I began in §4.1 by examining an objection to the unity judgement based on the claim that introspection is an unreliable guide to the capacity of consciousness. According to this objection, the introspectively based sense we have of enjoying a rich stream of consciousness is illusory. I suggested both that the evidence in favour of the austere conception of consciousness is far from decisive, and that introspection might provide us with a reliable guide to the structure of consciousness even if it should turn out to be unreliable with respect to its capacity. In §4.2 I examined a threat to the unity judgement provided by introspectively inaccessible experiences. Putting to one side the recherché possibility of deeply inaccessible experiences, I focused on the challenge of superficially inaccessible experiences. I argued that we might be able to explain the inaccessibility of such experiences by appealing to their 'size' rather than the fact that they are not phenomenally unified with the rest of the subject's (introspectively accessible) experiences. A final challenge to the unity judgement focused on Hurley's attack on the 'what it's like' conception of phenomenal unity. Despite its ingenuity, I argued that Hurley's objection is vulnerable at two points. First, it requires that phenomenal duplication is possible, and there is reason to doubt whether that is so. Secondly, even if phenomenal duplication is possible, Hurley's objection undermines the unity judgment only if we have good reason to think that we are subject to phenomenal duplication on a widespread scale, which we don't. I leave it to the reader to judge where these considerations leave the unity judgement, but my own view is that it is in quite good shape.

4.4 From the unity judgement to the unity thesis: I

The unity judgement might be secure, but how do we get from the unity *judgement* to the unity *thesis* given that the former is a claim about the structure of one's own consciousness and the latter is a claim about the structure of human consciousness in general? One might be forgiven for thinking that evidence about the structure of one's own consciousness—indeed, evidence about the structure of one's own consciousness that is limited to contexts of introspective attention—is rather too thin a reed on which to ground the unity thesis.

There is clearly some risk in adopting the unity thesis on the basis of the unity judgement, but—as Hume pointed out—a certain amount of risk attends each and every inductive generalization. The question is whether the amount of risk involved in this generalization is *excessive*. Let us begin by asking how an inference from the unity judgment to the unity thesis might go wrong. Two possibilities spring to mind. One way in which the unity judgement could be true but the unity thesis false is if the structure that consciousness possesses when the subject is introspecting is not representative of its structure at other times. I examine that challenge to the argument from introspection in the following section. In this section, I focus on a prior challenge to the argument: that the subject making the unity judgement might be unrepresentative of human beings in general.

First-year logic students are typically taught that induction on the basis of a single case is not to be trusted. There is some truth to this claim, for one-shot induction is often unreliable. The fact that I adore Vegemite gives me little reason to think that you too adore Vegemite, and even less reason to think that Vegemite is universally adored. But what every first-year logic student is told needs to be taken with a grain of salt, for there are contexts in which one-shot inference is perfectly legitimate. The fact that a certain substance is poisonous to me might make it reasonable for me to infer that it will also be poisonous to you, and even that it will be poisonous to human beings in general.

Whether or not one-shot inference is warranted depends on how the property in question is distributed in the relevant population (or, perhaps, on how it is believed to be distributed). Suppose that we are dealing with a property that is uniformly distributed in the relevant population: either every member of the population has it or no member of the population has it. For such a property, one-shot induction will be highly reliable (indeed, it will be infallible). If you want to know whether human beings are mortal, you need a sample of only one. Other properties, of course, are not homogeneously distributed. (Liking Vegemite would be one such property.) So, in order to know whether the unity thesis might be justified on the basis of one-shot inference (the unity judgement) we need to ask how likely it is that human consciousness has a uniform structure.

Let us approach this question by stages. I think we have good reason to suppose that there is a high degree of homogeneity in how the broad features of consciousness are realized in the members of our species. In fact, the very ascription of consciousness to other people depends on such an assumption. My warrant for thinking that you are conscious is based primarily on an inductive inference from my own case. I know that I am conscious, and I know that you and I are similar in ways that are highly germane to the possession of consciousness. Not only do we have various behavioural dispositions and physical properties in common, we also share a common evolutionary heritage (Sober 2000). These facts make it reasonable for each of us to engage in a one-shot inference when it comes to ascribing consciousness to our fellow citizens. (Indeed, not only is this one-shot inference warranted, it would be positively irrational to harbour serious doubts about it.)

One-shot inference is not just warranted when it comes to the ascription of consciousness per se, it is also warranted when it comes to the ascription of fine-grained conscious states. It is reasonable for me to suppose that the phenomenal states that I enjoy when hearing a trumpet are much like these which you enjoy when hearing a trumpet. Of course, such inferences *can* be derailed by the presence of individual differences. Some of these differences are obvious (those who are profoundly deaf lack auditory experience); others perhaps slightly less so (musical training can alter the phenomenology of auditory experience); still others are extremely surprising (individuals with synaesthesia might have musical experiences in contexts that are completely unknown to the rest of us). But esoteric cases to one side, one-shot inference is generally secure when it comes to the ascription of particular conscious states.

It seems reasonable to suppose that one-shot inference will be at least as reliable when it comes to the structure of consciousness as it is with respect to other features of consciousness—indeed, it may even be *more* reliable here than it is elsewhere. This is because the structure of consciousness is likely to be fixed by deep and stable features of our cognitive architecture, and thus to exhibit little variation within the normal range of adult human experience. Whether that homogeneity extends to (say) infants or those who have experienced cerebral insult is more of an open question. Here, I think, we can't expect the argument from introspection to have much force. In such cases, we will just have to determine the structure of consciousness as best we can from the agent's behaviour. (I return to this issue in the following section.)

There is a further point worth noting here. Although I don't have introspective access to your experiences, I do have access to your introspective reports. And if introspection can provide me with evidence for thinking that my current experiences are unified, then it can also provide you with evidence for thinking that your current experiences are unified. So in this sense my introspective evidence for the unity thesis is not limited to the results of my introspective endeavours but can include your introspective endeavours too. And if that is right, then the inference from the unity judgement to the unity thesis is not just a *one*-shot inference, but can draw on as many 'shots' as there are individuals who have reflected on the structure of their experience and have endorsed the unity judgement.

4.5 From the unity judgement to the unity thesis: II

If the unity judgement is correct then one's consciousness is unified when one introspectively attends to its structure. However, such occasions are surely highly unusual. Introspection, a critic might claim, is a pretty uncommon presence in ordinary waking life, and it is even less common for subjects to introspectively enquire into the structure of their own consciousness. With these thoughts in mind, one might wonder whether the unity judgement is representative of the normal structure of consciousness. Perhaps consciousness is unified only during periods of introspective attentiveness. And if that were so then the unity argument would be fatally flawed, for the unity judgement would provide a misleading picture of the typical structure of experience.

What should we make of this line of thought? First, I'm not so sure that introspection *is* that uncommon. True, we don't often explicitly attend to our own conscious states—our concern is generally with the world and not with our experience of the world—but arguably a background sense of one's own experience pervades normal waking life. Everyday experience often contains an implicit awareness of the fact that one is conscious, and also of various facts about the generic character of one's experience—that one is (e.g.), perceiving, or daydreaming, or thinking hard about a particular problem (although see Schooler 2002). And, it seems to me, we are also implicitly aware of the fact that our conscious states are unified with each other. Awareness of this form doesn't involve focal attention, but it is nonetheless a genuine form of introspection insofar as it takes as its objects (facts about) one's own conscious states.

'Fair enough', the critic might reply, 'but there is a further problem here. In order to be justified in thinking that the structure of introspected experiences is representative of the structure of unintrospected experiences, we need to reckon with the "refrigerator light" problem. How do you know that introspection (or the possibility thereof) isn't responsible for phenomenal unity in the way that opening the refrigerator door is responsible for switching on its light? If introspection (or the possibility thereof) were responsible for the unity of consciousness, then far from providing us with a reliable picture of the structure of consciousness introspection would provide us with exactly the wrong picture.'

Sceptical worries of this sort are most pressing when one has reason to think that the conditions of epistemic access to the scenario in question might themselves play a role in bringing it about. The refrigerator light problem is a problem only because our background knowledge of refrigerators makes it plausible to suppose that they might be designed with lights that are triggered by opening the door. We would have reason to take the refrigerator light objection seriously if—and perhaps only if—we had reason to suppose that either introspection itself or the mechanisms underlying introspective accessibility were responsible for the unity of consciousness. Do we have any such reason?

I am inclined to think not. Introspection, as I am conceiving of it, is a faculty whereby the phenomenal character of experience becomes available to the mechanisms of judgement (more specifically, to the mechanisms of self-ascription). It is, I think, more plausible to suppose that introspection reveals the unity within consciousness that exists independently of it than it is to suppose that phenomenal unity is a product of introspective accessibility (see also Dainton 2006: 34–41). I suspect that the mechanisms responsible for introspection (and conscious thought more generally) are relatively late additions to the architecture of consciousness. They are grafted onto those mechanisms responsible for the creature's awareness of its perceptual and bodily environment, and it is these more primitive mechanisms that ensure that the creature's experiences are unified. On this view, the unity of consciousness is not imposed on it by introspection but is a feature of consciousness that can be found even in creatures who enjoy only primitive forms of sensory experience.

Of course, even if phenomenal unity is independent of introspective capacities per se it might nonetheless depend on the kinds of integrative capacities whose presence is highly *correlated* with the presence of such capacities. Suppose, for example, that the unity of consciousness depends on working memory. If so, then it is likely to be compromised precisely in those conditions—such as delirium, dreaming, and the minimally conscious state—in which the mechanisms of working memory are disrupted. And if the unity of consciousness depends on the capacity for first-person thought (to take another possibility), then it is likely to be compromised in those syndromes—such as schizophrenia, dementia, and the dissociative disorders—in which the mechanisms underpinning first-person thought are also disrupted. In other words, even if the unity of consciousness doesn't depend on introspection *per se*, there may be reason to think that it is most likely to break down in precisely those conditions in which introspective access to the structure of consciousness is least reliable.

In my view this objection poses the most serious challenge to the argument from introspection. However, it is very difficult to say just *how* serious this challenge is, for we are largely ignorant of the mechanisms that might be implicated in the unity of consciousness, and thus we have relatively little grip on the conditions under which that unity is most likely to be lost or impaired. (Indeed, we are in something of a methodological bind here, for in developing such an account we will need to make assumptions about when the unity of consciousness might be lost and when it is retained.) My hunch, however, is that phenomenal unity is a rather basal phenomenon, one that requires little in the way of either working memory resources or the capacity for first-person thought. But to the extent that this is merely a hunch, the inference from the unity judgement to the unity thesis is certainly open to question.

4.6 Conclusion

This chapter has examined the first-person motivation for the unity thesis. As we have seen, providing introspective justification for the unity thesis turns out to be a rather challenging affair. Let us review the central points at which the argument from introspection is vulnerable—or at least apparently so.

The first half of this chapter examined three challenges to the unity judgement. An initial challenge involved the charge that introspection might be an unreliable guide to the structure of consciousness. A second challenge to the unity judgement came in the form of unintrospectible experiences. Inspired by Hurley's treatment of partial unity, a third challenge focused on the claim that the contrast between unity and its absence is not the sort of thing that might be introspectively discernible, even in principle. I argued that there are plausible responses to each of these challenges.

In the second half of this chapter I examined the inference from the unity judgement to the unity thesis. We saw that there are two gaps here: a gap between oneself and others, and a gap between contexts in which one enjoys introspective access to consciousness and contexts in which one doesn't. In §4.4 I argued that the first of these gaps can be adequately bridged, for inductive inferences from claims about the structure of one's own consciousness to that of others' are warranted even if they are one-shot inferences (which they needn't be). The most serious challenge to the argument from introspection involves the second of these two gaps. If the unity of consciousness were dependent on either introspection itself or the kinds of integrative capacities that are correlated with the presence of introspection then claims about the structure of consciousness based on introspection would not be a reliable guide to its structure in the context of non-standard background states. Is it likely that the unity of consciousness does depend on the kinds of integrative capacities that are correlated with introspection? My own view is that although it is not likely it is certainly an open possibility. Given our ignorance about the mechanisms underpinning consciousness, it would be foolish to suggest otherwise. Perhaps what we ought to say is that the 'pre-theoretical' case for thinking that a target individual has a unified consciousness will be a function of its background state of consciousness: the further we stray from normal waking consciousness, the weaker the case provided by the unity judgement for supposing that the individual in question retains a unified consciousness.

Where does that leave the unity thesis? It would be premature to put too much faith in it, but I do think that the foregoing considerations show that it ought to be taken seriously. Not only does it provide us with a respectable focus for third-person investigations into the structure of consciousness, we might even go so far as to say that it ought to be accorded a kind of default status— 'innocent until proven guilty'. Let us turn now to the question of how we might go about establishing whether or not it is guilty.

5

How to Evaluate the Unity Thesis

Determining whether or not a creature has a unified consciousness is an empirical task that demands close and careful attention to its cognitive and behavioural profile. The structure of a creature's consciousness cannot be 'read off' from its behaviour in any direct fashion, but instead requires bridging principles that link consciousness to behavioural and cognitive capacities. Such principles will invariably be contested. The goal of this chapter is to examine some principles that might plausibly link phenomenal unity to cognitive and behavioural capacities, and in so doing develop a framework for the third-person assessment of the unity thesis that can be deployed in the following chapters. This chapter is very much a 'ground clearing exercise', and many of the ideas introduced here will be developed in following chapters.

Although it has multiple manifestations, when stripped to its core there is really only one kind of argument against the unity thesis. The argument is by counter-example, and has two 'moments': a *positive* moment and a *negative* moment. The positive moment involves establishing that the target creature has conscious states e_1 and e_2, and the negative moment involves establishing that e_1 and e_2 are not phenomenally unified. In short, the positive moment involves an argument for consciousness, whereas the negative moment involves an argument against conscious unity.

5.1 The positive moment

The positive moment faces us with the vexed problem of measures or criteria for the ascription of consciousness—the problem of other conscious minds. What would constitute adequate evidence that another creature is in conscious states of a certain kind?

The first point that must be made here is that there is no short and snappy answer to this question. The conditions under which we ought to ascribe conscious states to a creature will need to take into account the kind of creature that we are dealing with, the background state of consciousness that it would be in if it were conscious, and the kind of fine-grained conscious state in question. For example, the considerations that might be relevant to determining whether a linguistic creature is conscious are likely to differ in important ways from those that might be relevant to determining whether a non-linguistic creature is conscious. Similarly, the considerations that might be relevant to determining whether a creature enjoys (say) auditory experiences are likely to differ in important ways from those that might be relevant to determining whether it enjoys (say) affective experiences. However, in order to make the following discussion manageable I will leave these complexities largely to one side, and will assume that we can sensibly refer to measures or criteria for the ascription of conscious states in the abstract. However, readers are urged to keep this idealization firmly in mind in this (and following) chapters.

The received view within consciousness studies is that the only legitimate tool for measuring consciousness is introspective report. Frith and colleagues state that 'to discover what someone is conscious of we need them to give us some form of report about their subjective experience' (Frith et al. 1999: 107). According to Weiskrantz, 'we need an *off-line* commentary to know whether or not a behavioural capacity is accompanied by awareness' (Weiskrantz 1997: 84). Naccache tells us that 'consciousness is univocally probed in humans through the subject's reports of his or her own mental states' (Naccache 2006: 1396). Finally, Papineau claims that the 'canonical way of finding out what someone experiences is to take note of their *reports*' (Papineau 2002: 189), and he clearly has introspectively based reports in mind. Let us call this the *introspective criterion*.

There is certainly much to be said for treating introspective reports as a central guide to both the presence and absence of consciousness. Not only are they one of the most useful tools for studying consciousness, they are arguably also one of the most reliable. But there is reason to doubt whether introspection is the only—or even the most fundamental—means that we have for ascribing conscious states to creatures.

Note first that formulating a plausible version of the introspective criterion is far from straightforward. We clearly don't want to say that we are justified in ascribing a conscious state with content <p> to S only if S has *actually* produced an introspective report to the effect that she is in conscious state <p>. More plausible is the thought that we are justified in ascribing a conscious state with content <p> to S only if S has the *capacity* to produce introspective reports to the effect that she is in conscious state with content <p>. But what exactly is it to have the capacity to produce introspective reports? We don't want to demand that subjects can produce the relevant kind of introspective report right here and now, for surely we can be justified in ascribing conscious states to creatures who are unable to produce such reports due to distraction, inattention, or indeed the fact that they are introspecting some other aspect of their overall experiential state. Should we then require only that subjects have the capacity to produce introspective reports in general? That would surely be too weak, for the fact that a creature might have the capacity to produce a certain type of introspective report doesn't tell us much about its *current* states of consciousness. In short, nailing down a plausible version of the introspective criterion is not easily done (see also Schooler & Fiore 1997).

A further problem with the introspective criterion is that it does not sit easily with the thought that the introspective judgements that subjects make are often wrong. Inattentional and change blindness—to name just two of the many phenomena that might be mentioned in this connection—suggest that introspection may mislead us about what particular conscious states we are enjoying at any one time. Indeed, the debate about the existence and nature of cognitive phenomenology suggests that introspection might even mislead us about the *kinds* of phenomenal states that we possess (Bayne & Montague 2011). These claims are of course controversial, but leaving to one side the debate about these particular examples, there is good reason to think that introspection might not furnish us with quite the direct and immediate access to consciousness that it is often thought to.

A third challenge for the introspective criterion concerns its inability to accommodate our pre-theoretical assumptions concerning creatures—such as young children and non-linguistic animals—that lack introspective capacities at all. Taken in its unrestricted form, the introspective criterion entails that the question of consciousness in such creatures is a purely theoretical one—a possibility that must be forever beyond our ken. That, I think, would be a highly unpalatable view. Of course, one could restrict the scope of the introspective approach, and hold that it applies only to creatures with the capacity to produce introspective reports. But although restricting the introspective criterion in this way might accommodate our intuitions about non-linguistic creatures, the very act of restricting the scope of the account raises questions of its own. Once we have recognized that there are non-introspective means of detecting consciousness in non-linguistic creatures, why shouldn't we allow that those same means can also be applied to linguistic creatures? Introspective reports may play a core role in the ascription of consciousness—especially when it comes to creatures who possess introspective abilities—but they are *not* the sole basis on which conscious states can be legitimately ascribed.

A final criticism of the introspective criterion is that it doesn't reflect what those who study consciousness actually *do*. Although the introspective criterion represents something akin to the official self-understanding of consciousness science, most consciousness scientists actually demand only environmental reports from their subjects. Typically, subjects will be asked to report when (say) the light is red, rather than when they have an experience (as) of a red light.

Of course, one might argue that environmental reports can be substituted for introspective reports without loss. Subjects who are able to report (say) that the light in front of them is red will typically also be able to report that they had an experience (as) of a red light. In this way, perhaps, a suitably constrained formulation of the introspective criterion might be able to account for experimental practice. But although this proposal might be able to account for experiments involving self-conscious subjects who appreciate the relations between introspective and environmental reports, the science of consciousness also concerns itself with creatures who are not able to substitute introspective reports for environmental reports. Indeed, the science of consciousness draws on data from creatures whose ability to produce any kind of reports is questionable.

In an influential set of experiments designed to identify the neural correlates of visual consciousness, Logothetis and colleagues examined the neural responses of rhesus monkeys to binocular rivalry (Sheinberg & Logothetis 1997; Logothetis et al. 2003). The monkeys were first trained to press bars in response to various images—horizontal and vertical gratings, for example—and then presented with rivalrous stimuli. As expected, their responses closely modelled those of human observers to the same stimuli. The question that concerns us here is not what this research tells us about the neural correlates of visual experience, but what we should say about the monkeys' button-presses. Logothetis and colleagues describe the monkeys as *reporting* their mental states, but I would want to resist this interpretation. It seems to me that there is little reason to suppose that the monkeys were producing reports of any kind let alone introspective reports. Arguably, to report that such-and-such is the case one has to conceive of the one's behaviour as likely to bring about a particular belief in the mind of one's audience—indeed, as likely to bring this belief about in virtue of the fact that one's audience appreciates that one's behavior carries the relevant informational content—and I know of no good reason to believe that the monkeys conceived of their button-presses in these terms.

Does it follow that we have no grounds for thinking that the monkeys were experiencing binocular rivalry? Not at all; in fact, I think the monkeys' button-presses qualify as very good evidence for the claim that they had rivalrous experiences. However, their button-presses constitute evidence of consciousness not because they were reports of any kind but because they were *intentional actions*. Intentional agency, I suggest, functions as a legitimate ground for the ascription of consciousness. Indeed, it is utterly commonplace to suppose that the non-verbal behaviour of an organism can give us evidence about its experiential life. We take the lioness to be conscious of the gazelle as she tracks its movements across the savannah, we take the bloodhound to be conscious of the scent that it follows through the woods, and we take the infant to be conscious of his mother's voice as he orients towards her. Let us call the claim that intentional agency can underwrite ascriptions of consciousness the *agentive criterion* of consciousness. Note that unlike the introspective criterion, the agentive criterion does not place necessary conditions on the ascription of consciousness, but only sufficient conditions.[1]

The notion of agency is of course a very broad one, and includes both environmental and introspective reports within its ambit. Because of this, adopting the agentive criterion in no way implies that we cannot use a creature's reports to determine its states of consciousness. Indeed, there will be many situations in which what a creature 'says'—that is, reports—may be the most useful way of getting the measure of its conscious states. But the important point is that from a theoretical perspective the agentive criterion treats reports as merely one tool among many when it comes to identifying what a creature might or might not be conscious of. Reports—even introspective reports— have no privileged status, and they are most certainly *not* the 'gold standard' of consciousness research.

Although it has its advocates, the agentive criterion does not command widespread support. I suspect that this is because it is widely thought that cognitive science has shown that the bulk of cognitive and behavioural control is under the control of so-called 'zombie systems'—systems that operate on the basis of unconscious representations (Koch & Crick 2001; Koch 2004). And if consciousness has little role in guiding thought and action, then—so the thought goes—we can hardly use agency as a legitimate marker of consciousness.

How forceful is this argument? Let us start by examining the evidence for zombie systems. Much of the contemporary enthusiasm for zombie systems began with blindsight, a condition that involves damage to the primary visual cortex that produces a scotoma (Weiskrantz 1986/2009). Although patients with blindsight deny that they are conscious of stimuli that are presented within the scotoma (the 'blind field'), they can reliably discriminate them when prompted to guess, at least when those stimuli are reasonably elementary.

---

[1] For discussion of the ways in which agency might function as a marker of consciousness see Clark (2001, 2009); Dretske (2006); Flanagan (1992); Morsella (2005); and van Gulick (1994).

Indeed, in some cases the acuity threshold of the patient's blind field can exceed that of his or her sighted field (Weiskrantz et al. 1974; Trevethan et al. 2007).[2]

Another influential source of evidence for the existence of zombie systems comes from work on the two visual systems—the dorsal stream and the ventral stream (Goodale & Milner 2003; Milner & Goodale 2006, 2008). Much of our knowledge of the two visual systems derives from the study of D.F., a woman who at the age of 35 experienced anoxia due to carbon monoxide poisoning. The anoxia damaged D.F.'s ventral stream, leading to impairments in her ability to see the shape, orientation, and location of objects, but it left intact those dorsal stream processes that are responsible for fine-grained online motor control. In one particularly striking study, D.F. was able to 'post' a letter through a slot despite being unable to report the slot's orientation or say whether it matched the orientation of another slot. D.F., we might say, has 'blindsight for orientation'. Numerous studies have shown that normal subjects also draw on dorsal representations that lie outside of consciousness for fine-grained visuomotor control. Much of this research is summarized—somewhat misleadingly, as we shall see—by suggesting that dorsal stream processing is 'for action' whereas ventral stream processing is 'for perception'.[3]

A third field of research that has provided evidence for the existence of zombie systems involves masked stimuli.[4] Such stimuli have been shown to trigger not only simple movements requiring only one muscle group, but also more complex movements 'requiring simultaneous activity in at least two sets of muscles on opposite sides of the body' (Taylor & McClosky 1990: 445). A number of other studies have demonstrated that stimuli of which the subject reports no conscious awareness are able to activate motor programmes, and thus influence reaction times and error rates (see e.g. Klotz & Neumann 1999). As Wilhelm Wundt's student Hugo Münsterberg wrote in the late nineteenth century:

When we apperceive [consciously perceive] the stimulus, we have usually already started responding to it; our motor apparatus does not wait for consciousness, but does restlessly its duty, and our consciousness watches it and is not entitled to order it about. (quoted in Neumann and Klotz 1994: 143)

---

[2] See Kolb & Braun (1995) and Lau & Passingham (2006) for evidence of blindsight-like phenomena in normal subjects.

[3] See e.g. Aglioti et al. (1995); Bridgeman et al. (1979); Bridgeman et al. (1981); Castiello et al. (1991); Fourneret & Jeannerod (1998); McIntosh et al. (2004a); Slachevsky et al. (2001); Schenk & McIntosh (2010).

[4] See also Ansorge et al. (1998); Lau & Passingham (2007); Leuthold & Kopp (1998); Miller et al. (1992); Schlaghecken & Eimer (1997); Smid et al. (1990); Taylor & McClosky (1996).

So much for zombie systems—how much pressure do they really put on the agentive criterion? Not a great deal, in my view. The study of zombie systems may give us reason to *reconfigure* our intuitive conception of the relationship between consciousness and agency (see e.g. Clark 2001), but by no means does it show that 'in order to discover what someone is conscious of we need them to give us some form of report about their subjective experience' (Frith et al. 1999: 107).

The first point to note is that even when online visuomotor activity is not grounded in visual experience it is still likely to be *correlated* with the existence of such states, at least in normal human beings. Although one's grip on a cup might be guided by unconscious dorsal stream representations, such representations are likely to be accompanied by ventral stream representations of the cup, and those representations will be conscious. And as far as the ascription of consciousness is concerned, all we need is the claim that agency is reliably correlated with the presence of consciousness. Secondly, very little behaviour is under the *exclusive* control of zombie systems. Zombie systems are not homunculi—'mini-me' who form and execute their own plans. Instead, their operations are very much under the control and guidance of the contents of perceptual and intentional consciousness. Milner and Goodale liken the dorsal stream to the robotic component of a tele-assistance system: the ventral stream selects the goal object from the visual array and the dorsal stream carries out the computations required for the assigned action (2006: 232). Left to its own devices the dorsal stream is capable of little. We can see this by considering just how impoverished D.F.'s behavioural capacities are when she is unable to draw on conscious information. She can pick up a screwdriver, but she fails to pick it up from the appropriate end for she is unable to recognize it *as* a screwdriver. She can post a 'letter' through a slot without error, but she has difficulty posting T-shaped objects (Goodale et al. 1994) or grasping X-shaped objects (Carey et al. 1996; McIntosh et al. 2004b). To contrast 'vision for action' with 'vision for (conscious) perception' is somewhat misleading, for there is very little action without conscious perception, and the vast majority of D.F.'s actions involve a great deal of conscious perception.

Close inspection of the blindsight data reveals the same story. Not only are blindsight subjects unable to discriminate complex shapes in their blind field, even those properties that they can unconsciously identify are not spontaneously integrated into their practical and theoretical reasoning. We might say that the availability of unconscious perceptual content is not 'manifest' to the patient, and as a result it is not really available to *them* as such. Blindsight subjects take themselves to be 'merely guessing', a fact that is reflected in their reluctance to incorporate blind field content into their spontaneous behaviour.

What would we say if zombie systems did start to act 'under their own steam', that is, independently of the control and guidance of conscious states? Suppose that certain blindsighters began to develop 'superblindsight' (Block 1995), and incorporated the contents of their blind field into their action plans. To the best of my knowledge, human blindsight patients do not exhibit 'superblindsight', but perhaps Humphrey's monkey Helen did (Humphrey 1972, 1974).

> Helen, several years after the removal of visual cortex, developed a virtually normal capacity for ambient spatial vision, such that she could move around under visual guidance just like any other monkey. This was certainly unprompted, and in that respect 'super' blindsight. (Humphrey 1995: 257)

Was Helen visually conscious of her environment? One might argue that she wasn't, on the grounds that her visual cortex had been removed. But one might equally argue that her spontaneous activity—the fact that she could move around under visual guidance 'just like any other monkey'—suggests that she was visually conscious. Far from undermining the agentive criterion, blindsight actually reveals the depth of intuitive support that it enjoys.

At this point a critic might allow that although intentional agency can ground the ascription of consciousness in the absence of introspective reports, introspective reports ought always to be privileged over any other form of agency. Warming to this theme, the theorist might point out that Helen showed spontaneous behavioural guidance in the absence of introspective report, and we don't know what introspective judgements she might have produced had we been able to ask her about the nature of her experiential states. Had she been able to produce introspective reports, the critic might continue, we ought surely to have trusted her reports ('I don't have any awareness in this area of my visual field') over her spontaneous behaviour.

I'm inclined to agree that introspective reports ought in general to be accorded *some* kind of privilege over other forms of behaviour as far as the ascription of consciousness is concerned. But it is, I think, a rather delicate matter about just what to say when introspective reports dissociate from non-introspective forms of behavioural control.

As an aid to reflection, let us consider some actual cases of 'agentive fragmentation'—instances in which the agent's overall behavioural profile provides conflicting cues about their state(s) of consciousness. In a series of unpublished masking experiments Cummings presented a row of five letters to subjects in rapid succession. Subjects were instructed to press one key if the letter 'J' (for example) was present in the display and to press another key if no 'J' was present.

When urged to respond as fast as possible, even at the cost of making a good many errors, subjects now tended to respond to the occurrence of a target letter in the 'blanked' positions with a fast (and *correct*) press of the 'target present' key, and then, a moment later, to apologize for having made an error. (Allport 1988: 174–5)

On the face of things this study involves a dissociation between environmental reports and introspective reports. The subject (correctly) reports that the display contained (say) a 'J', but then (incorrectly?) reports that she did not consciously perceive a 'J'. Which of these two reports provides us with a better measure of the subject's experience: the initial action, which appears to be an environmental report, or its subsequent introspectively based retraction?

Here is one argument—a bad argument, as it turns out—for privileging introspective reports over any other form of behaviour. Distinguish two kinds of errors that might be produced by a method for detecting consciousness: false positives and false negatives. A method produces a false positive when it says of a creature who is not in conscious state K that it is in conscious state K, and it produces a false negative when it says of a creature who is in conscious state K that it is not in conscious state K. Both errors are to be avoided, but which type of error is worse? If one thought that false positives were worse than false negatives, then one might be inclined to argue that introspection ought to be privileged over other possible measures of consciousness, for only by so doing could we be sure of avoiding false positives.

Here are two reasons why the argument is a bad one. First, it is far from clear that the introspective criterion *is* guaranteed to be more conservative—that is, to generate the fewest false positives—than its rivals. Arguably, a maximally conservative approach to the ascription of consciousness would insist that we should ascribe conscious states to a creature only when each of the various possible markers of consciousness point in the same direction. Secondly, there is no reason to think that we should be looking for a (maximally) conservative marker of consciousness in the first place. The concern to avoid false positives must be balanced against the concern to avoid false negatives, and as far as I can see there is no reason to regard one of these two errors as more serious than the other.

So, what *should* we do when introspective reports dissociate from other forms of behaviour? I'm not sure that there is any simple answer to this question. Dissociations of this kind—and we will come up against many such dissociations in future chapters—will need to be evaluated on a case-by-case basis. There are few rules to guide us here, and we will need to proceed largely by instinct. That being said, let me sketch some considerations that might be of some use to us as we attempt to find a clear path through the undergrowth.

Perhaps the most important point to keep in mind is that the agentive criterion grounds the ascription of consciousness in the exercise of *personal-level* agency. This isn't to say that our evidence for the existence of consciousness in a creature is *restricted* to intentional agency, but it is to say that our evidence for ascribing consciousness to a creature will be strongest when we are most sure that we are responding to something that *the agent* has done. By contrast, our evidence for consciousness will be correspondingly weaker to the extent that we are unsure about whether we are dealing with something that the agent has done as opposed to something that some sub-personal component of the agent—some 'mechanism inside them'—has done. Consider here the control of eye-movements. Some eye-movements are controlled by low-level mechanisms that are located within the superior colliculus; others are directed by high-level goal representations (Kirchner & Thorpe 2006; de'Sperati & Baud-Bovy 2008). Arguably, the former are more properly ascribed to sub-personal mechanisms within the agent, whilst the latter are better thought of as things that the agent does—as instances of 'looking'.

In drawing this distinction between the personal agency and sub-personal motor control I am *not* suggesting that we think of 'the agent' as some kind of homunculus, directing the creature's behaviour from its director's box within the Cartesian theatre. Nor am I suggesting that we should identify personal-level agency with 'willed', 'deliberate', or 'endogeneous' agency and exclude from its domain 'stimulus-driven', 'automatic', and 'exogenous' action. That would also be a mistake. As agents we are not 'prime movers' but creatures that behave in either reflexive or reflective modes depending on the dictates of the environment. The agent isn't to be identified with the self of rational reflection or pure spontaneity, but is to be found by looking at how the organism copes with its environment. Although there is evidence that the circuits involved in stimulus-driven agency are distinct from those that subserve self-generated agency (Jahanshahi & Frith 1998; Lengfelder & Gollwitzer 2001), few of our actions are either purely self-generated or purely stimulus-driven. Instead, the vast majority of what we do involves a complex interplay between our goals and environmental affordances (Prochazka et al. 2000; Haggard 2008). (Think of a typical conversation, where what one says is guided by both the behaviour of one's interlocutor and one's own goals and intentions.) Consciousness might manifest itself most obviously when deliberative, reflective control is required, but many stimulus-driven, automatic, and exogenous actions are also guided by conscious representations, zombie systems notwithstanding. Absent-mindedly making myself a cup of coffee whilst chatting to a colleague counts as a stimulus-driven automatic action on any reasonable construal of the notion, but there is little reason to deny that I draw on my perceptual experience of the world—and, indeed, my own body—in performing such a task.

A better approach to the contrast between personal and sub-personal control, I suspect, invokes the notion of cognitive integration. What it is for an action to be assigned to the agent herself rather than one of her components is for it to be suitably integrated into her cognitive economy. Where we have behaviour that is not suitably integrated into the agent's wider mental life, there is some temptation to think that it shouldn't be assigned to the agent, at least not without reservation.

Consider in this respect the following pair of studies. In one study, three blindsight patients were required to report when they saw a light that had been flashed into their blind field (Zihl & von Cramon 1980). The patients were instructed to produce eye-blink reports on some trials, key-press reports on other trials, and verbal reports (saying 'yes') on a third set of trials. Although the subjects were able to perform well by blinking and key-pressing (after practice), their verbal responses remained at chance. In the second study cognitively unimpaired subjects were required to report the onset of a light (illuminated for 200 milliseconds) in three ways at once: by blinking, by pressing a button, and by saying 'yes' (Marcel 1993, 1994). Surprisingly, the reports that subjects gave via one report modality often failed to cohere with those they produced via other report modalities. For example, in a single trial a subject might press the button but fail to say 'yes'. Furthermore, subjects were often unaware that they had failed to produce consistent responses across the three response modalities.

Although it is certainly possible that the subjects in these studies were conscious of the stimuli that they reported, the fact that their reports were in some sense 'autonomous'—that is, could not be matched by behaviour implicating other response modalities—does entail, I think, that it is *less* plausible than it would otherwise have been. The more widely available the contents of a representation are, the more comfortable we will be in ascribing it to the agent rather than one of their components. The agent *as such* seems to recede when dealing with representations that are able to drive only a restricted range of consuming systems, and with it our evidence that we are dealing with consciousness may also recede. Arguably this will leave the borderlands between personal-level agency and sub-personal agency murky, but perhaps that is how it should be.

These comments are obviously highly abstract, and in many cases they will offer us little concrete guidance about what kinds of conscious states, if any, to ascribe to the creature in question. We will often have to muddle through as best we can, and in many cases we may simply not be in a position to say anything about the nature of the subject's consciousness with any significant degree of warrant.

5.2 The negative moment: representational disunity

I turn now from the question of how the presence of consciousness might be established to the question of how the presence of disunity within consciousness might be established. What would count as evidence that a subject has conscious states that are not phenomenally unified?

One line of argument for phenomenal disunity appeals to failures of representational integration. Here, we need to distinguish different forms of representational integration. Perhaps the most basic form of representational integration takes the form of conjunction. In Chapter 3 we examined the idea that phenomenal unity goes together with the closure of phenomenal content under co-instantiated conjunction. According to closure, if experiences with contents <p> and <q> respectively are phenomenally unified then the subject will also have an experience with the content <p&q>. Although I rejected the closure-based analysis of phenomenal unity, I did allow that phenomenal unity will typically be accompanied by the conjunction of phenomenal content, particularly when the states in question belong to the same perceptual modality.

But there are other forms of representational integration besides conjunction. Consider Nagel's gloss on the unity of consciousness:

Roughly, we assume that a single mind has sufficiently immediate access to its conscious states so that, for elements of experience or other mental events occurring simultaneously or in close temporal proximity, the mind which is their subject can also experience the simpler relations between them if it attends to the matter . . . The experiences of a single person are thought to take place in an experientially connected domain, so that the relations among experiences can be substantially captured in experiences of those relations. (Nagel 1971: 407)

Examples of the idea that Nagel has in mind are not hard to find. An experience of two colour patches is typically accompanied by an awareness of their relative intensities; an experience of two sounds is typically accompanied by an awareness of their spatial relations; an experience of two bodily sensations is typically accompanied by an awareness of whether or not they occur in the same limb. Even when one is not actually aware of the simpler relations between the contents of unified experiences, one usually has the capacity to become aware of those relations.

What holds of the simpler relations between perceptual features also extends to the awareness of categories and gestalt relations that are mediated by e_1 and e_2. Suppose that e_1 and e_2 are representations (as) of the first and second halves of the word 'cobweb'. A subject who enjoys both e_1 and e_2 and who has the ability to recognize the word 'cobweb' as such will typically enjoy an experience (as) of the word 'cobweb'—at least, if e_1 and e_2 are phenomenally unified. If these experiences are not phenomenally unified then the subject will be restricted to experiences of the words 'cob' and 'web' and will not experience the perceived word as 'cobweb'.

With these thoughts in mind we can now see how we might argue for phenomenal disunity by appealing to failures of representational integration. Such an argument will require a principle connecting phenomenal unity with representational unity, along the lines of the following:

> *Representational Integration Principle* (RIP): For any pair of simultaneous experiences e_1 and e_2, if e_1 and e_2 are phenomenally unified then, *ceteris paribus*, their contents will be available for representational integration.

Developing a plausible argument from representational disunity to phenomenal disunity requires three things. Firstly it requires showing that the subject does indeed have experiences e_1 and e_2. Secondly it requires showing that these experiences are not representationally integrated. And, thirdly, it requires showing that the various *ceteris paribus* clauses cannot be activated. The first two tasks raise issues that have already been dealt with in §5.1, so I will focus here on the third: when might failures of representational unity fail to provide evidence of phenomenal disunity?

Begin by noting that some creatures simply won't have the cognitive machinery required to integrate the contents of their mental states in the appropriate manner. The degree to which a creature's states can be integrated will be a function of its integrative abilities—on what categories and concepts it has. Someone who cannot recognize elephants will not be able to synthesize experiences of the front and back ends of an elephant so as to recognize the presented animal as an elephant. Similarly, someone who suffers from prosopagnosia will be unable to synthesize the perceptual features of a face into a face percept. Of course, if certain forms of feature binding are necessary for perceptual consciousness—as has sometimes been claimed—then anyone with any perceptual experience at all must possess certain integrative capacities. But even if some forms of feature binding are essential to perceptual consciousness—it is clear that there are many others forms of binding that are not required for the possession of consciousness as such.

Secondly, even when the creature in question does have the machinery to integrate the contents of e_1 and e_2, it might not have the capacity to deploy that machinery on the occasion in question. Certain kinds of integration might require that the experiences in question have a certain temporal duration (which they might not have), or that the creature can attend to the relevant objects and properties (which they might not be able to). We also need to be particularly mindful of the role played by background states (or 'levels') of consciousness. Although we have some basic familiarity with the kinds of capacities for representational integration that creatures possess in the context of normal wakefulness, this is only one of many background states of consciousness and it would be naïve to expect that the kinds of representational integration and coherence that we find in ordinary waking consciousness also characterize all other background states of consciousness. In light of these considerations we would do well to exercise especial caution when arguing from representational disunity to phenomenal disunity outside of normal attentive wakefulness.

Let us take stock. The lack of representational integration—and closure, in particular—will often provide us with a reason to think that the states in question are not phenomenally unified, but just how strong that reason is will depend on the details of the case, and we certainly shouldn't expect that representational integration will follow from phenomenal unity with strict necessity.

5.3 The negative moment: access disunity

A second—and perhaps more potent—line of argument for phenomenal disunity concerns the *uses* to which a subject's conscious states can be put. In general, the contents of each of a creature's conscious states are available to the same range of cognitive and behavioural systems. But suppose that we came across a subject who appeared to be in two conscious states at the same time (e_1 and e_2), where the contents of these two states were not available to the same systems of cognitive and behavioural consumption. For example, the contents of e_1 might be available for verbal report but not memory consolidation, whereas the contents of e_2 might be available for memory consolidation but not verbal report. It would be tempting to take this selective accessibility—this breakdown in 'access unity'—as evidence that e_1 and e_2 were not phenomenally unified.

The key component in any argument from access disunity will be a principle that links phenomenal unity to access unity, such as the following:

> *Conjoint Accessibility Principle* (CAP): For any pair of simultaneous experiences e_1 and e_2, if e_1 and e_2 are phenomenally unified then, *ceteris paribus*, their contents will be available to the same consuming systems.

Assuming CAP, we can use the fact that the contents of e_1 and e_2 are not available to the same consuming systems as evidence that they are not phenomenally unified. As with arguments from representational disunity, arguments from access disunity will rarely—if ever—be demonstrative.

Developing a plausible argument from access disunity to phenomenal disunity requires three things. First, it requires showing that the subject does indeed have experiences e_1 and e_2. Secondly, it requires showing that these experiences are 'access disunified'—that their contents are not available to the same consuming systems. And, thirdly, it requires showing that the various *ceteris paribus* clauses cannot be activated. Given that the first task raises issues that were dealt with in §5.1, we need now to examine the second and third tasks.

Let us start with the question of what it is for states to be 'access disunified'. Take a creature with two experiential states (e_1 and e_2) and five consuming systems ($CS_1 \ldots CS_5$). States e_1 and e_2 will be fully access unified if their contents are available to all and only the same consuming systems, and they will be fully access *dis*unified if their contents are not available to any of the same consuming systems. But suppose that the contents of e_1 and e_2 are available to *some* of the same consuming systems but not others. For example, e_1 might be available to CS_1–CS_4, and e_2 might be available to $CS_2 \ldots CS_5$. We might think of such states as *partially access unified*. What should we make of such states? We could take the fact that the contents of both e_1 and e_2 are accessible to CS_2, CS_3, and CS_4 as evidence that they *are* phenomenally unified, but we could equally invoke the fact that some consuming systems have access to only one of these two experiences as evidence that they are not phenomenally unified. Neither response seems entirely appropriate.

One might attempt to defuse the force of this worry by arguing that partial co-accessibility is unlikely to occur, and hence that this issue can be set to one side notwithstanding its theoretical interest. Although tempting, I suspect that this kind of optimism is misplaced; in fact, given the complex nature of the architecture underlying cognitive and behavioural control there is reason to expect that breakdowns of access unity will usually be partial rather than complete. If one looks hard enough, one is likely to find some kind of cognitive task on which otherwise disunified states can be jointly brought to bear. Rather than being a theoretical problem that can be safely brushed under the carpet, partial co-accessibility needs to be confronted (as we will see).

A second response to the challenge of partial unity would be to suggest that degrees of access unity can be equated with degrees of phenomenal unity: the more access unified two states are, the more phenomenally unified they are. But this response can also be set to one side. For one thing, it is highly doubtful whether phenomenal unity can come in degrees. Two conscious states are either phenomenally unified with each other or they are not, and it is not possible for one pair of experiences to be more phenomenally unified with each other than another. And even if phenomenal unity can come in degrees, there is no reason to assume that degrees of phenomenal unity will be correlated with degrees of access unity.

In my view, the most reasonable response to partial unity is epistemic: the strength of any argument from access disunity will be a function of the degree to which the contents of the relevant states are co-accessible: the less co-accessible the contents of the states, the stronger our evidence for thinking that they are not phenomenally unified.[5] We should allow that phenomenal unity is *compatible* with some degree of access disunity—indeed, in some cases it might even be reasonable to suppose that phenomenal unity coexists with a high degree of access disunity—but the more radical the access disunity the better our evidence for phenomenal disunity. In some situations it might be rational to think that phenomenal unity coexists with a high degree of access disunity (see further §5.5), but in such cases one would be under an obligation to explain why phenomenally unified states are not also access unified.

Let us turn now to the third issue raised by the argument from access disunity: the question of *ceteris paribus* clauses. Under what conditions might things not be equal?

First, any argument from access disunity needs to factor in the possibility of processing bottlenecks. Consider a complex phenomenal state (e_3) and a simpler phenomenal state (e_1) that is subsumed by it. Although e_3 and e_1 will be phenomenally unified, they may not be access unified due to the fact that e_3 is more complex than e_1. (Given the disparity in the 'size' of their contents, certain consuming systems might be able to access the contents of e_1 but not those of e_3.) Of course, the same point holds with respect to experiences that are not part-whole related: two experiences might not be co-accessible due simply to the fact that one of them is more complex than the other. In light of this, arguments from access disunity will be most secure when dealing with

---

[5] Thanks to Ian Phillips for pushing me to say more here.

conscious states that are roughly of the same 'size'. The greater their size—especially their combined size—the more reason we will have for supposing that failures of access unity might be due to processing bottlenecks rather than failures of phenomenal unity.

A particularly important processing bottleneck is implicated in the psychological refractory period (Pashler 1992, 1998; Spence 2008). When two stimuli that are presented in close temporal succession require different responses, the response to the first stimulus almost always retards the response to the second stimulus, suggesting that there is a central bottleneck which prevents people from 'doing two things at once'. However, there are contexts in which the psychological refractory period can be minimized and perhaps even eliminated altogether. For example, the refractory period is notably reduced when the stimuli can be grouped together as aspects of a single object (here, subjects appear to be able to 'compile' the two responses into a single response), and when the responses involve high degrees of 'stimulus-response' compatibility, for example moving one's eyes in the direction of a visual stimulus.[6]

A second respect in which 'things might not be equal' involves differences in the representational format of the states in question. The means by which a state can influence thought and behaviour depends in no small part on the kind of state that it is. Suppose that we have two states, e_1 and e_2, where e_1's content is conceptual and e_2's content is non-conceptual. Given the link between conceptual content and reasoning, it would be no surprise to discover that e_1's content was able to drive (say) the mechanisms of belief-revision in ways that e_2's content was not. Conversely, assuming a link between non-conceptual content and action, it would not be surprising to discover that e_2's content could drive online behavioural control in ways that e_1's content could not. The lesson to be learnt from this is that failures of access unity will provide better evidence of failures in phenomenal unity when the states in question share a common representational format. Discovering that e_1 and e_2 couldn't (say) be jointly reported would give us better reason to think that they are not phenomenally unified if they were both conceptual states as opposed to one of them being conceptual and the other non-conceptual.

A final point that demands attention concerns the individuation of consuming systems. The problems here are not just the practical ones of knowing the neuropsychological means by which a particular behavioural response was produced, but the theoretical challenge of knowing what to do with

---

[6] For studies that establish the former point see Fagot and Pashler (1992) and Schumacher et al. (2001); for studies that establish the latter point see Kornblum et al. (1990), Greenwald & Shulman (1973), and Greenwald (2003).

such information. What does it take for actions to count as manifestations of a single consuming system as opposed to manifestations of distinct consuming systems?

Differences between motor systems might provide us with a rough guide to the individuation of consuming systems, but it would be most unwise to assume that consuming systems bear a one-to-one relation to motor systems. Most obviously, a single consuming system can be implicated in multiple behavioural responses. For example, introspective reports can be expressed by what one says, which buttons one presses, or where one looks. Less obviously, a single type of motor response can involve the activity of quite distinct systems. In some contexts a hand movement might realize a grasping action, in other contexts it might realize an attempt to communicate. The gross behavioural profiles of these two actions might be identical but the consuming systems implicated in them will not be. Indeed, grasping and communicating involve mechanisms that can be differentially disabled: some patients with somatosensory processing deficits are able to grasp the affected limb but unable to point to it when asked to indicate the site of damage (de Langavant et al. 2009), whilst other patients show the converse dissociation (Anema et al. 2009). The individuation of consuming systems is ultimately an empirical matter. Although pre-theoretical intuitions might be of some help in delimiting the rough borders between them, the fine-grained distinctions between consuming systems will be revealed only as the details of our cognitive architecture are filled in. An implication of this is that arguments from access disunity will be hostage to fortune, for our current assumptions about the borders between consuming systems might be quite wide of the mark.

Let us take stock once more. Access disunity provides us with an argument for phenomenal disunity, for there is reason to think that the contents of phenomenally unified states will generally be co-accessible to the subject's various consuming systems. The strength of such arguments, however, may often be difficult to determine, for not only is it plausible to suppose that phenomenal unity can coexist with some degree of access disunity, it might also be difficult to determine the degree to which the states in question are access disunified in the first place.

5.4 Probe-dependence

In the previous sections I examined two ways in which one might make a case for phenomenal disunity: by appealing to representational disunity or by appealing to access disunity. I also noted that neither type of argument is straightforward, for in each case the crucial principles involved—namely RIP and CAP—involve 'other things being equal' clauses, and in each case there is more than one way in which things may not be equal. I turn now to a further matter that complicates the evaluation of potential counter-examples to the unity thesis.

Most objects of study are independent of our attempts to study them. The number of bricks in a wall, the number of passengers on a train, and the number of monkeys up a tree are not typically dependent on the tools that one uses to measure them. Although it is natural to assume that consciousness is likewise independent of our attempts to detect it, there is reason to think that this assumption is false, and that the very contents of a subject's conscious states may be modulated by the tools that one uses to identify them. In other words, consciousness exhibits what we might call 'probe-dependence'.[7]

Probe-dependence can be illustrated by the phenomenon of extinction, a mild form of perceptual neglect that usually affects the left side of the patient's visual field (Vuilleumier & Rafal 2004; Mattingly et al. 1997). Patients with 'extinction' may be aware of stimuli that occur in their left hemi-field when such stimuli are presented singularly, but they will cease to be aware of them when they are presented concurrently with right hemi-field stimuli. However, the degree to which a patient manifests extinction can depend on just how they are tested. In one particularly striking case, Halligan and Marshall (1989) examined the ability of a patient to bisect a series of lines at the mid-point. When the patient was asked to bisect the lines using his *right* hand he veered into the right side of his visual field, suggesting that he was not aware of the left half of the lines. However, this extinction was no longer apparent when he was required to bisect identical lines using his *left* hand. In another study, five patients with neglect for the left side of visual space were asked to give same/different responses to pairs of line-drawn pictures of animals (Vallar et al. 1994). The two pictures were shown one above the other. One of the two pictures in each pair represented an intact animal, while the other represented a chimera in which the left half of one animal had been replaced by that of another animal. All patients misjudged the two members of the pair as identical to each other, but three of the five patients noticed the incongruous drawing when asked which of the two drawings more properly corresponded to the name of the animal depicted in the non-chimeric picture. A number other studies of extinction and neglect have found that the severity of a patient's symptoms are a function of how they are 'probed'.[8]

---

[7] The following is indebted to Dennett (1991), Hurley (1998) and especially Bisiach (1997).

[8] See Bisiach et al. (1989); Bottini et al. (1992); Duhamel & Brouchon (1990); Halligan et al. (1991); Joanette et al. (1986); Ricci & Chatterjee (2004); Smania et al. (1996); Tegnér & Levander (1991).

What accounts for such findings? One possibility is that although patients are always aware of the so-called 'extinguished' or 'neglected' stimulus, this awareness is difficult to tap. It is there, but is revealed only when patients are probed in particular ways. Another—and to my mind rather more attractive—possibility is that the very fact of asking the patient to respond to the stimulus in one way rather than another influences whether or not they are conscious of it. Asking the patient to (say) use their left hand rather than their right hand to bisect a presented line may activate the patient's right hemisphere and thus facilitate the awareness of objects in the patient's left visual field. Similarly, requiring patients to name an object might trigger right hemisphere activity, leading to the temporary amelioration of left visual field neglect.

The probe-dependence of consciousness is not restricted to brain-damaged patients but is also to be found in normal subjects of experience. Consider, for example, the Colavita effect (Colavita 1974; Spence et al. forthcoming). In the basic Colavita paradigm subjects are presented with a random series of visual, auditory, and audio-visual stimuli, and are required to make one response to the audio stimuli and another to the visual stimuli. Surprisingly, visual stimuli often 'extinguish' auditory stimuli on bimodal trials, despite the fact that subjects have no difficulty in detecting these auditory stimuli on unimodal trials. An account of the Colavita effect needs to explain why only one stimulus is reported on certain bimodal trials, and why it is the visual stimulus that invariably 'extinguishes' the auditory stimulus (rather than vice versa).

Spence (2009) provides a 'probe-dependence' account of the Colavita effect that contains plausible answers to both questions. His account draws on the finding that subjects who are instructed to respond to visual targets will be aided by the presence of an accessory sound (that is, subjects are quicker to respond to visual stimuli on bimodal trials than on unimodal trials), but the presence of an accessory visual stimulus *retards* responses (Sinnett et al. 2008). This suggests that on bimodal trials subjects initiate their response to the visual stimulus before they are in a position to respond to the auditory stimulus. So, under time-pressure to respond, vision-only responses will be expected to occur more often than audition-only responses. Moreover, Spence suggests, the representation of the auditory event will fail to generate an auditory experience on certain bimodal trials precisely because it is not responded to—or rather, because the subject has already responded to the visual stimulus. By 'responding' to the visual stimulus the subject's perceptual system has in effect 'decided' that there was only the one stimulus, and allows the representation of the auditory stimulus to fade into neuronal obscurity.

Probe-dependence might also account for some of the examples of agentive fragmentation discussed earlier in this chapter, although the devil will be in the details. It is possible that the dissociation between response modalities observed in Zihl and von Cramon's (1980) blindsight study (see p. 104) might have been a function of the pre-motor programming of reports. Perhaps the motor preparation required for verbal reports had the effect of reducing the sensitivity of the patients to stimuli in their blind field, whereas the motor preparation required for eye-blink or key-press reports did not. A similar kind of story might account for the dissociation between report modalities found by Marcel (1993). Perhaps the information concerning the stimulus began to activate the subjects' eye-blink responses prior to activating their verbal or button-press responses, with the result that subjects not only failed to produce consistent reports across these three modalities, but they also failed to monitor the fact that their responses had not been consistent. I should add that these comments are primarily intended to serve as examples of how probe-dependence might bear on agentive fragmentation, rather than as serious proposals about how to account for these findings.

Some commentators associate the notion of probe-dependence with an anti-realist conception of consciousness. Having suggested that 'probing the stream of consciousness at different times and places produces different effects', Dennett goes on to say that it is a mistake to suppose 'that there must be a single narrative (the "final" or "published" draft, you might say) that is canonical—that is the actual stream of consciousness of the subject, whether or not the experimenter (or even the subject) can gain access to it' (1991: 113). Whether or not this assumption is mistaken—and I would argue that it is not—the probe-dependence of consciousness certainly doesn't give us any reason to reject it. As far as probe-dependence is concerned, facts about consciousness could be as robust and determinate as you like.

So much for probe-dependence—what bearing does any of this have on the evaluation of the unity thesis? Probe-dependence requires that we must exercise caution in using any one response as our measure of consciousness, for the presence of the very thing being measured might be modulated by the nature of the probe(s) that we have employed. Requiring a subject to attend to a certain region of perceptual space or to prepare to initiate a particular motor response may affect the balance of activation between the two hemispheres, thus modulating how the patient's awareness is (say) distributed across their visual field. The experiences e_1 and e_2 might *appear* to be available to different consuming systems, but that appearance might be an illusion generated by the probe-dependence of consciousness. Suppose that we show a subject a light at the same time as we play a sound to him. We want to know whether he experienced both the sound and the light, and—if so—whether or not these two experiences were phenomenally unified. How are we to test him? Requiring him to produce a verbal report might bias him to report the light (and perhaps also extinguish the sound), but requiring him to produce a button-press report might bias him to report the sound (and perhaps also extinguish the light). We might be tempted to think that these two experiences were simultaneous but not phenomenally unified with each other, but in fact there may have been no single trial on which the subject was simultaneously aware of both the light and the sound. So, in evaluating any argument from access disunity we need to keep one steely eye on just how consciousness is being probed.

5.5 Imperial versus federal models

A final issue that complicates any evaluation of the unity thesis has hovered in the background of the entire chapter, but must now be brought into the clear light of day. The issue in question concerns the cognitive architecture of consciousness.

Painting with a broad brush, there are two ways in which one can think of the structure of consciousness: in 'imperial' terms or in 'federal' terms. The imperial approach conceives of consciousness in terms of a centre into which all processing flows and from which all control emanates. The contents of consciousness—and perhaps only the contents of consciousness—are located in a domain-general 'reservoir of experience'. This reservoir need not have a particular anatomical address—it might be spread across various neural regions—but it is a functional unit of sorts. Any content that it contains will be available to the same range of systems of cognitive and behavioural consumption. Certain forms of control might be decentralized, but on the imperial conception of things any such decentralized control must be located firmly outside of consciousness. Conscious control, according to this view, resides only within an imperial centre.

Advocates of a federal conception of consciousness operate with a very different view of things, according to which conscious states exert influence in the form of multiple 'domain-specific' circuits. Instead of being routed through a single domain-general workspace or central executive, the federalist thinks of conscious control on the model of a political system in which order is maintained by 'loose federations of centers of control and integration', to use Block's (1997: 162) evocative phrase. According to this approach, the ability of a state to drive various cognitive and behavioural programmes may be a function of the kind of state it is, with certain types of conscious states more readily available for some forms of cognitive and behavioural control than others. Of course, content-specific control might be hidden from sight in everyday contexts due to various mechanisms of integration, and it may take brain damage or the constraints of laboratory-induced cognitive load to reveal it.

Imperial models of one form or another are exceedingly common, with the 'centre' being variously identified with working memory, the global work-space, or the supervisory attentional system. But despite its widespread endorse-ment, the evidence in support of the approach is less than decisive. Certain versions of analytic functionalism notwithstanding, there is no *a priori* reason to assume that the contents of each of a subject's conscious states *must* be available for the same forms of cognitive and behavioural control. If the imperial approach to consciousness is not a conceptual requirement, then the case for it must be made on empirical grounds. Has that case been made? No doubt opinions will differ on this question, but my own view is that it has not. The studies that are cited in its support invariably operationalize consciousness in terms of global availability, which is to *assume* the truth of the imperial model rather than to provide evidence for it.

To cast doubt on global availability conceptions of consciousness is not to deny that there is an intimate connection between consciousness and global availability when it comes to neurologically intact adult humans in the normal waking state. The question, however, is how tight that connection remains once we step outside that rather restricted domain. For all we know, the correlation between consciousness and global availability breaks down when dealing with non-human animals, neonates, or adult members of our own species who have suffered trauma of some kind or another. We should remain alive to the possibility that the correlation between consciousness and global availability seen in the context of the normal waking state is generated by 'imperial' mechanisms of integration that are *superimposed* on top of the rela-tively more 'federal' mechanisms responsible for the construction of conscious-ness itself. The appearance of a 'centre' may be generated by the interaction of a number of modular-ish channels that are 'patched together' by working memory, inner speech, and other domain-general mechanisms of integration. When all goes well, the contents of these channels are widely—indeed, perhaps even *globally*—available for the control of thought and action, but control may 'go local' when these patches are put under pressure. The imperial conception of consciousness might capture an *idealized* conception of the relationship between consciousness and control, but we mustn't lose sight of the fact that we are often far from ideal subjects.

It seems to me that certain very general considerations provide reason to think that consciousness has at least a partly federal structure. For one thing, the selectional pressures driving the evolution of consciousness are likely to have been content-specific. This is perhaps most plausible with respect to bodily sensations. It would not be unreasonable to suppose that pain experiences are in the business of driving damage-avoidance behaviour, hunger experiences are in the business of driving grazing behaviour, and full bladder experiences are in the business of driving bladder-emptying behaviour. Similar kinds of functional specialization may also have shaped the architecture of perceptual experience. The various perceptual modalities are not merely specialized in the detection of particular kinds of information, they are also (and relatedly) specialized in the production of certain kinds of behaviours. For example, olfaction appears to be prepotent for memory whereas audition is prepotent for the perception of danger.

In fact, we might already have seen manifestations of our federal architecture earlier in this chapter. In discussing the psychological refractory period, I noted that it is generally impossible to produce two responses at once (§3.3). However, exceptions to this rule can be found in contexts of high 'stimulus-response' compatibility, as when subjects are required to move their eyes in the direction of a visual stimulus. Perhaps high SR-compatible actions can be executed without mutual interference because they involve distinct circuits of consciousness.

Even apparently imperial treatments of consciousness might turn out to have something of a federal structure on closer examination. Consider, for example, accounts that tie consciousness to working memory. Such accounts have an imperial sound to them, for working memory is often thought of as a single faculty. However, many models posit some kind of domain-specific fractionation within working memory. For example, Baddeley's influential account takes working memory to have four components: a central executive and three temporary storage systems (a visuospatial sketchpad, a phonological buffer, and an 'episodic buffer') (Baddeley 2003, 2007). Even the so-called central executive may turn out to have domain-specific structure. Although some theorists take executive control to be structured along *functional* lines, with different subsystems responsible for (say) manipulating, storing, and then distributing representations, others argue that it is structured along *domain-specific* lines, with subsystems of executive control being individually responsible for the manipulation, storage, and distribution of particular kinds of representations.[9] There is a similar debate about the structure of response-selection. Whereas some accounts treat response-selection as a unitary mechanism that schedules responses to various stimuli irrespective of their content, others hold that response–selection can be broken down along modality-specific lines, with different components of the cognitive architecture involved in scheduling

[9] For examples of the former approach see Owen et al. (1998); Owen et al. (1999); and Petrides (1995); for examples of the latter approach see Levy & Goldman-Rakic (2000); Adcock et al. (2000), and Gilbert et al. (2006).

responses to some kinds of stimuli but not others.[10] My concern here is not to weigh into these debates, but to point out that some of the mechanisms implicated in apparently imperial accounts of the architecture of consciousness might turn out to have an underlying federal structure.

So much for the contrast between imperial and federal conceptions of consciousness—how might this debate bear on the evaluation of putative counter-examples to the unity thesis? It is clear that representational and access disunity arguments against the unity thesis will be most straightforward on the assumption that one is dealing with a subject whose consciousness has an imperial structure. Should that assumption be challenged, then the inference from representational or access disunity to phenomenal disunity will be that much more problematic. If conscious states are grounded in content-specific circuits of control and integration, then we shouldn't expect conscious states of different kinds to be generally available for representational integration or joint behavioural and cognitive control. To put the point slightly differently, when it comes to federal subjects we will be justified in inferring a break-down in phenomenal unity from a break-down in representational unity or access unity only if we are also justified in assuming that the states in question are 'circuit-mates'. This is an important point, for establishing that the states in question are circuit-mates might be far from easy.

At this point a critic might be tempted to suggest that to endorse a federal conception of consciousness is not to complicate the evaluation of the unity thesis but to give up on it. After all—she might say—how could conscious states be unified unless consciousness has an imperial structure—unless there is a single workspace in which it 'all comes together'?

The question is a fair one, for there clearly are functional architectures that would prevent consciousness from being phenomenally unified. Nonetheless, the suggestion that the unity thesis *requires* an imperial conception of consciousness should be resisted. The unity thesis does indeed demand that any conscious subject have a single total state of consciousness, but this state need not be the product of a single workspace—even a virtual workspace. The unity of consciousness does not require that all conscious content flow towards a single location in functional space, nor does it require that the contents of each of a subject's experiences will be available to the same range of consuming systems. For all we know, the unity of consciousness may involve the integration of states that are grounded in the activity of multiple, domain-specific, circuits. To assume that phenomenal unity requires an 'imperial' conception of conscious

---

[10] For examples of the former approach see Pashler (1994) and Jiang & Kanwisher (2003); for examples of the latter approach see Meyer & Kieras (1997) and Schumacher et al. (2003).

control is to assume that the personal-level structure of consciousness must be preserved or mirrored at a sub-personal level of analysis. That assumption could turn out to be correct, but it has little *a priori* warrant. Indeed, to suppose that the unity of consciousness demands a centralized workspace is to make the same mistake that Descartes made when he located the seat of the soul in the pineal gland on the grounds that it is the only undivided organ in the brain.

5.6 Conclusion

Let us attempt to pull together some of the various themes developed in this chapter. Our focus has been on the question of how one might go about showing that the unity thesis is false. I began with the 'positive' moment— the task of showing that a creature enjoys certain conscious states. According to received wisdom, the only legitimate evidence of consciousness takes the form of (the capacity for) introspective report. I rejected this introspective criterion as being implausibly restrictive, and in its place I defended an agentive approach to the ascription of consciousness, according to which attributions of consciousness can be underwritten by intentional agency. Introspective report and intentional agency will typically point in the same direction as far as consciousness is concerned, but there may be occasions in which they point in different directions. I suggested that there are few rules about what to do in such contexts: in some cases it might be appropriate to invest one's faith in introspective report, in other cases it might be more appropriate to trust the 'testimony' of the subject's non-verbal behaviour.

In §5.2 I turned to the 'negative' moment—the task of establishing that some of a creature's conscious states are not unified. We saw that there are two ways in which the negative moment can be developed: the first involves an inference from representational disunity and appeals to RIP, the second involves an inference from access disunity and appeals to CAP. Neither route is unproblematic, for both RIP and CAP are hedged with *ceteris paribus* clauses, and it will often be unclear whether *cetera* are *paria*. Some failures of representational integration might be best explained by supposing that the subject lacks the capacity to integrate the contents of the states in question; other such failures might be best explained by supposing that although the subject has such capacities she is unable to exercise them at the time in question. Some failures of co-accessibility might be accounted for by invoking processing bottlenecks of various kinds; other such failures might be accounted for by differences in the representational format of the states in question. The presence of these 'get-out' clauses complicates the evaluation of putative counter-examples to the unity thesis, for it is difficult to distinguish legitimate appeals to such clauses from hollow exercises in 'ad hocery'.

§5.4 and §5.5 considered two more issues that further 'problematize' the evaluation of the unity thesis. Firstly, the very manner in which one probes a subject can have an impact on what that subject is conscious of. As we saw, the probe-dependence of consciousness cannot be ignored when asking whether a subject has certain experiences, and—if so—whether they are phenomenally unified. The second issue concerned the architecture of consciousness. Painting with a very broad brush, I distinguished two models of the architecture of conscious control: centralized (or 'imperial') models and decentralized (or 'federal') models. Deploying the arguments from representational and access disunity will be most straightforward on the assumption that consciousness has an imperial structure. By contrast, if consciousness has a federal structure—and we saw that there is some reason to suspect that it might—then the link between phenomenal unity on the one hand and representational integration and co-accessibility on the other will be that much more tenuous. Phenomenal unity might go hand-in-glove with representational integration and co-accessibility for 'circuit-mates'—that is, for conscious states that are located within the same circuits of consciousness—but there is little reason to expect this relation to hold for states that are nestled within distinct circuits.

Let me conclude by noting one final complication. In this chapter I have treated the negative and positive moments as though they are independent of each other. Although heuristically useful, this assumption is built on a fiction, for the question of whether a creature has experiences e_1 and e_2 cannot be disentangled from the question of whether those experiences—if indeed they occur—are unified with each other. Here's why. Suppose that we know that the creature is in mental states m_1 and m_2, but we want to know whether these two mental states are also conscious states. Suppose, further, that m_1 and m_2 are not co-accessible: the contents of m_1 are available to CS_1 but not CS_2, whereas the contents of m_2 are available to CS_2 but not CS_1. The fact that m_1 and m_2 are not co-accessible gives us some reason to think that if they are conscious then they are not co-conscious, but it might also give us some reason to think that they are not conscious in the first place. Perhaps m_1 and m_2 are examples of unconscious states that are able to drive (high-level) consuming systems. The upshot of this is that in order to produce a convincing counter-example to the unity thesis one must walk the following tightrope. On the one hand, one must show that there is sufficient disunity within a subject's cognitive economy to justify the thought that it contains states that are not phenomenally unified with each other. On the other hand, one must also establish that those states are conscious in the first place, and arguably that requires showing that their contents are at least widely available for the control of thought and behaviour. This does *not* mean that the unity thesis is 'methodologically secure'—a thesis whose falsehood could never be demonstrated—but it does mean that securing the evidence required to show that it is false is a far from trivial undertaking.

This concludes my discussion of how to evaluate the unity. I have presented two lines of argument that might be deployed against the unity thesis, and have identified some of the challenges we confront in attempting to determine the force of those arguments. In the following four chapters I put these ideas to work by examining the case for disunity, both within the normal human subject and in the context of various disorders of consciousness.

6

Fragments of Consciousness?

Irrespective of the modality from which they are drawn or the representational format in which they are couched, conscious states are not sealed off from each other but occur as phenomenally unified components of the subject's stream of consciousness. At least, that's how it seems. But perhaps we might be able to find evidence of disunity within consciousness if only we look hard enough. Might there be occasions in which the unity of consciousness breaks down?

This chapter provides an initial assault on this question—an assault that is followed up in subsequent chapters. The first half of the chapter examines the case for phenomenal disunity within normal forms of consciousness. In such cases the focus is not on the positive moment (are the states in question conscious?) but on the negative moment: are the states in question phenomenally unified with each other? The second half of the chapter turns to the question of whether the unity of consciousness might break down in the context of global impairments of consciousness. In such cases it is often an open question whether we are dealing with a conscious subject at all, but—as we will see—there is reason to suspect that if consciousness is present in these syndromes at all it is present in the form of phenomenal fragments.

6.1 The microstructure of perception

The brain faces multiple challenges in constructing a coherent model of its world. Different kinds of information make the journey from environment to subject at different speeds (light travels though air at 300,000,000 metres per second; sound travels at only 330 metres per second), and hence the subject will receive information about one and the same perceptual event at different times. This difference is most obvious for perceptual objects that are some distance away—think of the delay between seeing lightning and hearing thunder—but it is far from negligible even at close quarters. Once information has arrived at the relevant receptors it must then be processed before it can enter consciousness, and there is no reason to suppose that the time required for this will be invariant across modalities or even across features within a modality. In fact, there is evidence to suggest that features of different types *do* require different amounts of processing time: information about the colour of a stimulus is available to downstream systems about 80 milliseconds before information about its motion is available (Zeki & Bartels 1998a, 1998b; Arnold et al. 2001; Arnold & Clifford 2002).

These considerations raise the question of whether normal perception might not contain fragments of phenomenality—extremely brief experiences that are only later bound together to form phenomenal wholes. The stream of experience seems unified to introspection, but introspection has a coarse temporal grain. Perhaps a fine-grained model of perception will reveal the stream of experience to be built up out of 'shards of subjectivity'.

Something very much like this view is suggested by Dennett's multiple drafts model of consciousness. The foil for the multiple drafts model is what Dennett calls 'Cartesian Materialism', the view that there is a crucial finish line or boundary in the brain; that there is one place where it 'all comes together' (1991: 107). In place of Cartesian Materialism Dennett argues for a picture in which consciousness involves 'multiple channels in which specialist circuits try, in parallel pandemoniums, to do their various things, creating Multiple Drafts as they go' (1991: 253–4; see also 106 & 113).

These distributed content-discriminations yield, over the course of time, something rather like a narrative stream or sequence, which can be thought of as subject to continual editing by many processes distributed around in the brain, and continuing indefinitely. This stream of contents is only rather like a narrative because of its multiplicity; at any one point in time there are multiple drafts of narrative fragments at various stages of editing in various places in the brain. (1991: 113; see also 126, 132–5)

Dennett is cagey about whether the subject's multiple drafts—these 'narrative fragments'—are determinately conscious. Although his account is a multiple drafts account of *consciousness*, he also says that it is 'always an open question whether any particular content thus discriminated will eventually appear as an element in conscious experience' (Dennett 1991: 113). Indeed, at base Dennett appears to deny that there is a *determinate* fact of the matter as to whether or not these multiple content-discriminations are conscious. Having noted this component of Dennett's account I will leave it to one side, and will take the multiple drafts model to be a model of conscious states as such.[1]

---

[1] Indeed, in some passages of *Consciousness Explained* Dennett comes close to endorsing the claim that consciousness is unified: 'a conscious human mind is a more-or-less serial virtual machine implemented—inefficiently—on the parallel hardware evolution has provided for us' (1991: 218).

Dennett's case for the multiple drafts model is motivated by a pair of puzzling visual phenomena: the colour phi and meta-contrast masking. The colour phi is an illusion of apparent motion. When one looks at two small spots that are separated by a small visual angle and are illuminated in brief succession, one will experience a single point of light that appears to be moving from the location of the first spot to that of the second (Kolers & von Grünau 1976). Astonishingly, if the first spot is red and the second is green the moving point of light will appear to change colour from red to green at the *mid-point* of its trajectory. At least, that is what subjects *report* experiencing—whether such reports ought to be trusted is very much up for debate (as we will see).

Meta-contrast masking is a species of backwards masking in which a target stimulus is masked by a subsequent stimulus on account of the contiguity relations between them (Breitmeyer 2007; Breitmeyer & Ögmen 2006). In the standard meta-contrast paradigm, the target will be a disk and the mask will be a surrounding ring (see Fig. 6.1). Reports of the target's visibility will typically have a U-shaped function. In other words, when the SOA (stimulus onset asynchrony) between the disc and the ring is either very small (roughly, 0–20 milliseconds) or very large (roughly, over 150 milliseconds) subjects report that both the disk and the ring are visible, but at intermediate SOAs (roughly 40–70 milliseconds) subjects report that the disk is either invisible or only partially visible. Although apparent motion and meta-contrast masking are superficially quite different, both phenomena involve the visual system treating sequentially presented perceptual objects as a single object.

Dennett contrasts two models of these phenomena: an 'Orwellian' model and a 'Stalinesque' model (1991: 120–6). Taking its cue from George Orwell's *1984*, the Orwellian regards the reports that subjects give as the product of *post-experiential* editing. In the colour phi, subjects first experience a red spot being followed by a green spot, but a 'revisionist historian of sorts' replaces this

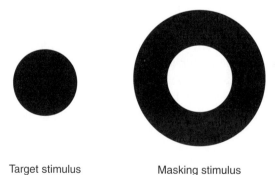

Target stimulus   Masking stimulus

Figure 6.1 Meta-contrast masking stimuli

narrative with a more convincing story in which a single spot moves from one location to another, changing colour at the mid-point of its trajectory. According to the Orwellian account of meta-contrast masking, subjects first experience a disc and then a ring, but this narrative is replaced by a more convincing account in which there is only a single perceptual object—namely, a ring. The proponent of the Stalinesque model shares the Orwellian's commitment to the thought that these phenomena involve editorial revision, but she locates that revision in a 'show trial' that the brain creates *prior* to consciousness. Whereas the Orwellian holds that subjects misreport their experiences, the Stalinist takes the reports of subjects to accurately reflect their experiences: colour-phi subjects experience only a single point of light moving from A to B, while meta-contrast subjects who report seeing only the mask in the meta-contrast trials do in fact experience only the mask.

Stalinesque models posit no disunity within visual experience but the same cannot be said of the Orwellian treatment of these phenomena. According to the Orwellian, subjects have visual experiences (of the green light at the mid-point in the colour phi; of the target disk in the meta-contrast paradigm) that are independent of their other visual experiences. These 'inaccessible' experiences would not be integrated with the rest of the subject's visual experiences, nor would they be available to the consuming systems that the rest of their experiences are available to. They would not be reportable, nor would they register in memory. In short, Orwellian treatments of these phenomena put pressure on the unity thesis. But are they plausible?

Before addressing that question we need to examine the prior question of whether the contrast between these two models is as substantive as it appears to be. Dennett himself argues that it is 'merely verbal':

> The two theories tell exactly the same story except for where they place a mythical Great Divide, a point in time (and hence a point in space) whose *fine-grained* location is nothing that subjects can help them locate, and whose location is also neutral with respect to all other features of their theories. This is a difference that makes no difference. (1991: 125; emphasis in original)

Dennett's position here is in part motivated by the thought that each of these two models can account for all of data, 'not just all the data we already have, but the data we can imagine getting in the future' (1991: 124). It seems to me that even if the debate between these two accounts were intractable it wouldn't follow that it is 'merely verbal'—that the two accounts would be merely notational variants of each other. This would follow only if we had reason to adopt a verificationist conception of consciousness—which we don't.

So, I will assume here that the debate between the Orwellian and the Stalinist is substantive. Indeed, Dennett's own treatment of the colour phi sheds some light on just what the contrast between these two approaches amounts to. Dennett suggests that apparent motion involves a 'misalignment' between the temporal order of experiences and the experience of temporal order (1991: 137; see also Dennett & Kinsbourne 1992). The thought is that the subject's experience of the *spot-as-green* occurs prior to their experience of the spot as *red-turning-to-green*, even though the contents of these experiences do not follow that temporal order. This model is clearly not an alternative to the Orwellian and Stalinesque models, but instead functions as a framework in which the contrast between the Orwellian and Stalinist accounts can be clearly appreciated. Both the Stalinesque and the Orwellian can agree that the temporal order of experiences is not aligned with the temporal order of their contents. The crucial issue that divides them concerns the status of the representations that occur prior to the occurrence of the representation of the light as green. The Orwellian holds that at this point in time the subject has a conscious (and indeed veridical) representation of the fact that there is a location at which there is no light, whereas the Stalinist holds that at this point in time the subject has no conscious representation of the stimulus. That contrast is hardly 'merely verbal'.[2]

Dennett might be wrong to suggest that the debate between these two accounts is merely verbal, but perhaps he is right in thinking that it is intractable. What should we make of this claim?

Note first that psychologists don't think of this debate as intractable; indeed, they don't even think of it as an open one. Instead, the Stalinesque account is the received view of both apparent motion and meta-contrast masking. Not only do researchers assume Stalinesque accounts of *these* phenomena, they also assume Stalinesque treatments of other phenomena that could in principle be accounted for in Orwellian terms. Consider the well-known McGurk effect, in which dubbing the sound of someone saying /ba/ onto the lip movements for /ga/ produces the experience of hearing /da/ (McGurk & MacDonald 1976). At least, this is what subjects *report* hearing. But perhaps—the Orwellian might suggest—subjects actually have a brief experience of /ba/ that is immediately

---

[2] Note also that Dennett's claim that the contrast between the Orwellian and Stalinesque models is 'a difference that makes no difference' is not easily reconciled with other things he says about consciousness. In some places he ascribes to subjects a certain kind of *infallibility* about their phenomenal states: 'we are giving you total, dictatorial authority over the account of how it seems to you, about what it is like to be you' (Dennett (1991): 96); in other passages he defends an operationalist approach to consciousness that 'brusquely denies the possibility in principle of consciousness of a stimulus in the absence of the subject's belief in that consciousness' (1991: 132). These comments leave little room for Orwellian speculation.

replaced by an experience of /da/. But there is little to recommend an Orwellian account of the McGurk effect and in fact Dennett himself describes it effect in starkly Stalinesque terms (Dennett 1991: 112).

Why do researchers adopt Stalinesque accounts of the colour phi and meta-contrast masking phenomena? Is it because they assume—either explicitly or implicitly—that introspective reports are to be regarded as some kind of gold standard when it comes to determining the contents of consciousness (see Chapter 5)? Perhaps so, but the case for Stalinism needn't rest on such a foundation. Instead, all the Stalinist need assume is that introspective reports about simple stimuli that are produced under conditions of full alertness and undivided attention—as these reports are—ought to be taken very seriously. They may not be infallible, but surely they provide pro tanto justification for Stalinism. The onus is on the Orwellian to show why we should doubt what subjects say about their experiences.

One reason for taking the Orwellian position seriously is that the degree of 'masking' seen in meta-contrast experiments can be manipulated not merely by changing the stimuli and SOA (as one would expect), but—more surprisingly—by modulating how awareness of the target is *measured*. In the typical meta-contrast experiment subjects are required to say whether or not the target was present (or seen). Such studies produce the standard U-shaped function in which awareness of the target is reported at low and high SOAs but not at intermediate SOAs. However, this U-shaped function frequently disappears when subjects are in-structed to respond in some other way—(say) by being told to 'hit a button as soon as anything appears'. Studies that employ such measures often find that awareness of the target shows monotonic improvement within increases in SOA rather than a U-shaped function. This is the 'meta-contrast dissociation effect'.[3]

How might the meta-contrast dissociation effect be explained? As Ansorge and colleagues (1998) note, studies which report U-shaped functions tend to differ from those that do not in two ways. Firstly, the former usually require subjects to produce verbal responses, whereas the latter typically employ non-verbal motor responses, such as button-presses. Secondly, in standard studies subjects are required to report the presence of the stimulus, whereas non-standard studies often instruct subjects to treat the stimulus as something to which they must respond rather than as an event about which they must make a judgement (Neumann & Müsseler 1990). In other words, the contrast between U-shaped and non-U-shaped performance could be accounted for by appealing

---

[3] See Erikson et al. (1970); Eimer & Schlaghecken (1998); Fehrer & Biederman (1962); Fehrer & Raab (1962); Harrison & Fox (1966); Neumann & Klotz (1994); Schiller & Smith (1966); and Taylor & McCloskey (1990).

to differences in output mode (verbal report vs. button press), differences in task mode (reporting vs. responding), or some combination of the two.

In an elegant study, Ansorge et al. (1998) attempted to disentangle these two variables by pitting a judgement task that involved motor-output against a response task that involved verbal-output. They found that output mode had no affect on subjects' awareness of (or, perhaps better, 'sensitivity to') the target, but that the meta-contrast dissociation effect could be fully accounted for by appealing to differences in task mode. Subjects appeared to be 'aware' of the target when they were encouraged to treat it as an object of response but not when they were led to treat it as an object of report.

The distinction between responding and reporting might not be the only factor at work in generating the meta-contrast dissociation effect. Lachter and Durgin conducted a series of meta-contrast studies in which subjects were required to press a button in order to indicate whether a 'masked' disc had been presented to the left or the right of fixation (Lachter & Durgin 1999; Lachter et al. 2000). When responding slowly (roughly 1,050 milliseconds) subjects produced a typical U-shaped function with significant amounts of masking at SOAs of about 40–50 milliseconds. However, when subjects were encouraged to produce speeded responses (roughly 400 milliseconds) performance improved monotonically with increasing SOA. In other words, the degree of masking could be manipulated by modulating *when* subjects responded to the target. (Just how this account of the meta-contrast dissociation effect might be related to that suggested by Ansorge et al. (1998) is something of an open question).[4]

These results might appear to support the Orwellian cause. If we have evidence that subjects are conscious of the target on speeded and responding trials, then (so the thought goes) perhaps we also have evidence that they were conscious of it on unspeeded and reporting trials—that is, on trials in which they deny having seen it.

This line of thought is tempting but we should resist its allure. Crucially, it relies on the assumption that the structure of consciousness remains invariant across speeded/unspeeded and responding/reporting trials, and that assumption ignores the possibility that consciousness might be probe-dependent (§5.4). If consciousness is probe-dependent, then whether or not the subject experiences the target might depend on task constraints, such as the speed at which

---

[4] Note too that if the principles underlying apparent motion are similar to those underlying the meta-contrast effect, and if one can abolish the latter by requiring speeded responses from subjects, then there is some reason to think that one can also abolish—or at least modulate—apparent motion by requiring speeded responses. As far as I know this has not been tested.

they are primed to react to it, or whether or not they take themselves to be responding to it rather than reporting it. On speeded trials the subject knows that she has little time to make a decision about the nature of the stimulus. Because the visual system is 'instructed' to construct the first available account of the stimulus that it can, it produces a visual experience of the target—that is, a *conscious* representation of the target—before information about the mask is registered. On unspeeded trials, however, the visual system is under no such pressure. As a result, it can and does draw on information about the mask to construct its conscious narrative—a narrative that fails to mention the target. A similar story can be told concerning the dissociation between responding trials and reporting trials: on responding trials perception is primed to generate an experience of the stimulus on the basis of its 'initial take', whereas on reporting trials perception generates an experience only once confirmation from 'higher-processes' has been received. In other words, one's very experience of the world may depend on the 'instructions' that the visual system is given. We might think of this as a probe-dependent version of Stalinism.

In certain respects this account of meta-contrast masking is not dissimilar to that which Dennett himself develops, for Dennett invokes precisely these phenomena in order to introduce the thought that consciousness might be probe-dependent (1991: 113; see also 136, 169). However, Dennett's conception of probe-dependence is 'anti-realist' in orientation—he takes it to show that the nature of consciousness is indeterminate at this level of temporal precision. My appeal to probe-dependence, by contrast, is resolutely realist. The nature of the subject's experience is a function of probe-involving facts, but probe-involving facts are themselves perfectly determinate: given how a subject is (or expects to be) probed on a particular trial, there will be a corresponding fact about what they experienced on that trial.

We now have the tools to respond to one of the more troubling objections to Stalinesque treatments of these phenomena—what we might call 'the loop objection'. Return to the colour phi phenomenon. As Dennett (1991: 121) points out, there can be a delay of up to 200 milliseconds between the two stimuli in the colour phi. This seems to be problematic for the Orwellian account, for one would have expected the visual system to have constructed a visual experience of the first (red) light by the time it received information about the second (green) light. It looks as though the Stalinist is committed to the view that perception involves a 'loop' of at least 200 milliseconds—and quite possibly much longer given that backward masking effects can occur with a SOA of 700 milliseconds (Weisstein & Wong 1986)—in order to deal with the (presumably unlikely) possibility that a 'show trial' might be needed. Not only does this proposal appear to be ad hoc, it is also hard to square with the thought that perceptual experience might play a role in the real-time guidance of action.

What should we make of the loop objection? First, it is far from clear that perceptual experience does play as central a role in the on-line guidance of action as common-sense assumes (see §5.1). More importantly, the objection assumes that whatever 'delay loop' there might be in perceptual experience is invariant across contexts. We can now see that this assumption is problematic. Not only might the parameters of the delay loop depend on the speed with which a subject probes his or her perceptual system, it might also depend on the perceptual content particular to that context. Given that certain types of perceptual features take longer to be processed than others, it is possible that the temporal window open for Stalinesque revision will depend on the features implicated in the particular perceptual state in question. We can accept Stalinism without positing a perceptual delay of 200 or more milliseconds that might hold in all perceptual contexts (Phillips forthcoming).

Where does this leave us? Orwellian models of the colour phi and meta-contrast masking may well be at odds with the unity thesis, but on balance the Stalinist treatment of these phenomena seems preferable to the Orwellian one. In fact, rather than finding evidence of disunity within perceptual experience we have seen just how much effort the perceptual system invests in the task of telling a coherent story about the world. Perceptual systems *do* harbour 'multiple drafts of narrative fragments', but those drafts are highly edited before they find their way to consciousness.

6.2 The emergence of thought

Cognition provides another locus in which to look for evidence of disunity within consciousness. I leave until later chapters the question of whether pathologies of cognition might furnish us with examples of breakdowns in the unity of consciousness, and will restrict my attention here to evidence from developmental psychology.

The unity of thought and action is not given to the child from birth but emerges only gradually during the first years of life. Children are agents, but they are less-than-fully integrated agents. Three distinct experimental paradigms seem to suggest that young children may have conscious thoughts that are not fully knit together within a single stream of consciousness. I begin by reviewing the relevant behavioural evidence before turning to questions of interpretation.

The first of the three paradigms is Piaget's (1954) famous A–not–B task.[5] In this task the infant watches a toy being hidden at one location (A) and after a brief delay is allowed to reach for it. When the toy is then hidden at a second location (B) and the infant is again allowed to reach for it, she will typically reach for it at location A rather than B, even when it is hidden in full view of her. In fact, the A–not–B error can occur even when the toy is 'hidden' in a transparent container and *remains* visible to the infant (Butterworth 1977).

Despite the fact that the infant searches for the toy at A, there are reasons to think that she might be aware that the toy is located at B. First, infants who are given a chance to correct themselves after reaching to A usually do so immediately. Secondly, having reached for A, infants often do not even look to see if the toy is there but instead reach directly for it at B. Thirdly, infants occasionally look towards B even as they reach for A. Such trials would be scored as correct if the dependent measure were looking rather than reaching. In fact, infants' looking behaviour is generally *more* accurate in such studies than is their reaching behaviour (Ahmed & Ruffman 1998; Baillargeon & Graber 1988; Hofstadter & Reznick 1996). As Adele Diamond notes, 'infants appear to be telling us with their eyes that they know where the toy is, but their hand goes to the old place anyway' (Diamond 1985: 881).

A second experimental paradigm in which behavioural dissociations can be found involves the deployment of rules. In the dimensional change card-sorting task, children are required to sort a series of cards based on one dimension (say, colour), and are then told that the game has changed and that the cards must now be sorted according to a second dimension (say, shape).[6] Three-year-olds will typically be able to report what the new rule is but will continue to sort the cards according to the old rule. Their verbal behaviour suggests one under-standing of what rule is currently in effect, yet their sorting behaviour suggests another. Interestingly, the same dissociation can also be found in the behaviour of patients with pre-frontal damage, who may be able to report the new rule even while they persist in using the old one to sort cards (Milner 1963).

A final experimental paradigm of interest to us here concerns children's appreciation of others' false beliefs (Wimmer & Perner 1983; Wellman et al. 2001). Standard false belief tests proceed as follows. The child watches as a protagonist places an object in one location (say, a cupboard). The protagonist then leaves the scene, and the object is moved to another location (say, a shelf) by a third party. While the protagonist is absent, the child is asked to either report or point to where the protagonist will search for the object on her return.

---

[5] See Diamond (1985, 1990); Diamond et al. (1994); Harris (1986); Wellman et al. (1986).

[6] See Frye et al. (1995); Zelazo et al. (1996); and Zelazo & Reznick (1991).

Typically, children under 4 years of age say that the protagonist will search for the hidden object where it is (that is, on the shelf), rather than where the protagonist would believe it to be (that is, in the cupboard), whereas children over the age of 4 say that the protagonist will search for the object where she last saw it. Such results seem to indicate that children under the age of about 4 lack the ability to reliably ascribe false beliefs to other agents.

Clements & Perner (1994) wondered whether young children who fail the standard false-belief task might nonetheless have an implicit understanding of false beliefs. In order to test this hypothesis, they measured where 3-year-olds looked in false-belief contexts. Their study featured a mouse called Sam who was unaware that a piece of cheese had been moved from one box (A) to another (B). Although 3-year-olds said that Sam would search for the cheese in box B, over 70 per cent of them looked in expectation towards box A. In a true-belief control, the children did not look in the direction of A (Garnham & Ruffman 2001). In a follow-up study, Garnham and Perner (2001) substituted the two boxes with mouse-holes at the bottom of which they placed slides. Now, children were not only asked where Sam would look for his cheese, but they were also allowed to move a small mat to the bottom of each of the two slides (in order to catch Sam's fall). Of the forty-three children in the study twenty spontaneously moved the mat to the bottom of the correct slide and eighteen looked in the right direction, but only ten were able to correctly say which of the two mouse-holes Sam would emerge from. Again, where children looked and what they did seemed to manifest an understanding of others' false beliefs that was not reflected in what they said (see also Freeman et al. 1991; Robinson & Mitchell 1995).

It might be tempting to suppose that these findings constitute evidence of phenomenal fragmentation—scenarios in which children have simultaneous conscious states that are not contained within a single stream of consciousness. Perhaps infants in the A-not-B task have two conscious representations of the toy's location: one that governs where they reach and another that governs where they look. Similarly, one might be tempted to think that the behaviour of children in the card-sorting task is guided by two conscious representations: one that determines how they actually sort the cards and another that determines how they say that the cards ought to be sorted. And perhaps 3-year-olds in the false-belief task have two conscious representations of where the protagonist will search for the target: one that directs where they look (or where they move a mat) and another that governs what they say. Not only do these studies appear to involve failures of access unity insofar as the children concerned seem to have representations whose contents are available to distinct consuming systems, they also appear to involve failures of representational unity; in each case, children seem to have thoughts whose contents are not integrated with each other in ways that one would expect them to be if they were phenomenally unified.

In order to evaluate the strength of this case for disunity we need to consider what might underlie these behavioural dissociations. Let us begin with the A-not-B error. Three lines of evidence suggest that this error is best explained by supposing that infants have difficulty inhibiting previously successful motor responses (Diamond 1990; although see Munakata et al. 1997). First, the more trials an infant has with A before switching to B, the harder it will be for her to make the switch. Secondly, infants no longer make the A-not-B error when they merely observe the object being hidden at A and are not allowed to search for it until it is hidden at location B. Thirdly, on trials involving *three* locations the infant will automatically reach for the object at the correct location having failed to find the object at A. If the infant's problems were cognitive—that is, if they involved only an inability to keep the object's location in mind—then one would expect infants who had failed to find the object at A to randomly distribute their searching between locations B and C. Taken as a whole, the evidence suggests that infants may be aware of the object's true location (at least on those trials in which behavioural dissociations are manifest), but be unable to inhibit the prepotent response to reach towards a location that has, until now, delivered the goods.

Problems with inhibitory control also explain the dissociations seen on the dimensional change card-sorting task. It is crucial to note both that sorting responses and reporting responses are tested on different trials, and that sorting trials are likely to be harder for children than reporting trials. The reason for this is that sorting trials contain conflicting cues that are not likely to be present on reporting trials. Suppose that the rule has changed from sorting on the basis of shape to sorting on the basis of colour. Although the child must now pay attention to the colour of the cards and ignore their shape, in looking at the cards their shape will continue to be highly salient to the child. By contrast, the child need not look at the cards in order to answer the question 'Where do trucks go in the shape game?' Hence, the child is more likely to be able to report the new rule correctly than she is to be able to employ it correctly, for reporting requires less inhibitory control than sorting does. This account is supported by an elegant study that sought to control for the effects of cue conflict. Instead of asking children where the trucks go, Munakata & Yerys (2001) asked them where the *red* trucks go, thus introducing into verbal trials the kind of distraction that is present on sorting trials. Modifying the task in this way did not completely eliminate the dissociation between verbal and non-verbal measures, but it did significantly reduce it, for children now did much worse on reporting trials than they had without the distraction.

What about the false-belief task? How are we to explain the dissociation between what 3-year-olds say and what they do in such contexts? One ingenious suggestion is that it represents a calculated response to uncertainty. Perhaps 3-year-olds give two 'answers' to the question put to them because they are unsure which of two possible answers is correct. (We might say that they are of 'two minds' were that metaphor not highly misleading in this context.) Ruffman and colleagues tested this ingenious proposal by giving tokens to 3-year-olds and allowing them to 'bet' on where they thought the protagonist would search. However, rather than 'hedge' their bets by putting some tokens on where they looked and others on what they said—as this proposal would have predicted—the children 'bet' all of their tokens in line with their verbal reports (Ruffman et al. 2001).

So how should we explain this behavioural dissociation? There is reason to think that at least part of the explanation of the behavioural dissociations seen in false belief studies might also involve inhibitory difficulties. Carlson and colleagues found that 3-year-olds did much better on a false belief task when they were required to place a sticker on the container in which they expected the protagonist to search rather than report or point to it (Carlson & Moses 2001; Carlson et al. 1998). The authors argue that children performed better on the sticker trials because they required less inhibitory control than is required by pointing or naming trials. Young children have had extensive practice pointing and reporting, and the directive that one ought to point to and describe only how things are is one that has been drilled into them. This directive needs to be inhibited on false belief tasks in which the child's understanding is measured by what they say or where they point. Placing stickers on objects, by contrast, is not guided by the same prepotent drive to conform to reality, and thus the young child requires less inhibitory control in order to override the tendency to act on what they know to be true of the world.

I have argued that inhibitory difficulties lie at the heart of the three dissociations examined in this section. Suppose that this proposal is correct: what bearing might it have on whether these dissociations involve breakdowns in the unity of consciousness?

Begin by noting that inhibitory failures are not restricted to young children (or patients with pre-frontal damage). Instead, inhibitory failures of various kinds—what Reason (1979) called 'slips of action'—are familiar from everyday life. As William James noted in his *Principles of Psychology*, 'absent-minded persons in going to their bedroom to dress for dinner have been known to take off one garment after another and finally to get into bed, merely because that was the habitual issue of the first few movements when performed at a later hour' (1890/1950: 119). Inhibitory failures involve a breakdown in what we might think of as 'the unity of agency', but they do not bring with them a corresponding breakdown in the unity of consciousness. There is no reason to think that such agents have conscious thoughts or intentions that are contained within separate streams of consciousness. Rather, the absent-minded agent has either lost awareness of their goals or is unaware that what they are doing is at odds with those goals.

With these thoughts in mind, let us return to the behavioural dissociations exhibited by young children. In the A-not-B task, the infant seems to be aware that the object is at location B but nonetheless reaches towards location A. Here, however, there is no reason to suppose that the infant has two conscious representations of the object's location, each of which is responsible for directing distinct behaviours. Instead, it seems plausible to suppose that the infant has at most a single conscious thought about the object's location, but inhibitory difficulties prevent this thought from directing where she reaches.

A similar diagnosis seems plausible with respect to the dimensional change card-sorting task. The child may be aware of the new rule, but that awareness may be prevented from guiding the child's sorting behaviour in the way that it should by the presence of highly salient cues (that is, cues that are highly salient with respect to the old rule). Does the presence of such cues cause the new rule to recede from the child's consciousness, or is the child still aware of the new rule but just unaware that she is no longer sorting cards according to that rule? It is difficult to say. But whatever the truth of the matter, this inhibitory failure seems unlikely to bring with it a breakdown in the unity of consciousness.

What about the false belief studies? Should we say that children have a conscious grasp of the protagonist's false belief that is manifest by where they look but not by what they say or where they point? This is certainly a defensible interpretation of the data. Asking the child to report or point to where the protagonist will look for the object increases the salience of the object's actual location, and once the child's attention has been drawn to the object's real location she may find it very difficult to draw on her understanding of where the protagonist will think the object is located. Instead, her responses to false belief questions may be 'commandeered' by her own conception of the object's location. For the reasons given in the previous two paragraphs, we shouldn't think of this as involving any kind of breakdown in the unity of consciousness.

However, this is not the only account of the dissociations seen in false belief studies. Another interpretation of the data—and one that is perhaps favoured by the majority of developmentalists—is that the child's looking (and mat-moving) behaviours reflect only an 'implicit' grasp of the protagonist's state of mind, a grasp that in no way involves any *awareness* on the part of the child. This interpretation garners some support from evidence which indicates that some kind of appreciation of the fact that others might have false beliefs is in place significantly before the age of 3. Studies using a violation-of-expectation paradigm have reported sensitivity to the false beliefs of others in the looking behaviour of 2-year-olds (Southgate et al. 2007), 15-month-olds (Onishi & Baillargeon 2005), and even 13-month-old infants (Surian et al. 2007). These studies are methodologically controversial (see e.g. Hood et al. 2003; Perner & Ruffman 2005), but their results are consistent with evidence derived from studies that have used other paradigms. For example, Buttelmann et al. (2009) found evidence of sensitivity to the false beliefs of others in 18-month-olds using a helping behaviour paradigm. It is difficult to credit 18-month-old infants with a conscious appreciation of others' false beliefs.

Just what bearing these results have on the looking behaviour of older infants is something of an open question. It is certainly possible that looking behaviour manifests a conscious appreciation of false beliefs only in older infants, and that the looking patterns of young infants reveals only unconscious representations of false beliefs. But if the looking behaviour of older infants is driven by purely unconscious representations, then there would be even less reason to think that these studies put pressure on the unity thesis, for they cast doubt on the unity thesis only on the assumption that the states that govern where children look are conscious.

It is time to draw this section to a close. I have examined a number of experimental paradigms that tap failures of behavioural integration in young children. These failures reveal ways in which the threads that bind thought and agency are not yet fully knitted together; they also point to ways in which those threads can unravel due to cerebral insult. But they don't demonstrate that the young child has multiple fragments of conscious thought. Future research within these paradigms—not to mention a better grip on the relationship between conscious thought and cognitive and behavioural control—might overturn this verdict, but thus far the case against the unity thesis is unproven.

6.3 Minimally responsive patients

Our search for fragments of consciousness within normal waking experience has been inconclusive. Although we have found evidence of certain failures of co-accessibility and representational integration within both perception and cogni-tion, none of these failures constitutes strong evidence against the unity thesis. But perhaps we have been looking in the wrong place. Arguably, we are most likely to find fragments of consciousness in the context of global impairments to consciousness—conditions in which the subject's 'background state' or 'level' of consciousness is aberrant. Many such conditions could be examined here, but I will focus on just three: the vegetative state, the minimally conscious state, and states brought about by epileptic absence seizures. This section provides an overview of these conditions; the following considers whether they might involve fragments of consciousness.

The vegetative and minimally conscious states

It is not uncommon for patients who have suffered a major head trauma or hypoxic-ischaemic brain damage to spend a period of time in a vegetative state.[7] The crucial clinical signs of the vegetative state are negative: there should be no evidence of awareness of self or of the environment, no responses to external stimuli of a kind that would suggest volition or purpose (as opposed to reflexes), and no evidence of language expression or comprehension. Unlike coma patients, vegetative state patients show a normal sleep-wake cycle; when awake, their eyes open and may rove around the room in a haphazard manner.

If he is peaceful when you enter the room, he may be aroused by the sound of your entry, opening his eyes if they are closed, quickening his breathing, grimacing or moving his limbs. Once he is calm again, you may notice a range of spontaneous movements: chewing, teeth grinding, swallowing, rapid movements of the eyes, fleeting fixation. More distressingly he may smile, shed tears, grunt, moan or scream without any discernable reason. Yet despite this varied repertoire of behaviours, you will be unable to convince yourself that you can communicate with him, or he with you; beyond his indiscriminate arousal to prominent stimuli and a flick of the eyes towards them, you will see no sign of perception or purposeful action: in short, you will find no convincing evidence of mind. (Zeman 2002: 215)

Patients often emerge from the vegetative state after a period of weeks, but in some cases the condition persists for months or even years. Patients who have been in a vegetative state for one month are said to be in a *persistent* vegetative state; those who have been in a vegetative state for longer—twelve months after a traumatic brain injury and six months after a non-traumatic brain injury—are said to be in a *permanent* vegetative state.

Those who recover from the vegetative state often spend a period of time in what is known as the *minimally conscious state* before returning to full consciousness (Giacino et al. 2002; Giacino 2005). As the terms indicate, the boundary between the vegetative state on the one hand and the minimally conscious states on the other is intended to coincide with that between the loss of consciousness and its reacquisition. However, it is recognized that this boundary is indistinct,

---

[7] For reviews see Bernat (2006); Jennett (2002); Zeman (2002).

not least because the reacquisition of consciousness in the minimally conscious state is often an unstable and fluctuating affair (Noirhomme et al. 2008). In order to determine whether this border has been crossed clinicians look for the presence of goal-directed behaviour: the ability to follow simple commands; gestural or verbal yes/no responses regardless of accuracy; intelligible verbalization; purposeful behaviour, such as appropriate smiling or crying in response to the content of emotional but not neutral stimuli; reaching for objects in a manner that is appropriate to their location; and holding objects in a manner that accommodates their size and shape (Giacino et al. 2002: 351). (Not surprisingly, there is disagreement about precisely which behavioural measures mark the transition from the vegetative state to the minimally conscious state. In the United Kingdom, diagnostic criteria regard visual fixation as an 'atypical but compatible' feature of the vegetative state, whereas in the United States sustained (but not brief) visual fixation suffices for a diagnosis of the minimally conscious state.)

Neuroimaging studies provide additional evidence of consciousness in the minimally conscious state (Owen & Coleman 2008). In one event-related potential (ERP) study, minimally conscious patients and controls were read sequences of words that contained either the patient's own name or other (unfamiliar) names (Schnakers et al. 2008). These sequences were presented in two conditions, a passive condition and an active condition. In the passive condition the names were merely presented to the subjects, whereas in the active condition subjects were instructed to count instances of particular names. Both controls and minimally conscious state patients (but not vegetative state patients) exhibited a larger P3 response for the to-be-counted names than for the not-to-be-counted names, and as compared to the passive listening trials. Given that the P3 response is a marker of attention, this result suggests that these patients—some of whom showed only visual fixation as a behavioural sign of consciousness—were able to direct selective attention in response to task commands. This finding doesn't prove that these patients were aware of the names being read to them, but it is certainly suggestive.

In fact, there is also evidence that certain *vegetative state* patients—that is, patients who are correctly diagnosed as being in the vegetative state according to current clinical guidelines—might be conscious. The most convincing findings to date come from an fMRI study of a 23-year-old female victim of a car accident who had been in a vegetative state for five months (Boly et al. 2007; Owen et al. 2006). The study involved two kinds of trials. On some trials the patient was played a pre-recorded instruction to 'imagine playing tennis'; on other trials she was instructed to 'imagine visiting the rooms in your home'. In each case, after 30 seconds she was told to relax ('now just relax') and given a

30-second rest period. In this paradigm, the patient's BOLD responses from those areas preferentially involved in motor imagery and spatial navigation were indistinguishable from those seen in thirty-four healthy volunteers: the instruction to imagine playing tennis produced increased activation in the supplementary motor area whereas the instruction to imagine walking around the home produced increased activation in the parahippocampal place area.

Should we conclude that minimally conscious state patients and perhaps even a few vegetative state patients have 'islands of consciousness'—fragments of phenomenality that are not knit together into a single stream of consciousness—or should we instead take these findings to be evidence of nothing more than unconscious activity? Before addressing this question let us examine another condition in which patients are minimally responsive.

Epileptic absence seizures

Epileptic absence seizures are so-called because patients appear to be 'absent' or disengaged from their immediate environment. They will typically fail to respond to questions or commands, and will have amnesia for the period in question. Absences can occur in the context of both partial (or focal) seizures, which arise in a circumscribed region of the brain (often the temporal lobe), and generalized seizures, in which the seizure permeates widespread regions of the brain. Absence periods that occur in the context of generalized seizures are often very brief (lasting for 5–10 seconds), whereas those that occur in the context of partial seizures can last for minutes.[8]

Although absence seizures are often said to involve a complete loss of consciousness, there is reason to think that in many cases the patient might retain rudimentary forms of experience. Consider the following description of a seizure in a 9-year-old boy:

He had a vacant look on his face. I asked him to close his eyes but he did not comply even though the command was repeated forcefully four times. I then said, 'Ricky, can you hear me?' to which he replied promptly by saying 'yes,' but when the command to close his eyes was again repeated, twice, there was still no compliance. After the attack, questioning revealed that he remembered that I had asked him to close his eyes. (Gloor 1986: S19)

In this instance, auditory perception, memory, and the ability to comprehend simple statements was preserved, but the patient was either unwilling or unable to perform the simple act of closing his eyes. In some cases patients are able to

---

[8] For overviews of impairments to consciousness in absence seizures see Blumenfeld (2005); Fried (2005); Gloor (1986, 1990).

execute quite elaborate forms of behaviour while in the grip of an absence seizure. Hughlings-Jackson (1889) recounts an episode in which a doctor undergoing an absence seizure examined a patient and wrote up the diagnosis in his notes—a diagnosis that accorded with the one that he made when he re-examined the patient the following day. A more recent case concerns a patient who experienced seizures while riding his bicycle to work.

[The patient] stated that after setting out in the morning he would occasionally find himself riding back home. Clearly, in the space of a relatively short time he had turned around and ridden back home, all the while maintaining his ability to operate a bicycle with the concomitant demands of contact with the environment. Yet he was unable to recollect this period of time. (Fried 2005: 114)

A recent review reinforces the anecdotal impression that the impairments to cognitive and behavioural capacities in absence seizures can be highly selective, with patients losing some capacities whilst retaining others (Blumen-feld 2005). The capacity to produce verbal responses to questions is more likely to be disrupted than is the capacity to read or count aloud, and both of these capacities are in turn more likely to be disrupted than is the capacity to encode items in short-term memory, which is in turn more likely to be disrupted than is the capacity to perform simple motor tasks on command. But insofar as any one of these capacities is retained we have some reason to suppose that consciousness is preserved, even if only in a rudimentary form.

A second reason for thinking that consciousness can be retained in periods of 'absence' is specific to seizures with a temporal lobe origin. Such seizures often begin with an 'aura' in which the patient might have a sudden emotional experience, hear a snippet of music, or undergo visual imagery. Some auras involve relatively simple perceptual fragments; others take the form of complex and structured multimodal percepts. Although it is sometimes stipulated that auras take place only in 'that portion of the seizure which occurs before con-sciousness is lost and for which memory is retained afterwards' (Bancaud et al. 1981), there is reason to suspect that auras—or at least aura-like phenomena— might persist even after the capacity for memory consolidation has been lost. If isolated bursts of electrical activity can trigger experiential fragments when the patient is able to both report and remember their experiences, perhaps they can also trigger such states when these capacities are no longer intact. Indeed, Gloor et al. (1980) speculate that the patient's very unresponsiveness during temporal lobe seizures might result from the fact his or her attention has been captured by such hallucinations.

6.4 The flickering flame

Although the disorders of consciousness just examined differ greatly in aetiology and cognitive profile, in each of these cases there is some reason to think that we are dealing with fragments of consciousness: autonomous slivers of awareness that may not be unified with each other, either at a time or through time. Normal human experience may be fully unified, but perhaps that unity breaks down in the context of abnormal background conditions.

In the previous chapter I suggested that arguments for phenomenal disunity will involve two moments: a 'positive moment' in which the case for consciousness is made and a 'negative moment', in which the case for disunity in consciousness is made. Let us begin with the positive moment.

The prima facie case for thinking that minimally responsive patients might often be conscious in some form or another is a strong one. Certainly clinicians regard patients in the minimally conscious state as manifesting rudimentary forms of awareness. By definition, persistent vegetative state patients do not show overt behavioural evidence of awareness, but as we noted certain patients may show covert evidence of awareness that can be detected via neuroimaging. Similarly, absence seizure patients often appear to retain a basic kind of perceptual contact with their own body and environment. In each minimally responsive condition, we have reason to think that some flicker of experience might remain.

Of course, this prima facie case is open to various challenges. Although each form of minimal responsiveness would need to be examined on its own terms, let us consider some general reasons for denying that minimally responsive patients are conscious.

One route to scepticism proceeds by way of appeal to the introspective criterion. There is clearly no evidence for consciousness here if introspective report is the only legitimate basis on which to ascribe consciousness. Naccache dismisses the claims of Owen et al. (2006) to have found evidence of consciousness in a persistent vegetative state patient (in the form of neural activity indicative of willed action) by stating that 'consciousness is univocally probed in humans through the subject's reports of his or her own mental states' (Naccache 2006: 1396). Although Naccache doesn't apply his comments to other minimally responsive patients they readily lend themselves to such extension. But the claim that consciousness can be probed only via introspective report is not a compelling one. There is something to be said for placing a great deal of weight on introspective report in the context of self-conscious subjects who are alert and cognitively unimpaired (see §6.1), but minimally responsive patients obviously do not answer to that description.

Another line of objection takes as its point of departure the connection between consciousness and rationality. According to Shoemaker, any conscious state must

belong to some reasonably rich set of mental states with all the members of which it is co-conscious. The set of states must be rich enough for it to be possible for there to be rational thought which draws its premises from the set, and action which is rationalized by members of the set. And a state's being co-conscious with a particular other state is a matter of these states being members of some larger set whose members are integrated in such a way that each is inferentially promiscuous relative to the others and each is available to participate with the others in the rational control of behavior. (Shoemaker 2003: 64)

Do minimally responsive patients possess a set of states the members of which are able to participate in the rational control of behaviour? Perhaps certain patients do occasionally meet this condition in some highly attenuated sense of rationali-ty, but it is clear that none of these patients can be said to possess a *rich* set of conscious states, far less a rich set of mental states that might conspire to produce robustly rational behaviour. But is Shoemaker right to demand that any con-scious state must be able to rationalize behaviour? This claim doesn't seem to be a conceptual truth. As best I can see, there is no incoherence in the thought that minimally responsive patients might have conscious states that fail to rationalize thought or action. Is it an empirical truth? Perhaps, but I know of no evidence in support of it. It is certainly true that conscious states which occur in the context of normal levels of arousal and wakefulness are typically integrated with each other so as to participate in the rational control of behavior, but we should not assume that what holds in the context of unimpaired background states of consciousness will hold also in impaired background states.[9]

Pursuing a similar theme, the sceptic might appeal to the correlation between consciousness and global availability in order to cast doubt on claims that minimally responsive patients are ever conscious. As we noted in the previous chapter, it is widely held that the contents of any conscious state must be globally available for cognitive and behavioural consumption, and on the face of things few if any of these patients enjoy mental states whose contents answer to this description. But this objection fails for the same reasons that the previous objection did: we should not assume that the properties conscious states possess in the context of unimpaired background states will transfer to impaired

---

[9] I am grateful to Ian Phillips and Lizzie Schechter for pressing me to say more here.

background states. The objector must specify a notion of global availability that minimally responsive patients fail to meet and which is also correlated with consciousness across *all* background states (levels) of consciousness. I very much doubt whether that can be done. There are certainly notions of global availability that these patients fail to meet—notions that require globally available content to be encoded in short-term memory, for example—but such forms of global availability are not plausibly regarded as necessary conditions on the possession of consciousness. Any notion of global availability that *is* plausibly regarded as necessary for consciousness as such is, I suspect, likely to be satisfied by at least some minimally responsive patients.[10]

A final line of argument on behalf of the sceptical position takes a rather different tack. Rather than attempt to show that minimally responsive behaviours couldn't have been carried out consciously, one might instead argue that they could have been performed unconsciously. One might attempt to assimilate minimally responsive behaviour to the kinds of automatized behaviour seen in cognitively unimpaired subjects that arguably takes places outside of consciousness. How plausible might such an attempted assimilation be?

The first thing to note is that some 'minimally responsive' behaviour may go beyond the over-learned and automatized. Consider the persistent vegetative state patient who showed neural activity suggestive of 30-second bursts of content-specific mental imagery in response to command (Owen et al. 2006). Such behaviour is clearly neither over-learned nor automatized, which is precisely why the authors of the study took it to provide solid evidence of consciousness. Secondly, the force of the analogy is limited even with respect to those 'minimally responsive' behaviours that are over-learned and automatized, for we need to distinguish different senses in which an action might be carried out unconsciously. In common parlance, to do something unconsciously is to do it without being aware of doing it—it is for the action to be unaccompanied by any *conscious monitoring* on the part of the agent. But actions that are not consciously monitored might nonetheless be triggered and guided by perceptually conscious states. The central question is not whether minimally responsive behaviours are consciously monitored but whether they are governed by

---

[10] Part of the problem here is that we are not entirely sure what to say about the relationship between consciousness and 'global availability' when most of the patient's cognitive and behavioural systems are 'off-line'. Must the contents of globally available states be available for the guidance of the creature's thought and behaviour 'right here and now', or does global availability require only that the creature could use the content in question to direct its thought and behaviour if it were able to direct its thought and behaviour? Those who embrace global availability accounts of consciousness have said little about which of these two conceptions of global availability they favour.

conscious representations of the patient's environment. And surely there is good reason to think that they are. Even taking into account the influence of zombie systems (see §5.1), it is highly implausible to suppose that the behaviours seen in minimally responsive patients might be carried out in the absence of any awareness whatsoever. I conclude that the prima facie case for thinking that minimally responsive patients enjoy occasional 'flickers of awareness' appears to survive critical scrutiny.

The 'positive moment' in an argument from disunity looks to be safe but what about the 'negative moment'? Do these phenomenal flickers occur as isolated slivers of sentience or are they phenomenally unified with each other within a single stream of consciousness? It goes without saying that any answer to this question is bound to be highly speculative. Our ignorance about the neurofunctional basis of consciousness conspires with our ignorance about these syndromes to render us incapable of anything more than half-educated speculation. That said, let us speculate.

In the previous chapter I sketched two ways in which one might attempt to secure the negative moment: by appeal to *representational disunity* (failures of representational integration) and by appeal to *access disunity* (failures of co-accessibility). Do we have the tools to construct either sort of argument here? In principle we might. We can imagine finding evidence for the claim that a minimally responsive patient was simultaneously in conscious states <p> and <q> but not in conscious state <p&q>, or that such a patient had pairs of conscious states whose contents were not available to the same consuming systems. And, depending on the details, such evidence might indicate that the patient had simultaneous experiences that were not phenomenally unified. But what evidence along these lines do we actually have?

Consider first the question of representational integration. As best one can tell, where consciousness occurs in the context of minimal responsiveness it does so in a rather unintegrated form. A minimally conscious state patient might enjoy a fleeting awareness of the voice of a loved one, a rather vague and indeterminate sense of the orientation of their limbs, and perhaps occasional experiences of thirst, hunger, and pain. And although the auras that occur in complex partial seizures can involve the representational integration of perceptual, mnemonic, and affective content, they can also take a fragmentary form. A patient might 'see' a familiar face, experience an 'odd feeling' in her body, and have a sudden sensation of fear without these contents being structured around a common thematic focus (Gloor et al. 1982).

But although these conscious states might not be integrated in the ways in which the contents of consciousness usually are, I doubt that we have the materials here for a compelling argument from representational disunity. The fact that a patient's experience of (say) a familiar face, an 'odd feeling', and fear may lack any underlying thematic unity does not indicate that they are phenomenally disunified. After all, even within the context of everyday experience it is not uncommon to enjoy phenomenally unified states—perceptions, emotional experiences, and memories—that share no thematic focus. The kind of representational disunity needed for evidence of phenomenal disunity requires more than the lack of 'thematic unity'.

There may be more potential to secure the 'negative moment' by focusing instead on access disunity. As we noted, the boundary between the vegetative state and the minimally conscious states is not a sharp one, and it is not uncommon for patients to meet some of the clinical signs of the minimally conscious state but not others. One patient might be able to reach for objects in an apparently purposive manner but fail to follow simple commands; another patient might be able to produce intelligible responses to questions but fail to respond to emotionally laden stimuli in appropriate ways. It is not implausible to suppose that such patients might have experiences whose contents are not accessible to the same sets of consuming systems. For example, experiences in one modality might be able to drive selective attention but not appropriate emotional responsiveness, whereas experiences in another modality might be able to drive appropriate emotional responsiveness but not selective attention.

Although I know of no clinical description that does support such speculations, this counts for little given the fact that few studies of minimally responsive patients provide the kind of detail that would be required here. However, even if such a case were to be found we would need to tread carefully before concluding that the patient in question had a disunified consciousness, for—as we noted in Chapter 5—certain failures of co-accessibility are compatible with the presence of phenomenal unity. Consider again the contrast between 'imperial' and 'federal' conceptions of the architecture of consciousness. Whereas imperial models take all forms of consciousness to converge on a single domain-general reservoir, federal models conceive of the contents of consciousness as distributed across a network of domain-specific circuits. If consciousness has a federal architecture, then it is possible that the flame of consciousness might re-emerge before the domain-general systems responsible for cognitive integration—systems that are secondary to those of consciousness itself—do. And if that were to happen, then one might expect certain failures of co-accessibility—not because the states in question weren't contained within a single stream of consciousness, but because that stream would contain contents drawn from distinct circuits of experience.

Let me note one final point in conclusion. It seems plausible to suppose that the 'stream of consciousness' will be rather narrower—more restricted in capacity—in contexts of minimal responsiveness than it is in the normal waking state. This, in turn, suggests that any flickers of phenomenology that patients might enjoy are more likely to be sequential rather than simultaneous. The 'flame of consciousness' might flicker in and out of existence in response to salient stimuli—turning on a light might trigger a momentary visual experience; an uncomfortable position might generate an experience of pain; hearing one's own name might generate a brief burst of auditory experience—but it is unlikely that any single flicker will represent more than a few features of the world at once. This in turn provides us with additional reason to think that the unity of consciousness is retained in these conditions, for there will simply be fewer states to be unified with each other.

6.5 Conclusion

This chapter has explored the case for phenomenal disunity within three quite different domains. I began with ordinary perceptual experience and the question of whether either apparent motion or meta-contrast masking provides evidence against the unity thesis. I then examined examples of cognitive and behavioural dissociations drawn from developmental psychology, and asked whether they too might be at odds with the unity thesis. And in the final two sections of this chapter we have examined the case for phenomenal disunity provided by minimally responsive conditions.

I have argued that none of these cases provides us with good evidence against the unity thesis. In the first case, we saw that the standard 'Stalinesque' interpretation of apparent motion and meta-contrast masking are preferable to Orwellian treatments of them. With respect to the behavioural dissociations manifested by young children, I suggested that in general these are best thought of in terms of inhibitory failures, and that as such they are consistent with the unity thesis. Finally, I argued that although minimally responsive patients might enjoy 'flickers of awareness', it is unlikely that such flickers involve conscious states that are both simultaneous and disunified with each other.

It should go without saying that these conclusions are *highly* tentative and provisional. In many cases we lack the cognitive and behavioural data that we would need in order to have a comprehensive assessment of the case against the unity thesis, and even where we possess the required data its interpretation with respect to questions of phenomenal unity is highly problematic. So, I cannot claim to have *demonstrated* that these conditions don't involve breakdowns in the unity of consciousness. Nevertheless, the foregoing does at least suggest that the unity of consciousness may survive even the most profound impairments to consciousness. The flame of consciousness might flicker into life by fits and starts, but even in that flickering it may retain the kind of elemental unity captured by the unity thesis.

7

Anosognosia, Schizophrenia, and Multiplicity

This chapter is concerned with a triad of clinical disorders in which the unity of consciousness appears to fall apart in fundamental ways. I begin with anosognosia, a syndrome in which patients are unaware of fundamental changes in the contents of their own conscious states. I then turn to schizophrenia, with a focus on two of its so-called 'positive symptoms'—namely, thought disorder and thought insertion. The chapter concludes with an examination of dissociative identity disorder (or 'multiplicity'), a condition in which individuals seem to manifest multiple conscious selves. As in previous chapters, my focus will be on the unity thesis: do these syndromes show that it is possible for human beings to have simultaneous states of consciousness that are not phenomenally unified? Along the way, we will pause to consider whether other forms of the unity of consciousness might be disrupted in these conditions.

7.1 Anosognosia: 'blind to one's blindness'

It was very striking that the patient did not take any notice of extreme and, later on, complete loss of vision. The patient, who was otherwise complaining a lot, was almost unaffected by this loss. When objects were presented in front of her, she—probably according to habit acquired during recent years—immediately tried to touch them, but she did not make an effort to recognize something by looking at it . . . It was obvious that she, like many blind people, had become an experienced guesser . . . She confirmed, calmly and faithfully, that she could see the presented objects, whereas almost daily examination proved the opposite (Anton 1899, trans. David et al. 1993: 267).

Anton called this impairment 'soul blindness' (*Seelenblindheit*), but it was a term coined by Babinski some fifteen years later—'anosognosia', literally, lack of knowledge of impairment—that stuck. (Curiously, Anton's own name is reserved for a particular form of anosognosia, namely anosognosia for blindness.) Anosognosia can occur in the context of any number of deficits; it is possible to be anosognosic for paralysis, deafness, aphasia, and prosopagnosia (the inability to recognize faces). Patients can be unaware of their physical impairments, of their behavioural consequences, and—what is most important from our point of view—even of the alterations to their own conscious states that result from those impairments and their behavioural consequences.[1]

These components of anosognosia are clearly exhibited by the following patient, an 80-year-old woman who was anosognosic for paralysis to the left side of her body due to a right-hemisphere stroke.

> Examiner: Where are we?
> C.C.: In the hospital.
> Examiner: Which hospital?
> C.C.: Santa Orsola.
> Examiner: Why are you in the hospital?
> C.C.: I fell down and bumped my right leg.
> Examiner: What about your left arm and leg? Are they all right?
> C.C.: Neither well nor bad.
> Examiner: In which sense?
> C.C.: They are aching a bit.
> Examiner: Can you move your left arm?
> C.C.: Yes, I can.
> Examiner: [The examiner puts her right index finger in C.C.'s right visual field.] Can you touch my finger with your left hand? [C.C. does not move.]
> Examiner: What happens?
> C.C.: It happens that I am very good.
> Examiner: Have you touched my finger?
> C.C.: Yes.

Later in the interview:

> Examiner: Could you clap your hands?
> C.C.: I am not at the theatre.
> Examiner: I know. But we just want to see whether you are able to clap your hands. [C.C. lifts her right arm and pits it in the position for clapping, perfectly aligned with the trunk midline, moving it as if it were clapping against the left hand. She seems perfectly satisfied with the performance.]
> Examiner: Are you sure that you are clapping your hands? We did not hear any sound.
> C.C.: I never make any noise. (Berti et al. 1998: 28–9)

---

[1] For reviews and cases see Bisiach & Berti (1995); Bisiach & Geminiani (1991); Forde & Wallesch (2003); Goldberg & Barr (1991); Heilman et al. (1998); Jehkonen et al. (2000); Marcel et al. (2004); McDaniel & McDaniel (1991); McGlynn & Schacter (1989); Papagno & Vallar (2003); Prigatano & Schacter (1991); Redlich & Dorsey (1945); Swartz & Brust (1984); Venneri & Shanks (2004); Vuilleumier (2000, 2004).

This transcript is representative of many involving patients with anosognosia. What might explain such reports?

Motivational accounts of anosognosia hold that patients are aware of their impairments and their consequences, but refuse to acknowledge them because their consequences are so overwhelming.[2] Although some cases of anosognosia may have a motivational component, it is implausible to suppose that motivational factors lie at the heart of the disorder. One problem with the motivational story concerns the selectivity of anosognosia. One patient may deny that they have hemianopia (blindness in one half of the visual field) but accept that they have hemiplegia (paralysis on one side of their body), whilst another might acknowledge their hemiplegia but deny their hemianopia (Nathanson et al. 1952; Jehkonen et al. 2000). Anton's own patient U.M. was 'blind to her blindness' but acknowledged her dysphasia. It would seem rather ad hoc to suppose that patients are less willing to acknowledge their blindness than they are their dysphasia.

Another account holds that although anosognosia does involve impairments of awareness, these impairments are limited to the encoding and retrieval of information in memory. On this view, patients are aware of their impairments when their behavioural consequences are obvious (say, because they fail to be able to dress themselves), but this awareness fails to make any impact on their long-term beliefs about their bodily state or capacities. This proposal receives some support from studies involving epileptic patients who have undergone the Wada procedure in preparation for temporal-lobe surgery. In this procedure, one hemisphere of the brain is anaesthetised, with the result that subjects suffer weakness in the contralateral side of the body. Because left-side injections produce language impairments in addition to right-side weakness, in many studies patients are questioned only after the effects of the barbiturate have resolved. A typical finding is that patients fail to remember that they had earlier experienced weakness in one half of their body. In one study, twenty-seven of thirty-one patients (who had had a right-sided injection) failed to recall having experienced left-arm weakness when questioned some fifteen minutes after the event (Carpenter et al. 1995; see also Meador et al. 2000).

Although this study suggests that memory problems might play *a* role in accounting for anosognosia, it is doubtful whether the condition can be fully explained in this way (Aimola Davies et al. 2008). Return to the transcript reproduced above. Not only did C.C. claim that she *could* move her arm and that she *had* moved her arm, she also claimed that she *was moving* her arm despite

---

[2] For classic statements of the motivational account of anosognosia see Weinstein & Kahn (1950, 1955). For recent defences of the approach see Ramachandran (1995) and Levy (2008).

the fact that it was immobile. As best one can tell, C.C.'s deficit wasn't merely one of failing to remember her impairment or its consequences, but included a problem of concurrent awareness.

Anosognosia appears to be a pathology of consciousness, but is it also a pathology of the *unity* of consciousness? Some authorities have thought so. Bisiach and Berti speculate that in anosognosia we might see a breakdown of phenomenal unity. 'Different mental states or events, although being individually endowed with phenomenal quality, are kept separate from one another within the stream of consciousness' (1995: 1338). The idea, I take it, is that patients are 'self-blind' to their impairments because certain components of their stream of consciousness have become dissociated from each other. The bulk of the patient's experiences remain introspectively accessible, but fragments of this stream have become isolated from the mechanisms responsible for introspection and cognitive influence more generally (see also Marcel 1993). This account might suggest that although C.C. retained some kind of awareness of her impairment (and perhaps also of its consequences), this state of awareness was not fully integrated with the rest of her conscious states. Let us call this the *phenomenal disunity* account of anosognosia.

Bisiach and Berti do not develop this proposal in much detail. As best I can tell, the only argument that they provide for it is an argument from 'dim' or 'clouded' knowledge—what Anton called 'dunkle Kenntnis'. Although anosognosia is characterized in terms of a lack of awareness of impairment, many patients possess an implicit appreciation of their impairment(s). For example, a patient with hemiplegia may deny that there is anything wrong with him, but he might nonetheless acknowledge that he doesn't retain the full suite of behavioural capacities that he once did. Other patients who also insist that there is nothing wrong with them will admit that the examiner would be unable to perform certain tasks had he or she been affected by the same impairment (Marcel et al. 2004). Still other hemiplegic patients might acknowledge their paralysis when directly questioned about it, but they will attempt to rise from bed or engage in other activities—such as knitting—that are obviously beyond them. Finally, when asked to account for their inability to carry out certain kinds of action, patients will often provide a justification that suggests that they have some awareness of their deficit. For example, a patient might explain her failure to move her arm by insisting that 'it has a cold' (Vuilleumier 2004).

I suspect that the argument from dim knowledge is meant to proceed along the following lines. The 'implicit awareness' of impairment that patients often manifest is best explained by supposing that there has been a division within the patient's stream of consciousness. The main tranche of this stream is available for the normal forms of cognitive and behavioural consumption (verbal report, belief revision), but there is a subsidiary tranche—a tranche that contains a representation of the patient's impairment(s)—whose contents are able to exert only indirect influence on the patient's thought and action.

What should we make of this argument? The central problem with it concerns an assumption about how cognitive and behavioural control might be related to phenomenal fragmentation. The argument assumes that conscious states that are 'kept separate' from the rest of the subject's conscious states are likely to play only a restricted role in cognitive and behavioural control. It is not clear to me why we should accept this assumption. Prima facie, one would expect the contents of phenomenal states to be widely available for cognitive and behavioural control whether or not they are isolated from the bulk of the subject's conscious states. In short, it is not at all clear that phenomenal fragmentation provides any—let alone the *best*—explanation of dim knowledge.

So, how *should* we think of dim knowledge? That depends on the kind of dim knowledge in question. Some patients exhibit dim knowledge of their impairment in the sense that they are aware of certain aspects of it but not others. For example, a patient might seem to be oblivious to the impairment itself but aware of its behavioural consequences. This kind of dim knowledge does not seem to be particularly difficult to account for, at least in broad outline. The patients in question have simply failed to 'put two and two together'. They are aware of some facts about themselves (say, that they can no longer walk to the store), but not others (say, that one of their legs is weak). Admittedly, the facts of which they are unaware are intimately related to the facts of which they are aware—someone who is aware that they cannot walk to the store ought to wonder why this is the case—but anosognosic patients would not be alone in failing to draw out the implications of what they are aware of in the ways that they should.

However, other instances of dim knowledge are not easily explained by appealing to distinctions in the content of awareness. For example, a patient might appear to be aware of his impairment when required to produce a verbal report of it but not when required to engage in certain kinds of non-verbal behaviour. In such cases it looks as though the patient both is and is not aware of one the same fact. How might we explain this kind of dim knowledge?

The notion of probe-dependence might be of some assistance to us here (see §5.4) Consider a patient who is anosognosic for unilateral visual neglect due to right hemisphere damage. The patient might appear to be aware of her neglect when asked to copy a design but not when required to say whether anything is wrong with her. This dissociation may occur because verbal report activates the left hemisphere (which is responsible for speech production) and 'sucks' attention away from the damaged right hemisphere in which information about the damage is represented. Without the demands of verbal report, attention can be restored to the damaged right hemisphere, and the patient will once again be conscious of the stimulus (Ricci & Chatterjee 2004). Attention can also be restored to the damaged hemisphere by caloric stimulation of the inner ear—either by stimulating the contralateral ear with cold water or the ipsilateral ear with warm water.[3] The probe-dependent perspective also suggests that even when a representation of the impairment does break through to consciousness it may do so only in a fairly weak and ineffectual manner, and as a result fail to possess the kind of influence on thought and action that is typical of conscious states.

Where does this leave the anosognosia-based challenge to the unity thesis? Not in particularly good shape, it seems to me. The central argument for thinking that patients with anosognosia might be subject to phenomenal fragmentation is the argument from dim knowledge, but we have seen that dim knowledge can be adequately accounted for in ways that involve no phenomenal disunity. Anosognosia is a pathology of consciousness, but it is not a pathology that puts any serious pressure on the unity thesis.

However, there is a sense in which patients with anosognosia might be said to have suffered from a loss in the unity of consciousness, broadly construed. The unity in question is not phenomenal unity but rather a kind of unity that is bound up with introspective awareness. Anosognosic patients are often oblivious to major changes in the contents of their own conscious states. They either overlook experiences that they have, or they fail to notice that they no longer have the kinds of experiences that they once did. For example, the anosognosic patient described above seems to be unaware of the fact that she was not clapping, despite the manifest difference in experience that typically accompanies the contrast between clapping and not clapping. Not only does this patient seem to be impaired in tracking what the world is like, she also appears to be impaired in tracking her own states of consciousness. Following Nikolinakos (2004), we might say that anosognosia involves a breakdown in the unity of *reflexive* consciousness.

In response to this proposal, a critic might challenge the assumption that the impairments seen in anosognosia will normally be introspectively manifest. Levine, for one, argues that the sensory impairments implicated in anosognosia are 'never phenomenally immediate but instead must be discovered by observation and inference' (1990: 234). This may be true of some of the impairments that occur in the context of anosognosia, but surely the fact that one is hemiplegic or blind ought to be apparent—indeed, manifestly apparent—to

---

[3] See Bisiach et al. (1991); Cappa et al. (1987); Rode et al. (1992); Rubens (1985); Silberpfennig (1949); Vallar et al. (1990); Vallar et al. (1994).

anyone with normal introspective abilities. How could anosognosia *not* involve some kind of impairment of the mechanisms underlying introspection?

One answer to this question takes the form of the 'imagery hypothesis', according to which patients are unaware of their impairments because the missing perceptual content has been replaced by internally generated experiences that 'mimic' the kinds of states that the patient expects and would have otherwise enjoyed (Heilman 1991; Goldenberg et al. 1995). Consider the following dialogue between a physician and H.S., a 46-year-old woman who appeared to be anosognosic for complete cortical blindness.

> Examiner: (Moves a bunch of small keys, producing a sound): I am holding an object. Do you have any idea what it might be?
> H.S.: Could that be a key?
> Examiner: (Silently moves the keys beneath the table): What does it look like?
> H.S.: On top there is a big ring, and it has a dark key-bit.
> Examiner. Do you see the key well?
> H.S.: I am seeing that it is a key.
> Examiner. (Opens and shuts scissors): Do have any idea what that might be?
> H.S.: Are those scissors?
> Examiner: Do you see them?
> H.S.: Only vaguely. I guessed a little.
> Examiner: (Silently hides the scissors beneath the table): What can you see of these scissors?
> H.S.: Upside are the handles where you take them, and below them is the part for cutting.
> Examiner: Are you seeing this?
> H.S.: Yes. (Goldenberg et al. 1995: 1378)

The authors of this paper suggest that H.S. had mistaken her imagery experiences for perceptual experiences, and that suggestion seems eminently reasonable. The objects that she described seeing were either the kinds of objects likely to be encountered in the environment in which she found herself, or—as in this extract—suggested by what she could hear. Arguably, H.S's blindness was not introspectively manifest to her because the missing perceptual content had been filled in by visual imagery, in something akin to the way in which the missing perceptual content in the blind spot is filled in by the mechanisms responsible for perceptual completion.

The imagery hypothesis has the resources to account for other forms of anosognosia as well. Consider again C.C, the hemiplegic patient described above, who—despite obvious evidence to the contrary—appeared to believe that she had just clapped. Perhaps C.C. had this false belief because she had the kind of proprioceptive and agentive experiences that normally accompany clapping, although these experiences would not be 'perceptual' but 'imagistic'. Certainly some patients have such experiences. In response to a request to raise her arm a patient who had recently recovered from anosognosia for hemiplegia observed, 'It feels like it's rising, but it's not' (Chatterjee & Mennemeier 1996: 229). Such reports are not unusual in the literature.

But the imagery hypothesis does have its limitations. Consider the fact that C.C. *admits* that she's not making any sound when she 'claps'. Although she could be hallucinating motor experience, she does not appear to be hallucinating a sound, and not being able to hear yourself clap would alarm someone who was otherwise cognitively normal.[4] Similarly, one might have thought that the evident failure of H.S.'s visual experiences to support reliable action ought to have alerted her to the fact that they were internally generated rather than accurate representations of her environment (as she mistakenly believed them to be). So, even allowing for the fact that involuntarily generated imagery might plug the experiential gaps created by the patient's impairments, there is still a good case to be made for thinking that anosognosia may involve a 'breakdown' in the unity of reflexive consciousness.

Thus far I have considered cases in which patients appear to be unaware that they have *lost* certain forms of conscious experience. However, there are also patients who appear to be unaware that they *retain* certain kinds of conscious states. Consider the following case of 'inverse Anton's Syndrome' (Hartmann et al. 1991). The patient in question complained that he was completely blind, and took himself to be aware of the world only by non-visual means. One of his interests involved the buying and selling of horses. When asked how he judged the horses he said 'by their sound and their feel'. However, testing demonstrated that he had a relatively large area of preserved vision. He could name objects, colours, and famous faces that were presented in an area of 30 degrees in the right upper quadrant of his visual field. When confronted with his abilities he continued to deny that he had visual experience and insisted that he identified the stimuli in question by feel. The patient was neither disoriented nor hysterical, and the clinicians could not discern any plausible motive for his denial.

Was this patient conscious of various stimuli but merely unaware that he was conscious of them, or were his visual representations unconscious in the way in which the blindsight patient's visual representations appear to be? It is not clear. It is certainly tempting to contrast this case with that of blindsight, for unlike blindsighters this patient did not need to be prompted in order to use his visual

---

[4] I am indebted to Lizzie Schechter and Fiona Macpherson here.

information. Arguably, the most natural interpretation of the case is that the patient had conscious visual representations to which he lacked introspective access. He seems to have been aware of the features of the world that his visual experiences represented, but unaware of his visual experiences themselves. (To put it another way, he seems to have been unaware that his awareness of certain environmental features was visually mediated.) This self-blindness appears to have been selective, for there is no evidence that he was unaware of his experiences in other sensory modalities.

By way of drawing this section to a close, let me mention one implication that these findings might have for treatments of introspection. There are two broad perspectives one might take to introspection. On the one hand, one might think of introspection as a domain-general faculty (Schacter 1989; McGlynn & Schacter et al. 1988). On this view, selective failures of introspection would result from impairments to the connections between this faculty and particular perceptual systems. On the other hand, one might think of introspection as involving the operation of a number of domain-specific faculties. Furthermore, one might think of these domain-specific faculties as redeploying the very machinery used to generate experiences of the relevant domain in the first place (Bisiach 1988; Bisiach & Geminiani 1991). On this picture, the introspection of visual experience would involve a kind of reactivation of those experiences themselves. Following Bisiach, I submit that anosognosia provides some support for this domain-specific approach to introspection. Unlike the domain-general conception, the domain-specific model predicts that disruptions to a domain of experience will be accompanied by difficulties in the introspective detection of those disruptions. This is precisely what one finds in anosognosia: damage to certain modules not only impairs the individual's ability to form perceptual or sensory representations in a particular domain, it also impairs their ability to detect that impairment. This thought is actually hinted at by Anton himself, who remarked that in anosognosia for unilateral neglect 'not only the perception related to one side of the body or to one extremity but also the corresponding concepts are lost' (Anton 1898, trans. Förstl et al. 1993).

7.2 Schizophrenia: 'an orchestra without a conductor'

Another syndrome that is frequently said to involve a breakdown in the unity of consciousness is schizophrenia. The disease takes its name from the Greek for 'splitting of the psyche' and Kraepelin (1896), one of its earliest commentators, considered the loss of the unity of consciousness to be one of its core features.

Schizophrenia is a complex and heterogeneous disease, and many theorists have suggested that it is best thought of as a collection of loosely related disorders rather than a single entity.[5] Even those who argue in favour of retaining a single diagnostic category typically grant that the symptoms of schizophrenia cluster into two groups: negative symptoms and positive symptoms (Andreasen 1985; Crow 1980; Liddle 1987). Whereas the positive symptoms are characterized by a surfeit of affect and thought, the negative symptoms involve deficits in affect and thought, such as a reduction in the ability to experience pleasure (anhedonia), lack of motivation (avolition), and poverty of speech (alogia). Discussions of the structure of consciousness in schizophrenia typically restrict their attention to the positive symptoms, and it is on two such symptoms—namely thought disorder and thought insertion—that I will focus here.[6]

Thought disorder involves impairments in the ability to structure thought and action around goals. The cognitive and perceptual focus of patients is guided by associations and irrelevant stimuli that capture their attention, rather than by the logic of the task that they have set themselves. At root, thought disorder appears to involve a disturbance in selective attention.[7] Patients become 'engrossed' or 'entranced' by stimuli that should be disregarded. Attention is 'sticky', and cannot be easily moved from one stimulus to another:

If I am reading I may suddenly get bogged down at a word. It may be any word, even a simple word that I know well. When this happens I can't get past it. It's as if I am being hypnotized by it. It's as if I am seeing the word for the first time and in a different way from anyone else. It's not so much that I absorb it, it's more like it is absorbing me. (McGhie & Chapman 1961: 109)

Another patient remarked that

the mind must have a filter which functions without our conscious thought, sorting stimuli and allowing only those which are relevant to the situation at hand to disturb consciousness. And this filter must be working at maximum efficiency at all times, particularly when we require a high degree of concentration. What happened to me . . . was a breakdown of the filter, and a hodge-podge of unrelated stimuli were distracting me from things which should have had my undivided attention. (MacDonald 1960: 218)

Whereas normal cognition is tuned to be sensitive to stimuli that are either intrinsically salient or important to the subject, in thought disorder attention is drawn to mundane matters—a stray remark, a vase, or the pattern on some

---

[5] See Andreasen & Carpenter (1993); Boyle (1990); Bentall (1990); and Poland (2007).
[6] See Freedman (1974) and McKay et al. (1996) for first-person perspectives on these symptoms.
[7] See Anscombe (1987) and Gray et al. (1991). However, see Cutting (1985) and McKenna (1994) for reservations about this account of thought disorder.

brickwork. The patient may be confused as to why her attention has been drawn to an insignificant stimulus, and in order to make sense of her own behaviour she might come to believe the stimulus *is* significant, that it possesses a hidden meaning that is manifest only to her.

As far as I can see, thought disorder does not put any real pressure on the unity thesis. There is no reason to think that patients have multiple conscious states that are not contained within an overall phenomenal field. What thought disorder does demonstrate is the importance of what we might call the *narrative unity* of consciousness—the ability to keep one's thoughts on track. But narrative unity is not phenomenal unity, and the unity thesis is only concerned with the phenomenal structure of consciousness.

The breakdown in conscious unity exemplified by thought disorder is of a relatively recognisable kind, for we are all familiar with difficulties in screening out distracting information. A second positive symptom—thought insertion—involves forms of mental fragmentation that are rather more alien (Graham 2004; Mullins & Spence 2003). Jaspers characterizes thought insertion as follows:

Patients think something and yet feel that someone else has thought it and in some way forced it on them. The thought arises and with it a direct awareness that it is not the patient but some external agent that thinks it. The patient does not know why he has this thought nor does he intend to have it. He does not feel master of his own thoughts and in addition he feels in the power of some incomprehensible external force. (Jaspers 1962: 122–3)

Mellor gives the following oft-cited example of thought insertion:

I look out the window and I think that the garden looks nice and the grass looks cool, but the thoughts of Eamonn Andrews [a well-known TV presenter from the 1960s] come into my mind. There are no other thoughts there, only his . . . He treats my mind like a screen and flashes his thoughts into it like you flash a picture. (Mellor 1970: 17)

Before addressing the question of whether thought insertion might put any pressure on the unity thesis, we need to gain a clear conception of just what it involves. That turns out to be a far from straightforward task.

One account of thought insertion holds that it involves a loss of the sense of subjectivity or 'my-ness' that is said to accompany thought. On this view, patients are to be understood as denying that thoughts of which they are introspectively aware—thoughts that occur in their stream of consciousness—are theirs. This account is implicit in Freud's description of thought insertion as a condition in which 'portions of [the patient's] mental life—his perceptions, thoughts, and feelings—appear alien to him and as not belonging to his own ego' (Freud 1962: 13). Let us call this the *no-subjectivity* account. Another account of thought insertion holds that patients should not be understood as denying that they are the *subjects* of the thoughts in question, but merely that they are the *agents* of those thoughts (see e.g. Gallagher 2000; Stephens & Graham 2000). On this view, we should take 'the thoughts of Eamonn Andrews' to refer to the thoughts that Eamonn Andrews *produces*, not the thoughts that Eamonn Andrews *has*. As we shall see, this account can be developed in a number of ways.

The statements of the patients themselves do not clearly favour one model over the other. Although some expressions of thought insertion suggest that a sense of passivity lies at the root of the patient's experience—one patient may say that his mind is being treated like a screen; another may say that thoughts are put into his mind—other expressions of thought-insertion point in favour of the no-subjectivity model, insofar as these patients appear to deny ownership of the relevant thoughts and are inclined to attribute ownership of the thoughts to other individuals.

One might be inclined to reject the no-subjectivity account on the grounds that it ascribes to patients thoughts that are quite obviously fantastical—indeed, thoughts that may even be pragmatically self-defeating. But the force of this worry is uncertain, for patients with thought insertion are delusional, and by their very nature delusions involve gross departures from rationality. If it is possible for those with delusions of somatoparaphrenia to sincerely deny ownership of body parts that they admit are connected to their own bodies, why should it not also be possible for individuals with delusions of thought insertion to deny ownership over thoughts of which they are directly aware? As far as I can see, both the no-subjectivity and the no-agency accounts provide us with viable conceptions of what patients might mean in denying that certain thoughts are their own.

That being said, the no-agency account is prima facie more attractive than the no-subjectivity account, for it appears to make thought insertion *relatively* comprehensible. It is easier to understand why someone might come to think that their own thoughts are under the control of alien forces (and hence not their own in an agentive sense) than it is to understand how they might come to believe that their 'own' thoughts are not their own in a subjective sense. So, let us examine the prospects of the no-agency model.

Perhaps the most straightforward version of the no-agency account conceives of conscious thinking as an action that is typically accompanied by a 'feeling of doing'. According to this version of the account, it is the absence of this feeling that leads patients to suppose that their thoughts are not under their own control but are instead under the control of alien forces. Frith provides an influential presentation of this idea:

> Thinking, like all our actions, is normally accompanied by a sense of effort and deliberate choice as we move from one thought to the next. If we found ourselves thinking without any awareness of the sense of effort that reflects central monitoring, we might well experience these thoughts as alien and, thus, being inserted into our minds. (Frith 1992: 81)

I think it is rather debatable whether conscious thought lives up to this description. In saying this I don't mean to deny that thinking *can* be accompanied by a sense of effort and deliberate choice; the experience of suddenly realizing that one's mind has been wandering and as a result setting oneself to concentrate on the task at hand is a familiar one. But, generally speaking, thought seems to be no more accompanied by a 'feeling of doing' than does perception or bodily sensation. For the most part one thought replaces another and the will seems to be a largely passive bystander. Even in the context of 'directed thinking'—which, it seems to me, is the exception rather than the rule—one does not experience oneself as the agent of particular thoughts but merely as having thoughts that are in line with one's overall cognitive goals.

Rather than develop the no-agency account in terms of 'a sense of effort and deliberate choice', we might do better to think of it in terms of a disruption to the intentional control of thought. We may not experience particular thoughts as 'things we do', but we do normally experience ourselves as having a certain kind of control over the general direction and evolution of our thoughts. We might call this kind of control 'metacognitive control.' Perhaps patients say that other agents are putting thoughts into their minds because they experience a lack of metacognitive control with respect to those thoughts.

The obvious objection to this proposal is that there are many contexts in which we take our thoughts to be inconsistent with our cognitive goals without ascribing them to other agents. Lying in bed at night I might curse my inability to control my thoughts, but I am not tempted to suppose that these thoughts are those of someone else. Moreover, as Stephens and Graham (2000) note, patients with obsessive thoughts experience their thoughts as escaping their metacognitive control, but they don't disown them in the way that patients with thought insertion do. An additional challenge for this account is that passivity phenomena are not restricted to judgements but include impulses and emotional states, so-called 'made emotions'.

> I cry, tears roll down my cheeks and I look unhappy, but inside I have a cold anger because they are using me in this way, and it is not me who is unhappy, but they are projecting unhappiness into my brain ... You have no idea how terrible it is to laugh and to look happy and to know that it is not you. (Mellor 1970: 17)

Unhappiness is not normally experienced as a state that is under one's control. Given this, it is hard to see how one might explain why a patient might come to believe that unhappiness is 'being projected into their brain' by supposing that they have experienced a disruption to the sense of metacognitive control.

A final variant of the no-agency approach can be found in Campbell (1999) and Stephens and Graham (2000), who suggest that thought insertion results from the patient's inability to reconcile the thoughts of which she is aware with her self-conception. As Stephens and Graham put it, the subject 'will not accept as agentically her own thoughts whose occurrence she finds inexplicable by reference to her conception or self-referential description of her intentional states' (Stephens & Graham 2000: 170).

In my view this is the most promising version of the no-agency account. Although it is not without problems—we often have thoughts that are neither explained by nor consistent with our self-conception without being at all tempted to alienate them—it does account for the fact that thought insertion can occur for mental states that we do not experience as under our direct control. However, this version of the no-agency view has departed so far from the origins of the approach that it is no longer clear that it is really an *alternative* to the no-subjectivity account. Suppose that one thought of oneself as an intentional system (Dennett 1971). On this conception, it is not clear that one could think of a mental state as one's own without also representing it as being caused by oneself in a certain kind of way. Arguably, belonging to an intentional system *just is* being produced by it. And if that is right, then perhaps this version of the no-agency account is best viewed not as an alternative to the no-subjectivity account but as a way of fleshing it out.

So much for the question of what might lie behind claims of thought insertion: do such claims—however they are to be understood—put pressure on the unity thesis? I think not. Although thought insertion reveals aspects of the unity of consciousness (broadly understood) that are easily overlooked, there is little reason to suppose that it involves any kind of phenomenal fragmentation. The aspect of the unity of consciousness that is lost or at least compromised in thought insertion is what we might call the unity of 'subjectivity' or 'reflexivity'—the sense that each of one's experiences are one's own. But—as we have remarked before (§1.3)—this form of the unity of consciousness ought not be confused with the phenomenal unity of consciousness.

The twin symptoms of thought disorder and thought insertion go some way towards justifying Kraepelin's description of 'the schizophrenic mind' (to use a dangerous phrase) as 'an orchestra without a conductor', but we have found nothing in our examination of schizophrenia that might call the *unity thesis* into question. Certain forms of the unity of consciousness might be compromised in schizophrenia, but the kind of unity in which we are most interested here— phenomenal unity—appears to be left intact.

7.3 Multiplicity: 'the delusion of separateness'

The clinical syndrome most closely associated in the popular mind with break- downs in the unity of consciousness is multiple personality disorder (MPD), now officially known as dissociative identity disorder (DID). Both of these terms are cumbersome, and I will refer to the condition simply as 'multiplicity'.

Multiplicity is sometimes confused with schizophrenia. The confusion is understandable, for there are certain parallels between multiplicity and the positive symptoms of schizophrenia (see p.169). Nevertheless, the disorders are regarded as distinct in clinical practice. Roughly speaking, schizophrenia involves a 'fragmentation' or 'disintegration' of the psyche, whereas multiplicity involves a 'multiplication' of the psyche (David et al. 1996). In order to qualify for a diagnosis of multiplicity, a person must have two or more distinct identities or personality states. These identities—or 'alters' as they are also known—'each have their own relatively enduring pattern of perceiving, relat- ing to and thinking about the environment and the self' (American Psychiatric Association 2004). Alters take turns directing the behaviour of the multiple, and while a particular alter is 'out' the multiple's behaviour will generally be guided only by the memories, beliefs, plans, and other intentional states of that alter.

The earliest reports of what might now be classified as cases of multiplicity were both published in 1791. The first involved a young man known to us only as 'Captain Miller's son', who was described as having 'two distinct minds, which acted by turns independently of each other'. When in dissociative 'fits' he could remember what had occurred during previous 'fits' but had no memory for the periods between fits (Carlson 1981). The second case involved a young German woman who suddenly exchanged her own personality for the manners and ways of a French-born lady. 'In her French personality, the subject had complete memory of all that she had said and done during her previous French states. As a German, she knew nothing of her French personality' (Ellenberger 1970: 127).

Interest in multiplicity flourished in the late nineteenth century, with theor- ists on both sides of the Atlantic—mostly notably Binet and Janet in France and James and Prince in the United States—arguing that dissociative phenomena are at odds with the claim that consciousness is necessarily unified (Crabtree 1986). This turn-of-the-century fascination with multiplicity reached its apex with Morton Prince's (1905/1978) study of 'Christine Beauchamp' (whose real name was Clara Fowler) and W. F. Prince's (1915/16) study of Doris Fischer. After 1915, multiplicity enjoyed a dramatic decline; although some cases—such as Thigpen and Cleckley's (1954) 'Eve'—enjoyed a wide amount of attention, no more than fifty-four cases of multiplicity were reported between 1900 and 1970. By the 1970s 'double consciousness' had become 'multiple personality disorder', a change of name that was in part prompted by an increase in the average number of personality states manifested by 'multiples'; although multiple personalities were not unknown in the nineteenth century, the norm was two. Reports of duality are now infrequent, and the typical multiple is said to have between five to ten personality states, with some multiples reported to have hundreds of personalities.

How might multiplicity be at odds with the unity thesis? The most direct threat involves taking alters to have (or perhaps be) distinct streams of consciousness that might be 'out' at one and the same time. Let us call this the *phenomenal disunity* account of multiplicity. The phenomenal disunity account is at odds with the unity thesis, for if the unity thesis is right then the conscious states enjoyed by a subject at any one time must be phenomenally unified with each other. Of course, one could attempt to reconcile the phenomenal disunity account of multiplicity with the unity thesis by identifying subjects of experience not with human beings but with (say) psychological networks or intentional systems. (Indeed, on this view the advocate of the unity thesis might even *expect* alters to 'have' their own stream of consciousness.) Just what to say about the connection between the unity of consciousness and the self should we allow that a single organism might 'house' multiple subjects of experience raises many complex issues, not least of which is the problem of how to individuate intentional systems. However, I will leave these issues to oneside here and focus solely on the question of whether the phenomenal disunity account of multiplicity is correct. If it is not—as, indeed, I shall argue is the case—then these issues are moot.

Although discussions of multiplicity often assume that the phenomenal disunity account is true, the view has rarely been defended. In fact, the only developed defence of the view that I know of is to be found in Stephen Braude's book *First-Person Plural*. Braude's account of multiplicity is nuanced. Although he argues that alters have their own streams of consciousness—indeed, that they are independent loci of *self*-consciousness (1995: 78 f.)—he also argues that multiples have a single, underlying self, which he describes as a 'Kantian ego'. I will leave the Kantian components of Braude's account to one side, and focus only on his arguments for the claim that alters possess autonomous streams of consciousness, streams that can run in parallel to each other.

On my reading *First-Person Plural* contains four arguments for the claim that alters are distinct loci of consciousness. The first of these arguments appeals to the intentional disunity exhibited by alters. Not only do alters claim to be

distinct persons (and not merely personalities); they will disavow the interests and activities of other alters and pursue goals of their own, sometimes even holding different jobs. Moreover, different alters seem to be of different ages and sexes and appear to have distinct overall body-images. For example, one alter might feel he or she is the wrong sex, or too young, short, or fat, to wear the clothes of another alter. (1995: 67; see also 253)

Call this 'the argument from intentional disunity'. The argument starts from a firm foundation, for alters do indeed possess their 'own' traits, beliefs, memories, goals, and self-conceptions. The problem arises when we attempt to move from that claim to the claim that alters are distinct loci of consciousness. Should we think of these sets of psychological states as organized around 'discrete centres of self-consciousness'?

I think not. Although some authors have suggested that 'the grounds for assigning several selves to [a multiple] can be as good as—indeed the same as—those for assigning a single self to a normal human being' (Dennett & Humphrey 1998: 54, emphasis suppressed), in my view the urge to reify alters in this way should be resisted. Alters ought to be regarded as personality 'states' or 'files' rather than bona fide subjects of experience. It might be tempting to argue that since by definition any multiple will have a number of self-conceptions, he or she will also have a number of conscious selves. However, we can see that this inference is fallacious by considering self-deception. Jane has good reason to believe that her husband is having an affair, yet she 'keeps the truth from herself', as we say. When Jane is being honest with herself she recognizes that her marriage has fallen apart, but when in the grip of self-deception she thinks of herself as someone who is happily married. Jane has distinct self-conceptions, but there is no reason to regard these self-conceptions as picking out different selves in any robust sense of the term. Similarly, we can regard alters as self-conscious without being committed to the view that the first-person thoughts 'had by' a multiple's various alters refer to distinct entities.

Self-deception not only undermines the argument from intentional disunity, it also provides us with a lens through which to view multiplicity: perhaps multiples are simply massively self-deceived. By this I do not mean that multiples are deceived *by* themselves (although this may indeed be true), but rather that they are deceived *about* themselves (Heil 1994). In one alter state a white middle-aged male multiple might believe that he is black; in another alter state he might believe that he is a woman; and in a third alter state he might take himself to be a child. As Putnam et al. (1986) put it, multiplicity is a 'delusion of separateness'. The most striking manifestation of this delusion is 'internal homicide', in which one alter tries to kill a fellow alter, oblivious to the fact that any such act would bring about his or her own demise.

Even if it were sound, the argument from intentional disunity could at best establish only that multiples have *successive* rather than *simultaneous* streams of consciousness—in the terminology of the nineteenth century, that patients have *alternating* rather than *double* consciousness. Braude's second argument, if successful, would make good on this lacunae. The argument appeals to certain features of the way in which multiples 'switch' between alter states:

one can actually observe and clearly identify the participants in the struggle. For example, as two alters vie for executive control, the multiple's face might shift rapidly between the distinctive features of each. Even more importantly, the clear personality shifts on the subject's face often reflect the alters' idiosyncratic contributions to the conflict. For example, one personality might show anger, tension or confusion, and the other might display amusement and contempt. And those dispositions can be exhibited in a manner characteristic of the respective personalities. (Braude 1995: 67 f.)

The idea, I take it, is that multiples harbour multiple *agents*, and where we have multiple loci of agency it is likely that we also have multiple loci of consciousness.

Even if switching lives up to Braude's description of it—see Hacking (1995) for a rather different picture—I suspect that the conflict Braude describes is merely an exaggerated form of the struggle for emotional control with which many of us are familiar. Consider a person who has been deeply insulted in a context in which anger is not an appropriate emotion to manifest. One might witness a struggle between anger and self-control being played out on the subject's visage. Braude's comments suggest that inter-alter conflict is 'deeper' than this, but I am not convinced. For one thing, the agentive disunity described by Braude and other commentators appears to be superimposed on a base of sensorimotor integration. To the best of my knowledge, multiples do not demonstrate the kind of agentive disunity seen in (say) the anarchic hand syndrome.

Even if there is a sense in which alters vie for control of the multiple, it doesn't follow that we should conceptualize switching in terms of a struggle between two centres of apperception—two self-conscious agents. Rather than describing *alters* as vying for executive control, it might be more perspicuous to describe the multiple's behaviour as successively informed by competing intentional structures. Indeed, in some passages Braude describes *alters* as switching (as though alters themselves are loci of agency), while in other passages he describes *the multiple* as switching between alter states. It is this latter locution that seems to be most common in the experimental literature. In a representative study, patients were 'required to select two personalities unaware of each other' (Dorahy 2001: 777; see also Loewenstein et al. 1987). It is not clear to me how the patients could comply with this request if it is their alters—rather than 'they themselves'—that are the basic units of agency.

A third argument for phenomenal disunity—perhaps more suggested by what Braude says than endorsed as such—concerns the role that switching might play within the life of the multiple.

> Switching personalities enables a multiple to cope with exhaustion, pain, or other impairments to normal or optimal functioning. For example, if A is tired or drugged, B can emerge fresh or clear-headed. When in pain, A can switch to an anesthetic personality. Or, personalities can keep passing the pain to each other in turn, switching when the persistent pain becomes intolerable. (Braude 1995: 45)

Braude's comments have their roots in a common account of the aetiology of multiplicity, according to which multiplicity arises out of the attempt to cope with the psychic pain occasioned by horrific abuse. The victim of the abuse deals with the pain by creating other personalities to whom it can be transferred. The thought behind this passage, I take it, is that switching could play this role only if alters qualify as distinct loci of consciousness.

This proposal might contain a kernel of truth, but it is difficult to make sense of if taken literally. Pains are not the sorts of things that can be passed from one subject of experience to another. I can *cause* you to be in pain, but I cannot *give* you my pain in the way which I can give you my sandwiches, my shoes, or even the shirt off my back. Moreover, even if pains were transferable, we have no conception of *how* they might be passed from one alter to another. Nor is it clear how the multiple might be better off by transferring pain between their alters. Wouldn't the multiple him- or herself still be in pain irrespective of which of their alters 'had' the pain?

However we can salvage something from the proposal. Drawing on an approach that dates back to the work of Theodule Ribot (1891), suppose that we think of alters as behavioural schemas—networks of intentional states that govern an organism's responses in particular environments.[8] Behavioural schemas are not unique to multiples, but structure all our interactions with the environment. Switches between one schema and another can be triggered by changes in environment, as when a teacher takes on a pedagogical persona upon entering a classroom, but they can also be endogenously elicited, as when one adopts a certain mood state in order to cope more effectively with a

---

[8] See also Putnam (1986); Bower (1994); Silberman et al. (1985).

challenging situation. What marks out multiplicity as a form of pathology is the fact that the patient's schemas are abnormally insulated from each other, and also the fact that the multiple's schemas frequently contain delusional content. The multiple often deals with her environment by taking on a schema that misrepresents her true identity.

On this picture of things, what it is for one alter to 'transfer' its pain to another is just for the multiple to switch from one schema state to another. And now we can understand how the 'transfer' of pains might be of benefit to the patient, for some personality states might be better equipped to deal with noxious stimuli than others. We know that certain types of pain can be ameliorated by various cognitive strategies, and the patient might be better at implementing such strategies when in some personality states than in others. Indeed, by switching from one alter state to another the multiple might not only be able to handle psychic distress more effectively but in fact avoid it altogether.

We have made sense of the idea that alters can 'transfer' their pains, but in so doing we have also deflated any hope that the argument might have established phenomenal disunity. The transfer of a pain from one alter to another involves a single stimulus being processed within the context of distinct behavioural schemas, rather than the movement of a single conscious state from one stream of consciousness to another. There is no evidence of phenomenal disunity here.

Braude's fourth and final argument for the view that multiples have multiple streams of consciousness appeals to introspection. Consider the following quotation, taken from W. F. Prince's description of his patient Doris Fischer. The narrator is one of Fischer's alters, Sleeping Margaret [S.M.], and the initials refer to her other alters.

S.D. [Sick Doris] watched when R.D. [Real Doris] was out. There would be three of us watching her, each with thoughts of her own. S.D. watched R.D.'s mind, M. [Margaret] watched S.D.'s thoughts of R.D., and I watched all three. Sometimes we had a disagreement. Sometimes a jealous thought would flit through S.D.'s mind—she would think for a moment that if R.D. would not come out any more M. might not like her (S.D.) as well as R.D. She never tried to hinder R.D.'s coming out, though, but always to help, and only a slight thought of the kind would flit through her mind. But M. would see it and get cross with S.D., and so the disturbance inside would make R.D. go in. (Prince 1915/16: 109)

The phenomenon referred to here in which one alter appears to be directly aware of the thoughts of a co-alter is often known as 'co-consciousness'. However, this term is less than ideal, for not only is 'co-consciousness' often used as a synonym for 'phenomenal unity', the term implies that the kind of access in question is symmetrical, which is not the case. Indeed, this kind of access is typically asymmetrical, with alter A having access to alter B's mental states but not vice versa. For lack of a better term, I will call this relation 'inter-alter access'.

Inter-alter access is often presented as a kind of telepathy, as if alters who enjoy it are 'able to peek into a private room of experiences, or access or "read" a stream of experiences distinct from their own' (Braude 1995: 82).[9] The idea, I take it, is that alters occasionally have introspective (or, if you like, 'quasi-introspective') access to two kinds of mental states: their own and those of certain co-alters. In the Doris Fischer case, the narrating alter (S.M.) would have introspective access both to her own thoughts and to those of S.D., R.D., and so on. Not only would S.M. be aware of *what* each of these alters is thinking, she would also be aware of *which* particular alter was thinking each of the various thoughts to which she had 'quasi-introspective' access. For example, S.M. would know that a certain thought was flitting through S.D.'s mind rather than through (say) R.D.'s mind.

Although the telepathic model of inter-alter access has a certain charm, there is no shortage of objections to it. How might introspection go about tagging thoughts as the thoughts of particular alters? Why might such a mechanism have evolved? How could one be introspectively aware of a thought without being aware of it as one's own? It is far from clear that there are good answers to any of these questions. We might be forced to endorse the telepathic model even in the face of these challenges if it were the only game in town, but it isn't. In fact, there are a number of other ways in which inter-alter access can be conceptualized.

One alternative to the telepathic account holds that reports of inter-alter access are confabulations—'mere hallucinations'—of mental states (Stephens & Graham 2000). The introspective state that the multiple is reporting might be real enough, but the mental state that is its target might be a figment of the multiple's imagination. Support for this proposal is provided by the fact that alters can be created in hypnotic contexts as merely intentional entities (Mers-key 1992). Pierre Janet describes the evolution of a secondary personality in a woman, called Lucie, whom Janet was treating for fits of terror.

'Do you hear me?' asked Janet.
'No,' she answered (in writing).
'But you have to hear in order to reply.'
'Yes, of course.'

---

[9] For other 'telepathic' treatments of inter-alter access see Rovane (1998); Greenwood (1993); Wilkes (1988); and Zemach (1986).

'Then how do you do it?'
'I don't know.'
'Must there not be someone who hears me?'
'Yes.'
'Who is it?'
'Someone other than Lucie.'
'Oh, indeed. Another person. Should we give this person a name?'
'No.'
'Yes. It is more convenient.'
'All right then—Adrienne.'
'Adrienne, do you hear me?'
'Yes.' (Janet 1913: 318)

Braude (1995: 25) describes Janet as using automatic writing to discover Adrienne, but it seems more fitting to describe Janet as 'aiding materially in the formation of a person', as Binet (1890/1977b) put it in his rather understated way. Here, as elsewhere, fiction may give rise to fact. Alters might begin life as purely intentional entities, figments of hypnotic hallucination, but thereafter acquire a degree of reality as the multiple begins to live out her fantasy (Velleman 2006).[10]

Another alternative to the 'telepathic' account holds that in inter-alter access multiples are aware of genuine mental states, but these states are their own rather than those of some other subject of experience. This proposal receives some support from the fact that the line between inter-alter access on the one hand and the schizophrenic symptoms of thought insertion and auditory hallucination on the other is far from sharp (David et al. 1996). Patients with schizophrenia are often aware of thoughts or voices that they take to be self-referential ('She's so mean...'), and it is not hard to see how such states might be taken as manifestations of inter-alter access by a sympathetic theorist. Bliss et al. (1983) studied forty-four patients with auditory hallucinations, thirty-five of whom had received a diagnosis of schizophrenia at some point. Of these thirty-five patients, the authors identified twenty as having multiple personality disorder on the grounds that they manifested multiple personalities under hypnosis—'the voices could be contacted, engaged in conversation, and would readily admit to being the culprit' (1983: 30). I very much doubt that this study shows what its authors take it to show—namely, that many individuals with multiplicity are falsely diagnosed with schizophrenia—but it does suggest that the distinction between auditory hallucinations and inter-alter

---

[10] See Braude (1995); Harriman (1942); Kampman (1976); and Putnam (1986) for discussion of the creation of alternate personalities in hypnotic contexts.

access is neither sharp nor easily discerned. This point is reinforced by other studies of dissociative identity disorder. One study of thirty patients found that thirty per cent of the patients heard voices commenting on their actions and forty-three per cent took the thoughts of others to be inserted into their minds (Kluft 1987); another study of 102 patients found that seventy-nine per cent of patients reported voices commenting on their actions while sixty-five per cent reported experiencing thoughts that they ascribed to others (Ross et al. 1990). Bizarrely, this latter study also found that those patients who had received a diagnoses of dissociative identity disorder had *higher* levels of first-rank symptoms of schizophrenia than had those patients who had been diagnosed as suffering from schizophrenia, a finding that has been confirmed by other studies (Steinberg et al. 1994).[11]

What does this show? Well, we have little hesitation in regarding the inner speech and thoughts of which the subject is apparently aware in auditory hallucinations and thought insertion as actually belonging to the patient, notwithstanding her protestations to the contrary. The patient is talking or thinking to himself, unaware that this is what she is doing. Why shouldn't we say precisely the same thing about inter-alter access? Why should we not say that S.M. is aware of her own thoughts and is simply mistaken in ascribing them to another 'alter'?

The obvious response is that there is a sense in which multiples *do* have multiple minds whereas patients with schizophrenia do not. Although there is something to this response, I don't think that it undermines the force of this proposal. Returning to the Doris Fischer case, we can ask whether S.M.'s reports of being aware of S.D.'s jealous thoughts 'answered' to anything. They might, if Prince's account of the case is to be believed. Doris Fischer had an alter called (by Prince and herself) 'Sick Doris', and she may well have had jealous thoughts while in this alter state. But this does not show that S.M. had any kind of 'telepathic access' to S.D's mind, for there are many 'third-person' ways in which Doris Fischer could, as S.M., divine that she had an alter called S.D. with jealous thoughts. Most obviously, she could have acquired this information from her therapist, Prince. Having represented herself as having an alter with jealous thoughts, Doris Fischer now has reason to create such an alter if she wants to be seen by Prince as a good patient. Moreover, it is entirely possible that she doesn't want to acknowledge or identify with those jealous thoughts that she might have when S.M. is 'out', and hence ascribes them to another alter—'*I'm* not jealous, S.D. is'.[12]

---

[11] As Kennett and Matthews (2003) note, there are also deep commonalities between inter-alter access and the phenomenon of depersonalization, a condition in which patients experience themselves as alienated from their own mental states (see Chapter 11).

[12] Thanks to Ian Phillips here.

A final account of inter-alter access—in some ways a variant of the model just discussed—is that inter-alter access involves the mental states of one alter 'leaking' into those of another alter. Let me explain, I have suggested that we should conceive of alters as 'psychological schemas': semi-autonomous clusters of behavioural traits, dispositions, beliefs, memories, and other intentional states. Suppose that while Doris Fischer is in one alter state a thought that 'belongs to' another alter is activated for some reason. The intruding thought will seem alien to her, for it won't sit well with her self-image—that is, the self-image that is currently structuring her overall thought and action. And if indeed the thought doesn't 'belong' to the psychological schema that is currently directing her behaviour then there may be *a* sense in which she is right to reject it as not fully hers.

Something akin to this phenomenon may not be uncommon in everyday life. Suppose that one is in a sexually intimate context when thoughts appropriate to a very different context—say, a philosophical discussion—suddenly enter one's head. Such thoughts might seem alien, as not truly one's own. If one also had a model of oneself as having a philosophical personality for which such thoughts would be appropriate, one might be tempted to ascribe such thoughts to that personality and not one's current personality. In this respect it is interesting to note that the kind of states for which inter-alter access is reported tend to be affectively laden. Perhaps this is because it is affectively laden states that are most at odds with an alter's self-conception—that is, with 'its' conception of the multiple's identity.

I conclude that the argument from inter-alter access fails to support disunity interpretations of multiplicity. Where does this leave Braude's defence of the phenomenal disunity treatment of multiplicity? Braude's case in favour of the disunity account of multiplicity is advanced as a cumulative one, and it is entirely possible that although none of his arguments is individually convincing his overall case is. I will leave readers to judge for themselves whether that might be so, but my own view is that the unity thesis is unscathed by what we know of multiplicity.

7.4 Conclusion

The disorders of consciousness seen in anosognosia, schizophrenia, and multiplicity are frequently said to involve a breakdown in or fragmentation of the unity of consciousness. There is *some* truth in such claims given that certain elements of the unity of consciousness—broadly construed—are impaired in each of these syndromes. In anosognosia we see a breakdown in the integration that normally holds between the contents of a person's consciousness and their intro-spective access to those contents. In schizophrenia we see a disruption to the narrative unity of consciousness brought about by impairments to selective atten-tion in the context of thought disorder, and a disruption to the unity of self-consciousness brought about by the patient's inability to keep track of their own in the context of thought-insertion. Multiplicity presents us with an even more profound impairment to the unity of self-consciousness. Here, the patient suffers from the delusion that he or she is in some way multiple subjects of experience. In varying ways, each of these syndromes involves notable departures from the coherence and integration that consciousness—particularly *self*-consciousness—normally displays.

But none of these syndromes threatens the unity thesis. In none of these cases do we have good reason to posit a breakdown in the *phenomenal* unity of consciousness. The kinds of failures in representational integration and co-accessibility of content that are required to construct a plausible case against the unity thesis are notably missing from the clinical literature on these syn-dromes. Perhaps the strongest evidence against the unity thesis found thus far derives from the behaviour of individuals with multiplicity. But even here, I have suggested, it is more plausible to suppose that the agentive disunity seen in multiplicity is best accounted for in terms of a single stream of consciousness that is successively informed by a variety of psychological schemas, rather than by appeal to parallel streams of experience. This switching between schemas may produce the *appearance* of phenomenal disunity, but I suggest that this appearance masks an underlying phenomenal unity.

8

Hypnosis

The modern practice of hypnosis derives from Anton Mesmer, but it was his student, Marquis de Puységur, who first speculated on the structure of consciousness in hypnosis (Crabtree 1985). In his *Memoirs*, published in 1784, Puységur referred to the hypnotic state as involving a second consciousness. References to this 'second' or 'double' consciousness were commonplace in the wave of interest in the unity of consciousness that swept psychology in the late nineteenth century. In France, Pierre Janet published a series of articles on the alterations of consciousness seen in hypnosis and other forms of 'sleep-waking'; Alfred Binet discussed automatic writing in his *Double Consciousness* (1889–1900) and *Alterations of Personality* (1896); while Théodule Ribot argued in his *Diseases of Personality* (1891) that the 'double consciousness' seen in hypnotic phenomena tells against the existence of a transcendent ego. Not to be outdone, William James and Morton Prince in Boston argued at length that the dissociations of mentality seen in automatic writing and hypnosis demonstrate that consciousness can be split into parts 'which coexist but mutually ignore each other' (James 1890/1950: 204;). Scientific interest in hypnosis waned in the early decades of the twentieth century only to be rekindled in the 1970s with the work of Ernest Hilgard, who—in places at least—reaffirmed the claims of his nineteenth-century predecessors that hypnosis often brings with it a breakdown in the unity of consciousness. This chapter examines those claims, with a particular focus on the so-called 'hidden observer.'

8.1 The 'hidden observer'

The hidden observer has its roots in the nineteenth-century phenomenon of automatic writing that most impressed the nineteenth-century theorists. William James recounts the following examples of what he termed 'the secondary consciousness' in action:

A young woman who had been writing automatically was sitting with a pencil in her hand, trying to recall at my request the name of a gentleman whom she had once seen. She could only recollect the first syllable. Her hand meanwhile, without her knowledge, wrote down the last two syllables. In a perfectly healthy young man who can write with the planchette, I lately found the hand to be entirely anaesthetic during the writing act; I could prick it severely without the Subject knowing the fact. The *writing on the planchette*, however, accused me in strong terms of hurting the hand. Pricks on the other (non-writing) hand, meanwhile, which awakened strong protest from the young man's vocal organs, were denied to exist by the self which made the planchette go. (James 1890/1950: vol. I: 205 f.; italics in original)

The hidden observer paradigm takes automatic writing and relocates it to a formal laboratory setting. In a typical hidden observer experiment the subject is hypnotized and informed that he or she will be agnosic (or analgesic) for some stimulus, typically pain produced by immersion of a hand in icy water (cold-pressor pain). The subject is then given a 'hidden observer' induction, on the model of the following:

When I place my hand on your shoulder, I shall be able to talk to a hidden part of you that knows things that are going on in your body, things that are unknown to the part of you to which I am now talking. The part of you to which I am now talking will not know what you are telling me or even that you are talking. (Knox et al. 1974: 842)

The hidden observer induction makes explicit what was left implicit in automatic writing experiments: that the subject should be able to report the stimulus in some ways, but not in others. Hidden observer experiments typically find that many highly hypnotizable subjects do indeed have a 'hidden part', just as the induction suggests. The subject's normal reports will indicate that he or she is agnosic for the stimulus, but their hidden observer reports will suggest levels of awareness of the stimulus similar to those reported in conditions of hypnosis without agnosia.[1]

What should we make of these results? The late nineteenth-century theorists took them to be evidence of a 'secondary' or 'double consciousness'—a separate, dissociated, stream of experience. Here is Prince, describing the manifestations of the 'split-off' or 'doubled' consciousness.

Subconscious ideas are dissociated or split-off ideas; split off from the main personal consciousness, from the focus of attention—if that term be preferred—in such fashion

---

[1] Crawford et al. (1979); Knox et al. (1974); Hilgard et al. (1975); Hilgard et al. (1978); Laurence & Perry (1981); Nogrady et al. (1983).

that the subject is entirely unaware of them, though they are not inert but active. These split-off ideas may be limited to isolated sensations, like the lost tactile sensations of anesthesia; or may be aggregated into groups or systems. In other words, they form a consciousness coexisting with the primary consciousness and thereby a doubling of consciousness results. The split-off consciousness may display extraordinary activity. The primary personal consciousness as a general rule is of course the main and larger consciousness; but under exceptional conditions, as in some types of automatic writing, the personal consciousness may be reduced to rudimentary proportions, while the secondary consciousness may rob the former of the greater part of its faculties and become the dominant consciousness. (Prince 1907a: 23)

According to this account, hidden observer subjects enjoy two streams of consciousness at one and the same time: a 'central' stream that is responsible for the subject's 'overt' reports, and a 'hidden stream' responsible for their 'covert' reports. I will call this the *two-streams model* of the hidden observer. Prince's twentieth-century successors have tended to be rather cagier about assigning two streams of consciousness to hypnotic subjects. For the most part, contemporary theorists conceive of the mental states underlying hidden observer reports as unconscious. Call this the *zombie model*.

The debate between the zombie and two-streams models has an important bearing on whether hypnosis undermines the unity thesis. If the zombie model can be sustained, then the case against unity would be in poor shape: hypnosis might involve a breakdown in the unity of *cognition* but it would not involve any breakdown in the unity of *consciousness*. If, however, the two-streams model can be sustained, then there may be good reason to think that hypnosis is at odds with the claim that consciousness is necessarily unified. So, our first task is to examine the prospects of the zombie model.

8.2. The zombie model

Although there are passages in Hilgard's work in which he describes the hidden observer as a 'hidden consciousness' (Knox et al. 1974: 847), there are places in which he seems to endorse what I have called the zombie model. For example, he suggests that the 'hidden observer' is 'a metaphor for something occurring at an intellectual level but not available to the consciousness of the hypnotized person' (Hilzard 1977: 188; see also 1992: 21). What inclines Hilgard to the view that hidden observer behaviours are produced by unconscious states?[2]

---

[2] Hilgard is not the only authority to be somewhat equivocal in his descriptions of the structure of consciousness in hypnosis. Kihlstrom describes hypnosis as involving 'a division of consciousness into

Hilgard's main argument for the zombie model seems to turn on the claim that hidden observer 'reports' are not really reports. They are not actions of the hypnotic subject—instead, '. . . the experimenter makes contact with a cognitive system that is hidden from the subject himself as well as from the experimenter' (1973: 406; see also Hilgard 1977: 244). The argument, I take it, is that because hidden observer 'reports' are not made by the subject they cannot provide evidence for claims about the subject's conscious states, and hence we must regard them as generated by unconscious representations of stimuli.

I find the argument unconvincing. Hidden observer behaviours certainly appear to be reports, and it is not clear who produces them if not the hypnotized subject. In fact, distinguishing hidden observer or 'covert' reports from 'overt' reports is a far from straightforward business. One cannot differentiate the two by appealing to the motor systems employed, for Hilgard and collaborators have elicited hidden observer reports via automatic writing, button-pressing, and even 'automatic talking' (Hilgard et al. 1975). Nor can hidden observer reports be distinguished from overt reports by reference to the fact that the former occur *after* the latter, for in some studies hidden observer reports are given (roughly) simultaneously with overt reports (Hilgard et al. 1975). Theorists sometimes remark that hidden observer reports do not occur spontaneously (see e.g. Spanos 1983: 171), but as far as I can tell spontaneous reports simply would not be coded as hidden observer reports. In order to qualify as a hidden observer report a behaviour must conform to a pre-assigned hidden observer prompt. But prompted or not, hidden reports still qualify as genuine reports as far as I can tell.

A second argument for the zombie model comes from Freud. Although Freud defended the two-streams model at one point (Breuer & Freud 1893), he came to think of the secondary stream of mentality in zombie terms. Freud's change of heart seems to have been prompted by the following line of argument:

One did not hesitate to ascribe mental processes to other people, although one had no immediate consciousness of them and could only infer them from their words and actions. But what held good for other people must be applicable to oneself. Anyone who tried to push the argument further and to conclude from it that one's own hidden processes belonged actually to a second consciousness would be faced with the concept of a consciousness of which one knew nothing, of an unconscious 'consciousness'—and this would scarcely be preferable to the assumption of an 'unconscious mentality'. (Freud 1910/1955: 31 f.)

multiple, simultaneous streams of mental activity', but in the very next sentence he appears to endorse the zombie model, saying that 'dissociation proper occurs when one or more of these streams influences experience, thought, and action *outside phenomenal awareness* and voluntary control' (1985: 406; my emphasis).

Freud describes the postulation of a second consciousness as 'scarcely preferable' to the postulation of purely unconscious processes, but it is clear that he regards the two-streams model as rather less attractive than the zombie account.

Freud's argument is no more convincing than Hilgard's. Its Achilles' heel, of course, is the claim that the subject of the second consciousness would know nothing about this 'unconscious consciousness'. In one sense this is right; in another it is wrong. The subject's primary consciousness would have no direct acquaintance with the mental states of the secondary consciousness, but this is entirely to be expected: subjects have direct access only to those mental states that occur within their own stream of consciousness. Does this mean that the secondary consciousness is completely unknown? Of course not. Two-streams theorists will argue—as in fact they did—that one could have strong third-person grounds for ascribing a secondary consciousness to oneself.[3]

The most plausible case for the zombie model turns on the supposed parallels between hidden behaviours and the various forms of normal behavioural control that can take place outside of consciousness. The kinds of studies that are of most relevance here are not the implicit perception studies found in cognitive neuroscience (see §5.1), but the high-level priming studies drawn from social psychology.[4] In a representative experiment, Bargh et al. (1996) asked participants to complete a scrambled sentence test, with half of the participants given sentences that contained words that primed stereotypes of old-age ('wrinkle', 'grey', 'wise') and the other half given sentences containing only age-neutral words. The participants left the unscrambling task believing that they had completed the experiment. However, as they left, the time that it took for them to walk from the experimental room to the end of the hall was measured. As Bargh and colleagues predicted, those who had been given sentences containing old-age primes took significantly longer to reach the end of the hall than did control subjects, who had not been primed in this way.

Although the parallel between high-level priming and hidden observer behaviours is not unattractive, I am not convinced that it runs all that deep. For one thing, in social psychology experiments the prime influences the subject's behaviour by *modulating* how the subject acts (e.g. by walking more

---

[3] See Barresi (1994) for a fascinating discussion of the debate between Freud and Prince on the status of the 'secondary consciousness'.

[4] For reviews see Bargh & Ferguson (2000); Dijksterhuis & Bargh (2001); Hassin et al. (2004); Kihlstrom (1987).

slowly), but it doesn't provide the subject with a goal. The participant's in Bargh's study weren't walking slowly *on purpose*. In contrast, hidden observer content seems to provide subjects with a goal around which their hidden observer behaviour is focused. Secondly, subjects in the Bargh study were not unaware of the prime itself, they were merely unaware of how the prime influenced their behaviour. So even if we were tempted to assimilate hidden observer behaviour to the kinds of unconscious behavioural modulation found in Bargh's study, we would still be forced to ascribe conscious states of some kind to the hidden observer.

Taking another tack, the proponent of the zombie model might liken hidden observer behaviour to the kinds of behavioural routines seen in various pathologies of consciousness, such as epileptic absence seizures. But as I argued in Chapter 6, the jury is out on whether such patients really are unconscious. Individuals in the grip of an absence seizure might lack the capacity for conscious reflection, but one can certainly lack that capacity without lacking consciousness altogether. Despite the ample evidence for thinking that certain kinds of cognitive control can occur outside of consciousness, we should baulk at the thought that unconscious states can guide the kinds of behaviours seen in hidden observer contexts. The cognitive unconscious might be smart (well, relatively smart), but I doubt that it is smart *enough* to generate hidden observer behaviours.

In fact, the framework for ascribing consciousness developed in Chapter 5 provides us with grounds to reject the zombie model. In that chapter, I argued that goal-directed behaviour provides us with good reason to ascribe consciousness to a creature, and hidden–observer behaviours are clearly goal-directed. Here is Binet, describing an experiment involving a hypnotized subject with an 'insensible' hand:

Let us make ten punctures in the insensible hand and thereupon let us ask the subject, who, as a matter of course, has not seen his hand, which is hidden behind a screen, to think of some number and name it; very frequently the subject will think of the number 10. In the same manner let us put a key, a piece of coin, a needle, a watch into the anaesthetic hand, and let us ask the subject to think of any object whatsoever; it will still happen, yet less frequently than in the preceding experiment, that the subject is thinking of the precise object that has been put into his insensible hand . . . How shall we explain this result? . . . We have to admit . . . that when we excite the anaesthetic hand, in different ways, by puncture or by contact with an object, the second consciousness perceives the sensation, counts the punctures, recognizes the objects, and, for the purposes involved, abandons itself to more or less complicated intellectual acts. (Binet 1890/1977a: 32)

In fact, we needn't even appeal to the agentive criterion in order to reject the zombie model, for the 'traditional' introspective criterion also puts the zombie model under pressure. As the nineteenth-century advocates of the two-streams model pointed out, one can coax the hidden observer to produce introspective reports. Indeed, the conversations that James, Binet, Hilgard, and others report having with the 'hidden observer' suggest that it would even be able to pass versions of the Turing test! Morton Prince went so far as to claim that one would have no grounds for ascribing consciousness to one's fellows unless one were prepared to grant it to the automatic writer (see also Zemach 1986):

The only grounds that I have for believing that my fellow beings have thoughts like myself are that their actions are like my own, exhibit intelligence like my own, and when I ask them they tell me that they have consciousness, which as described is like my own. Now, when I observe the so-called automatic actions, I find that they are of a similar character, and when I ask of whatever it is that performs these actions, Whether it is conscious or not? the written or spoken reply is that it is and that consciously it feels, thinks and wills the actions, etc. The evidence being the same in the one case as in the other, the presumption is that the automatic intelligence is as conscious as the personal intelligence. (Prince 1907b: 69)

As far as I can see, proponents of the zombie model could attempt to resist this line of argument only by appealing to the claim that the contents of consciousness must be globally available for cognitive and behavioural control. As I noted in Chapter 5, it is widely held that conscious content differs from unconscious content in that only the former is available for the global control of thought and behaviour. Given that hidden observer content appears to be available for only restricted forms of cognitive and behavioural control, one might argue that we have reason to doubt that it is conscious.

The problem with this line of argument is that the global availability conception of consciousness is far from secure. We can grant that there is a fairly strong correlation between consciousness and global availability where normal background states of consciousness are concerned, but we are clearly not here dealing with such a state. Rather than concluding that hidden observer content is unconscious because it is not globally available, one might equally well reject the global availability conception of conscious content on the grounds that it is at odds with the hidden observer phenomenon. In light of the fact that hidden-observer content is available to high-level consuming systems—systems implicated in introspective report and personal-level agency—I think that we should conclude that the balance of evidence is against the zombie model.

8.3 The two-streams model

If the states that lie behind hidden observer behaviours are conscious then we have in effect established the 'positive moment' in an argument for phenomenal disunity. The question is whether the negative moment can also be established. Are the conscious states implicated in the hidden observer unified with the subject's other conscious states in a single stream of consciousness, or does the hidden observer subject have two independent streams of consciousness?

We can begin by noting that if the two-streams model is right then the structure of consciousness in the hidden observer context involves a departure—a quite radical departure—from that which it possesses outside of such contexts. It is quite unclear what features of either the hypnotic context in general or the hidden observer induction in particular might account for this departure. As we will see in the following chapter, many theorists claim that split-brain patients have two streams of consciousness, but in this case we have a plausible account of how this division might have been brought about, for split-brain patients have had surgery in which the main route of communication between the two hemispheres has been severed. Hypnotized individuals, of course, have had no such surgery. In response, the two-streams theorist might point out that hypnosis can lead to quite astonishing changes in the *contents* of consciousness. Hypnosis can both insert unusual experiences into the stream of consciousness (as in vivid imagery) and remove normal experiences from the stream of consciousness (as in hypnotically induced analgesia for surgical pain). But it is one thing to allow that hypnosis can alter the contents of consciousness and quite another to suppose that it can alter the structure of consciousnes. In sum, we have reason to treat the two-streams model with some suspicion.

Let us turn from these indirect considerations to the question of the evidence in favour of the two-streams model. The ingredients for one argument can be found in the fact that hypnotized subjects frequently report a diminished sense of agency for actions performed as the result of hypnotic suggestions.[5] Two-streams theorists appear to have a ready explanation for this fact: hypnosis has split the subject's 'central executive', together with their stream of consciousness, into two executive systems. Here is how Kirsch and Lynn put the idea (which, note, they do not themselves endorse).

Responses to suggestion are produced by a division of the executive ego into two parts, separated by an amnesiac barrier. On one side of the barrier is a small hidden part of consciousness that initiates suggested actions and perceives the self and the external

---

[5] Bowers et al. (1988); Comey & Kirsch (1999); Spanos & Barber (1972); Zamansky & Ruehle (1995).

world accurately. On the other side is the hypnotized part of consciousness that experiences suggested actions as involuntary and is not aware of blocked memories or perceptions to which only the hidden part has access. (Kirsch & Lynn 1998: 67)

According to this line of thought, we should not expect the subject to report normal experiences of agency, for the part of the subject that is responsible for the report is distinct from that part which initiated the action. The subject's sense of agency is unreportable (at least, via overt reports) because it has been relegated to the 'hidden' part of their consciousness.

What should we make of this 'phenomenology of agency' argument? One response to it is provided by the dissociated control account of hypnosis, according to which the subject's diminished sense of agency for hypnotic actions merely reflects the fact that hypnotic suggestions bypass executive agency altogether. Dissociated control theorists claim that we should not expect hypnotized subjects to experience a sense of agency, for—the thought goes— hypnotic actions don't involve executive control, and only such actions are accompanied by a sense of agency.[6]

This dissociated control response is ingenious, but I don't think it succeeds. For one thing, it assumes that the lack of agentive experience is a general feature of hypnotic responding as such. This is not the case. Rather, the loss of agentive experience attaches to particular actions as a result of the hypnotist suggesting that the subject will lose the sense of agency for that particular action. More-over, hypnotic subjects *can* lose the experience of agency for executive actions. For example, subjects can be induced to 'forget' their concept of the number 4, and will count 1, 2, 3, 5, and so on (Evans 1980). Behaviour of this kind counts as executive by anyone's lights.

In my view, the phenomenology of agency argument fails because it assumes that actions must be accompanied by an experience of agency. I see no reason to grant this assumption. Arguably, the phenomenology of agency is not a neces-sary concomitant of agency itself, even when the actions in question are 'executive'. I suspect that the hypnotic suggestion has simply removed (or at least dampened) the subject's sense of agency whilst leaving untouched the subject's capacities for executive agency (Bayne & Levy 2006). In other words, hypnotized subjects fail to report a sense of agency for certain actions not because it has been relegated to a 'hidden' part of their consciousness, but because it has been removed from their experience entirely.

A second argument for the two-streams model appeals to Martin Orne's notion of so-called 'trance logic'. Orne claimed that hypnosis involves states

---

[6] Bowers (1990, 1991); Bowers & Davidson (1991); Miller & Bowers (1993).

which are characterized by the 'apparently simultaneous perception and response to both hallucinations and reality without any apparent attempts to satisfy a need for logical consistency' (Orne 1959: 295). For example, the 'duality reports' of age-regressed subjects indicate that they feel no inconsistency between the experience of themselves as both a child and an adult (Perry & Walsh 1978; Laurence & Perry 1981). Perhaps such subjects feel no need to resolve the tension between these experiences because they occur within different streams of consciousness. We appear to have here the seeds of a representational disunity argument.

But a closer look at the reports of age-regressed subjects reveals that they provide little support for the two-streams model; indeed, they may even be at odds with it. Consider the following reports of age-regressed subjects.

Subject 21: I became small again, small, small. Physically, . . . I saw myself again with my curls at school . . . I felt 5, and I felt 23 also . . . I knew I was 5 years old at school, but I knew I was 23 years old, also, that I was an adult . . . I really felt 5 years old. I would not be able to say that I was solely 23 years old.

Subject 17: (Did you really feel you were 5 years old?): I felt . . . you know, I was two people, one standing off looking at the other, and the other that was standing was saying, you idiot, you can write your name, why are you taking so long? Yet the one that's writing it is struggling away, to form these letters . . . can't. (Laurence & Perry 1981: 338)

Although these statements are somewhat obscure, they do seem to indicate that both the experience of being a child and the experience of being an adult occur as components of a single conscious state. For one thing, the subjects appear to be aware of the composite character of their overall experiential state. Further, these experiences seem to be available to at least some of the same systems of cognitive consumption, most noticeably those involved in verbal report. Rather than occurring within separate streams of consciousness, 'trance logic' states seem to be phenomenally unified with each other.

Now, if age-regressed subjects can maintain two separate identities within a single stream of consciousness, then it might also be possible for hidden observer subjects to do likewise. According to this proposal, hidden observer subjects have two clusters of experience, one for 'covert' experiences and another for 'overt' experiences, but these two clusters of experience coexist within a single unified stream of phenomenology. The connection between duality reports and the hidden observer is supported by evidence indicating that subjects who produce duality reports in age regression also show significant differences between levels of pain as reported by the hidden observer and as reported normally (Laurence & Perry 1981; Nogrady et al. 1983; although see Spanos et al. 1985).

I suspect that this proposal might capture the phenomenology of *some* hidden observer subjects. Although they are far from crystal clear, certain hidden observer reports do suggest that 'hidden observer' experiences can be unified with the other experiences. 'I felt . . . that I was hypnotized but that there really was a clear side of me' (Laurence & Perry 1981: 339); 'After you put your hand on my shoulder I felt much lighter, as though I was floating . . . It is as though you were contacting someone else outside of me but part of me at the same time; as though I had a twin 'me' and in a way I could not immediately communicate with each part at the same time' (Spanos et al. 1985: 1161). These reports indicate that at least some consuming systems—viz. memory systems—have access to both normal and hidden observer experiences. How else would subjects be able to report both normal and hidden observer experience? Although these facts are difficult to reconcile with the two-streams model, they do fit comfortably with a model on which covert and overt experiences exist side-by-side as components of a single stream of experience. We might perhaps compare the relations between these experiences to those that obtain between one's perceptual and imaginative experiences when gazing out a train window in a reverie. There is *some* sense in which one might want to think of such a scenario as involving two streams of experience, for there will be a kind of intentional coherence within each of these sets of experiences—the environmentally constrained perceptual experiences on the one hand and the internally generated reverie experiences on the other—that doesn't hold between them. But these two streams are not distinct streams of consciousness in the sense that the two-streams theorist has in mind, for one's perceptual experiences will be phenomenally unified with one's imaginative experiences, bound together as parts of a total phenomenal state.

Might it be possible to account for *all* hidden observer studies in this way? I have my doubts. Consider a hidden observer subject (H.O.) whose 'overt' reports indicate hypnotic analgesia but whose 'covert' reports indicate high levels of cold-pressor pain. I take it that when H.O. produces an overt report of not being in pain he does so on the basis of a conscious judgement that he is not in pain. Call this state 'm_1'. Further, when H.O. generates a 'hidden observer' report of being in pain, we can take this to indicate that he has an experience—a conscious representation—of being in pain. Call this state m_2. How are m_1 and m_2 related?

It seems unlikely that m_1 and m_2 could be phenomenally unified with each other, for there is a deep and obvious tension between their contents: m_1 represents an absence of pain, whereas m_2 represents the presence of pain. It is, of course, possible for an experience of pain and an experience of its absence to be phenomenally unified with each other when they are directed at different body parts, but that is not the case here. On the plausible assumption that inconsistent representations within the same perceptual modality cannot be phenomenally unified (see Chapter 3), we have good reason to think that H.O. has two separate streams of consciousness. Further, even if inconsistent representations within the same perceptual modality can be phenomenally unified, one would expect them to give rise to an awareness on the part of the subject that he has inconsistent experiences. The typical hidden–observer subject, however, appears to be completely unaware of the fact that he is both experiencing cold-pressor pain and also experiencing his arm as free of pain. Given the representational contents of m_1 and m_2, it is unlikely that they are components of a single conscious state.

Let us take stock. In §8.2 I argued that the zombie treatment of the hidden observer is implausible, and that we have good reason to suppose that hidden observer behaviours are manifestations of consciousness. I then turned in §8.3 to the question of what the relationship between those conscious states and the subject's 'overt' experiences might be: are states of both kinds contained within a single stream of consciousness, or do subjects have two streams of consciousness, as two-streams theorists hold? There may be certain contexts in which both 'overt' and 'covert' experiences are contained within a single stream of consciousness, but I have argued that there are other hypnotic contexts concerning which this proposal is highly implausible. But if this is right, it seems to follow that the unity thesis is false.

8.4 The switch model

Perhaps, but perhaps not: there is one final account of the hidden observer still to be considered. Rather than taking hidden-observer subjects to have two streams of consciousness that run in parallel, we might suppose that they have two streams of *unconscious* processing, with the contents of their consciousness drawing sequentially on each of these two streams. According to this proposal, the subject's consciousness switches between overt and covert states (Bayne 2007b). The hidden observer prompt—e.g. hand on the shoulder—changes the content of the patient's experience by directing his or her attention to stimuli that had previously been neglected. It functions as an alarm bell, causing the subject to become aware of stimuli that they had represented only unconsciously. Although the first full presentation of the switch model is to be found in Spanos & Hewitt (1980), the general idea dates back to Freud, who suggested that cases of 'double consciousness' involve a splitting of mental activity into two groups, with the same consciousness 'turning to one or other of these groups alternately' (1915/1955: 170–1).

Although the switch model has not received the attention that it deserves, Hilgard does devote several pages of *Divided Consciousness* to it. On my reading, Hilgard presents three objections to the switch model. First, he points out that in some hidden observer experiments the hidden observer probe occurs *after* the trial has been completed (1977: 238 f.). Since only the *memory* of the stimulus is available, it follows that the information must have been stored while the analgesia persisted, and thus that awareness of the target information could not depend on the presence of a probe as demanded by the switch model.

In making this objection, Hilgard assumes a 'bottom-up' account of hidden observer experiences, according to which such states are veridical perceptions rather than hallucinations prompted by the subject's expectations. This assumption has been undermined by a series of hidden observer studies conducted by Spanos and collaborators. In an initial study, Spanos & Hewitt (1980) were able to modulate the levels of pain reported in a cold-pressor experiment merely by changing the content of the hidden observer induction, a finding replicated by Spanos et al. (1983). In later work, Spanos and colleagues provided additional evidence of top-down influence on hidden observer reports by showing that hidden observers could be led to breach hypnotic amnesia if the possibility of such breaches was explicitly allowed for by the hidden observer induction (Spanos et al. 1985). In a delightful twist on this paradigm, Spanos et al. (1985) gave subjects a hidden observer induction in which they asserted that concrete words were stored in one hemisphere of the brain and abstract words in the other hemisphere, with each hemisphere having its own hidden observer. Subjects were then asked to memorize a list containing both concrete and abstract words. Following this, they were given an amnesia suggestion, in which they were told that they would not be able to remember any of the items on the list. As predicted, subjects were amnesic for the items on the list. However, on certain trials the experimenter contacted one or other of the two hidden observers, and asked them whether they could recall the words. Breaching of amnesia was now category-specific, with subjects able to remember only concrete or abstract words depending on which of the two hidden observers had been contacted.

Some commentators are unconvinced by these studies, pointing out that even if hidden observer behaviours can be influenced by the content of the induction, it doesn't follow that the hidden observer is an 'experimental creation', as Spanos (1983) puts it.[7] Quite so. But the results that Spanos and

---

[7] For this observation see Laurence et al. (1983) and Kihlstrom & Barnier (2005).

collaborators found do not show merely that the contents of hidden observer reports are subject to top-down *modulation*, they show rather that such reports can be *fully accounted for* in top-down terms. Consider an experiment in which subjects were not given *any* cues about how much access their hidden observer had to the pain (Spanos et al. 1983). If, as Hilgard held, it is the hidden observer induction itself that enables subjects to access previously inaccessible experiences, then one would expect those subjects who had been given a hidden observer induction to have reported higher levels of pain than control subjects who had been hypnotized but not given a hidden observer induction. But this was not the case: the levels of pain reported by those subjects who had been given a hidden observer induction were not significantly different from those reported by hypnotized controls. The results of these experiments suggest that even when hidden observer reports are 'veridical' they are likely to be so only because the experimental context contains the appropriate cues. In sum, the hidden observer manipulations conducted by Spanos and colleagues undermine Hilgard's objection to the switch model.

A second objection to the switch model is that in at least one hidden observer experiment subjects are said to have produced overt and covert reports *simultaneously* (Hilgard et al. 1975). It is hard to see how the switch model might account for this finding if the reports really were simultaneous, but I have doubts on that point. Hilgard's papers contain no quantitative data about the timing of reports, and when hidden observer studies have specified simultaneity measures they have operationalized it to within 500 milliseconds (Spanos & Hewitt 1980), which is certainly long enough for the subject's attention—and with it their stream of consciousness—to switch from one stream of processing to another.

Hilgard's final objection to the switch model is that although hypnotic subjects do report the occasional intrusion of the stimulus into consciousness, such reports are not given 'when the covert experience is accounted for' (Hilgard 1977: 238). I am not completely sure what Hilgard has in mind here, but I think his point is this: although hidden observer reports are easily distinguished from the spontaneous reports that hypnotic subjects give when the suppressed stimulus spontaneously enters consciousness, the switch model predicts that hidden observer subjects would give the same kinds of reports that subjects give when reporting intrusions.

The objection underestimates the resources of the switch model. There are two ways in which a previously suppressed stimulus might intrude into the subject's consciousness: spontaneously, or via a hidden observer probe. It is plausible to suppose that the phenomenology of these two forms of intrusion differ. When the subject's attention is spontaneously drawn to the stimulus the subject will be inclined to describe the stimulus as intruding into consciousness, but when the subject's attention is drawn to the stimulus by a hidden observer probe they will, I suspect, be inclined to describe themselves as accessing the experiences of a 'hidden part of them'. Those administering the hidden observer induction may not endorse homuncular conceptions of the hidden observer, but what they tell their subjects certainly suggests that they do, for the experimenter contrasts 'the hidden part of you' with 'the part of the subject to which I am now talking'. No wonder that some subjects are drawn to report their experiences in homuncular terms—the very induction that they are given suggests that good subjects will do no less!

8.5 Conclusion

This chapter has focused on the claim that the hidden observer phenomenon involves a breakdown in the unity of consciousness. I began by noting that disunity interpretations of the hidden observer begin on the right foot, for it is certainly plausible to suppose that hidden observer behaviours are manifestations of conscious states. In the terms introduced in Chapter 5, the 'positive moment' of the case for disunity seems secure. I then turned to the question of whether the 'negative moment' can be established. Are the subject's conscious states contained within a separate stream of consciousness—one that runs in parallel to the subject's overt stream—or are both 'covert' and 'overt' states contained within a single stream of consciousness? I argued that it is unlikely that these states will always occur within a single stream of consciousness if they are simultaneous, for there are contexts in which the contents of the subject's 'covert' experiences are at odds with those of their 'overt' experiences, and obviously so. If the states were parts of a single stream of consciousness then one would expect the subject to be aware of the inconsistency between them.

But do hidden observer subjects have both 'covert' and 'overt' experiences concurrently? I suspect not. Instead, I suggested that we can account for the hidden observer data by supposing that the subject's stream of consciousness switches back and forth between two streams of mental processing, an 'overt' stream whose contents are manifest in the subject's ordinary reports and behaviour, and a 'covert' stream, whose contents are manifest only in the subject's hidden observer reports. Not only might such switches be rapid, they might also be relatively independent of the subject's control. And if that were the case, then subjects themselves might be oblivious to the fact that their stream of consciousness was switching between 'overt' and 'covert' contents.

From an external point of view these switches might generate the appearance of distinct streams of consciousness running in parallel—as the two-streams model has it—but that appearance would be an illusion. The hidden observer phenomenon certainly involves deep and surprising changes in the contents and structure of consciousness, but it does not undermine the unity thesis.

9

The Split-Brain Syndrome

Whereas discussions of the unity of consciousness in the late nineteenth century focused on various dissociative phenomena, discussions of the unity of consciousness since the late twentieth century have centred on the results of so-called 'split-brain' operations. First performed on humans by van Wagenen and Herren in the 1930s, the split-brain procedure involves severing the corpus callosum in order to prevent epileptic seizures spreading from one hemisphere to another. However, van Wagenen's and Herren's version of the operation was not particularly successful (Bogen 1995), and the procedure was abandoned until it was resurrected by Vogel and Bogen at Caltech in the late 1950s (Bogen & Vogel 1962). The revised form of the operation proved more effective, and in early 1970 Donald Wilson of Dartmouth Medical School commenced another series of split-brain operations (Wilson et al. 1977; Wilson et al. 1982). The last forty years have provided neurologists with a new range of weapons for controlling epilepsy, but the split-brain procedure remains a treatment option of last resort (Spencer et al. 1987).

Astonishingly, the split-brain operation has little impact on the patient's ability to cope with the demands of everyday life. Patients can drive, hold down jobs, and carry out routine day-to-day tasks. Bogen remarks on their 'social ordinariness', and early researchers were baffled by the apparent lack of cognitive impairment arising from the operation (Akelaitis 1943, 1944). The split-brain case against the unity of consciousness derives not from the everyday behaviour of split-brain patients but from the cognitive and behavioural disunities that they exhibit in carefully controlled studies.[1] Most commentators take such studies to show that split-brain patients no longer enjoy a unified consciousness. In this chapter I argue that this assessment of the split-brain syndrome is open to challenge.

---

[1] For reviews of the split-brain syndrome see Baynes & Gazzaniga (2000); Beaumont (1981); Gazzaniga (1995, 2005); Seymour et al. (1994); Spencer et al. (1988); Wolford et al. (2004); Zaidel et al. (2003).

9.1 Setting the stage

Most split-brain studies have drawn on a pool of eleven patients, six from the Caltech series and the remainder from the Dartmouth series. The procedure performed on the original Caltech patients is known as a 'commissurotomy', and involves severing all of the corpus callosum, together with various other interhemispheric tracts, including the anterior commissure, the hippocampal commissure, and (in some cases) the massa intermedia of the thalamus. In another form of the procedure, referred to as a 'callosotomy', only the corpus callosum is sectioned. The differences between commissurotomy and callosotomy patients are not pronounced, and I will refer to them all as 'split-brain patients'. Behaviourally speaking, the important division is between patients in whom the anterior portion of their corpus callosum has been sectioned and those in whom only the posterior portion of the corpus callosum has been sectioned. The former tend to exhibit the classic split-brain syndrome, while the latter show only minimal dissociations.

The split-brain syndrome is most clearly revealed under carefully controlled experimental conditions. In the typical split-brain experiment, information is presented to the patient in such a way that it is processed by only one hemisphere.[2] In vision this is typically achieved by means of tachistoscopic presentation, in which the patient is required to maintain a central focus whilst information is flashed into one hemi-field long enough to be registered but not long enough to permit eye movements. For example, the word 'key-ring' might be presented to the patient such that 'key' falls within the patient's left visual field (LVF) and 'ring' falls within the patient's right visual field (RVF). The contralateral structure of the visual system ensures that stimuli projected to the LVF are processed in the right hemisphere and vice versa (see Figure 9.1). Other modalities can be studied in a similar fashion. Tactile perception in the split-brain is studied by presenting stimuli to only one of the patient's hands, or by presenting different stimuli to each hand. Typically, the patient will be unable to either name aloud objects correctly identified with the left hand, or select with their right hand an object palpitated by their left hand. With respect to olfactory information, the patient may be unable to match odours presented to one nostril with those presented to the other (Gordon & Sperry 1969). The situation with respect to audition is rather more complicated, and I will defer discussion of it until §9.5.

---

[2] See Zaidel et al. (1990) for a detailed account of the various methods used to test commissurotomy patients.

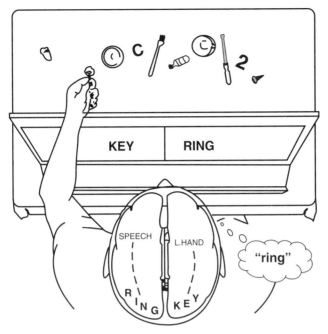

Figure 9.1 The subject reports (through the speaking hemisphere) having seen only the visual stimulus flashed to the right half of the screen (ring) and denies having seen the left-field stimulus or recognizing objects presented to the left hand (key). At the same time, the subject uses his left hand to correctly retrieve the left-field stimulus (key). When asked to name the object selected by the left hand the subject identifies the stimulus flashed to the right half of the screen (ring)

Source: Sperry (1974)

These experimental paradigms reveal the two kinds of disunities that constitute the classic split-brain syndrome: *representational disunities* and *access disunities* (see Chapter 5). Representational disunities involve a lack of integration and inferential promiscuity in the contents of the patient's mental states. In the key-ring experiment, the patient may have a representation of the words 'key' and 'ring' without having a representation of the word 'key-ring'. To take another example, a patient might be aware that her LVF contains the numeral 9 and that her RVF contains the numeral 6, but be unaware of which hemi-field contains the higher numeral. Access disunities occur when the contents of the patient's conscious states are not available to the same range of consuming systems. For example, a patient in the key-ring experiment who is asked to report what she sees will typically say that she sees only the word 'ring', yet with her left hand she may select a picture of a key and ignore pictures of both a ring and a key-ring. Generally speaking, information presented in the RVF will be unavailable for left-handed grasping behaviour while information presented in the LVF will be unavailable for verbal report.

Although the precise nature of such disunities may vary from patient to patient—for example, patient L.B. can name LVF stimuli but cannot compare stimuli presented to different halves of his two visual fields, whereas patient N.G. can compare stimuli across her two visual hemi-fields but cannot name LVF stimuli (Johnson 1984a, 1984b)—this description captures the 'classic' split-brain syndrome and provides a useful anchor for discussion. What might it tell us about the structure of consciousness in the split-brain?

The first question to ask is whether both left-hemisphere (LH) and right-hemisphere (RH) representations are conscious. (In the terminology introduced in Chapter 5, this is the challenge of meeting 'the positive moment'.) Some of the early split-brain commentators expressed doubts about an affirmative answer to this question. According to some authorities, only the patient's right hemisphere is conscious. The 'non-speaking' left hemisphere is unconscious, and the behaviours that it generates are produced by 'zombie mechanisms' (Eccles 1965; MacKay 1966; see §5.1 for discussion of zombie mechanisms).

The problems with this account of the split-brain are daunting. Although speech production is generally lateralized to the left hemisphere, certain split-brain patients (P.S., V.P., L.B., J.W.) have some capacity for both LH and RH speech production (Baynes & Gazzaniga 2000; Levy et al. 1971; Zaidel et al. 2003). More importantly, we should not make linguistic production—or, for that matter, linguistic comprehension—a precondition on the possession of consciousness. Such a principle would, implausibly, remove pre-linguistic children and aphasics from the realm of the conscious. One might argue that if a creature that is capable of verbal report cannot verbally report the contents of state P then one has reason to think that P is not a conscious state, but even this principle is contentious. Appealing to any such principle in this context is particularly problematic, for right-hemisphere guided behaviour in the split-brain is a plausible counter-example to the claim that the contents of consciousness must be verbally reportable.

Can the zombie model be defended by assimilating right-hemisphere guided behaviour to other instances of unconscious behavioural control? Perhaps the right hemisphere behaviour of split-brain patients is of a piece with the non-conscious motor control that has been found in normals (see §5.1). However, on close examination the parallel between right hemisphere behaviour and unconscious motor control turns out to be rather weaker that it might have seemed at first. Normal subjects who demonstrate motor control outside of awareness remain aware of the stimulus; what is lost is merely awareness of the *response* to the stimulus. In other cases, such as blindsight, the subject is not conscious of the stimulus, but is conscious of his response to it. The split-brain case would be unique in that the subject would be unaware of both the stimulus *and* their response to it.

The fundamental problem with the zombie model, however, is that split-brain patients can produce complex goal-directed behaviour under right hemisphere control. Indeed, right hemisphere behaviour far surpasses in cognitive complexity the kinds of tasks that elsewhere occur outside of consciousness. Summarizing an experiment testing the right-hemisphere based abilities of split-brain patients (with left hemisphere language), Sperry et al. write, 'The overall level of the right hemisphere's ability to identify test items and also the quality of the accompanying emotional and evaluative responses were of the same order approximately as those obtained from the right visual field and left hemisphere' (Sperry et al. 1979: 163). We would have little hesitation in saying that a patient in a persistent vegetative state had emerged from the vegetative state if they were to perform actions that were as purposeful and environmentally sensitive as those that split-brain patients perform under right hemisphere control. In light of this, I conclude that both the left and right hemispheres in the split-brain can support consciousness. In other words, the 'positive moment' in the argument for disunity can be met.

What about the negative moment? Can it also be met? The dominant view within both neuropsychology and philosophy is that it can. Most commentators are united in the view that there are times at which the split-brain patient has phenomenally disunified conscious states. Let us call such views *disunity accounts* of the split-brain. Within the broad family of disunity accounts we need distinguish *two-streams* accounts from *partial unity* accounts. Proponents of the two-streams account hold that the conscious states that a split-brain patients has at any one time can be assigned to one of two non-overlapping sets, where the members of each set are mutually unified but no member of either set is phenomenally unified with any member of the other set. Although few theorists put their views in quite this way, the two-streams model is arguably the received account of the split-brain syndrome.[3] In the words of one paper, '. . . the disconnected hemispheres in both animal and human subjects are separately conscious in parallel at a moderately high and approximately equal

---

[3] See also Davis (1997); Gazzaniga & LeDoux (1978); Marks (1981); Puccetti (1981); Schechter (2010); Sperry (1974, 1977); Tye (2003); Zaidel et al. (2003).

value' (Sperry et al. 1979: 153). By contrast, proponents of the partial unity account hold that consciousness in the split-brain has a branching structure: patients have simultaneous experiences (e_1, e_2, and e_3) such that e_1 and e_2 are each phenomenally unified with e_3 but not with each other (see §2.4). To the best of my knowledge the partial unity model of the split-brain was first explicitly presented by Lockwood (1989), although there are earlier hints of it in both the philosophical and neuropsychological literatures.[4]

Both the two-streams and partial unity models are at odds with the unity thesis, for each model holds that there are times during which patients have experiences that are not phenomenally unified with each other. However, one could attempt to reconcile these models with the spirit behind the unity thesis by rejecting the identification of subjects of experience with organisms. For example, one could follow neo-Lockeans in identifying subjects of experience with psychological networks or intentional systems. On such accounts, the truth of phenomenal disunity treatments of the split-brain need not spell the end of the unity thesis, for it could turn out that severing the corpus callosum not only splinters the patient's stream of consciousness but also creates multiple—and perhaps even overlapping—subjects of experience. Just what to say about the unity thesis should we identify subjects of experience not with organisms but with intentional systems raises many complex issues, not least of which is the problem of how to individuate such systems. However, I will leave this issue for others to pursue, for if the account of the split-brain that I offer in §9.5 is sound then the unity thesis can be saved without denying that subjects of experience can be counted by counting conscious organisms. But before we get to that, we must first examine what there is to be said on behalf of disunity accounts of the split-brain.

9.2 The case for disunity

Common to the two-streams and partial unity models is the claim that split-brain patients are phenomenally disunified—that the 'negative moment' can be sustained. So our first order of business is to examine the case for phenomenal disunity. I will consider three arguments for thinking that split-brain patients have phenomenally disunified conscious states.

---

[4] For philosophy see Moor (1982); for neuropsychology see Sperry (1976, 1984); Trevarthen (1974a) and (1974b). It is also possible to read Nagel's (1971) account of the split-brain as prefiguring the partial unity model in certain ways, although the central thrust of Nagel's position is that consciousness in the split-brain has no determinate structure.

The argument from agentive disunity

Although split-brain patients generally display a high degree of agentive unity, there are contexts in which this unity is lost, or at least impaired to some degree. One manifestation of agentive disunity in the split-brain is inter-manual conflict, in which the patient's left hand becomes anarchic and interferes with what the patient is trying to do with his or her right hand. For example, the anarchic hand might interfere with the patient's attempts to button up his shirt. Anarchic hand behaviour is common in the weeks immediately after surgery, but typically subsides within a few months (Bogen 1998; Wilson et al. 1977; Fergusen et al. 1985).

A second form of agentive disunity is spatial decoupling. Although cognitively intact subjects find it difficult to simultaneously draw distinct spatial patterns (for example, a square and a circle) with each hand, split-brain patients have no such difficulties (Preilowski 1972; Zaidel & Sperry 1977). In one study, patient J.W. and three normal controls were required to draw with each hand pairs of lines that differed in orientation (Franz et al. 1996). As expected, control subjects were impaired on trials in which the two stimuli had divergent orientations (relative to when they had identical orientations), whereas J.W. showed *improved* performance on such trials.

It seems to me that neither inter-manual conflict nor spatial decoupling provide much support for thinking of split-brain patients as phenomenally disunified. The behaviour of the anarchic hand is best thought of as triggered by stimulus-driven intentions: seeing a button elicits a prepotent response to undo it; seeing a fork elicits a prepotent response to pick it up, and so on. The intention might be triggered by a conscious perception of the stimulus, but the subject herself need not be conscious of the intention. Indeed, we are frequently unaware of stimulus-driven intentions. (Consider what it is like to navigate a crowded street whilst engaged in conversation.) Spatial decoupling is likewise consistent with phenomenal unity. Again, the kind of motor independence seen here involves only subconscious mechanisms; we needn't posit separate conscious intentions or goals in each hemisphere. We might also note that although split-brain patients can produce *spatially* decoupled actions, they do not produce *temporally* decoupled actions (see Franz et al. 1996; Kennerley et al. 2002; Tuller & Kelso 1989). Split-brain patients may be less 'agentively unified' than cognitively intact individuals, but we should not think of each hemisphere as harbouring an autonomous agent. Each of the two hemispheres may be able to process perceptual information autonomously, but they are not able to select motor responses independently and simultaneously (Ivry et al. 1998; Pashler et al. 1994; see also Reuter-Lorenz 2003).

Paradoxically, the most striking form of agentive disunity in the split-brain may involve inter-hemispheric *cooperation* rather than inter-hemispheric *conflict*. In a phenomenon known as 'cross-cuing', patients employ environmental cues to transfer information between hemispheres. For example, the patient may run a fingernail down the teeth of a comb in order to produce a characteristic noise by which the object can be identified (Zaidel et al. 2003: 365). Employing the perceptual space shared by both hemispheres, the right hemisphere may attempt to 'tip-off' the left hemisphere by visually fixating on a related object. Cross-cuing can also be mediated by movements of the head or tongue, subvocal speech, and various forms of imagery (Bogen 1998; Corballis 1995; Gazzaniga & Hillyard 1971). Like bridge partners trying to tip each other off about their hand or members of a jazz duo attempting to keep each other 'in the pocket', we could think of the two hemispheres as distinct agents intent on securing a common goal.

But as tempting as it might be, I think we have good reason not to model cross-cuing on intersubjective communication. For one thing, the cuing hemisphere does not take itself to be communicating with another agent, nor does the receiving hemisphere think of itself as the recipient of a communicative act. In a revealing comment, J.W. exclaimed, 'Are you guys trying to make two people out of me?' (MacKay & MacKay 1982: 691). If we were to accept the intersubjective conception of cross-cuing, we would have to think of J.W. as (self?) deluded in taking himself to be a single agent. That, I think, would be an unwelcome result. (Contrast the kind of cross-cuing carried out by J.W. with that which occurs between conjoined twins, which clearly does take place between different agents.) Although there is some evidence that split-brain patients may have distinct RH and LH self-conceptions (LeDoux et al. 1977; Sperry et al. 1979), there is no evidence that each of the patient's hemispheres thinks of itself—or, indeed, of its neighbour—as an autonomous locus of agency.

Unwelcome or not, we might be forced to model cross-cuing on intersubjective communication if it were the only account going. However, it turns out that it's not. In fact, there are two alternatives to the 'communicative' conception of cross-cuing. On the one hand, we could model cross-cuing on the kind of information transfer that occurs between sub-personal homunculi in (say) decision-making or memory retrieval. On the other hand, we could model cross-cuing on self-directed agency; in other words, we could think of cross-cuing as a technique by means of which the *patient* attempts to manipulate his or her own mind. Just as one might try to jog one's memory by engaging in certain types of imagery or by talking to oneself, so too the split-brain patient might deliberately deploy various tricks in order to transfer information between hemispheres. It is not clear to me which of these two models best fits cross-cuing, but each of them seems preferable to the communicative model.

Split-brain patients depart from the norms of unified agency in a number of ways, but none of these departures indicates that we should think of patients as 'housing' two distinct conscious agents. Instead, the evidence suggests that split-brain patients are single agents who are attempting to get by as best they can (Gillett 1986). Split-brain patients might enjoy significantly less agentive unity than you or I, but we should not conceive of them as 'composites' of two conscious agents.

The representational disunity argument

Another argument for phenomenal disunity appeals to a lack of representational integration between left hemisphere and right hemisphere representations. Consider a typical split-brain patient ('S') in a key-ring experiment.

(1) S has, simultaneously, an experience with the content <'key'> and an experience with the content <'ring'>.

(2) Any subject with simultaneous experiences of <'key'> and <'ring'> that are phenomenally unified with each other will also have an experience with the content <'key' & 'ring'>.

(3) S does not have an experience with content <'key' & 'ring'>.

Therefore,

(4) S's experiences of 'key' and 'ring' are not phenomenally unified.

(1) appears to be secure. Since the two words were flashed to S simultaneously, it seems to follow that if S was indeed aware of both words then she was aware of them simultaneously. And, as I argued in §9.1, there is good reason to think that each hemisphere in a split-brain subject can support consciousness.

The truth of (2) seems to follow from what in Chapter 5 I called RIP:

> Representational Integration Principle (RIP): For any pair of simultaneous experiences e_1 and e_2, if e_1 and e_2 are phenomenally unified then, ceteris paribus, their contents will be available for representational integration.

Note that the kind of integration in question here is rather undemanding. The argument does not even require that S be aware of the presented word as 'key-ring'. All (2) requires is that S be aware of the words 'key' and 'ring' together in the form of a representation that has as its content <'key' & 'ring'>. But S doesn't even appear to possess this representation.

Is (3) secure? Is it possible that S could in fact have a conjunctive experience of the words 'key' and 'ring', but simply be unable to report this content because of cognitive bottlenecks of the kind seen in the Sperling experiments (see §4.2)? Although I was at one point attracted to this proposal (Bayne & Chalmers 2003), I now regard it as unsatisfactory. Bottleneck models might be able to explain why *S* cannot report an experience of <'key-ring'> or an experience of <'key' & 'ring'>, but they are ill-equipped to explain why she cannot use the contents of her representation of 'key' in ways in which she can use her representation of 'ring' and vice versa. It is not as if saying 'key' or picking out a ring with one's left hand is more cognitively demanding than saying 'ring' or selecting a key from amongst an array of objects. *S* would presumably have little difficulty forming a conscious representation of 'key-ring' were we to project it into either her LVF or her RVF. Furthermore, where there are cognitive bottlenecks, we are usually able to *report* that we are aware of more than we can directly report. Subjects in the Sperling experiments cannot report the contents of their experience of the entire matrix, but they can (and do) indicate *that* they had an experience of the matrix whose contents outstripped what they could report. But *S* fails to have even this indirect form of access to her experiential content. She doesn't, for example, say that she was aware of two words, only one of which she could identify. It seems reasonable to conclude that *S* manifests no evidence of having an experience of <'key-ring'> because she has no such experience.

In sum, premises (1) (2) and (3) are individually plausible, and together they entail phenomenal disunity. The representational disunity argument looks to be secure.

The access disunity argument

A third argument for phenomenal disunity appeals to the relationship between access unity and phenomenal unity. Once again we can use the key-ring experiment as our 'template'.

(1) *S* has, simultaneously, an experience with the content <'key'> and an experience with the content <'ring'>.

(2) If simultaneous experiences of <'key'> and <'ring'> are phenomenally unified with each other then they will be access unified: their contents will be available to the same range of consuming systems.

(3) *S*'s representations of 'key' and 'ring' are not access unified: although the contents of both states are available for high-level consumption, they are not available to *the same* consuming systems.

(4) So, *S*'s experiences of 'key' and 'ring' are not phenomenally unified.

Given that the first premise of this argument is identical to that of the previous argument we need not comment any further on it here. But what about (2) and (3)?

In arguing for (2) we might appeal to the Conjoint Accessibility Principle:

> *Conjoint Accessibility Principle* (CAP): For any pair of simultaneous experiences e_1 and e_2, if e_1 and e_2 are phenomenally unified then, *ceteris paribus*, their contents will be available to the same consuming systems.

As I argued in Chapter 5, the force of the inference from access disunity to phenomenal disunity depends on the degree to which the states in question are access disunified: the less co-accessible the contents of the states, the more reason we will have for denying that they are phenomenally unified. So, that leads us to premise (3): are there any consuming systems to which the subject's experiences of <'key'> and <'ring'> might both be available? Given the difficulties in individuating consuming systems it would be premature to give a definitive answer to this question (see p. 213), but the evidence suggests that few consuming systems will have access to both contents. In short, the access disunity argument also seems to be secure.

It's time to recap. I have examined three arguments for the claim that split-brain patients are phenomenally disunified. Although none is decisive, the arguments from representational and access disunity are strong, and their combined force goes some way towards explaining—not to mention justifying—the dominance of disunity models. So let us temporarily proceed on the assumption that the typical split-brain patient is indeed phenomenally disunified. The question I turn to now is whether the split-brain patient has two separate streams of consciousness or a merely partially unified consciousness. As we will see, neither proposal is unproblematic.

9.3 Everyday integration

In the period immediately following surgery (right-handed) patients typically experience unilateral apraxia—an inability to execute with their left hand actions that are verbally described or named by the examiner, despite being able to imitate these actions when demonstrated. Long-term deficits following the split-brain procedure include impairments in making and executing decisions, problems with short-term memory, and frequent absent-mindedness.[5] Nonetheless, the split-brain procedure has surprisingly little impact on the everyday lives of patients. They can cook, cycle, swim, and play the piano, and naïve observers are rarely aware that they suffer from cognitive impairments. It is far from clear how

---

[5] See Mark (1996); Fergusen et al. (1985); Zaidel (1994).

disunity models might account for this 'social ordinariness'. How is it possible that individuals with a disunified consciousness are able to exhibit such high degrees of cognitive and behavioural unity?

Although the challenge of everyday unity confronts both two-streams and partial unity theorists alike, it is most pronounced with respect to the two-streams account, and I will focus my discussion on two-streams responses to it. However, many of the points that apply to two-streams accounts of everyday unity also apply *mutatis mutandis* to partial unity accounts.

There are two treatments of the everyday unity of the split-brain patient to be found within the two-streams literature: a 'contextualist' treatment and a 'duplication' treatment. Both treatments take as their point of departure the fact that in everyday contexts the two hemispheres will have access to (roughly) the same environmental features, and hence their contents will 'mirror' each other. As Sperry notes, 'the two retinal half-fields of the eyeball move as one, and eye movements are conjugate, so that when one hemisphere directs the gaze to a given target the other hemisphere is automatically locked in at all times on the same target' (Sperry 1974: 7). Further, the restrictions that prevent cross-cuing in the laboratory do not apply outside of the laboratory, and thus the patient can ensure that information is duplicated between the hemispheres even when their environmental relations fail to ensure this.

From this common starting point the two accounts proceed in quite different directions. Contextualists hold that split-brain patients have two streams of consciousness only in certain experimental conditions, and that in everyday life they enjoy a single, fully unified consciousness (Marks 1981; Tye 2003). As such, contextualists argue that the inter-hemispheric mirroring of content is conducive to conscious unity. Duplicationists, by contrast, take the mirroring of content to result in (disunified) phenomenal duplicates—conscious states whose contents are fully identical. In other words, they attempt to account for everyday unity without restricting the scope of the two-streams account. Let us begin with contextualism.

Marks captures the contextualist position in the following question, 'Why should neural processes unrelated by direct causal routes not be the physical basis for a single mental state?' (Marks 1981: 23). The idea, I take it, is that split-brain patients have what we might call 'scattered experiences'. Consider two neural states, N_1 and N_2, located in the left and right hemispheres respectively. Although each of these states could have realized a K-type experience on its own had the other state been inactive, the patient has only a *single* token of a K-type experience even when both N_1 and N_2 are active. Rather than N_1 constituting one K-type experience and N_2 constituting another K-type experience, their 'sum' or 'composite' realizes a single K-type experience, despite the fact that there are no direct causal connections between them.

The plausibility of this proposal surely depends in no small measure on how experiences ought to be individuated. I have recommended that experiences ought to be individuated in tripartite terms—that is, by reference to times, subject, and phenomenal properties. This conception of experience does leave conceptual space for scattered experiences to inhabit, for it doesn't require that the physical basis of token experience have any kind of internal causal unity. But even if scattered experiences are possible, it is far from clear that they will be able to do the work that the contextualist requires of them. How could the patient's K-type experience produce integrated thought and action if its causal basis is distributed between two causally isolated hemispheres?

Things may be even worse for those attracted to a vehicular conception of experience, as I suspect most contextualists are. How could the mereological sum of N_1 and N_2 realize a single token experience given the lack of causal commerce between them (Schechter 2010)? N_1 and N_2 might individually realize a K-type experience, but given that N_1's causal influence is restricted to the patient's left hemisphere and N_2's causal influence is restricted to the patient's right hemisphere it is difficult to see how the sum or composite of these two states could realize a K-type experience. It looks as though N_1 and N_2 must realize the K-type functional role as individuals, and if that is right then it is hard to see how their composite—N_1 & N_2—could itself realize that functional role. The only real loci of causal powers here are N_1 and N_2. The 'sum' of these two events is not itself a neural event in any non-gerrymandered sense, and even if it were it seems not to possess psychologically relevant causal powers of its own.

Further shortcomings of the 'scattered experiences' proposal can be brought into view by comparing N_1 and N_2 with another pair of neural states, N_3 and N_4, where N_3 realizes a K-type experience in one patient and N_4 realizes a K-type experience in another patient. Contextualists need to explain why it is that the sum of N_1 and N_2 constitutes a scattered K-type experience but the sum of N_3 and N_4 does not. In response, contextualists might be tempted to point out that N_3 and N_4 occur in the context of different minds—different psychological economies—whereas N_1 and N_2 do not, but it is precisely this latter claim that stands in need of explanation. Indeed, in a sense the objection from everyday integration *just is* the challenge of explaining how activity in two (disconnected) hemispheres could give rise to a single mind (or the appearance thereof).

Contextualists don't only need to provide an account of how the appeal to scattered experiences might explain everyday unity in the split-brain, they also need to explain how the transition between everyday and experimental contexts could bring about changes in the structure of the patient's consciousness

(Nagel 1971). How could moving back and forth between experimental and everyday environments transform the structure of the patient's consciousness from one in which the patient's experiences are all contained within a single stream to one in which they are parcelled out between two streams? After all, it is plausible to suppose that phenomenal structure supervenes on neural structure, and the patient's neural structure appears not to be fundamentally altered by the transition between everyday and experimental contexts.

As I understand their position, Marks and Tye reject the assumption that phenomenal structure supervenes on neural structure. On their view, the transition between unity and disunity occurs merely as a result of changes in the *contents* of the respective hemispheres. The patient has a unified consciousness in everyday life because—to put it somewhat loosely—the conscious content of the one hemisphere is 'mirrored' by that of the other hemisphere, whereas the patient's consciousness is disunified in laboratory conditions because the contents of the one hemisphere differ from those of the other. But as we have noted, it is unclear why we should interpret this 'mirroring' in terms of scattered (or 'disjunctive') experiences whose neural bases are distributed between the hemispheres as opposed to duplicate experiences that are fully located in one or the other hemisphere.

There is, however, another way in which the contextualist might attempt to account for transitions in the structure of the patient's consciousness, a way that does not involve giving up on the thought that the neural activity in one hemisphere must be causally integrated with that in the other in order for the subject to have a unified consciousness. Drawing on Hurley's 'vehicle externalist' account of consciousness, the contextualist might hold that the unity of consciousness involves a 'dynamic singularity in the field of causal flows that is centred on but not bounded by a biological organism' (1998: 207). This kind of contextualist might suggest that the difference between everyday and laboratory environments resides in the fact that only in everyday contexts does the 'causal flow' that underpins consciousness include both hemispheres within its orbit, whereas it is unable to extend beyond the reach of a single hemisphere when the patient is (say) required to maintain central fixation.[6]

Although I myself am not much attracted to vehicle externalism, I do think that it ought to be taken seriously. Moreover, being able to ground a plausible account of the split-brain would itself speak in its favour. But in fact the vehicle externalist proposal just sketched is really more of a promissory note than anything else, and it may not be one that is easily cashed. The contextualist who is tempted to go externalist needs to explain why the 'causal flow' that

---

[6] I should add that I am considering here a contextualist appropriation of Hurley's vehicle externalism. I am not suggesting that this was Hurley's own position.

constitutes the patient's phenomenal field might be able to straddle both hemispheres in everyday contexts but not in experimental contexts.

As far as I can see, the only plausible move to be made here appeals to the thought that the cognitive demands that split-brain patients face in experimental contexts are more taxing than those that everyday life places on them, and that it is these demands that govern the structure of the relevant causal flows. Although there is *something* to this suggestion (as we will see in §9.5), it is highly implausible to suppose that high cognitive load could generally lead to phenomenal division. Think of shadowing tasks, in which one has to repeat the words presented to one's left ear while listening for target words in the auditory stream presented to one's right ear. Such tasks are taxing, but they don't cause one's auditory states to divide into two distinct streams of consciousness. A further difficulty with the 'cognitive load' proposal is that one can elicit representational and access disunities of the sort the two-streamer appeals to even under conditions of minimal cognitive load. After all, identifying the word 'key-ring' does not seem to be particularly onerous.

It is time for an interim summary. I have argued that contextualist versions of the two-streams model are not promising. Neither the 'isolated realizers' version of contextualism developed by Marks and Tye nor the vehicle externalist version of contextualism that we have just examined provide us with a plausible account of everyday unity in the split-brain.[7]

Does this mean that the two-streams model is sunk? No. Contextualism is in fact something of a minority view within the two-streams camps, and most two-streamers attempt to account for everyday unity in the split-brain by adopting what I call the duplicationist account. To return to our earlier example (see p. 200) rather than supposing that N_1 and N_2 form the basis of a single K-type experience (as the contextualist does), the duplicationist takes N_1 to form the basis of one K-type experience and N_2 to form the basis of another, numerically distinct, K-type experience.[8]

This duplicationist strategy avoids many of the objections that troubled the contextualist's treatment of the inter-hemispheric mirroring of content, but it has troubles of its own. The primary objection to it is that the very notion of duplicate experiences is of dubious coherence. As I pointed out in Chapter 3, the tripartite account of experiences leaves no conceptual space for duplicates, for by definition duplicates have the same content, are had by the same subject of experience, and occur simultaneously. (Remember that we are here identifying the subject with the split-brain patient.) So, in order to embrace the

[7] See Schechter (2010) for additional discussion of the isolated realizers proposal.
[8] See e.g. Davis (1997); Puccetti (1981); Moor (1982); Sperry (1974).

duplication gambit the two-streams theorist must either reject the tripartite conception of experience, or argue that each stream is to be identified with a distinct subject of experience.

Of course, the duplicationist *could* reject the tripartite account of experience. She could, for example, individuate experiences in neural or functional terms. Such views might allow a person to have multiple experiences with the same phenomenal content as long as the various experiential tokens involve (supervene on; are grounded in) distinct neural events. Although the issues here are complex, I think that we have good reason to retain the tripartite account. Experiences are properties of subjects of experience—they are not properties of neuronal assemblies or sub-personal homunculi. Talk of 'the left hemisphere doing this' or 'the right hemisphere knowing that' is tempting—indeed, I myself have engaged in it on occasions—but it needs to be taken with a large pinch of salt. And the fact that experiences are states of subjects ought to be reflected in their identity conditions.

Should the two-streamer allow that the split-brain subject might be or 'house' two subjects of experience? I think the costs of going down this road are high. As we have already noted, the patients don't think of themselves as multiple. There is no sense in which the left hemisphere thinks of itself as one subject and the right hemisphere thinks of itself as another subject. Not only do patients themselves not think of themselves as multiple, experimentalists do not typically think of them as multiple either. Although researchers are sometimes inclined to think of themselves as dealing with two subjects, such contexts are very much the exception to the rule. For the most part, there is little doubt that 'I'-thoughts associated with the left hemisphere refer to the same individual as 'I'-thoughts associated with the right hemisphere, and if 'I'-thoughts associated with each hemisphere are co-referential then we must be dealing with a single subject of experience. These considerations fall short of *demonstrating* that split-brain patients cannot enjoy duplicate experiences, but they do put that proposal under significant pressure.

There are two final issues to consider before I draw this section to a close. The first is this. At the start of this section I noted that contextualist and duplicationist accounts of everyday unity in the split-brain share a common assumption—namely, that in everyday environments the contents of the patient's two hemispheres will 'mirror' each other. I have proceeded by granting this assumption, but in fact there is good reason to challenge it. The two hemispheres might enjoy a *partial* mirroring of content in everyday environments, but given hemispheric specialization in perceptual processing it is very unlikely that their contents will *fully* mirror each other. Secondly, even when the two hemispheres *do* receive the same perceptual input, this may not lead to behavioural integration, for the behavioural upshot of perceptual information is not a function of that information alone but depends on the broader psychological context in which it is processed. For example, stimuli that the left hemisphere regards as aversive might not be so regarded by the right hemisphere, or vice versa. Given that the two hemispheres have different memory stores and cognitive styles (Roser & Gazzaniga 2004; Schiffer et al. 1998), even complete mirroring of content might be expected to lead to behavioural disunity were both hemispheres conscious in parallel.

We have seen that there are two lines of response open to the two-streams theorist in accounting for everyday behavioural unity in the split-brain: a 'contextualist' response, according to which split-brain patients enjoy phenomenal disunity only in laboratory contexts, and a 'duplicationist' response, according to which everyday unity is accounted for by supposing that the subject's two streams are mirror images of each other. In my view, neither proposal succeeds. Let us turn now from the prospects of the two-streams account of the split-brain to those of the partial unity model.[9]

9.4 Partial unity

The two-streams model goes hand in glove with the assumption that the split-brain operation bisects a single cognitive-behavioural workspace into two such workspaces, each of which is sealed off from the other. According to this picture, information presented to each hemisphere can be integrated only with information available to that hemisphere, and each of the patient's consuming systems has access to the contents of one and only one workspace. This picture is problematized by the phenomenon of inter-hemispheric integration.[10]

First, some background. Particular sections of the corpus callosum are responsible for the transfer of distinct types of information. The anterior mid-body transfers motor information, the posterior mid-body transfers somatosensory information, the isthmus transfers auditory information, and the splenium transfers visual information.[11] This specialization suggests that it should be possible for patients to exhibit domain-specific splitting, and indeed this turns out to be the case.

Gazzaniga and LeDoux describe a patient (D.H.) with a partial callosotomy, who appeared to be split for touch but not vision:

---

[9] The material in this section has benefited greatly from discussions with Lizzie Schechter.

[10] See Corballis (1995); Sidtis (1986); Zaidel (1995); and Zaidel et al. (2003) for useful surveys of inter-hemispheric integration with a focus on vision.

[11] See Funnell et al. (2000a, 2000b); de Lacoste et al. (1985).

Tactual information in the left hand and right hemisphere remained isolated from the right hand and the left hemisphere. Yet, when a visual stimulus, such as the picture of an apple, was lateralized to either hemisphere, either hand could manually retrieve the apple, unaided by visual exploration. (Gazzaniga & LeDoux 1978: 10; see also Gazzaniga & Freedman 1973)

Even patients with a complete callosotomy appear to be capable of selective inter-hemispheric integration. Gazzaniga et al. (1963) describe a patient who was unable to localize with the one hand brief touches that had been applied to the foot, leg, arm, hand, and trunk of the contralateral side of his body, but was able to both localize with either hand and verbally report touches that had been applied to any region of his head or face. Selective inter-hemispheric integration is not restricted to touch but can also be found within vision. Ambient (peripheral) information about relative motion and size can be transferred between hemispheres (Trevarthen 1970; Trevarthen & Sperry 1973), as can information about visual field location (Holtzman 1984). Apparent motion can also occur across the visual hemi-fields: stimuli that are presented to each hemi-field sequentially can generate a percept of a single stimulus moving from one hemi-field to the other.[12]

Finally, there is evidence for the integration of perceptually based categorical information. In one experiment, patients were required to determine which of three pictures shown in one hemi-field matched a picture shown in the other hemi-field (Cronin-Golomb 1986; see also Zaidel & Iacoboni 2003). For example, the patient might be presented with a picture of a fish in his LVF and pictures of a pig, spider, and duck in his RVF. (The duck matches the fish, for both animals are associated with water.) Each of the three patients could match inter-field stimuli to high levels of reliability, suggesting that high-level, categorical information could be transferred between hemispheres.

Inter-hemispheric integration suggests that the 'split' of consciousness seen in the split-brain might be partial rather than complete—that some patients might have a single, partially unified stream of consciousness rather than two streams of consciousness. To convert inter-hemispheric integration into an argument for partial unity we need only suppose that inter-hemispheric integration involves token experiences that 'straddle' the two hemispheres. Consider again D.H., who is split for touch but not vision. Suppose that D.H. has, at the one time, tactile experiences in both hands and visual experiences in both hemi-fields. We have some reason to think that although his visual experiences *are* unified with each

---

[12] Ramachandran et al. (1986); Corballis (1995); Naikar & Corballis (1996); but see also Gazzaniga (1987).

other this is *not* the case for his tactile experiences. But what is the relationship between D.H.'s *visual* experiences and his *tactile* experiences? Presumably each of his visual experiences is unified with both his left hand tactile experience *and* with his right hand tactile experience, even though those experiences are not unified with each other. But if that is right, then D.H has a partially unified conscious-ness, for (at a single time) he will have a pair of experiences that are unified with each other but not with a third experience (see §2.4). Although D.H. is unusual among split-brain patients in being split for touch but not for vision, we have seen that even the most split of split-brain patients appears to retain the ability to integrate certain types of information, and comparable arguments could be constructed for them also.

The argument from integration is provocative. Without doubt, it demon-strates that the partial unity model of the split-brain needs to be taken seriously— much more seriously than it is usually taken. But it is not, I think, wholly decisive. To provide a watertight argument from integration one needs to show both that the relevant behavioural responses are indeed a manifestation of inter-hemispheric integration *and* that the integration in question is conscious. Neither of these tasks will be at all trivial to accomplish.

There are (at least) two ways in which an apparently integrative response might actually result from the operation of a single hemisphere. On the one hand, individual hemispheres sometimes have a wider range of processing abilities than is often suspected. For example, there is evidence that the right hemisphere has some ability to monitor the full visual field even when the corpus callosum is severed (Mangun et al. 1994). Given this, one has to ensure that visual field judgements that appear to involve the integration of LVF and RVF content cannot be produced by the right hemisphere under its own steam.

Even when behaviour does involve both hemispheres it may not involve inter-hemispheric *integration*. In an elegant study, Kingstone and Gazzaniga (1995) showed just how easy it is for split-brain patients to produce integrative behaviour in the absence of true representational integration. In an initial experiment, their subject (J.W.) appeared to demonstrate inter-hemispheric integration. For example, when the word 'ten' was presented to his left hemi-sphere (RVF) and the word 'clock' was presented to his right hemisphere (LVF) J.W. drew a clock showing 10 o'clock. However, Kingstone and Gazzaniga showed that J.W. produced his 'composite' pictures not by integrating infor-mation between hemispheres, but by transferring control of his drawing hand from one hemisphere to another. Using a single hand, J.W. would first sketch a clock under the guidance of his right hemisphere, and then add clock-hands indicating 10 o'clock under the guidance of his left hemisphere. As Kingstone and

Gazzaniga put it, the only integration to be found here occurred 'on the sheet of paper in the drawing itself' (1995: 324; see also Miller & Kingstone 2005).

Moreover, even when inter-hemispheric integration occurs it may not involve a 'phenomenal bridge' between the patient's two hemispheres (Corballis 1994). The argument from integration turns on the assumption that bilateral integration involves experiential events that 'straddle' the patient's two hemispheres, but conscious states in one hemisphere might have an effect on those in the other hemisphere even in the absence of inter-hemispheric phenomenal unity. A plausible example of this involves the inter-hemispheric transfer of affect. In one oft-cited vignette, a patient was unable to verbally identify a picture of Hitler that had been presented in his left visual field, but his description of it was clearly influenced by negative affect—affect that had presumably been generated in the right hemisphere (Sperry et al. 1979). Rather than suppose that the patient had a single experience of negative affect that bridged his two hemispheres, perhaps a right hemisphere state of negative affect merely primed a similar state in his left hemisphere. In other words, it seems plausible to suppose that inter-hemispheric integration can take place outside of consciousness.

In fact, Naikar (1996) advances just this treatment of apparent motion across the vertical midline in patient L.B. Rather than supposing that L.B.'s experience of the first light (as located in one hemifield) was phenomenally unified with an experience of the second light (as located in the other hemifield), Naiker suggests instead that (unconscious) sub-cortical mechanisms registered a shift of spatial attention from one hemi-field to the other, giving rise to a *judgement* of apparent motion across the vertical midline.

Might *all* instances of inter-hemispheric integration be explained in this deflationary manner? Perhaps; it is difficult to tell from the experimental literature. In principle, there are two ways in which one could rule out priming treatments of inter-hemispheric integration. One way to block priming accounts of integration would be to show that the *kind* of integration in question could not have occurred unless the states involved were phenomenally unified with each other. For example, one could undermine the 'priming' account of apparent motion by showing that visual representations cannot produce a representation of apparent motion unless they are both conscious and phenomenally unified with each other. In practice however, this line of response will be difficult to establish, for we know so little about the kinds of information transfer that can occur outside of phenomenal integration. Another strategy one might employ in order to block priming interpretations would be to show that the representations produced by the relevant instance of inter-hemispheric integration are not only integrated with both right- and left-hemisphere conscious states, but that their contents are also available to both right- and left-hemisphere 'consuming systems'. Although perhaps more feasible than the previous strategy, this strategy is also likely to be difficult to implement. Not only would one need to show that the consuming systems in question are unique to each hemisphere (rather than shared between the hemispheres), but one would also need a principled way of assigning consuming systems to hemispheres (and, by implication, to streams of consciousness). Although we can be reasonably confident that some behavioural capacities—such as control of the contralateral hand for fine motor movements—involve consuming systems that are unique to each hemisphere, other forms of motor control can be passed back and forth between hemispheres, so we cannot individuate consuming systems in terms of coarse-grained behavioural capacities. In short, it will not be easy to rule out deflationary 'priming' interpretations of inter-hemispheric integration.

But the deepest challenges facing the partial unity model are not empirical but conceptual. In weighing the overall plausibility of the approach we need to consider both its empirical credentials and its intrinsic plausibility (or the lack thereof). In Chapter 2 I noted that the question of whether the model is even coherent is far from settled. Contrary to what has often been claimed, the problem with partial unity is not that we cannot imaginatively project ourselves into a partially unified phenomenal perspective. Rather, the problem with partial unity is that it seems to be inconceivable. It seems to be central to our notion of a phenomenal perspective that phenomenal unity cannot fragment in the way that partial unity would require. This worry is far from decisive—after all, when it comes to consciousness, inconceivability judgements are notoriously controversial—but it surely has some force. Perhaps it would be reasonable to waive such worries if the evidence in favour of the partial unity model were overwhelming, but that is far from being the case if the considerations presented above are sound.

Where does this leave us? Although §9.2 appeared to provide a solid case for disunity interpretations of the split-brain, we have seen that both the two-streams and the partial unity versions of the disunity approach face formidable challenges. In light of this, perhaps we ought to reconsider the assumption that split-brain patients do indeed have a disunified consciousness. Maybe the case for disunity developed in §9.2 was not quite as solid as it appeared to be.

9.5 The switch model

In the previous chapter I suggested that the cognitive and behavioural disunity seen in hypnosis is best accounted for by supposing that hypnotised subjects have a single stream of consciousness that switches between two streams of processing. Drawing on ideas that were first advanced by Jerrre Levy (Levy 1977, 1990), I suggest that we can account for the cognitive and behavioural disunities seen in the split-brain in precisely the same way (Bayne 2008b). Rather than suppose that the patient's two hemispheres are conscious in parallel, we should think of consciousness in the split-brain as moving or switching from one hemisphere to another. Although both hemispheres can process information concurrently, they take turns supporting consciousness. In effect, the switch model paints patients as suffering from a kind of fluctuating perceptual extinction: when the left (right) hemisphere is activated stimuli in the LVF (RVF) are typically ignored in favour of stimuli in the RVF (LVF). The patient might be conscious of the word 'key' (due to right hemisphere activity), or she might be conscious of the word 'ring' (due to left hemisphere activity), but she will not be conscious of both 'key' and 'ring' *at once*, even when the two words are simultaneously presented to her.

An important source of evidence for the switch model is to be found in an experiment conducted by Levy and colleagues involving chimeric stimuli—that is, stimuli that are created by conjoining two similar half-stimuli at the vertical midline (Levy et al. 1972). A chimeric face might be constructed from the left side of one person's face and the right side of another person's face. On some trials subjects were asked to point to a matching stimulus (either with their right or left hands), whilst on other trials subjects were required to name the stimulus. On almost all trials, subjects indicated only one match for each of the chimeric stimuli.

In their original report, Levy and co-authors suggested that the non-responding hemisphere had a rival percept that it failed to express, and it is this interpretation of the experiment that seems to have entered the literature (see e.g. Marks 1981). However, in subsequent work Levy argued for a very different account of the data:

With one half-stimulus joined at the mid-line to a different half-stimulus to make a 'chimera,' each hemisphere would receive equivalent, but different stimulus input, and if two perceptions were gained, they would be in conflict as evidence concerning the object of interest, and the motor responses guided by these percepts would be in conflict... [But] if... perception is the preparation to respond, then, except in special circumstances, there should be a single perception linked to a single response under conditions of competitive stimulus input... Our studies overwhelmingly confirmed the predictions of this conceptual model. For all patients examined, and for tasks including the perception of faces, nonsense shapes, pictures of common objects, patterns of Xs and squares, words, word meaning, phonetic images of rhyming pictures, and outline drawings to be matched to colors, patients gave one response on the vast majority of competitive trials. Further, the nonresponding hemisphere gave no evidence that it had any perception at all. Thus, if the right hemisphere responded there was no indication, by words or facial expression, that the left hemisphere had any argument with the choice made, and, similarly, if the left hemisphere responded, no behavior on the part of the patient suggested a disagreement by the right hemisphere. (Levy 1990: 235; see also Levy 1977)

Levy's 'switch' account of this data strikes me as rather more elegant than her earlier 'non-responding' account. Rather than take the non-responding hemisphere to have a conscious percept that it was either unable or unwilling to express, it seems simpler to suppose that whatever percepts it might have had were unconscious.

Levy's experiments are not the only evidence of perceptual extinction in the split-brain. In a follow-up experiment, six split-brain subjects were given a mixture of dot and numeral counting exercises via the usual tachistoscopic method (Teng & Sperry 1974). Between one and five dots were flashed either in the LVF or RVF alone, or in the two visual fields simultaneously. All but one of the six split-brain subjects showed massive amounts of extinction, with patients reporting only those stimuli restricted to a single hemi-field. Gazzaniga and colleagues also found perceptual extinction in a study that examined the bilateral integration of tactile stimuli in a split-brain patient. The authors noted that 'it was as if a strong shift of attention to one hemisphere had tended to extinguish perceptual awareness in the other' (Gazzaniga et al. 1963: 211).

The dynamics of switching in the split-brain appears to depend on a number of factors, one of which is the response required of the subject. Some studies have noted that differences between *motor* responses can influence the lateral-ization of awareness in the split-brain. For example, Levy et al. (1972) reported that verbal responses tended to favour completion of the right half of the stimulus, while manual responses favoured completion of the left half of the stimulus. Trevarthen found that the lateralization of conscious perception could be switched merely by requiring subjects to respond with one hand rather than the other (Trevarthen 1974b: 195). In another series of studies, Levy and Trevarthen found that the lateralization of awareness could also be switched by modulating the *cognitive* content of the responses required by patients (see Figure. 9.2). For example, asking patients to match chimeric stimuli based on their visual appearance favoured the LVF (implicating the right hemisphere) whereas instructing them to match stimuli based on their function favoured the RVF (implicating the left hemisphere) (Levy & Trevarthen 1976; see also Sperry 1974 and Iacoboni et al. 1996). As Teng and Sperry put it, 'the apparent distribution of attention between the two hemispheres is not static, but may change with the nature of the task . . .' (Teng & Sperry 1973: 137). The response-dependence in evidence here is not unique to the split-brain—we have seen it previously in unilateral neglect (Chapter 5) and anosognosia (Chapter 7)—but it does seem to be remarkably pronounced in the split-brain syndrome.

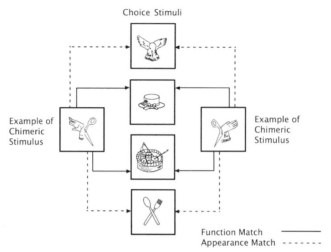

Figure 9.2 When instructed to match chimeric figures on the basis of their function (or meaning) subjects employed the right-hand side of the figure indicating left-hemisphere capture of awareness, whereas subjects employed the left-hand side of the figure when instructed to match on the basis of appearance (or form), indicating right-hemisphere capture of awareness

Source: Based on a figure in Levy 1977

Something akin to inter-hemispheric switching can also be elicited in normal subjects. Milner & Dunne (1977) used chimeric stimuli in which the vertical join was hidden by a white strip, the purpose of which was to hinder detection of the incongruity between the two sides of the stimulus. At 100 milliseconds exposure normal subjects had great difficulty detecting that the stimuli were chimeric. On trials in which no awareness of asymmetry was present, the subjects indicated (either manually or verbally) only one face, which was always perceived as complete. Milner and Dunne's subjects also manifested response-dependent processing akin to that seen in Levy's experiment, with verbal responses favouring RVF stimuli and left-handed responses favouring LVF stimuli. One *could* take Milner & Dunne's study to show that normal subjects have two streams of consciousness under these experimental conditions, but it is surely more reasonable to conclude that this study provides further evidence for the switch model.[13]

Further support for the switch model is provided by studies of auditory processing in the split-brain. Because information from each ear projects to both hemispheres, commissurotomy does not itself lead to the lateralization of

[13] See also Landis et al. (1979) and Landis et al. (1981) for other split-brain-like effects in normal subjects.

auditory information. However, lateralization can be achieved by means of a dichotic listening paradigm, in which patients are simultaneously presented with competitive stimuli to each ear. Under these conditions, ipsilateral processing is suppressed in favour of contralateral processing, with inter-hemispheric competition ensuring that information from only a single ear enters consciousness at any one point in time. Moreover, which of the two hemispheres dominates auditory processing can be modulated by task demands. In one study, Milner and colleagues found that patients presented with different digits to each ear complained that they could hear nothing in the left ear even though they had expected to hear numbers in both ears (Milner et al. 1968; see also Milner et al. 1990). Because patients were required to verbally report the numbers, the left hemisphere suppressed input from the ipsilateral ear in favour of input from the contralateral ear. However, right hemisphere activation could be elicited by changing the response required of patients. Subjects were presented with pairs of competing instructions, one to each ear, with each instruction naming an object to be retrieved by touch from amongst a group of nine objects hidden behind a screen. Subjects who were instructed to use their left hand to retrieve objects tended to follow the instruction given to the left ear, with partial to complete neglect of the instruction presented to the right ear. In other words, use of the left hand appears to have favoured right hemisphere processing, leading in turn to the suppression of auditory information entering through the right ear.

We can now see where the arguments for the disunity models of the split-brain go wrong. Consider again the key-ring experiment. The representational and access disunity arguments assume that the patient's two hemispheres must be simultaneously conscious because the stimuli are simultaneously projected to the patient's visual hemifields, and because each hemisphere can respond to the stimulus in its hemi-field as and when required. But both inferences are contentious. Perhaps the ability of patients to respond in this way is the result of consciousness switching rapidly and effortlessly between hemispheres in response to the demands of the patient's context. The hemisphere that is silent on any one trial may be so because it is unconscious rather than because it is unable (or unwilling) to 'speak'.[14]

So much for how the switch model might account for the experimental data—how might it explain everyday unity in the split-brain? There are three lines of

---

[14] Note that the role assigned to contextual demands by the switch account differs from that assigned to them by contextualist versions of the two-streams account (see §9.3). According to the switch account, context plays a role in determining which of the two hemispheres monopolizes consciousness and suppresses the other hemisphere, whereas the two-streams account holds that context determines whether or not the patient's consciousness is unified or divided.

thought we might appeal to here. Most straightforwardly, it is possible that split-brain patients generally get by on a single conscious hemisphere. Split-brain control is usually dominated by the left hemisphere, and experimenters often comment on the difficulties they confront in eliciting responses from the right hemisphere. Even when the right hemisphere does initiate a response, the left frequently takes over and finishes it, sometimes to the detriment of the patient's performance (Nebes & Sperry 1971; Sperry 1974; Zaidel & Sperry 1973).

Secondly, inter-hemispheric switches might be both smooth and rapid, generating the impression that the patient is conscious of more than she is—in much the way that our fluid interaction with the environment perhaps generates the impression that we are conscious of more than we are. The ability of some patients to control both arms from each hemisphere might also mask inter-hemisphere switching. A single right-handed action might be under the control of first one hemisphere and then the other (Kingstone & Gazzaniga 1995).

Finally, it may be that the lower cognitive demands of everyday life allow patients to deploy a kind of non-focal, low-level attention that can straddle both hemispheres. Trevarthen notes that in certain situations patients adopt a 'particular condition of mental orientation', in which awareness is bilaterally distributed. In this condition,

visual events were noticed by commissurotomy patients in an undivided bilateral and temporally unified space around the body and their strength, quality or motion, and general spatial configuration were related to this space much as they would be by normal subjects. (Trevarthen 1974b: 195)

Whereas experimental contexts generally require focused attention, everyday life may permit patients to enter into a state of non-focal awareness of the kind that Trevarthen describes. Moreover, although focal consciousness is restricted to a single hemisphere at a time, it might be possible for non-focal awareness to be distributed across the patient's two hemispheres.

The foregoing goes some distance towards establishing the switch model as a viable account of the structure of consciousness in the split-brain. I turn now to the question of whether this prima facie plausibility can withstand critical scrutiny.

9.6 Objections and replies

Let us examine some objections to the switch model.

First objection: 'We know that split-brain patients have independent attentional systems in each hemisphere. Given the intimate connections

> between attention and consciousness, surely attentional disunity in the
> split-brain constitutes strong evidence for phenomenal disunity.'

Do split-brain patients have independent attentional systems? There is certainly some evidence for this conclusion. An early study found that the two hemispheres could carry out visual discrimination tasks independently and in parallel, suggesting that there was some degree of attentional division in the split-brain (Gazzaniga & Sperry 1966). This finding is supported by a number of other studies that indicate that there is some degree of hemispheric independence in visual attention within the split-brain (Arguin et al. 2000; Luck et al. 1989; Luck et al. 1994; Mangun et al. 1994).

However, these findings need to be balanced against a number of other findings that suggest that attention remains fundamentally unified in the split-brain. Based on an experiment requiring split-brain subjects to either synchronize the taps of their two index fingers or to alternate them as rapidly as possible, Kreuter et al. (1972) concluded that 'a maximum effort by one hemisphere does withdraw capacity from the other, an effect which in the absence of the corpus callosum is presumably mediated by a "capacity distributing system" located in the brain stem' (Kreuter et al. 1972: 460). Holtzman & Gazzaniga (1982) found that cognitive load in one hemisphere interfered with performance in the other hemisphere on a task requiring the subject to match the presented stimulus to a template, and a follow-up study involving lexical memory produced a similar result (Gazzaniga 1987).

Semantic priming studies also suggest that there is attentional integration in the split-brain. In one experiment, L.B. was presented with two words, one to each visual hemi-field, and instructed to categorize (living vs. non-living) the RVF word but ignore the LVF word (Lambert 1991). His performance on this task showed an inhibitory effect from the unattended word that closely resembled that seen in neurologically normal individuals. A subsequent study found normal levels of negative priming in three split-brain patients: LVF items inhibited responses to categorically related items in the RVF (Lambert 1993). Lambert concluded that there is a single system of selective attention in the split-brain, involving sub-cortical connections.

Indeed, even studies of visual attention are far from unanimous in suggesting that the division of the corpus callosum brings about a corresponding division in visual attention. In a spatial priming study, patients were required to produce speeded responses to targets in either the LVF or RVF (Holtzman et al. 1984). Targets were preceded by spatial cues that directed the subject's attention to either the LVF or RVF (focused attention) or both visual fields simultaneously (divided attention). These conditions were compared with neutral trials on which the cue carried no information about the location of the target. The authors found that valid focused attention trials showed a response time advantage over divided attention and neutral trials, suggesting that some form of spatial attention remains unified in the split-brain.

Studies of sustained attention present a somewhat mixed picture. An early study concluded that complete commissurotomy patients had independent systems responsible for sustained attention with this state of divided attention being maintained for prolonged periods (Ellenberg & Sperry 1980). In contrast, a later vigilance study concluded that split-brain patients appear to have a single, and rather depleted, source of sustained attention (Dimond 1976). There were frequent occasions during the course of this study when one or other of the two hemispheres appeared to be completely unresponsive to external stimulation. Perhaps, the author suggested, these periods of unresponsiveness resulted from 'the loss of attentional capacity from one hemisphere, without at the same time leading to an overall loss of attentional capacity' (Dimond 1976: 354).

What should we make of all of this? I'm not sure that there is any tidy story to tell. Gazzaniga once claimed that 'attention remains largely integrated in the split-brain patient' (Gazzaniga 1987: 119). That claim may have been something of an over-statement but it is certainly true that many forms of attention appear to remain integrated in the split-brain. At the very least, split-brain patients do *not* have 'two attentional systems'. Some forms of attention may be split in the split-brain but others appear to remain 'intact', either because attention straddles both hemispheres or because it alternates between hemispheres. In fact, rather than *undermining* the claim that consciousness remains unified in the split-brain the work on attention may actually provide some *support* for the view.

> Second objection: 'The switch model is anatomically implausible. *How* could consciousness move between hemispheres given that the main band of fibres connecting the cortical regions has been severed?'

I don't have a model of how the switch model is neurophysiologically implemented, but it is possible to deflate the objection without such a model. As we have just seen, some attentional systems remain unified in the split-brain, and it is possible that these systems play an important role in 'shuttling' consciousness between hemispheres as and when required. Secondly, we have independent evidence that consciousness can be unified in the absence of a corpus callosum, for individuals born without a corpus callosum (acallosals) show few of the signs of behavioural disunity that characterize the split-brain syndrome.[15] And, third, we know that the mechanisms responsible for modulating wakefulness remain unified in the split-brain. Split-brain patients do not exhibit unihemispheric sleep (Sperry 1974), unlike dolphins, grey whales, white whales, southern sea lions, northern fur seals, and certain bird species.[16] Although the relationship between the mechanisms underlying wakefulness and those underlying consciousness is uncertain, it is possible that the sub-cortical systems implicated in modulating wakefulness and arousal play an important role in maintaining coherent relations between the hemispheres.

> Third objection: 'What about the data that appeared to motivate the partial unity account? How does the switch model account for bilateral integration in the split-brain?'

The first point to make is that the force of the evidence for *conscious* bilateral integration is somewhat uncertain. As I noted earlier (§9.4), it is possible that behaviour that appears to involve inter-hemispheric integration might actually be produced by a single hemisphere exerting control over (say) both the right and left hands. Furthermore, even where inter-hemispheric integration does occur, it might involve only inter-hemispheric priming rather than any kind of phenomenal bridge between the hemispheres.

But suppose that split-brain patients do occasionally have experiences that 'straddle' their two hemispheres: would that be at odds with the switch model? Not necessarily. The critical question is whether such experiences are also unified with experiences that are not themselves unified with each other. Consider D.H., who is split for touch but not vision. Suppose that, at a particular time, D.H. is presented with visual stimuli in both hemi-fields and tactile stimuli to both hands. Perhaps it is possible that D.H.'s visual experiences can be phenomenally unified with either the right hand stimulus or the left hand stimulus, but not both at once. More generally, it is possible that although consciousness can straddle the two hemispheres in different places at different times, it cannot fragment in the way demanded by partial unity. Of course, this is all very speculative. In order to evaluate this proposal we need to know more about what patients such as D.H. can be simultaneously conscious of—in particular, we would need to know whether D.H. can be simultaneously

---

[15] On this point see Ettlinger et al. (1974); Ferriss & Dorsen (1975); Gott & Saul (1978); Lassonde et al. (1988); Lassonde et al. (1991); Reynolds & Jeeves (1977); Saul & Sperry (1968); Chiarello (1980); although see Forget et al. (2009), Jeeves (1979), and Lassonde et al. (1995) for evidence of cognitive impairment in acallosals.

[16] See respectively: Mukhametov et al. (1977); Lyamin et al. (2000); Lyamin et al. (2002a); Lyamin et al. (2002b); Mukhametov et al. (1985); Rattenborg et al. (2001).

conscious of tactile stimulation to both right and left hands. The issue of partial unity must be left open here. Although it could turn out that we need to reject the full-unity version of the switch model in favour of one that allows partial unity, we ought not embrace partial unity just yet.

> Fourth objection: 'The switch model holds that the contents of consciousness are sequentially informed by processing in each hemisphere. If this were so, however, then one would expect patients to report sudden changes in the contents of their consciousness. After all, subjects who experience *binocular* rivalry are aware of the alteration between rival percepts, so why are split-brain patients apparently unaware of the alteration between rival percepts if, as the switch model claims, they are subject to inter-hemispheric rivalry?'

I regard this as one of the most challenging objections to the switch model, and I am not sure that I have a completely satisfactory solution to it. But the following observations do, I think, blunt its force.

For one thing, there is extensive representational overlap between hemispheres (as two-streams theorists have often noted). Perhaps the patient's perspective of the world when her consciousness is informed by right hemisphere processing will not in general be significantly different from that which she enjoys when it is informed by left hemisphere processing. But of course there will be occasions in which the contents of the patient's experience will undergo radical changes as consciousness switches from one hemisphere to another. Should we not expect the patient to notice such changes when they occur? Perhaps not. The distinction between changes in the contents of consciousness and the conscious representation of those changes is no mere formal nicety but has some psychological robustness, as we noted in discussing change blindness. Indeed, it is not uncommon for patients to be unaware of quite radical changes to the contents of their own consciousness (see Chapter 7). For example, patients with achromatopsia (agnosia for colour) frequently fail to realize that they have lost their experience of colour, and are often puzzled by questions about the reliability of their colour vision (Cowey 2009). Unilateral neglect furnishes us with even more striking examples of the failure to keep track of 'gaps' in one's own consciousness. In a famous study, patients were asked to imagine themselves standing in Milan's Piazza del Duomo with their back to the cathedral (Bisiach & Luzzatti 1978). As one might predict, they failed to describe buildings on their left. When asked immediately afterwards to describe what they would see if looking at the cathedral from the opposite end of the square, the same patients named the previously neglected buildings but neglected those that they had just mentioned. At no point did the patients attempt to integrate their successive reports, nor did they express any concern about the obvious inconsistency between them. In the same way that the ability to track perceptual continuity is impaired by the very damage that causes neglect, so too it is possible that the very operation which causes inter-hemispheric rivalry in the split-brain also prevents patients from becoming introspectively aware of that rivalry. Perhaps, as I noted in Chapter 7, it is possible that introspective access to an experience requires activating the very neural areas that generated it in the first place (Bisiach 1988). If that were the case, then in order to be aware of inter-hemispheric switches in consciousness the patient would be required to simultaneously activate both hemispheres—precisely what the switch account rules out.

> Fifth objection: 'Suppose that the contents of consciousness in the split-brain do switch between hemispheres in the way that you've been suggesting. Wouldn't it be more plausible to describe such a scenario as one in which the subject has *two* streams of consciousness which are sequentially active rather than a *single* stream of consciousness whose contents are drawn from each hemisphere in succession? Come to think of it, what exactly is the difference between claiming that consciousness in the split-brain switches between two streams of cognitive activity and claiming that split-brain patients have two streams of consciousness that operate sequentially?'

Let us begin with the question of what, if anything, distinguishes these two versions of the switch model. If we think of a stream of consciousness in purely phenomenological terms, then the difference between the one-stream and two-streams versions of the switch model reduces to the question of whether inter-hemispheric switching interrupts the continuity of consciousness. If the split-brain subject enjoys no interruption in the continuity of consciousness, then we ought to say that he or she has but a single stream of consciousness. Of course, it is difficult to know whether or not inter-hemispheric switching brings with it a phenomenal gap—a hiatus in experience. The patient *reports* no such gap, but this has little to no evidential weight, for if there were such a gap it would not be available for report.

If we individuate streams of consciousness in terms of the underlying mechanism(s) responsible for consciousness, then the difference between the one-stream and two-streams versions of the switch model turns on whether there is a single mechanism of consciousness in the split-brain or two. On this point there is a clear difference between the two versions of the switch model. The single-stream model holds that consciousness in the split-brain patient has a singular (presumably sub-cortical) ground, whereas the two-streams model holds that the left and right hemispheres have independent mechanisms of consciousness—that there is no common substrate of consciousness in the split-brain. On this conception of streams of consciousness, it seems to me that the evidence clearly favours the one-stream model. There is but one substrate of consciousness in the split-brain, and it is grounded in an (undivided) sub-cortical network. Right and left hemisphere activation in the split-brain generates conscious content only because it is suitably incorporated into that system (see also §10.6).

9.7 Conclusion

I have argued that the near-consensus in favour of disunity models of the split-brain is far from secure. Such models come in two forms: two-streams models and partial unity models. Two-streams models face challenges on two fronts: not only do they struggle to account for the unity of the split-brain patient's everyday behaviour they may also be at odds with the fact that patients demonstrate some degree of inter-hemispheric integration within experimental contexts. Does this mean that we should think of the split-brain in terms of partial unity? I think not. Although partial unity models may provide a better account of the behavioural evidence than two-streams models, it is not at all clear that such models are coherent. Preferable to both two-streams and partial unity models is the switch model, which—I argued—provides the best account of both the behavioural disunities that split-brain patients exhibit under experimental conditions and the behavioural unities that they exhibit outside of such contexts.

Of course, any claim about 'the' structure of consciousness in the split-brain must be at best provisional. Despite the undoubted utility of the notion of a 'split-brain syndrome', the individual differences between split-brain patients are not insignificant and should not be overlooked (Kinsbourne 1974). Indeed, there may not even be a single account of 'the' structure of consciousness in any one split-brain patient. Perhaps there are patients who have a single unified consciousness in some contexts, two streams of consciousness in other contexts, and a partially unified consciousness in still other contexts. Leaving these speculations to one side, it is undoubtedly the case that the split-brain data are extremely complex, and it would be foolish to pretend that the evidence points unequivocally in favour of the switch model. However, that is not my claim. My claim, rather, is that the switch model ought to be regarded as a serious rival to the two-streams and partial unity models. And if the switch model is right, then the split-brain syndrome does not undermine the unity thesis.

Does this mean that the unity thesis is secure? I think so. In Chapter 6 we saw that there is no good evidence of phenomenal disunity within everyday forms of conscious experience. In Chapter 7 I argued that although anosognosia, schizophrenia, and multiplicity involve the breakdown of certain forms of the unity of consciousness, none of these phenomena threaten the unity thesis. In Chapter 8 we saw that the appearances of disunity within hypnosis can be accounted for in terms of switches in consciousness. And in this chapter I have defended a parallel model of the structure of consciousness in the split-brain syndrome. The upshot of all this appears to be that there is indeed a deep and robust sense in which consciousness is unified, a sense that is captured by the unity thesis.

With the conclusion of this chapter I also conclude Part II of this book. In Part III I examine some of the potential implications of the unity of consciousness. In particular, I will explore ways in which the unity of consciousness might inform our understanding of consciousness, bodily experience, and the self.

PART III. IMPLICATIONS

10

The Quilt of Consciousness

Whether spun from the fabric of philosophical imagination or patched together on the basis of fMRI images, few theories of consciousness are constructed with the unity of consciousness in mind. This is rather odd, for if consciousness is unified—as I have argued it is—then our models of consciousness ought surely to be informed by this fact. Any adequate account of consciousness must be consistent with, and perhaps even explain, the unity of consciousness. In this chapter I examine theories of consciousness with respect to how well they might accommodate this constraint. In order to dampen down expectations, let me say from the outset that I am not in the business of solving 'the hard problem' (Chalmers 1996) or closing 'the explanatory gap' (Levine 1983). I am inclined to think that explaining how to get experience from neural activity is not unlike trying to get 'numbers from biscuits or ethics from rhubarb' (McGinn 1993: 155), and neither of those activities strike me as useful investments of either my time or yours. Instead, my aim is the rather more modest one of sketching a framework that might inform theory-building in consciousness studies. My hope is to dislodge some bad ideas, and put some better ones in their place.

10.1 Atomism versus holism

One way to distinguish between theories of consciousness is in terms of how they conceive of the structure of the phenomenal field. Let us distinguish two general orientations that can be adopted here: an *atomistic* orientation and a *holistic* orientation. Theorists who adopt an atomistic orientation assume that the phenomenal field is composed of 'atoms of consciousness'—states that are independently conscious. Holists, by contrast, hold that the components of the phenomenal field are conscious only as the components of that field. Holists deny that there are any independent conscious states that need to be bound together to form a phenomenal field. Holists can allow that the phenomenal field can be *formally* decomposed into discrete experiences, but they will deny that these elements are independent atoms or units of consciousness.[1]

The contrast between atomism and holism is no mere formal nicety but has important methodological implications. Atomists will be inclined to recommend a 'bottom-up' approach to the study of consciousness according to which we should focus on understanding the mechanisms responsible for generating the atoms of consciousness. Holists, by contrast, will have deep reservations about this approach. They will doubt whether we can understand consciousness by focusing on the components of the phenomenal field in a piecemeal manner. Instead, the holist will recommend a top-down methodology, according to which we should look for the mechanisms implicated in the construction of the entire phenomenal field.

The distinction between atomism and holism cuts across many of the standard ways of classifying theories of consciousness. Let us consider how the distinction might play out within the context of three broad approaches to consciousness: monitoring approaches, functionalist approaches, and neurally based approaches.

Monitoring accounts of consciousness hold that a mental state is conscious in virtue of being monitored in some way or another.[2] Discussion of this approach has focused on the nature of the monitoring representation ('Is it thought-like or perception-like?') and on the relationship between the monitored state and the monitoring state ('Might the monitoring state be identical to the monitored state or must they be distinct?'). In contrast, there has been rather little discussion of whether monitoring accounts of consciousness should be developed in atomistic terms or holistic terms. The monitoring approach as such can be developed in either direction, and in fact both atomistic and holistic versions of the monitoring approach can be found in the literature. Rosenthal (2003) defends an atomistic version of the monitoring approach, although his account has holistic elements insofar as he holds that the monitoring thoughts responsible for consciousness 'clump together' sets of monitored states. Van Gulick, on the other hand, defends a holistic version of the monitoring approach, according to which the 'transformation from unconscious to conscious state is not merely a matter of directing a separate and distinct meta-state onto the lower-order state but of "recruiting" it into the globally integrated state that is the

---

[1] This distinction has something in common with Shoemaker's (2003) distinction between atomistic and holistic theories of consciousness and even more in common with Searle's (2000) distinction between building block and unified field models of consciousness, but neither author quite captures the contrast that I am after here.

[2] For important collections of papers on monitoring accounts of consciousness see Gennaro (2004) and Kriegel & Williford (2006).

momentary realization of the agent's shifting transient conscious awareness' (van Gulick 2004: 74f.).

The functionalist approach to consciousness can also be developed in either atomistic or holistic directions. At the heart of functionalist accounts is the claim that a state is conscious in virtue of the functional role that it plays within the subject's cognitive economy, where this role is typically identified with some kind of capacity for broad cognitive and behavioural control. Much of the discussion of functionalism has focused on its epistemic status ('Is it an *a priori* truth or an *a posteriori* one?') and on the question of how to best characterize the functional role distinctive of conscious states ('What exactly does broad cognitive and behavioural control amount to?'), but there has been rather less discussion of the implications of functionalism for accounts of the structure of consciousness.

Many of the most influential versions of functionalism are most naturally understood in atomistic terms. Consider, for example, Dretske's (1995) account of consciousness, according to which phenomenally conscious mental states are identified with non-conceptual representations that supply information to a cognitive system for calibration and use in the control and regulation of behaviour (Dretske 1995: 19). On this account there is good reason to suppose that (say) a visual state and affective state might qualify as independent atoms of consciousness, for the two states are likely to control and regulate behaviour independently of each other. Consider also Tye's (1995) PANIC model of consciousness. This account qualifies as a version of functionalism in virtue of the fact that the 'P' in his acronym stands for 'poised', where a state is poised exactly when its content stands ready and in position to make a direct impact on the subject's belief/desire system (1995: 138). Tye's account of consciousness is *formally* holistic for he holds that the only states that qualify as experiences are entire streams of consciousness (see §2.1), but it is atomistic in spirit, for there is nothing in the account which ensures that various non-conceptual representations will be poised to control thought and action conjointly—that is, as the components of a single state. Other versions of functionalism are more naturally understood in holistic terms. For example, Shoemaker claims that 'the factors that go into making a particular mental state conscious are inextricably intertwined with those that go into making different states 'co-conscious', i.e. go into constituting a unified state of consciousness of which that state is a part' (2003: 58). Although Shoemaker's account falls short of a full-blown commitment to holism, it clearly has more of a holistic orientation than do the versions of functionalism developed by Dretske and Tye.

Finally, let us examine how the contrast between atomism and holism plays out in the context of neurally-inspired accounts of consciousness. A prominent (and indeed radical) version of atomism is defended by Zeki and Bartels (1999). They argue that activity at each node of a processing–perceptual system generates its own 'micro-consciousness'. These micro-consciousnesses are independent units of consciousness that involve only the registration of fine-grained conscious features—colour, motion, shape, and so on. A less extreme version of atomism appears to be implicit in Lamme's recurrent processing account of consciousness, according to which visual experience involves recurrent (or re-entrant) processing between lower and higher regions within the visual cortex (Lamme 2006; Lamme & Roelfsema 2000). Although Lamme's focus is on visual experience, the recurrent processing approach can be applied to consciousness more generally. When so extended it appears to generate an atomistic conception of consciousness, for there is nothing in the approach itself which limits the subject to one stream of recurrent processing at a time, or which requires multiple streams—streams located within different perceptual systems—to be bound together into a single recurrent cascade.

Other neurally based models of consciousness are more naturally understood in holistic terms. Consider the global workspace approach to consciousness, originally proposed by Baars (1988) and developed more recently by Dehaene and Naccache (2001). Global workspace accounts hold that 'conscious experience emerges from a nervous system in which multiple input processors compete for access to a broadcasting capability; the winning processor can disseminate its information globally through the brain' (Baars 1993: 282). This approach suggests a holistic picture of consciousness, insofar as its advocates typically insist that entry into the workspace is gated by a 'winner takes all' competition, with only a single representational state admitted to the workspace at any one point in time (see e.g. Dehaene & Changeux 2004).

We have seen that the contrast between atomistic and holistic approaches to consciousness cuts across many of the established classifications for theories of consciousness. My interest in this chapter is not with the question of whether theories of consciousness should be pursued within (say) a monitoring framework or a neural framework, but whether we should think of consciousness in holistic terms or atomistic terms. It will come as little surprise that I will argue in favour of holism. My case against atomism begins in §10.2 and §10.3, where I argue that various aspects of the representational unity of consciousness put pressure on some of the more extreme manifestations of atomism. However, these sections are best thought of as entrées to the main business of this chapter, which takes place in §10.4. There, I argue that atomistic accounts of consciousness are at odds with the unity thesis, and conclude that we should adopt a holistic conception of the structure of consciousness. §10.5 identifies and attempts to disarm a number of objections to holism, and §10.6 presents a sketch of what a plausible version of holism might look like. But before we turn to the unity thesis and its implications, we need to first examine possible constraints imposed by the representational unity of consciousness.

10.2 Binding

In a special issue of *Neuron* dedicated to the binding problem Adina Roskies asks, 'Will the solution to the binding problem be the solution to the mystery of consciousness?' (Roskies 1999: 9). Roskies has not been alone in suggesting that the connections between consciousness and the binding problem run deep, and it is widely held that a model of binding might shed essential light on the nature of consciousness itself.[3] Although I doubt that binding will unlock the puzzle of consciousness, I do think that it provides us with reason to reject certain radical versions of atomism.

Let us start with binding. Most generally, binding is the process of bringing information together—synthesizing it, as Kant would say. As Kant also noted, binding takes a number of forms. One form of binding occurs when one applies a concept on the basis of perceptual experience, and in so doing integrates conceptual and perceptual representations. Binding of another sort takes place when one integrates a sequence of perceptual experiences, and builds up a global representation of one's environment. But the kind of binding that has been the focus of 'the binding problem' is *feature binding*: the integration of perceptual features—colour, shape, texture, identity, and so on—into coherent percepts of objects. Feature binding is essential to object unity (Chapter 1).

Because distinct types of perceptual features are processed in different locations within cognitive architecture, there is a question about how the brain binds these features together so as to create representations of integrated perceptual objects. In fact, there are really two feature binding problems: a *selection* problem and a *tagging* problem (Robertson 2003; Treisman 1996, 2003). Suppose that you are looking at a grey donkey carrying a child who is wearing a blue jacket. Your visual system needs to do two things here. First, it needs to select the right features to put together: it needs to represent the donkey as grey and the jacket as blue rather than vice versa. Secondly, it needs to make sure that those features which have been selected are 'tagged'—that is, bound together as a functional unit and made available as such to downstream systems. Of most interest to us here is the tagging component of the binding problem.

---

[3] See e.g. Engel et al. (1999a); Revonsuo (1999); Sauvé (1999).

Some theorists have suggested that the binding problem is a pseudo-problem, a relic of a long-discredited commitment to some kind of Cartesianism.

Those for whom the consciousness module is a lost cause appeal to so-called 'binding', although they do see it as a 'problem'. Because the attributes of a perceived object appear bound, there must be some brain-glue (synchrony, co-oscillation?), that conjoins the separate and scattered representations of its attributes into the object representation . . . This would make sense if there were an inner observer for whose viewing pleasure the screens of the Cartesian Theatre display all this binding. But the brain is unsupervised and uncentered, and no one is watching. (Kinsbourne 2000: 546)

Kinsbourne is right to point out that there is no homunculus inspecting images projected onto the screen of subjectivity, but the binding problem survives the closure of the Cartesian Theatre. No matter how unsupervised and uncentred neural functioning might be, we still need an account of how distributed features are bound together to form representations of unified objects, and how—once bound—they are kept together so as to exert cognitive and behavioural influence as a unit.

So much for binding itself—why think that binding has anything to do with consciousness? As best I can tell, there are two reasons why theorists have been attracted to the thought binding might bear on the analysis of consciousness. The first of these reasons concerns the influence of temporal synchrony accounts of binding. Synchrony accounts of binding hold that the tagging of perceptual features is achieved by the phase-locked activation of distributed neural areas.[4] The temporal synchrony model replaces so-called 'grandmother cells' (that is, cells that fire only in response to particular objects such as one's grandmother) with clusters of neurons that respond to specific, 'low-level' features.[5] Suppose that one is viewing a scene containing a red square and a green circle. The idea is that the neurons that code for redness and squareness would fire in synchrony with each other as would the neurons that code for green and circularity, but the first sets of neurons would fire out of phase with the second set of neurons. However, temporal synchrony would provide a bridge between binding and consciousness only if there were evidence that synchronization is involved in both feature binding and consciousness. There is indeed some evidence in

---

[4] For representative defences of the temporal synchrony approach to binding see Milner (1974); von der Malsburg (1995); Eckhorn (1999); Engel et al. (1999a); Engel & Singer (2001); Roeflsema et al. (1997); Singer (2009); Singer & Gray (1995). For critical discussion of the approach see Gold (1999); O'Reilly et al. (2003); Shadlen & Movshon (1999).

[5] This account of binding is sometimes referred to as the '40Hz hypothesis' because the relevant synchrony is thought to occur at around 40Hz (in fact, between 35 and 70Hz). However this label is somewhat misleading in that it suggests that the hypothesis requires synchronized oscillations, but in fact non-oscillatory signals can also be synchronized (Engel et al. (1999b)).

favour of synchrony models of binding (although its force is highly disputed), but I know of no evidence implicating synchrony in the explanation of consciousness. In fact, the only reason to think that temporal synchrony might be implicated in models of consciousness involves appealing to a prior link between binding and consciousness, which is precisely what is in question at this point.

The second motivation for thinking that the mechanisms of binding and those of consciousness might be deeply connected derives from the fact binding and consciousness are robustly *correlated*. This thought has two components: feature binding occurs only in the context of conscious representations, and consciousness doesn't harbour unbound features. This correlation wouldn't demonstrate that there is an explanatory or constitutive connection between binding and consciousness, but it would certainly provide that view with some support. But is there a robust correlation between consciousness and binding? Let us begin with the question of whether binding requires consciousness. Is it the case that features must be conscious in order to be bound together, or can binding occur outside of consciousness?

Although influential discussions have assumed that consciousness is required for feature binding (Crick & Koch 1990a, 1990b), it is not difficult to find examples of feature binding outside of consciousness. Patients with blindsight appear to be capable of binding together primitive features in their blind field (Kentridge et al. 1999, 2004). Certain forms of priming also suggest that feature binding can occur independently of consciousness. In order for the word 'dog' to function as a semantic prime one must bind together its parts so as to form a representation of the word 'dog' as such (Neumann & Klotz 1994; Marcel 1983). Consider also the kind of priming that occurs in unilateral neglect (Ladavas et al. 1993; Farah 1997). Processing of a word presented in the right visual field can be facilitated by the brief presentation of an associated word in the neglected left visual field, even though the neglected word appears not to enter consciousness. In order for the neglected word to facilitate right visual field processing it needs to be represented as such, and this of course requires the binding of its constituent features. A further form of visual binding that occurs outside of consciousness concerns the integration of (unconscious) dorsal stream with (conscious) ventral stream representations. In short, there is ample reason to think that feature binding is not restricted to consciousness.

Consciousness may not be necessary for feature binding, but perhaps feature binding is necessary for consciousness. In fact, it is probably this claim that represents the most influential conception of the link between binding and consciousness:

Conscious access in perception is always to bound objects and events ... Experienced objects have colours, locations, orientations. They may not always be correctly bound;

in fact, when we first look at a complex multiobject scene they probably are not. But it seems impossible to even imagine free-floating shapes, colours, or sizes. Using language or other symbols, we can abstract particular properties (a kind of unbinding), but this is not part of our perceptual experience. (Treisman 2003: 97; see also Engel et al. 1999a, 1999b)

According to what we might call the *binding constraint*, perceptual features cannot enter consciousness without first being bound together in the form of objects. If true the binding constraint would demonstrate that the mechanisms of consciousness must be 'downstream' of the mechanisms responsible for feature binding. It would also have implications for the size of the minimal units of perceptual consciousness.

Is the binding constraint true? It is certainly extremely plausible. However, it is difficult to be more definitive than that without an account of what qualifies as a perceptual feature. We may have a rough and ready idea of what the features of visual experience are—although even here there is ample room for debate—but our grip on what counts as a feature is much less secure once we leave the domain of vision. What are the feature of auditory experience? Are they pitch, volume, and timbre? What are the 'features' of olfactory experience? And what about other forms of sensory consciousness, such as pain? Is the aversive character of a pain one feature, its felt bodily location another, and its qualitative character—its 'painfulness'—a third? These questions cannot be answered by appeals to introspection but require detailed accounts of the architecture of perception. Pending the development of such accounts any definitive verdict on the tenability of the binding constraint would be premature.

What we can say, however, is that there is at least a *prima facie* case for thinking that certain kinds of sensory features can enter consciousness without first being bound. Consider experiences of 'free-floating' anxiety. As best I can tell such features are not bound to anything. They are not bound to particular body parts, nor are they bound to one's body as a whole. Consider also olfaction. Whatever features olfactory experience might involve, it is far from clear that they must be bound together in the form of object- or event-involving percepts in order to enter consciousness. The fact that olfactory experience lacks the rich spatial structure of (say) visual experience raises questions about just what a binding-constraint for olfaction might even look like.

But even if certain kinds of sensory features can enter consciousness in an unbound form, feature binding can still provide us with a robust constraint on theories of consciousness, for there is good reason to think that perceptual features of most kinds are conscious only in the context of bound percepts.

And if this is right, then certain radical forms of atomism—such as Zeki and Bartels's 'micro-consciousness' approach—must be false. According to Zeki and Bartels, the units of visual consciousness can be identified with the perceptual features—colour, motion, shape, and so on—that are processed at the various 'nodes' of the visual system. But if that were so, then these features ought to be capable of independent existence within the stream of consciousness, and that doesn't seem to be the case. Contrary to what Zeki and Bartels suggest, we should not think of feature binding as a process of 'bringing different conscious experiences together' (Bartels & Zeki 1998: 2330), for there is in general no perceptual experience prior to feature binding. Binding might not be the sword that severs the Gordian knot of consciousness, but it is surely a form of conscious unity that no theorist can afford to ignore.

10.3 Inter-sensory integration

The binding constraint places pressure on some of the more extreme manifestations of atomism but it is not a particularly challenging constraint to meet and few versions of atomism fall foul of it. More challenging is a constraint to be explored in this section—a constraint of representational integration.

The commonplace distinction between the senses encourages us to think of the stream of experiences as divided into modality-specific chunks. We naturally fall into the temptation of referring to visual experiences, auditory experiences, and so on. Now, although there is a perfectly legitimate sense in which we can think of the stream of consciousness as containing modality-specific segments it would be a mistake to think of such states as atoms of consciousness.

We can see why by considering the phenomenon of inter-modal integration.[6] There is now a huge literature devoted to the complex and extensive ways in which the contents of experiences within one modality are intimately dependent on those in another modality. Consider first the temporal content of experience. In what is known as 'temporal ventriloquism', the subsequent presentation of an auditory stimulus changes the perceived temporal location of a previously presented visual stimulus (Morein-Zamir et al. 2003; see also Kamitani & Shimojo 2001). In fact, following a flash with a sound moves the perceived time of the flash back whilst following it with another sound moves it

---

[6]   For reviews of the empirical literature see Calvert et al. (2004); Driver & Noesselt (2008); Ernst & Bülthoff (2004); Lalanne & Lorenceau (2004); Macaluso & Driver (2005); Spence & Driver (2004); Spence and Squire (2003); Spence et al. forthcoming; Stein & Meredith (1993); Stein et al. (2009). For reflections on the theoretical implications of this research see Shimojo & Shams (2001); O'Callaghan (2008) and forthcoming.

forward in time (Fendrich & Corballis 2001). In another example of the intermodal dependence of temporal content, the perceived rate of visual flicker can be modulated by the rate at which a concurrent stream of auditory input is presented (Recanzone 2003; McDonald et al. 2005). The window within which the temporal structure of visual and auditory experience is integrated is not fixed but dynamic, its parameters change in order to accommodate the fact that sound increasingly lags behind vision as the source of the sound increases in distance (Sugita & Suzuki 2003).

Generally speaking, the temporal content of audition modulates that of vision rather than vice versa, but the converse is the case when it comes to the spatial content of perceptual experience. Here visual information generally dominates that of other perceptual modalities, such as audition (Howard & Templeton 1966; Bertelson 1999) and touch (Pavani et al. 2000; Rock & Victor 1964). Indeed, the influence of the spatial content of vision on other modalities can be quite profound. For example, the direction of visual motion can actually *reverse* the experienced direction of an auditory stream (Zapparoli & Reatto 1969; Soto-Faraco et al. 2004).

Intermodal effects are not limited to the spatial and temporal contents of experience but can even modulate the *number* of objects that subjects experience. In what is known as the auditory-flash illusion, subjects will misperceive a single flash of light as two flashes when it is paired with two beeps (Shams et al. 2000). Intermodal effects are not limited to properties that are available via more than one modality (the common sensibles) but can also be found for properties that are proprietary to a particular sense, such as colour. For example, tactile stimulation at a particular location can improve the perceptual discrimination of colour at that and nearby locations.[7]

Intermodal integration also occurs for high-level, categorical information. Perhaps the most well known of such effects is the McGurk effect, in which dubbing the phoneme /ba/ onto the lip movements for /ga/, produces, in normal adults, an auditory percept of the phoneme /da/ (McGurk & McDonald 1976). More recently, Chen and Spence (2010) have shown that semantically congruent auditory input can help subjects identify masked pictures. Subjects who had been played the sound of a barking dog were more likely to recognize a masked picture as that of a dog than were controls who had been exposed only to white noise.

Is the extent of inter-perceptual integration surprising? Perhaps. We might have assumed that a more reliable architecture would have entrusted the job of

---

[7] Spence et al. (2004); see also Frassinetti et al. (2002); Lovelace et al. (2003); McDonald et al. (2000).

adjudicating inter-sensory conflict to post-conscious executive systems. But this is not the cognitive architecture that we have inherited. Instead, the brain resolves most inter-sensory disputes prior to consciousness on the basis of '*a priori*' assumptions about the relative reliabilities of the various senses in particular contexts, with the result that 'the conscious subject' is unaware of the very existence of the disputes.[8] But although this arrangement might seem surprising, a moment's reflection reveals its advantages: eliminating inconsistencies prior to consciousness frees post-conscious mechanisms up for other tasks. (And of course some inconsistency does make it through to consciousness, as we noted in Chapter 3.)

The ubiquity of inter-modal integration puts further pressure on atomistic approaches to consciousness. Not only does it provide additional evidence against the view that perceptual features qualify as atoms of consciousness, it also tells against more moderate forms of atomism that conceive of the units of consciousness in modality-specific terms. Consider, for example, O'Brien and Opie's endorsement of the atomistic view:

our instantaneous phenomenal experience is a complex amalgam of distinct and separable conscious events; not a serial stream, but a mass of tributaries running in parallel...a conscious individual does not have a 'single consciousness,' but several distinct phenomenal consciousnesses, at least one for each of the senses, running in parallel. (O'Brien & Opie 1998: 387 see also O'Brien & Opie 2000.)

It is not obvious how this conception of consciousness might be squared with inter-modal integration. How could we account for the subtle interplay between the contents of the various modalities if the senses are a 'mass of tributaries running in parallel'? Inter-modal integration suggests that the stream of perceptual experience is best thought of as highly braided rather than as composed of sense-specific tributaries that generate experience in splendid isolation from each other. The senses are not hermetically sealed off from each other, but function as highly interdependent channels. A subject's perceptual experience in any one 'modality' is the result of complex interactions between any number of sensory channels, and the hope that one might be able to identify stable, modality-specific mechanisms underlying it is, I suggest, a vain one. Inter-sensory integration does not itself show that the atomistic conception of consciousness is untenable, but it does suggest that whatever atoms of consciousness there might be are unlikely to take the form of modality-specific chunks.

[8] See Alais & Burr (2004); Ernst & Bülthoff (2004); and Helbig & Ernst (2007).

10.4 Implications of the unity thesis

Although both the binding constraint and intermodal integration put pressure on certain manifestations of atomism, it would be stretching things to say that they are at odds with atomism as such. But let me turn now to a unity constraint that does put pressure on all forms of atomism: the unity thesis.

Atomists hold that the subject's total phenomenal state is built up out of units of consciousness. As we have noted, there are a number of ways in which atomists might conceive of the 'size' of these units. Radical atomists will hold that the atoms of consciousness are perceptual features. More moderate forms of atomism will suggest that the atoms of consciousness can be thought of in terms of modality-specific experiences, such as integrated visual representations of scenes. Still other forms of atomism might conceive of the units of consciousness as having a structure that cuts across the traditional distinction between the senses—for example, the atomist might suggest that the units of consciousness correspond to multi-modal representations of objects. But whatever their take on the units of consciousness, atomists of all stripes must account for the fact that those units don't occur as independent elements of consciousness but as the components of an overall phenomenal field. How might atomists respond to this challenge?

One response is to simply deny that the atoms of consciousness *are* unified within the context of an overall phenomenal field. According to this kind of atomist, the so-called unity of consciousness is nothing more than illusion. Readers who have made it thus far will not be surprised that I am inclined to simply set this response to one side. In my view the only tenable response to this challenge is to posit a mechanism that might account for the fact that the atoms of consciousness are generally—if not invariably—unified with each other. This mechanism would not be responsible for consciousness as such. Instead, its role would be to ensure that the subject's conscious states are phenomenally unified with each other—subsumed by a total phenomenal state. Holists, of course, have no need to posit a mechanism that is specifically responsible for phenomenal binding, for the holist holds that the components of a subject's total phenomenal state are brought into being *as* the constituents of that state.

Although some atomists have recognized the need for phenomenal binding (see e.g. Zeki and Bartels 1999), most atomists have been curiously reluctant to discuss, let alone posit, such a mechanism. There is good reason for this reluctance, for there is little evidence of its existence. If there were such a mechanism then we would expect it to occasionally malfunction, with the result that the subject would be left with phenomenal fragments—

units of consciousness that would no longer be integrated into phenomenal wholes. But to the best of my knowledge neuropsychology furnishes us with no examples of phenomenal fragmentation. As we have seen in the preceding chapters, although there are plenty of syndromes in which other forms of the unity of consciousness break down, there are no syndromes in which the *phenomenal* unity of consciousness breaks down—at least, so I claim.

Of course, my defence of the unity thesis is open to any number of challenges. A critic might argue that my treatment of (say) the split-brain syndrome is unsatisfactory, and that there are periods during which split-brain patients have two streams of consciousness. But even if this were right it would not provide much comfort for the atomist given that the kinds of breakdowns in phenomenal unity that could conceivably characterize the split-brain hardly reveal the *pre-existing* structure of consciousness. Although there is some elasticity within the atomistic approach as to how 'big' the atoms of consciousness are, on no plausible version of the view is the typical subject's total phenomenal state composed of only two atoms, one grounded in each hemisphere. Parallel points apply to each of the other syndromes that might provide counter-examples to the unity thesis. In each case, the kinds of splits that might be thought to occur would be imposed on the structure of consciousness 'from without' rather than along pre-existing fault-lines. (The appropriate analogy for such breakdowns in phenomenal unity would be that of splitting a coconut with an axe rather than segmenting an orange into pieces). Feature binding and inter-sensory integration 'problematize' certain radical forms of atomism, but the unity thesis suggests that the entire approach is wrong-headed.

This 'unity thesis argument' is the star witness in the case against atomism, but it does not carry the case on its own. Two further features of consciousness argue in favour of holism. We might call the first of these features the *dynamic* structure of consciousness. As Koch (2004) has argued, entry into the stream of consciousness can be thought of as taking the form of a competition between coalitions of contents, each one of which struggles to make its voice heard above that of its fellows. Coalitions that win this competition—whether by top-down control or stimulus-driven attention—enter the stream of consciousness; the losers hover in the wings, waiting for their moment. The forces behind these dynamic changes are global and domain-general in nature. Whether or not a particular coalition makes its mark on consciousness depends not on its intrinsic properties but on its strength relative to those with which it is in competition. These dynamic features are hard to square with atomism. Why should entry into consciousness be dynamically gated in this way if different types of conscious states are produced by autonomous mechanisms?

Holism also receives some support from the fact that background states (or 'levels') of consciousness are domain-general. Background states of consciousness typically characterize the full spectrum of a subject's conscious states rather than some particular subset of those states. It is *the subject* that is awake, dreaming, hypnotized, delirious, and so on. We might think of background states of consciousness as ways in which the subject's overall phenomenal field is modulated. The global nature of background states of consciousness is also evident in transitions between consciousness and unconsciousness. Typically, the re-acquisition of consciousness takes place all at once rather than in (say) modality-specific stages. Consciousness may dawn gradually, but it dawns gradually over the whole. Similarly, when consciousness is lost it is typically lost 'as a whole' rather than in (say) modality-sized chunks. Although their force may be difficult to quantify, these indirect considerations provide additional reasons to embrace a holistic approach to the structure of consciousness in favour of atomism.

10.5 Correlates, causes, and counterfactuals

Although few theorists might describe themselves as card-carrying atomists, the view has wide currency within the contemporary literature. In fact, one might even describe it as a kind of orthodoxy. In this section I consider three of the most influential—and, indeed, potent—motivations for the view.

The central argument for atomism takes as its point of departure the claim that the neural mechanisms underpinning consciousness—the neural 'correlates of consciousness', as they are often described—are not to be found at any one location but are scattered throughout the brain.

The multiplicity of cortical loci where correlations with awareness have been found provides some evidence against one of the oldest ideas about consciousness, that the contents of awareness are represented in a single unitary system. . . . Instead, the data described above seem more consistent with a view in which the contents of current awareness can be represented in many different neural structures. However, one could still argue that the neural correlates described above are not in fact the actual representations that constitute the conscious percept, but merely information that is likely to make it onto the (as-yet-undiscovered) screen of awareness, so the possibility of such a unitary awareness system is not definitively ruled out by these data. In contrast to the idea of a unitary and content-general Cartesian theatre of awareness, the data summarized above fit more naturally with the following simple hypothesis: *the neural correlates of awareness of a particular visual attribute are found in the very neural structure that perceptually analyzes that attribute.* (Kanwisher 2001: 97, emphasis in original)

Generalizing Kanwisher's comments beyond vision, we might put the challenge as follows: doesn't the fact that the neural correlates of consciousness are distributed across a multiplicity of cortical loci demonstrate that consciousness has an atomistic structure?[9]

I think not. Let us begin by noting that recent developments in cognitive neuroscience paint a rather more dynamic picture of the relationship between neural structures and the analysis of particular attributes than that suggested by Kanwisher's comments. According to a recent review, 'even classic sensory-specific areas (perhaps even primary cortices) can be influenced by multisensory interplay' (Driver & Noesselt 2008: 14). Receptive fields are rarely fixed and stable, but respond to changes in the creature's behavioural orientation. For example, eye position can modulate activity in primary auditory cortex (Fu et al. 2004; Werner-Reiss et al. 2003). In fact, many of the examples of inter-sensory integration reviewed in §10.3 are likely to result from the inter-sensory modulation of early perceptual areas.[10]

Even so, the atomist might respond, there is surely *some* sense in which the neural correlates of consciousness are localized to particular cortical areas. How might the holist account for this fact?

To fix ideas, let us consider one particular example of neural localization: the relationship between visual experiences of motion and activity in MT.[11] This relationship is clearly an intimate one. In order to selectively modulate such experiences one ought to target MT activity rather than activity in some other part of the brain. Of course, one needn't target MT if one wants to manipulate the subject's visual experience of motion but is not too particular about what other kinds of effects one might have on the subject's experience. For example, one could intervene on brain-stem systems. Not only would an intervention of this kind lead to the elimination of visual experiences of motion, it may also lead to the elimination of all forms of consciousness. These reflections show that we need an account of the neural correlates of consciousness that does justice to the

---

[9] Although I follow tradition and refer to the neural states underpinning consciousness as its neural *correlates*, I do not assume that these states are merely correlated with consciousness. In fact, I think it likely that they stand in a rather more intimate relation—such as realization, constitution, or even identity—to conscious states. However, I use the relatively non-committal 'correlate' in order to avoid taking a stance on the question of just how neural states and conscious states are related. See Chalmers (2000) and Hohwy (2007) for discussion of the notion of a neural correlate of consciousness.

[10] See Ghazanfar et al. (2005); Kayser & Logothetis (2007); Lakatos et al. (2007); Molholm et al. (2002); Schroeder & Foxe (2005); Senkowski et al. (2005); Watkins et al. (2006).

[11] For evidence connecting activity in MT with the visual experience of motion see Britten et al. (1992); Cowey & Walsh (2000); Heeger et al. (1999); Huk et al. (2001); Kammer (1999); Kourtzi & Kanwisher (2000); Rees et al. (2002); Théoret et al. (2002); Zihl et al. (1983).

fact that it is possible to intervene on consciousness both selectively and non-selectively. We need a conception of the neural basis of consciousness that captures the fact that MT activity is in some way essential to the visual experience of motion, but which also does justice to the fact that MT activity will generate experiences of motion only in the context of a conscious creature.

In light of the foregoing, let us distinguish between three types of neural correlates. A state's *total* neural correlate is that neural state that is *minimally sufficient* for its existence. (Note that a total neural correlate should not be confused with the neural correlate of a total phenomenal state.) We can divide a state's total correlate into two components: a *differentiating* correlate and a *non-differentiating* correlate.[12] A state's differentiating correlate is that component of its total correlate that accounts for its content. A state's non-differentiating correlate is that part of its total correlate that remains once its differentiating correlate is 'removed'. Whereas differentiating correlates *distinguish* one kind of conscious state from another, non-differentiating correlates are *shared* by a subject's conscious states. For example, visual experiences of motion and tactile experiences of one's feet will have unique differentiating correlates but common non-differentiating correlates (at least if we are considering experiences that are had by the same subject at the same time). Note that although I have contrasted differentiating correlates from non-differentiating correlates the distinction is actually a graded one, for one correlate can be more or less differentiating than another. Some non-differentiating activity might be implicated in (say) all and only visual experience; other non-differentiating activity may be implicated in all and only affective experience. I have ignored this complication in what follows in the interests of keeping the discussion manageable.

The distinction between differentiating and non-differentiating correlates is widely appreciated but not under these labels. Instead, theorists typically distinguish between 'core correlates' and 'enabling correlates' (see e.g. Chalmers 2000; Block 2005; Koch 2004). I think these terms are somewhat unhelpful, for they encourage an atomistic conception of the structure of consciousness. Referring to differentiating correlates as 'core' encourages us to view them as the fundamental mechanisms of consciousness—the systems that *really* generate consciousness—and we have seen that that assumption is problematic. Indeed, if either of these two types of correlates deserves to be thought of as 'core' it is *non-differentiating* correlates, for it is these correlates that are common to—and hence 'lie at the core of'—the subject's various conscious states. By the same token, referring to non-differentiating correlates as 'enabling correlates' down-

---

[12] I owe these labels to David Chalmers.

grades their status to that of the 'electrical supply'—systems whose primary job is to merely ensure that the differentiating correlates are activated. In other words, these terms encourage an atomistic picture of consciousness—a picture on which the fundamental mechanisms of consciousness are distributed across the cortex like so many lights on a Christmas tree.

Return to Kanwisher's claim that the neural correlates of awareness of a particular visual attribute are found 'in the very neural structure that perceptually analyzes that attribute.' We are now in a position to see why this claim is, at best, highly misleading. Any particular visual attribute might involve highly localized differentiating activity, but a state's differentiating correlate should not be confused with its total correlate. Consider once again the relationship between activity in MT and visual experiences of motion. Is it plausible to suppose that MT activity is not only the differentiating correlate of such experiences but is also their total correlate? Hardly. At the very least, the only evidence we have for linking MT activity with experiences of motion is evidence that MT functions as a differentiating correlate of such experiences—we have no evidence whatsoever that it constitutes a total correlate of experiences of motion. Moreover, the thought that MT activity might qualify as a total correlate of such experiences has little to recommend it. One wouldn't expect a slice of MT that had been put in a bottle to generate visual experience, no matter how much current might be run through it. In order to generate visual experience, MT activity must be suitably integrated with non-differentiating activity. Of course, none of the foregoing establishes that holistic approaches to consciousness are more plausible than atomistic approaches. My aim in this section has been merely to demonstrate that what we know about the role played by local neural activity in the generation of consciousness does not provide any support for atomism.

A second argument for atomism appeals to the fact that the components of a stream of consciousness will typically possess distinctive causal profiles. A pain in one's tooth will cause one to visit the dentist, a feeling of fatigue will cause one to take to one's bed, and a thirst for beer will cause one to inspect the contents of one's fridge. The atomist might argue that these commonplace observations indicate that the components of a subject's phenomenal field are atoms, for states with distinctive causal powers must be conceived of as having some kind of robust independence.

We do need to account for the distinctive causal powers of the various components of an overall phenomenal field but we need not embrace atomism in order to do so. States can possess distinctive causal powers without having independent existence; indeed, they can possess distinctive causal powers without having the *capacity* for independent existence. The weight of an object provides it with one fund of causal powers and its colour provides it with another, but an object's weight and its colour are not independent existents that must be fused in some way. Various features 'enter' consciousness in one fell-swoop, but having entered consciousness they bring with them different causal powers.

It might be useful here to consider a related debate concerning the structure of belief. Common sense (not to mention much philosophy) takes an 'atomistic' approach to the structure of belief, holding that a subject's total belief state is built up out of individual beliefs—the belief that 2+2=4, that Timbuktu is in Mali, that scrambled eggs are best made with a little bit of milk, and so on. On this conception of things, the subject's total belief state is, so to speak, secondary to their individual beliefs. But some have argued that we should instead think of subjects as having only a single state of belief (Lewis 1994; Stalnaker 1984). This state would be global in that its content would include everything that the subject believes. Does this 'top-down' conception of belief imply that the subject's 'sentence-sized' beliefs cannot have distinctive causal powers? I don't think so. Even if I believe that Timbuktu is in Mali and that scrambled eggs are best made with milk only in virtue of being in a single, global belief state which in some way includes each of these two beliefs as elements, it is nonetheless true that my vacation-planning behaviour implicates only the former state whereas my breakfast-making behaviour implicates only the latter state. The causal articulation of one's belief set does not require that that set be built up out of individual, fine-grained beliefs. Similarly, a subject's total phenomenal state is causally articulated, but we needn't think of this causal articulation in atomistic terms.

A final argument for the atomistic approach concerns the modal independence that various phenomenal states have from each other. Take a total phenomenal state (e_1). We can imagine another total phenomenal state (e_2) that is identical to e_1 apart for the fact that the subject lacks one of e_1's components—say, a pain in the left leg (e_3). In other words, we can think of e_2 as e_1 'minus' e_3. But if e_2 qualifies as an 'atom' of experience when it occurs on its own as a total phenomenal state, should it not also qualify as an atom of experience when it occurs in the context of e_1?

I think not. Begin by noting a rather odd implication of the argument. Let us assume that the argument is sound, and that e_2 does indeed qualify as an atom of consciousness when it occurs in the context of e_1. Now, what should we say about the status of e_3—the subject's experience of a pain in the left leg? Although e_2 might have the potential to constitute a total phenomenal state in its own right, it is highly doubtful whether the same can be said of e_3. Arguably, the experience of a pain in one's left leg can occur only in the context of certain other experiences (such as an overall sense of one's body). It seems to follow from this that e_3 isn't a phenomenal atom, for the argument appears to presuppose that a state qualifies as a phenomenal atom *only if* it has the potential to constitute a total phenomenal state. But if e_3 isn't a phenomenal atom then it's not clear just how we are to think of it. It looks as though the atomist will need to distinguish between two kinds of phenomenal states: phenomenal atoms (such as e_2) and states (such as e_3) that are not phenomenal atoms despite providing a distinctive contribution to the subject's overall experiential state. This position may not be incoherent, but it does not strike me as particularly attractive.

Although this objection suggests that something goes wrong with the argument from independence it doesn't identify where the argument goes wrong. The root of the trouble, however, is not difficult to locate: the fact that a state has the *potential* to constitute an independent unit of consciousness does not ensure that it *is* an independent unit of consciousness. We can see this by returning again to Tye's analogy between experiences on the one hand and statues and clouds on the other (see §2.1). As Tye points out, although certain undetached parts of statues and clouds would constitute statues and clouds in their own right were they suitably detached, as undetached parts they do not. The point generalizes beyond objects like statues and clouds to include events. Consider a football match involving five minutes of stoppage time. Call this event F_1. Now, had the referee blown the whistle at the end of the fourth of those five minutes of stoppage time, the game would have had only four minutes of stoppage time. Call this counterfactual game F_2. Should we hold that because F_2 would have qualified as an 'atom of football' when it occurs on its own then it also qualifies as an 'atom of football' when it occurs within the context of F_1? Surely not. When it comes to understanding football matches— not to mention statues and clouds—there is clearly a great deal to be said for starting with the whole rather than its parts.

Although the argument from independence fails, it does highlight an important feature of consciousness that any account must accommodate: tokens of a single fine-grained phenomenal state type can occur within the context of various total phenomenal state types. (At least, this is true for many fine-grained phenomenal state types; there may be content-based constraints on the types of conscious states that can co-occur within a total phenomenal state (Dainton 2006). However, the essential point is that this fact can be accommodated without embracing atomism.

10.6 Towards a plausible holism

The lesson to be learnt from the preceding sections is clear: our approach to consciousness should be holistic. Rather than begin with atomic states of consciousness that must be 'glued together' to form total phenomenal states we should regard total states as the basic units of consciousness. But what exactly might a plausible version of holism look like? My aim here is not to provide a 'worked-up' model of consciousness, but to develop a metaphor that might be of some use in guiding the construction of such a model.

The metaphor in question likens consciousness to a quilt. Just as multiple squares of cloth are patched together to form a quilt, so too multiple coalitions of content are woven together to form an overarching state of consciousness. One can identify particular fine-grained states of consciousness within this overarching state—just as one can pick out particular squares within a quilt—but these states are not independently conscious. The elements of a subject's total phenomenal state do not 'enter' consciousness as independent units but only *en masse*.

The key contrast between the quilted model and various versions of atomism concerns their respective conceptions of phenomenal unity. In order to account for the unity of consciousness the atomist must posit some kind of mechanism which functions to bind the atoms of consciousness together into phenomenal wholes. The advocate of the quilted model need posit no such mechanism, for the quilted theorist holds that the components of a total state of consciousness come into being *as* the components of that total state. One need no more bind the various components of consciousness together than one need bind the various organs of a body together—they come into being as unified with each other.

Within the contemporary landscape the account that is most congenial to the quilted conception of consciousness is Tononi's dynamic core model, according to which the neural basis of consciousness involves reciprocal interactions between thalamic and cortical processing ('thalamico-cortical loops'). The dynamic core is grounded in sub-cortical systems and reaches out to include various domain-specific processing nodes within its sweep. The very nature of this process ensures that any features that are made conscious are made conscious together—as the components of a single phenomenal state. The thalamico-cortical loops are integrated with each other, such that we should more properly speak of a *single* thalamico-cortical loop rather than multiple loops. Perhaps it should come as no great surprise that Tononi's account appears to fit most closely with the ideas that I have outlined here, for he is one of the few authors in the recent literature to have taken the unity of consciousness as a serious constraint on theorizing about consciousness (Tononi 2004, 2007; Tononi & Edelman 1998).[13]

Although the dynamic core may have a stable sub-cortical ground it does not have a unitary anatomical location, for the location of the thalamico-cortical loops may vary between subjects and indeed even within subjects across times. Nor does this account imply that we can identify consciousness with some kind of 'box' in an information-processing flow-chart. The architecture of cognition is relatively stable, but that of consciousness is highly labile and changes on a time-scale that is measured in hundreds of milliseconds. Certain phenomenal features such as one's sense of bodily presence and background mood might have an abiding presence in consciousness; others flutter in and out of consciousness depending on perceptual input and one's attentional focus. Further, the boxes of information-processing psychology typically have a restricted domain, whereas the dynamic core can bind an extremely heterogeneous range of content together. Rather than attempting to locate consciousness within the box-and-arrow diagrams beloved by cognitive neuroscience, it might be better to think of consciousness as involving a dynamic unity that is *superimposed* on the relatively static structure of thought and perception.

Does the dynamic core conception of consciousness qualify as a version of the 'imperial' approach to consciousness in the sense that I outlined in Chapter 5? It might appear to, for one might be tempted to think of the 'core' as some kind of 'seat of consciousness': a location within functional space towards which all content flows and from which all control emanates. But to conceive of the core in these terms would be to misunderstand its role, which is merely to generate a total phenomenal state. In this respect, the dynamic core model is perfectly consistent with what I called the federal conception of consciousness, according to which the various components of the stream of consciousness are contained within domain-specific circuits. The dynamic core is in the business of ensuring that contents of various kinds are fused together into a single phenomenal state, but it is not in the business of ensuring that each of these contents will be available to the same range of consuming systems. Nor, for that matter, is it in the business of solving the binding problem or ensuring that the contents of consciousness are consistent with each other. Although the dynamic core might

---

[13] Also congenial is Hurley's suggestion that consciousness involves a dynamic singularity in the field of causal flows: a tangle of multiple feedback loops of varying orbits (1998, 2003). However, Hurley weds her dynamical approach with a commitment to 'vehicle externalism', the thought that the vehicles of consciousness loop out into the world. Although not opposed to externalism in principle, I am not particularly enthusiastic about it.

play *a* role in ensuring that these kinds of unities are typically present in consciousness, these functions are not themselves the responsibility of the dynamic core.

The quilted model generates no specific methodological prescriptions but it does provide a very general framework for approaching the study of consciousness. Let me bring this section to a close by reflecting on one the questions posed by this framework (Bayne 2007a; Hohwy 2009).

Most investigations into the neural basis of consciousness employ what we might call a *content-based methodology*. Studies designed on this basis hold the presence of consciousness itself fixed and manipulate only the contents of consciousness. The binocular rivalry studies of Logothetis and colleagues that I mentioned in Chapter 5 provide an influential example of this approach.[14] In these studies Logothetis and colleagues trained monkeys to 'report' their visual experiences by pressing different levers, and then recorded from cells in the visual cortex whilst the monkeys were experiencing binocular rivalry. A more recent example of the content-based methodology is provided by a series of studies conducted by Rees and colleagues involving patients with perceptual extinction. The experimenters contrasted the neural activity seen when the visual stimulus was 'extinguished' (that is, not among the contents of the patient's consciousness) with that which occurred when the patient *was* conscious of it.[15]

This content-based approach is in a good position to uncover the differentiating correlates of consciousness, but it is rather more difficult to see how it might enable us to identify the *non-differentiating* correlates of consciousness. This wouldn't be so bad if one thought of non-differentiating activity as merely enabling, but we have found reason to reject that view. Differentiating activity represents only half of the story as far as the neural underpinnings of consciousness are concerned.

In order to identify the non-differentiating correlates of consciousness we need to employ the *creature-based methodology*. Studies conducted in accord with this rubric attempt to screen off the influence of the contents of consciousness and look instead for the domain-general neural activity that correlates with the presence of consciousness as such. An example of this approach is provided by the work of Alkire and colleagues, who have used anaesthesia-induced loss of consciousness to identify the mechanisms responsible for the transition between consciousness and unconsciousness.[16] Other examples of the creature-

---

[14]   See Logothetis (1998); Sheinberg & Logothetis (1997); see also Tong et al. (1998).
[15]   See Rees (2001); Rees et al. (2002); see also Driver & Mattingley (1998) and Sarri et al (2006).
[16]   See Alkire et al. (2000); Alkire & Miller (2005); White & Alkire (2003).

based methodology are provided by studies that attempt to identify the neural factors which account for the loss of consciousness in coma and the persistent vegetative state and its re-acquisition in the minimally conscious state (see §6.1).[17] Such studies aim to uncover the domain-general, non-differentiating correlates of consciousness rather than their content-specific counterparts.

It is clear that there should be a place for both content-based and creature-based methodologies within the science of consciousness: the former are needed in order to identify the differentiating correlates of consciousness, whereas the latter are needed in order to identify the non-differentiating correlates of consciousness. What is less clear is whether the independent deployment of these two approaches will provide us with a full account of the neural basis of consciousness. I have my doubts. What we really need to know is how differentiating neural activity *interacts* with non-differentiating activity so as to generate the subject's total phenomenal state. It is possible that such a picture will emerge as a result of the independent execution of content-based and creature-based studies, but it is also possible that we will need to develop new methodologies—methodologies that involve the conjoint manipulation of both 'state consciousness' and 'creature consciousness'—in order to determine just how the quilt of consciousness is knit together from the various fragments of content distributed throughout the brain. But just what such a methodology might look like is a question that must be left for another occasion.

10.7 Conclusion

Theory-building in consciousness studies has generally paid scant attention to the unity of consciousness. This is unfortunate, for the unity of consciousness provides us with important and much-needed constraints on accounts of consciousness. I began in §10.2 with a constraint based on object-unity. According to the binding constraint, perceptual features cannot enter consciousness without first being bound together to form percepts of unified objects. Although few accounts of consciousness fall foul of the binding constraint, it is at odds with the kind of radical atomism endorsed by Zeki and Bartels (1999). In §10.3 I provided a brief overview of the vast literature on inter-modal integration, and argued that this body of work puts further pressure

---

[17] See Laureys et al. (2000); Schiff (2004).

on atomism, for it indicates that the senses do not operate as a 'mass of tributaries running in parallel', as some atomists claim (O'Brien & Opie 1998), but as a network of highly entangled and inter-dependent channels.

But the real pressure on atomism derives from the fact that conscious states occur as the components of a single phenomenal field. How might atomists account for the phenomenal unity of consciousness? They have two options: they can either deny that consciousness is unified, or they can posit a mechanism that might be responsible for ensuring that the atoms of consciousness are brought together in the form of phenomenal wholes. Neither of these options has much to recommend it. The first option flies in the face of introspection, whereas the second generates an unwanted prediction: if the stream of consciousness involves the activity of mechanisms of 'phenomenal binding', then why are there no syndromes in which these mechanisms have broken down leaving the subject in question with phenomenal atoms? And even if—contrary to what I have argued in previous chapters—there are syndromes in which phenomenal unity is lost, the manner of its breakdown surely provides little encouragement for atomists.

The upshot, I suggested, is that the structure of consciousness is fundamentally holistic: there are no mechanisms responsible for phenomenal binding because the unity of consciousness is ensured by the very mechanisms that generate consciousness in the first place. Drawing on Tononi's 'dynamic core' model of consciousness, I suggested that we should think of the mechanisms of consciousness as producing a quilt of consciousness. This quilt is generated by sub-cortical systems that reach out into various cortical nodes and bind distributed fragments of content into a single, multifaceted phenomenal state. Although the various phenomenal states that can be distinguished within this quilt should not be thought of as phenomenal atoms, they do qualify as experiences in their own right, for they may possess distinct causal profiles and a certain degree of functional autonomy.

I brought this chapter to a close by examining one of the many methodological questions that it raises. Investigations into the neural basis of consciousness currently take one of two forms. Some studies ignore creature consciousness and focus on the differentiating correlates of certain kinds of fine-grained conscious states. Other studies ignore the contents of consciousness and focus on the non-differentiating correlates of consciousness that might be implicated in consciousness as such ('creature consciousness'). Both kinds of studies are important, but it is unclear whether either approach is able to reveal how the differentiating correlates of consciousness *interact* with the non-differentiating correlates. Although an account of this interaction might emerge from integrating the results of content-based studies with those of creature-based studies, but it is also possible that we may need to develop novel experimental approaches—approaches that in some way manipulate both creature consciousness and the contents of consciousness in tandem—in order to determine just how the dynamic core goes about stitching content that is distributed across a variety of neural circuits into a single quilt of consciousness.

11

The Body

In a poetic but somewhat puzzling passage in the *Principles of Psychology*, William James suggests that the unity of consciousness might be grounded in 'the warm animal feeling' of bodily self-consciousness (James 1890/1950: 317). There is much to recommend James's proposal. One's own body is not just one object among many, but occupies a core place within one's phenomenal field. The 'phenomenal body'—that is, the body as experienced—is that object within which one's bodily sensations are located and around which one's perceptual states are structured. Perhaps, as James suggests, bodily self-consciousness might explain—or at least constrain—the unity of consciousness. The aim of this chapter is to take the measure of this thought.

11.1 Bodily self-consciousness

Let us begin with the ways in which one's own body is present in experience. Most obviously, one's body enters into the content of bodily sensations. Pains, aches, and other bodily sensations are experienced as occurring within particular body parts and regions. Although some bodily sensations are precisely located, others—such as nausea—can be assigned only a gross and coarse-grained location; still other bodily sensations—such as those associated with fever and fatigue—are experienced as pervading the entirety of one's body. The body is also given in proprioceptive experience—that is, the awareness of how one's limbs are arrayed in space relative to each other. Even with one's eyes closed, one can be aware of one's arms as extending out before one, or of one's feet as arranged thus-and-so. The body is also present in the phenomenology of agency. In acting one's awareness will typically be focused on those objects that one is attempting to manipulate, but this experience will often be accompanied by a recessive awareness of those body parts by means of which one is acting.

Bodily self-consciousness is not restricted to the 'inner senses' but also enters into the contents of exteroception—the so-called 'external senses'. This is perhaps most evident in touch, in which one's own body forms a template for the external world. Touch has a Janus-faced nature, for one is aware both of the object being touched and of one's own body as the means by which one is aware of the world. Vision and audition also contain a bodily element, for one's body is tacitly experienced as that object which is located at the focus of these sensory fields. But although vision and audition represent the location of one's body they do not represent it as a spatially extended physical object. Instead, it is consistent with visual and auditory experience that one is nothing more than a mere point in space.

Arguably, the forms of bodily experience just surveyed are not merely bodily in the sense that they happen to represent one's own body, but in the deeper sense that they represent one's body *as* one's own body. We might say that these experiences have *de se* content (Lewis 1979). It is, I suggest, part of the very content of bodily sensations that they represent one and the same object as that which is given in the perspectival structure of perception. One need not engage in inference in order to determine whether (say) the object in which one's pains are located is one and the same as that which forms the vanishing point of the visual field.

So, the body is well positioned to contribute to the unity of consciousness, but how exactly might it play that role? A bold answer to this question holds that conscious states are phenomenally unified with each other in virtue of the fact that their contents exhibit what we might call the 'unity of bodily self-consciousness'. By this I mean that they represent one's body as a single, integrated thing. In effect, this proposal suggests that the unity of consciousness can be thought of in terms of a kind of global 'object-binding'.

The problem with this proposal is that there are forms of conscious content into which the body does not enter. Consider conscious thought, for example. Thoughts certainly take place within the confines of one's body, but arguably this fact is not reflected in their phenomenology. Trying to remember a telephone number does not bring with it a sense of oneself as an embodied being, not even implicitly. More controversially, it is doubtful whether the body is implicated in the experiential character of moods. The experiences associated with ennui, buoyancy, nervousness, and so on are grounded in bodily states, but this fact is not reflected in what it is like to be in these states. (At least, so it seems to me.) Indeed, the body may even be missing from certain types of perceptual experience. For example, smelling freshly ground coffee does not seem to bring with it any sense of oneself as a spatially located—let alone spatially extended—object. But if some kinds of conscious states have no bodily content then bodily self-consciousness cannot provide us with a *fully general* account of the unity of consciousness.

Nonetheless, bodily self-consciousness could still play an important role in grounding the unity of consciousness. However, that role would need to be restricted to accounting for the unity between particular types of conscious states. Perhaps bodily self-consciousness acts as a *filter* on conscious states, ensuring that those states with bodily content are phenomenally unified with each other only if they are also bound together by bodily self-consciousness. The idea, in other words, is that those conscious states that do contain implicit reference to one's own body—roughly, bodily sensations and perceptual states—must represent one's body as a single, integrated object in order to be phenomenally unified with each other. Call the claim that phenomenal unity is constrained by bodily self-consciousness in this way the *embodiment constraint*.

Although the embodiment constraint would not provide us with an account of the unity of consciousness as such, it would (if true) forge an intimate link between phenomenal unity on the one hand and a certain kind of representational unity—the unity of bodily self-consciousness—on the other. But is the embodiment constraint true? This chapter examines three challenges to it. §11.2 focuses on the worry that bodily sensations and perceptual experiences cannot be located within a single frame of reference; §11.3 examines challenges to the embodiment constraint that derive from what we know about pathologies of bodily experience; and §11.4 examines an objection from the possibility of multiple embodiment. I will argue that the embodiment constraint survives the first two challenges but succumbs to the third.

11.2 Egocentric space

In order for bodily self-consciousness to constrain phenomenal unity in the way required by the embodiment constraint it must be possible to map all forms of bodily self-consciousness onto a single frame of reference. If there were no way in which the contents of (say) visual experience could be located with respect to those of bodily sensations, then we would have no grounds for taking the object represented in bodily experience to be one and the same as that which forms the point of origin of the visual field. In this section I examine an analysis of bodily experience that puts some pressure on the claim that there is indeed such a frame of reference. The analysis in question is developed by José Bermúdez, who takes it to vindicate Merleau-Ponty's claim that the outline of one's body is 'a frontier which ordinary spatial relations do not cross' (Merleau-Ponty 1962:

85). I will suggest that although there is much of value in Bermúdez's analysis, it falls short of doing quite that.

Bermúdez begins with the plausible claim that there is no point in (or on) the body that counts as the centre of a frame of reference within which bodily sensations can be located. This fact, he suggests, illustrates an important contrast between the spatial structure of bodily experience proper ('somatic proprioception', in his terms) and that of perceptual experience. Bermúdez motivates this contrast by noting that certain questions that can be sensibly raised about perceptual experiences cannot be sensibly raised about bodily sensations. For example, one can ask which of two visually perceived objects is further away than the other, and whether or not they lie in the same direction. However,

neither question makes any sense with respect to proprioception. One cannot ask whether this proprioceptively detected hand movement is farther away than this itch, nor whether this pain is in the same direction as that pain. What I am really asking when I ask which of two objects is further away is which of the two objects is further away from me, and a similar tacit self-understanding is included when I ask whether two objects are in the same direction. But through somatic proprioception one learns about events taking place within the confines of the body, and there is no privileged part of the body that counts as *me* for the purpose of discussing the spatial relations they bear to each other. (Bermúdez 2005: 309)

Bermúdez concludes that whereas perceptual content is structured in terms of a body-centred frame of reference, the content of bodily experience is structured in terms of body parts. In fact, he suggests that bodily sensations can be assigned two locations: A-locations and B-locations (Bermúdez 2005: 311). The A-location of a bodily sensation is given relative to the joints that demarcate the borders of the body part in which it is located. For example, a pain in one's foot is experienced as occurring at the same A-location as long as it remains at the same location in the foot. The B-location of a bodily sensation is fixed by the relations between it and the subject's body as a whole, a notion that Bermúdez unpacks by appealing to the angles of the joints that lie between it and the torso. The A-location and B-location of bodily experiences that fall within the torso will coincide.

This account of the spatial content of bodily experience undermines the embodiment constraint, for it seems to cut the 'inner space' of bodily sensation adrift from the 'outer space' of perceptual experience. It is difficult to see how the body of bodily sensations could be experienced as identical to the body of perceptual experience if the body is 'a frontier which ordinary spatial relations do not cross'. And if the experiences delivered by the 'internal' and 'external' senses cannot represent a single object (as such), then the embodiment constraint seems to be in trouble. So, is Bermúdez's account of the structure of bodily sensations correct?

There is something to it, for it does seem plausible to suppose that the *fundamental* location of bodily sensations is given by reference to a body part. However, we can embrace that insight without also embracing the thought that the body is a frontier that 'ordinary spatial relations do not cross'. Good thing too—for there is ample reason to think that bodily sensations and perceptual experiences can be located within a single frame of reference.

One source of evidence is introspective. Suppose that you are visually aware of two objects on the table in front of you: a book on your left and a glass on your right. Let us also suppose that you are also aware of a pain in your right hand. I submit that when you pick up the glass with your right hand, you will experience the pain as being closer to the glass than it is to the book. If you should happen to put the glass down and pick up the book with your right hand, the pain will then be experienced as closer to the book than it is to the glass. The spatial relations between the pain and the objects on the table will be experienced as changing in response to changes in the experienced location of one's hand. So, introspection provides us with one reason to think that there must be *some* framework in which the objects of bodily and perceptual experience can be located.

This argument from introspection can be bolstered by an appeal to the interdependence between the spatial content of bodily sensation on the one hand and perceptual experience on the other, as illustrated by the cross-modal congruency effect (see Figure 11.1). This effect is studied by requiring subjects to hold a sponge cube in each hand. Embedded in each cube are two vibrotactile stimulators (black squares) and two visual distractors (red circles). While staring directly ahead, subjects are required to identify the elevation of a series of vibrotactile targets that are presented to the thumb or index finger (lower versus upper elevation, respectively) of either hand. A visual distractor is then presented randomly on each trial to one of the four possible locations from which a vibrotactile stimulus can be delivered. This visual distractor will be either congruent or incongruent with the vibrotactile stimulus that it is paired with. (For example, on a congruent trial an upper light will be presented with an upper touch, whereas on an 'incongruent' trial a lower light will be presented with the same upper touch.) When incongruent, visual distractors retard the speed with which subjects make tactile judgements and increase their error rates. Importantly, the size of the effect can be modulated by changing the subject's posture. When the hands are *uncrossed* visual distractors on the right hand interfere more strongly than visual distractors on the left hand for vibrotactile targets presented to the right hand, but when the hands are *crossed* visual

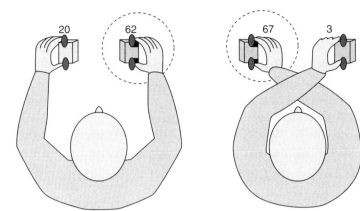

Figure 11.1 Crossed hands. Participants hold in either hand a sponge cube in which two vibrotactile stimulators (black squares) and two visual distractors (red circles) are embedded. They must then fixate a central point straight ahead while being required to discriminate the elevation of a series of vibrotactile targets presented unpredictably to the thumb or index finger (lower versus upper elevation, respectively) of either hand. A visual distractor is presented randomly on each trial together with the vibration from one of the four positions with participants instructed to ignore any visual event. The values given directly above each hand highlight the magnitude of the cross-modal congruency effect (in milliseconds) elicited by visual distractors placed on that particular cube. Note that the effect follows the right hand in space when posture is changed: visual distractors on the rightmost cube interfere more strongly if the cube is held in the right hand in an uncrossed position, but lights on the left cube interfere more when the hands are crossed and the right hand holds the leftmost cube instead

Source: Maravita et al. 2003

distractors on the leftmost cube (which is now held by the right hand) generate more interference than do visual distractors on the rightmost cube (which is held by the left hand) (Spence et al. 1998; Pavani et al. 2000; Maravita et al. 2003). In other words, the cross-modal congruency effect follows the hand when its overall location relative to the rest of the subject's body changes. Arguably, the spatial content of bodily experience can modulate that of perceptual experience and vice versa only because both forms of experience are located within a single frame of reference.[1]

---

[1] Illusions of various kinds also demonstrate that the spatial contents of bodily and perceptual experiences are interdependent. For example, de Vignemont and colleagues have shown that the perceived size of a touched object can be modulated by altering the perceived size of the touching finger (de Vignemont, et al. (2005b)). See also de Vignemont et al. (2005a) and de Vignemont (2007).

A final reason for thinking that body sensation and perceptual experience involve a common frame of reference appeals to the demands of agency. As Bermúdez himself notes (2005: 312), effective action requires that one integrate information about the location of perceived objects with information about the location of one's limbs, and that in turn requires that information about body parts and external objects be mapped onto a single frame of reference. Now, although there is no *a priori* requirement that this frame of reference will also be used to structure the contents of perceptual experience, it is not unreasonable to suppose that it might at least *influence* experiential content (even if the on-line control of action is also guided by frames of reference that are independent of consciousness).

The overall picture is clear: we need an account of how the spatial content of bodily experience is internally related to that of perceptual experience. Developing such an account goes well beyond the scope of this chapter, but let me provide a thumbnail sketch of what such an account might look like.

As Bermúdez suggests, it is plausible to suppose that the fundamental location of a bodily experience is given by reference to a body part (on the model of A-locations). However, one's body parts are themselves experienced as located with respect to each other within the context of one's body as an articulated whole (on the model of B-locations). The content of this bodily experience is itself structured by an egocentric frame of reference that infuses perceptual experience. It is likely that touch plays a particularly crucial role in aligning these two frames of reference, for touch informs one about the spatial properties of both one's own body parts and also those of the objects with which one is in contact. The resulting frame of reference will allow one to directly experience the spatial relations between perceptual events and bodily events—such as that the pain is now closer to the glass than it is to the book.

This is obviously a very rough sketch of what it might be for bodily experience and perceptual experience to inhabit a shared space, but despite its crudity it suffices to allay the worry that 'inner' and 'outer' experiences occur within two wholly incommensurate frames of reference. And insofar as it does that, it also removes an obstacle to the embodiment constraint. If, as I have argued, spatial relations can 'cross the frontier of the body', then it is possible that the sense of embodiment provided by the 'internal' senses (that is, bodily sensations) and the 'external senses' (that is, perceptual experience) might represent one's body as one and the same object.

11.3 The fragmented body

Although ordinary corporeal experience involves an awareness of oneself as a single, integrated physical object, there are conditions in which the unity of bodily experience appears to be compromised and perhaps even lost altogether. What happens to phenomenal unity in such cases? If the embodiment constraint is right then the fragmentation of bodily experience must bring with it a corresponding fragmentation in phenomenal unity. Is that so, or can phenomenal unity survive breakdowns in the unity of bodily awareness?

Let us approach this question indirectly by first considering pathologies of embodiment in which corporeal experience appears to retain its fundamental integrity despite being disrupted in profound ways. Perhaps the most familiar pathology of embodiment is the phantom limb experience.[2] Individuals who have 'lost' a limb due to amputation or congenital abnormality often experience the missing limb as replaced by a phantom. Such experiences are generally unwelcome, especially when unpleasant bodily sensations are located in the limb. Although the phantom typically replaces a missing body part, phantoms can be supplementary to the normal bodily form. In one case a woman experienced herself as having four phantom legs (Vuilleumier et al. 1997); in another case a man experienced himself as having six phantom arms (Sellal et al. 1996).

In the phantom limb syndrome the borders of the phenomenal body extend beyond those of the objective body. In other pathologies of bodily experience, however, the borders of the phenomenal body retreat inside those of the objective body. Patients suffering from 'asomatagnosia'—literally, agnosia for one's body—may complain that entire limbs (or parts thereof) are 'missing'—that is, have disappeared from awareness.[3] Similarly, patients suffering from personal neglect are often unaware of one side of their body (usually the left side), although this loss of bodily awareness may itself go unnoticed by the patient.

In these disorders the borders of the phenomenal body depart in drastic ways from those of the objective body, but there is no reason to think that patients suffer from a fundamental breakdown in the *unity* of bodily awareness. Insofar as these patients experience their body parts at all they continue to experience them as the parts of a unitary object, an object that they also experience as their own

---

[2] Melzack (1992); Melzack et al. (1997); Ramachandran & Hirstein (1998); Wade (2009).

[3] Critchley (1953); Arzy et al. (2006); Feinberg et al. (1990). See Moro et al. (2004) for a fascinating study of two patients suffering from asomatagnosia in the context of tactile neglect. Although their neglect could be ameliorated by requiring them to move their left hand into their right visual field (and thus bringing it within their attentional focus), this had no effect on the patients' sense of embodiment. The patients were now aware when their hand was touched but they continued to deny that it was theirs.

body. These syndromes involve changes to the size and configuration of the phenomenal body, but its fundamental structure—the sense of the bodily self as a single integrated object—appears to be undisturbed.

Indeed, patients can experience *gross* alterations in bodily experience without losing the sense of bodily unity and integrity. Consider two individuals, I.W. and G.Y., who suffer from impairments to the sense of touch and muscular proprioception due to global deafferentation (Cole & Paillard 1995). I.W. has no sensations of touch or proprioception below the collar-line, while G.L. has no such sensations from below her mouth. In order to navigate, they need to visually monitor the positions of their limbs and the relationship between their bodies and their environments. One might have thought that this loss of proprioception would lead I.W. and G.Y. to experience a loss of bodily unity—that they might experience their bodily sensations as 'free-floating' events—but that does not appear to be the case. I.W., at any rate, reports that his sense of body image—'his sense of wholeness and configuration' (Cole & Paillard 1995: 261)—remains fundamentally intact.

There are, however, pathologies of embodiment that *do* challenge the embodiment constraint. One such pathology is depersonalization. Depersonalization is characterized as involving an 'alteration in the perception or experience of the self, so that one feels detached from, and as if one is an outside observer of, one's mental processes or body' (DSM-IV-TR).[4] Echoing Hume, patients will describe themselves as a 'mere bundle of thoughts'. Some patients will complain that they 'no longer have an ego, but are mechanisms, automatons, puppets; that what they do seems not done by them but happens mechanically; that they no longer feel joy or sorrow, hatred or love; that they are as though dead, not alive, not real' (Schilder 1953: 304). Other patients will say that they feel 'like a piece of furniture'—that they don't feel like a human being or an animal (Sierra et al. 2002: 531). Galen Strawson cites the experience of a friend with this condition who found that the thought 'I don't exist' kept occurring to him. 'It seemed to him that this exactly expressed his experience of himself, although he . . . knew, of course, that there had to be a locus of consciousness where the thought "I don't exist" occurred' (Strawson 1997: 418).

Individuals with depersonalization are not delusional: they know that they are embodied, and they retain an accurate conception of where the borders of their body lie. However, there is another pathology of embodiment in which

---

[4] See Baker et al. (2003); Cappon & Banks (1965); Sierra & Berrios (1997, 2002); Schilder (1953); Shorvon (1946).

the experience of bodily alienation of the kind that depersonalization involves does lead to delusional fixation. The pathology in question is Cotard's delusion, named after the French psychiatrist who first described it (Cotard 1880, 1882).[5] Cotard's delusion is typically said to involve the belief that one is dead, but this characterization captures only the more extreme manifestations of the delusion, and it is useful to employ a rather broader conception of the condition. Cotard himself referred to the delusion as *le delire de négation*—the 'delusion of negation'. In its milder manifestations patients express feelings of self-deprecation and despair; in its more severe forms they will deny the reality of body parts or insist that their body is a corpse. Enoch and Trethowan (1991) describe a patient who referred to himself as 'a mere point in space'. Somewhat paradoxically perhaps, patients may also assert that they are immortal, a judgement that might also manifest the loss of corporeal experience.

Depersonalization and Cotard's delusion threaten the embodiment constraint for the following reason. On the one hand patients appear to have lost the unity of bodily self-consciousness. At the same time, there is no reason to doubt that their experiences are subsumed by a single phenomenal state. Patients don't display any of the representational or access disunities that occur in (say) the hidden-observer phenomenon or the split-brain syndrome. However, before we reject the embodiment constraint we need to consider in precisely what sense these patients might be said to have lost the unity of bodily self-consciousness.

Let us start with those components of bodily experience that patients appear to *retain*. As best one can tell, patients continue to experience their bodily sensations as located in their body parts; they continue to experience their body parts as the components of a single object; and they continue to experience their own bodies as the focal point of their visual and auditory fields. None of these components of bodily self-consciousness appear to be disrupted in either depersonalization or Cotard's delusion. Instead, the loss of bodily self-consciousness that occurs in these conditions appears to be restricted to what we might call the experience of *affective identification* with one's body. Rather than experiencing themselves as being 'at one' with their body—as 'embodied' in it—patients appear to experience themselves as lodged within it 'as a sailor might be lodged within his ship', to appropriate Descartes's memorable phrase. This account is supported by both what patients say and also by the fact that both disorders are associated with extremely high levels of depression. Cotard's patients have been described as 'stranded on an island of emotional desolation'

---

[5] See Berrios & Luque (1995a, 1995b); Gerrans (2000); Young & Leafhead (1996).

(Ramachandran & Blakeslee 1998: 167). We might say that although these patients continue to be aware of their own bodies as integrated objects, for them bodily awareness is no longer a form of genuine *self*-consciousness.

Now that we have a better grip on the sense in which these conditions involve pathologies of bodily experience, let us return to the embodiment constraint. The key issue here is whether the link between the unity of bodily awareness and the unity of consciousness requires affective identification with one's own body. James may have had this aspect of bodily awareness in mind when he suggested that the unity of consciousness might be grounded in the 'warm animal feeling' of bodily self-consciousness, but I did not build this component into the embodiment constraint. Instead, the embodiment constraint was only meant to capture the thought that the unity of consciousness might be grounded in the role that the phenomenal body plays in structuring the content of bodily sensation and perceptual experience. Given that this component of bodily self-consciousness seems to remain largely unscathed by depersonalization and Cotard's delusion, so too does the embodiment constraint.

Where does this leave us? Our brief survey of pathologies of corporeal awareness has failed to reveal any decisive objections to the embodiment constraint. This is not because we have found that the fragmentation of bodily awareness is also accompanied by a corresponding fragmentation in the unity of consciousness, but because we have failed to find any instances in which bodily awareness fragments in a manner that might put pressure on the embodiment constraint. There are various conditions in which the borders and structure of the phenomenal body depart from those of the objective body, but in none of these conditions do patients appear to lose the sense of their body as a single integrated object in which their bodily sensations are located and around which their perceptual experiences are structured. For all that has been said thus far, the embodiment constraint might capture a deep truth about human experience.

11.4 Multiple embodiment

But perhaps we have been looking for counter-examples to the embodiment constraint in the wrong place. Rather than asking whether it is possible for the unity of consciousness to coexist with the experience of corporeal *disunity*, perhaps we should instead ask whether it might be possible for the unity of consciousness to coexist with the experience of corporeal *multiplicity*. Could a set of phenomenally unified states be structured around multiple phenomenal bodies? If so, then the unity of bodily self-consciousness couldn't constrain phenomenal unity, and we would have to reject the embodiment constraint.

Let us begin with the question of whether multiple phenomenal embodiment is ever a feature of human experience. The strongest evidence that I know of for answering this question in the affirmative comes from the study of heautoscopy.[6] Heautoscopy is a form of autoscopy (literally 'self-seeing') in which patients feel as though they are located in two bodies, and that their spatial perspective is divided between that of their actual location and that of a 'hallucinated self'—a hallucinated person with whom they identify. Heautoscopy is to be distinguished from two other forms of autoscopy: out-of-body experiences on the one hand and autoscopic hallucinations on the other (see Figure 11.2). Patients in the grip of an out-of-body experience feel as though they have left their body and are located at some point above it, whilst those in the grip of an autoscopic hallucination are aware of a person which they experience as 'another me' (Kölmel 1985). In heautoscopy the subject experiences himself as located in both his actual body *and* in the visually presented body.

Brugger et al. (1994) describe the following case:

Turning around, [the patient] saw himself still lying in bed. He became angry about 'this guy who I knew was myself and who would not get up and thus risked being late at work.' He tried to wake the body in the bed first by shouting at it; then by trying to shake it and then repeatedly jumping on his alter ego in the bed. The lying body showed no reaction. Only then did the patient begin to be puzzled about his double existence and become more and more scared by the fact that he could no longer tell which of the two he really was. Several times his bodily awareness switched from the one standing upright to the one still lying in bed; when in the lying in bed mode he felt quite awake but completely paralyzed and scared by the figure of himself bending over and beating him. His only intention was to become one person again and, looking out of his window (from where he could still see his body lying in bed), he suddenly decided to jump out 'in order to stop the intolerable feeling of being divided in two.' At the same time, he hoped that 'this really desperate action would frighten the one in bed and thus urge him to merge with me again.' The next thing he remembers is waking up in pain in the hospital. (Brugger et al. 1994: 839)

(The case had a happy ending, for although the patient's window was three storeys up, he landed on a large bush.) In this case, the patient's experience of double embodiment seems to have been sequential, with his spatial perspective switching from that of one body to that of the other. However, there are also cases of heautoscopy in which it is unclear whether the experience of

---

[6] For autoscopy more generally see Brugger (2006); Blanke et al. (2004); Blanke & Mohr (2005) and Dening & Berrios (1994).

dual embodiment is sequential or simultaneous. Blanke et al. (2004) present the following description of a patient who experienced heautoscopy after an epileptic seizure.

[The patient] had the experience as if she were seeing herself from behind herself (seeing the back of her head and upper torso without arms). She felt as if she were 'standing at the foot of my bed and looking down at myself' and as if 'looking through a telescope.' During the same experience, [the patient also had] the impression of 'seeing' from her physical visuo-spatial perspective, which looked at the wall immediately in front of her. Asked at which of these two positions she thinks herself to be, she answered that 'I am at both positions at the same time,' without having the feeling of being out of her body. (Blanke et al. 2004: 247 f.; see also Lunn 1970)

Although the patient says that she experienced herself as located in both bodies at once, the authors of the report express some scepticism about the veracity of this claim, and suggest instead that her experience might have actually rapidly alternated between two bodily perspectives in the way in which the previous patient's experience seems to have. So, although these reports are intriguing, it is possible that true multiple embodiment—that is, *simultaneous* multiple embodiment—falls outside the limits of human experience.

But perhaps science fiction can take over where real science leaves off. Even if *we* cannot experience ourselves as multiply embodied, there doesn't seem to be anything incoherent in the idea. Consider an organism who I shall call 'Borgy'.

Autoscopic hallucination	Heautoscopy	Out-of-body experience
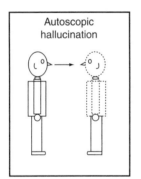	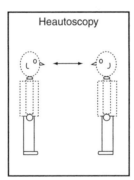	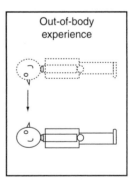

Figure 11.2 The phenomenology of autoscopic hallucination (left), heautoscopy (middle) and out-of-body experiences (right). For each form of autoscopy, the position and posture of the actual body is indicated by black lines and that of the merely experiential (or phenomenal) body by dashed lines. The arrows point away from the centre of the patient's apparent visual field, which is variously located in the actual body (autoscopic hallucination), the merely phenomenal body (out-of-body experiences), and both the actual and merely phenomenal bodies (heautoscopy)

Source: Blanke et al. 2004

Borgy is a 'scattered creature', for he has three bodies that are biologically independent of each other. (We might think of each of these bodies on the model of the human body.) However, the brains that are located in these three bodies can communicate with each other via miniature radio transmitters. In fact, Borgy's brains are functionally integrated with each other to roughly the same degree that our two neural hemispheres are. Although Borgy has three bodies, he is a single subject of thought, action, and experience. His perceptual states feed into a unitary cognitive system, and he has direct control over each of his three bodies (this, in part, is what makes the three bodies *his* bodies). He acts with his three bodies and their twelve limbs in the way that you act with your one body and its four limbs. The fact that he has three bodies allows Borgy to experience the world from the perspective of three non-contiguous locations at once. At one and the same time he might feel the sun beat down in Sydney, hear a plane flying over the Sonoran desert, and smell freshly baked croissants on the steps of Sacré Coeur.

Although Borgy's bodily and perceptual experiences will be structured around distinct bodies, I suggest that they might well be phenomenally unified. Borgy's three brains are distributed between his three bodies, but I see no reason to deny that they might jointly implement the kind of neurophysiological singularity that underlies the unity of consciousness. This 'sub-personal' integration might also have a 'personal' echo. Because Borgy's perceptual experiences feed into a single cognitive system, he will be able to experience certain relations between events that occur within his individual perceptual fields. Even though he doesn't experience the spatial relations between his three bodies, his phenomenal perspective could include a representation of (say) the relationship between the temperature in each of the locations in which he has a body. For example, he may be directly aware that it is hotter in Arizona than it is in Paris. To take another example, suppose that there is a duck in front of each of Borgy's three bodies. Borgy will not experience the three ducks as spatially related to each other, but he may be able to experience one of the ducks as bigger (or more colourful, noisier, etc.) than the others. The upshot of these considerations, I suggest, is that Borgy constitutes a counter-example to the embodiment constraint, for it is plausible to suppose that he could retain a phenomenally unified consciousness despite the fact that neither his perceptual experiences nor his bodily sensations will be be structured around a single physical object.[7]

---

[7] See Dainton (2006: 60–72) for a somewhat similar line of argument against the thought that the phenomenal unity of consciousness might be identified with some kind of spatial unity.

In presenting Borgy to various audiences I have discovered that he does not command universal approval. Critics generally allow that it might be possible for a single creature to experience itself as multiply embodied, but they find it implausible to suppose that such a creature could retain a unified consciousness. They are inclined to grant that Borgy could have three body-centred perceptual fields, but they baulk at the thought that his experiences could occur within a single *phenomenal* field. What might be said in support of such worries?

Those who doubt whether Borgy puts any pressure on the embodiment constraint would be ill-advised to put any weight on the fact that it is difficult to *imagine* what it might be like to be Borgy. True, the attempt to imagine what it would be like to inhabit three bodies at once seems to degenerate into imagining what it would be like to inhabit three bodies successively (which is a very different thing indeed), but these imaginative difficulties have little evidential force. As we noted in Chapter 3, we should not mistake the inability to project oneself into a certain phenomenal perspective for the inability to conceive that a certain type of phenomenal perspective is possible. (Moreover, when pressed this imaginative difficulty does not reveal a deeper worry about inconceivability in the way that the imaginative challenge posed by partial unity turned out to (see §2.4)). If we are to reject the thought that Borgy could retain a single phenomenal field we will need to do more than appeal to imaginative difficulties.

One line of argument for thinking that Borgy's experiences couldn't be phenomenally unified appeals to considerations of consistency. If one thought that phenomenally unified experiences must be consistent then one might also think that Borgy couldn't have a single phenomenal perspective on the grounds that his experiences couldn't be mutually consistent. But this objection is not convincing. Even if there were a consistency constraint on phenomenal unity—and I argued in §3.2 that there isn't—it is not at all clear that Borgy must flout it. Borgy has three bodies, and there is every reason to suppose that the representational contents of his perceptual experience would reflect this fact. In the same way that our bodily sensations are 'tagged' to body parts, so too Borgy's experiences would presumably be 'tagged' to one or other of his bodies. I might experience myself as having a pain in the big toe of my left foot, but Borgy would experience himself as having a pain in the big toe of the left foot of body A; whereas I might have a visual experience as of a monkey directly in front of me, Borgy would have a visual experience as of a monkey directly in front of body B, and so on.

But perhaps our imagined critic has been approaching matters from the wrong angle. Perhaps the problem with Borgy is that his phenomenal perspective *prevents* certain kinds of inconsistency from taking hold. The fact that our perceptual fields are structured in terms of a single egocentric frame of reference allows that the contents of any one sensory field can come into conflict with those of another. As we saw in §10.3, our cognitive architecture ensures that most inter-modal conflicts are 'ironed out' prior to consciousness; nonetheless, there remains some scope for inter-modal conflict within our experience. But Borgy's perceptual experiences are structured around distinct frames of reference, and thus the range of perceptual conflict that he is able to enjoy will be extremely limited in scope. Hence, the objection goes, we have reason to doubt whether his perceptual experiences could be phenomenally unified with each other. Those experiences that are structured around any one of his three bodies might be so unified, but those that are structured around distinct bodies could not be.

It seems to me that this objection simply begs the question against the claim that Borgy could have a unified consciousness. Why should we suppose that perceptual experiences can be phenomenally unified with each other only if they fall within a single frame of reference? As a rough parallel, consider the relationship between perceptual states and states of imagination. The contents of these states may not be located within a single frame of reference, but it is not uncommon for perceptual experiences to be phenomenally unified with imaginative experiences. Similarly, I suggest that Borgy's various perceptual experiences and bodily sensations could also fall within a single phenomenal field despite their lack of spatial unity.

Another reason for thinking that Borgy couldn't possess a unified consciousness concerns what we might call 'joint actions'. Although the term 'joint agency' is normally reserved for actions that involve the integrated activity of multiple agents, I use it here for actions that Borgy executes by means of the integrated activity of more than one of his three bodies. For example, Borgy might use all three of his bodies to manoeuvre a piano up a flight of stairs. In order to carry out joint actions, Borgy will need some way of keeping track of the spatial relations between his three bodies and their parts. Further, if we are to model Borgy's joint actions on our own actions, then this process of keeping track will need to be non-inferential—he will need to experience the relations between his bodies in the way in which we experience the relations between our hands. But—the objection runs—Borgy will be able to enjoy non-inferential awareness of the spatial relations between his bodies only if he has a single body image that represents each of his three bodies, and he will be unable to acquire or maintain any such body image because the spatial relations between his three bodies will be constantly changing. But if Borgy cannot carry out joint actions, then his repertoire of basic actions will be limited to actions that involve only a single body. And if that were the case, then—the argument continues—it is hard to see how he could also have a single phenomenal field. For surely part of what is entailed by the claim that Borgy has a single phenomenal field is that he would have command of each of his three bodies as a single agent—that he could realize his intentions via his several bodies in the direct manner in which we are able to realize our intentions through our several limbs.

There is much that might be said in response to this objection, but I will let the following two points suffice. First, it is far from obvious that Borgy couldn't possess a single body image that incorporates information about each of his three bodies. Remember that his three brains communicate with each other in much the way that our two hemispheres communicate with each other. And if inter-hemispheric communication is able to sustain a single body image in our case, then perhaps inter-cerebral communication is able to sustain a single body image in Borgy's case. Secondly, and more fundamentally, even if phenomenal unity brings with it some kind of conjoint availability for cognitive and behavioural control, we should not assume that it brings with it the capacity for joint agency as understood above. As I pointed out above, Borgy will be able to draw on the joint contents of his perceptual fields for various forms of theoretical reasoning. He will be able to work out whether the ducks in Paris are noisier than the ducks in Sydney, or whether it is hotter in Sydney than it is in Tucson. So, even if Borgy were unable to execute joint actions—and it is unclear whether this claim can be substantiated—this limitation must be set against the fact that the contents of his three perceptual fields will be jointly available for certain forms of cognitive consumption.

A final objection is that Borgy's experience of embodiment couldn't be *genuine*—that he would not experience any of his bodies as truly his own. The thought behind the objection is this. Each of Borgy's three bodies would be an 'external object' relative to his other two bodies. Bodies B and C would be part of the furniture of the world from the perspective of body A, and of course body A would have precisely the same status from the perspectives of bodies B and C. Might this not lead to a deep ambivalence within Borgy's corporeal experience?

It is, of course, difficult to know what Borgy's experience of embodiment would be like; as we have already noted, our ability to know what it might be like to be multiply embodied is limited at best. However, I see no reason why Borgy's experience of embodiment shouldn't be any less robust than yours or mine. Borgy would indeed have a 'third-person' perspective on each of his bodies, but we too enjoy such a perspective on our own bodies when we catch sight of ourselves in the reflecting glass of an office block or a subway train. Given that such experiences do not engender feelings of corporeal alienation in our own case I fail to see why they should do so in Borgy's case.

11.5 Conclusion

This chapter has explored some of the many links between the unity of consciousness and bodily self-consciousness. I began by considering the claim that bodily self-consciousness might ground the unity of consciousness as such. I rejected this thought on the grounds that certain modes of consciousness lack any bodily content, and focused instead on the embodiment constraint: the claim that in order to be phenomenally unified with each other those conscious states that are forms of bodily self-consciousness must represent one's own body as an integrated object.

I then examined three challenges to the embodiment constraint. The first of these challenges focused on Bermúdez's analysis of the spatial content of bodily experience. Drawing on Merleau-Ponty's claim that 'the outline of the body constitutes a border that ordinary spatial relations cannot cross', Bermúdez's analysis provided us with reason to doubt whether bodily sensations and perceptual experiences can be located within a single frame of reference. The key move in dissolving this worry, I suggested, lies in the realization that although the fundamental location of bodily sensations is given by reference to a body part, those body parts are themselves experienced as located within an egocentric frame of reference, thus allowing for spatial relations between the objects of 'inner' and 'outer' experience.

I then turned to pathologies of bodily experiences—most notably depersonalization and Cotard's delusion. These conditions appear to put pressure on the embodiment constraint, for those who suffer from them seem to have lost the normal integrity of bodily self-consciousness but do not appear to have suffered from a corresponding breakdown in the overall phenomenal unity of consciousness. However, I suggested that this pressure is more apparent than real, for the loss of bodily self-consciousness that occurs in these conditions appears to be restricted to the sense of 'affective identification' with one's body. These conditions put pressure on the proposal that the unity of consciousness is grounded in bodily self-consciousness only if that notion is understood to involve affective identification with one's body. James may have had something like that thought in mind in suggesting that the unity of consciousness is grounded in 'the warm animal feeling' of bodily self-consciousness, but this claim was not built into the embodiment constraint.

A third and final challenge to the embodiment constraint focused on the possibility of multiple embodiment—or rather, the experience of multiple embodiment. Whether or not such experiences fall within the range of those that we can enjoy—and we saw that there is tantalizing evidence to suggest that they might—they certainly don't seem to be deeply impossible. More to the point, there doesn't seem to be any incoherence in the thought that one could experience oneself as multiply embodied whilst retaining a fully unified stream of consciousness. And if that's right then the embodiment constraint is false. The upshot of this chapter, I suggest, is that phenomenal unity is fundamentally independent of the sense of embodiment. Bodily self-consciousness does make a vital contribution to our ordinary sense of self-consciousness, but the link between the unity of consciousness on the one hand and the unity of embodiment on the other is not indissoluble.

12

The Self

Thus far I have said rather little about 'the self', but no account of the unity of consciousness would be complete unless it had something to say about the connections between the unity of consciousness and the self. My treatment of the self can be read as a tale of two halves. In the first part of the chapter I argue that prominent accounts of the self are unsatisfactory insofar as they fail to ensure that the intimate relations between the self and the unity of conscious- ness are secured. §12.2 makes this case with respect to biological (or 'animalist') treatments of the self, and §12.3 makes this case with respect to psychological (or 'neo-Lockean') treatments of the self. In the second half of the chapter I sketch an account of the self that attempts to do justice to the essential connections between the self and the unity of consciousness. I call the view that emerges from these labours 'virtual phenomenalism'. Selves, on this view, are the central characters in a kind of phenomenal fiction.

12.1 Selves

What might we be looking for in looking for an account of the self? In this chapter I will focus on three roles that 'the self' or 'subject of experience' (I use these terms interchangeably) ought to play. These roles are not the only ones that are associated with the self, but taken together they are clearly central to the notion of the self. Anything that might hope to qualify as a bone fide self ought to play all three roles, and anything that does play all three roles will thereby qualify as a self.

Firstly, experiences don't occur as self-standing entities, but are 'had by' selves. Selves are the things to which we ascribe conscious states. Call this the *ownership* component of the self-role. Secondly, selves are the objects of first-person reflection—'I'-thoughts. What one thinks about when one thinks in the first-person is a self—indeed, it is oneself. Call this the *referential* component of the self-role. Thirdly, selves have a perspective or point of view on the world. A self is not merely an entity *in* the world, it is also something *for* which the world itself is an entity. Call this the *perspectival* component of the self-role.

What kind of thing might play these three roles? Two very different answers to this question dominate the contemporary landscape. According to some theorists, the entity that plays the self role—at least where you or I are concerned—is nothing less than an animal, the member of a certain species. According to this biological (or 'animalist') account of the self, the owner of one's mental states is an organism; first-person thought picks out a particular organism; and the perspective of any one self is none other than the perspective of a particular organism. You came into existence when a certain animal came into existence, and you will continue to exist only as long as that animal exists.[1]

The second of these two approaches to the self follows Locke in holding that selves are to be understood in broadly psychological rather than biological terms. Famously, Locke claimed that distinctness of consciousness suffices for distinctness of personal identity, although he was not terribly clear about just what 'identity of consciousness' involves. It is possible that Locke might have been looking to develop what I will call a 'phenomenalist' conception of the self (Atherton 1983), but this is not how 'neo-Lockeans' have developed his approach. Instead, neo-Lockeans think of the self in purely psychological terms. On this view, selves are minds—networks of causally and intentionally integrated mental states. Older strands in this tradition focused on the psychological unity and continuity provided by memory, whereas contemporary versions of the approach tend to employ a more inclusive conception of the kinds of mental states and relations that can bind together the parts of a person into unitary person-stages and in turn bind those person-stages together so as to form a temporally extended self.[2]

Although the biological and psychological treatments of the self dominate the contemporary discussion, there is a third approach that one can take to the self: a phenomenalist approach. According to the phenomenalist the identity conditions for selves involve essential reference to streams of consciousness— that is, sequences of phenomenal states that are bound together by chains of

---

[1] For examples of the biological approach see Ayers (1991); Johnston (1987); Olson (1997); van Inwagen (1990); and Snowdon (1990).

[2] For examples of the psychological approach see Lewis (1976); Noonan (1989); Nozick (1981); Parfit (1984); and Shoemaker (1984).

phenomenal continuity. As we will see in §12.4, the phenomenalist approach can be developed in various ways.

The contrast between these approaches to the self can be safely ignored in many contexts, for the kinds of organisms in which we are most interested are human beings, and human beings typically have only a single mind and a single stream of consciousness at any one point in time. But in seeking to understand our notion of a self we need to consider situations in which the links between biological, psychological, and phenomenal unity are severed. Reflection on such cases, I will suggest, motivates the thought that selves should be understood in phenomenal rather than biological or psychological terms.

12.2 The biological self

There are many circumstances in which it is perfectly legitimate to think of ourselves as animals. Indeed, this book itself provides an example of such a context, for in evaluating the unity thesis I equated subjects of experiences with animals of a certain species—human beings. But although the animalist conception captures a central strand in our conception of the self, it has important limitations.

These limitations can be revealed by considering an animal that possesses more than one stream of consciousness at a time. Peter van Inwagen has provided us with a portrait of such a creature—Cerberus. Cerberus has two heads, each of which has its own brain. These two brains

are for all practical purposes identical (they are at least as similar as the brains of monozygotic human twins), and each is the seat of all those functions of which a human brain is the seat (including ratiocination and the processing of sensory information and the control of voluntary motion) except one: neither contributes any direction to the homeodynamic processes that hold the organism together: neither exercises any control over metabolism or the healing of traumatic lesions or antisepsis or respiration or pulse rate or anything of that sort. All such 'maintenance'—insofar as it is localized—is under the control of a quite separate organ, M. (van Inwagen 1990: 191)

Although Cerberus is biologically unified he is phenomenologically disunified, for 'he' has two streams of consciousness, one in each of his two heads. How many selves does Cerberus have? Animalists such as van Inwagen hold that the only self here is Cerberus, but it seems to me that there is good reason to reject this answer.

Let us begin with the ownership component of selfhood. Suppose that Cerberus' right-brain stream contains an experience of severe pain, while his left-brain stream is entirely devoid of pain. The animalist is compelled to say that Cerberus is in pain in virtue of the fact that his right-brain stream contains a pain experience. But this description leaves out the fact that Cerberus has a stream that is free of pain. A better description of this scenario—it seems to me—is that we are dealing here with two conscious selves, one that is in pain and another that is pain-free. A world in which 'Cerberus' has experiences of pain in both streams of consciousness is worse than a world in which he has such experiences in only one stream, not (just) because there is more pain in such a world but, intuitively, because additional selves are in pain.

In response, the animalist might claim to have a perfectly adequate description of this case according to which the only subject of these experiences is Cerberus himself. Instead of thinking of experience in terms of a two-place relation between selves and the objects of experience, we should think of it as a three-place relation between selves, the objects of experience, and streams of consciousness. In other words, we should replace such claims as 'Cerberus is conscious of the dog', with 'Cerberus is conscious of the dog in the stream of consciousness located in his right brain'. Perhaps we could adopt this conception of Cerberus, but to do so would be to revise our ordinary conception of the relationship between consciousness and the self. As things stand we do not think of consciousness as a three-place relation. Moreover, it is arguable that in adopting this position the animalist is implicitly treating Cerberus as having two selves, for in relativizing ascriptions of experience to one or the other stream of experience we would in effect be taking streams to play the ownership component of the self-role.

What about the referential component of the self-role? Could Cerberus himself be the object of 'I'-thoughts located in each of 'his' streams of consciousness? Consider two thoughts, one of which occurs in his right brain and one in his left brain. These two thoughts are akin to 'I'-thoughts, but I will call them 'I★-thoughts' in order not to prejudge the question of whether or not they really are 'I'-thoughts. The question we need to ask is whether I★-thoughts really are 'I'-thoughts, and—if so—whether they might refer to Cerberus himself.

If I★-thoughts are indeed 'I'-thoughts then they ought to behave as 'I'-thoughts ought to behave. Can they? Suppose that Cerberus tokens the thought <I★ am hot> in one of his brains and the thought <I★ am hungry> in his other brain. Will Cerberus also token the thought <I★ am hot and hungry>? No. At least, he won't token this thought on the basis of tokening <I★ am hot> and <I★ am hungry>. These two thoughts could generate the conjunctive thought <I★ am hot and hungry> only if they were phenomenally unified, which—given that they occur in distinct brains—we are assuming is not the case. The lack of conjunctive availability extends from Cerberus' conscious thoughts to his perceptual and sensory states. Suppose that Cerberus has an experience of heat in one conscious stream and an experience of hunger in the other conscious stream. Cerberus might examine his behaviour and conclude <I★ am hot and hungry>, but he won't be able to form this thought on the basis of introspection, and as a result this thought won't have the kind of justification distinctive of introspectively based thoughts.

Their inability to generate conjunctive thoughts is not the only respect in which Cerberus' I★-thoughts fail to play to the functional role of 'I'-thoughts. Suppose that Cerberus believes that he is not thirsty, but suddenly experiences a sensation of thirst. Normally, the experience of thirst will lead a person to replace the belief <I am not thirsty> with the belief <I am thirsty>, but this will not happen in Cerberus' case if his sensation of thirst occurs in one stream of consciousness but his belief that he is not thirsty occurs in the other stream.

The point generalizes from theoretical reasoning to practical reasoning. Consider Perry's case in which he is inadvertently spilling sugar all over the supermarket floor (Perry 1979). Perry thinks to himself, 'The guy who is spilling sugar is a real idiot'. This thought is self-referential: it refers to Perry, for he is the person who is leaving a trail of sugar. But it refers to him under a demonstrative mode of presentation ('that guy who is spilling this sugar') rather than via the first-person ('I myself am leaving a trail of sugar'). Now, suppose that Cerberus is in Perry's situation: he too is leaving a trail of sugar in a supermarket. Unlike Perry, however, Cerberus realizes that he is responsible for leaving the trail of sugar. But there's a catch. Cerberus's realization is restricted to his right brain; his left brain has no inkling of this fact. Will Cerberus' realization lead him to form the intention to desist from spilling sugar on the floor? Not necessarily. Suppose that Cerberus' right brain has antisocial inclinations: *it* doesn't care about leaving a mess in the supermarket. Cerberus' left brain is civically minded, but the only representation of the culprit than it possesses is a demonstrative one ('that guy who is trailing sugar'), and a merely demonstrative representation of the situation won't lead him to act. So, although Cerberus has an I★-based representation of the culprit and an I★-based desire not to spill sugar he won't stop spilling sugar, for these two representations are not contained within the same stream of consciousness and as a result cannot be integrated in the way required for Cerberus to form the intention to stop spilling sugar.

A final respect in which the cognitive dynamics of I★-thoughts departs from those of 'I'-thoughts concerns inconsistency. Suppose that Cerberus' right brain contains an experience of being hot but his left brain contains no such experience. Assume, further, that Cerberus has two belief-forming systems, each of which has access to only one of these two streams of consciousness. Although it is clearly irrational to have obviously inconsistent 'I'-thoughts—if, indeed, it is even

possible to have obviously inconsistent 'I'-thoughts—it doesn't seem at all irrational for Cerberus to form the beliefs <I★ am hot> and <I★ am not hot>. After all,
both beliefs will be warranted given the experiential content of his two streams.

The upshot of the foregoing is that the functional role played by Cerberus'
I★-thoughts departs in fundamental respects from that played by 'I'-thoughts.
Relative to the organism as a whole, I★-thoughts do not play the direct role in
practical and theoretical reasoning that 'I'-thoughts ought to play. If these
thoughts refer to Cerberus, then they cannot also be 'I'-thoughts.

In response, the animalist might point out that we need to distinguish the
functional role that a thought *does* play from the role that it *should* play.
Famously, one can believe that there is petrol in the tank and that an open
flame is likely to ignite petrol fumes without putting these thoughts together in
the ways in which they ought to be put together. Developing this point, the
animalist might admit that although I★-thoughts don't play the functional role
that 'I'-thoughts ought to play, they should nonetheless be regarded as *degenerate*
'I'-thoughts rather than some other species of thought altogether.

I think this response fails to get to the heart of the matter. The crucial issue is
not that Cerberus' I★-thoughts aren't integrated with each other in the ways
that 'I'-thoughts that refer to Cerberus ought to be, but that they *cannot* be
integrated with each other in these ways. His problem is one of competence not
performance. Given this, we have good reason to think that the norms govern-
ing 'I'-thoughts don't apply to I★-thoughts, and hence that I★-thoughts are not
'I'-thoughts. Cerberus can think of himself by means of multiple modes of
presentation (as Ceberus; as the creature that he can see in the mirror; as his
mother's favourite son), but he cannot think of himself via 'I'-thoughts—he
cannot think of himself *as himself*.

What about the perspectival component of the self-role? Should we think of
Cerberus as having two experiential perspectives, or should we instead think of
Cerberus as supporting two selves, each of which has its own perspective on
the world? Although the former description of the case is not without merit, the
latter is preferable. In the relevant sense there is no single thing that it is like to
be Cerberus. There is something that it is like to enjoy the experiences that are
located in Cerberus' right brain, and there is something that it is like to enjoy
the experiences that are located in his left brain, but—given that these two sets
of experiences are not components of any overarching phenomenal state—
there is no single thing that it is like to enjoy both sets of experiences at once. In
other words, Cerberus *as such* has no phenomenal perspective.

We can perhaps better appreciate this point by considering members of our
own species whose situation resembles that of Cerberus' in relevant respects.

Consider conjoined twins, such as Abigail and Brittany Hensel.[3] Although the Hensel twins share a body (with two hearts and stomachs and a single liver, large intestine, bladder, and set of reproductive organs), they have separate heads and spinal cords. Despite the fact that the twins presumably enjoy many of the same types of experiences, there is little doubt that each twin has her own phenomenal perspective. I suggest that what holds true of the Hensel twins also holds true of Cerberus. The fact that Cerberus is one organism whereas the Hensel twins are arguably separate organisms who happen to share a body is irrelevant: we should no more assign a single self to Cerberus than we should assign a single self to the Hensel twins.

Where does this leave us? Reflection on Cerberus suggests that the self follows phenomenology rather than biology when these two kinds of unities are pitted against each other. The biological strand in our self-conception may be an important one, but a full understanding of the self must also do justice to those intuitions that are *at odds* with the biological approach to the self, and the considerations presented in this section suggest that those intuitions run deep.

12.3 The psychological self

As we observed in §12.1, many theorists follow Locke (1690/1975) in thinking that our identity is best captured not by appeal to biological notions but by appeal to psychological and causal notions. The neo-Lockean identifies selves with minds: networks of causally and intentionally integrated mental states. Might this neo-Lockean approach do a better job of capturing the intimate relations between the unity of consciousness and the self than the biological approach did?

The first thing we need to ask is whether minds (as neo-Lockeans conceive of them) *could* exhibit phenomenal disunity. Is it possible to construct a 'psychological analogue' of Cerberus, or are there reasons to think that there are constitutive relations between phenomenal unity ('co-consciousness') on the one hand and co-mentality on the other, such that a single mind couldn't sustain phenomenally disunified states at one and the same time?

Although advocates of the psychological approach have said surprisingly little about this issue, it is possible to identify two strands of thought within the

---

[3] See *Time Magazine* 25 March (1996).

literature. The first strand suggests that it is possible for a single mind to contain phenomenally disunified states, at least for short periods of time. Indeed, many theorists would claim that this is not merely possible but actual. According to a widely held view of the split-brain syndrome, split-brain patients have a single mind that sustains two streams of consciousness, at least for certain periods of time (§9.3). Whether or not this version of the two-streams model correctly describes the structure of consciousness in the split-brain—if the arguments presented in Chapter 9 are on the right track then it doesn't—it certainly seems to provide us with a *coherent* account of the split-brain.[4]

Running counter to this line of thought is another, which suggests that it might not be quite so easy for a single mind to contain two streams of consciousness as first appearances might indicate. The author who has done the most to develop this position is Sydney Shoemaker (1996, 2003). Although Shoemaker grants that 'co-mental' states need not be 'co-conscious', he also argues that there are constitutive relations between mental unity and the unity of consciousness.

If, perhaps per impossibile, there were [two] streams of consciousness realized in the two hemispheres of a brain in such a way that the two were causally insulated from each other, and there were no possibility of integrating their contents (other than the way in which the contents of the minds of two friends are integrated), what we would have is two minds, and two persons, in one body. (Shoemaker 1996: 191)

Why would causally insulated streams of consciousness bring with them two minds? Shoemaker doesn't spell out the argument behind this claim in full detail, but the thought he has in mind is this: the functional constraints on what it is for a mental state to be the kind of mental state that it is entail that there are principled limitations on the ways in which co-consciousness and co-mentality can dissociate from each other. Let us consider this issue in some detail.

How might a single mind support two streams of consciousness? The most straightforward answer to this question takes the form of what I will call the *static model*. Consider a mind whose unconscious mental states (beliefs, desires, intentions, and the like) can be divided into two discrete sets, A and B. The intentional states within each set are intentionally and causally integrated with each other, but no member of each set is intentionally or causally integrated

---

[4]   The apparent intelligibility of Parfit's physics exam case (1984: 247) provides further reason to think that it is coherent to suppose that a single mind could contain two streams of consciousness, even if only for brief periods.

with any member of the other set. In this mind, each of these two sets of states governs and is in turn governed by a distinct stream of consciousness, ST_a and ST_b respectively. Selection for entry into ST_a takes place from within the members of set A and selection for entry into ST_b takes place from within the members of set B. Further, once states from A and B have been selected for entry into ST_a and ST_b respectively they do not interact with each other—at least, not in the high-grade manner in which co-conscious states ('stream-mates') do. Finally, the components of each of these two streams of consciousness have only a limited influence on whether the mental states contained in this mind enter consciousness. For example, conscious states in ST_a can influence which members of A (but not B) enter ST_a, but they cannot have any influence on which mental states enter ST_b. Parallel constraints, of course, apply to the influence of conscious states that are contained within ST_b.

There are good reasons to doubt whether this static model of disunity is coherent. First, it is part of the functional role of mental states—at least, personal-level intentional states such as desires, intentions, and judgements—that they are able to be 'drawn into' consciousness as and when they ought to be. Where mental states m_1 and m_2 are appropriately related to each other the 'entry' of m_1 into consciousness ought to bring with it the 'entry' of m_2 into consciousness. Suppose, for example, that m_1 is the thought <Today is Tuesday> and m_2 the thought <The garbage ought to be put out on Tuesdays>. These two thoughts ought to lead one to token the thought <The garbage out to be put out today>. Secondly, it is part of the functional role of mental states that, when conscious, they are able to be co-conscious with each other. If the thoughts <Today is Tuesday> and <The garbage ought to be put out on Tuesdays> are simultaneously conscious then they ought also to be co-conscious—at least if they belong to the same mind. Thirdly, it is part of the functional role of mental states they are able to initiate the entry of appropriate unconscious states into consciousness. This component of a state's functional role would also be severely compromised within a statically disunified mind. Taken together, these considerations suggest that the static model of disunity is of dubious coherence. Even granting the fact that the functional constraints on the identity of mental states are somewhat loose, the amount of encapsulation present in a statically disunified mind would, it seems, prevent the states within it from playing the kinds of functional roles that they would need to play in order to qualify as bona fide, personal-level, mental states.

The static model of disunity might be incoherent, but it is not the only model of how a single mind could implement two streams of consciousness at a time. Rather than taking the division between the mind's two streams of consciousness to reflect an underlying intentional division, we might think of phenomenal disunity as superimposed on a single set of mental states the members of which are intentionally and causally integrated with each other. Call such a mind a *dynamically* disunified mind. A dynamically disunified mind also has two streams of consciousness, but in such a mind there are no fixed barriers that would prevent any two mental states from entering consciousness together in the way that there are within a statically disunified mind. Those mental states that can enter consciousness can enter either of the mind's two streams of consciousness. Further, in a dynamically disunified mind there are no fixed constraints on the ways in which conscious states are able to elicit the entry of unconscious mental states into consciousness. Activity within ST_a is capable of triggering the entry of any particular state into either ST_a or ST_b, and precisely the same is true of ST_b. The only encapsulation present in a dynamically disunified mind is that between simultaneously conscious states. Whereas high-grade integration between any two simultaneously conscious states will always be possible within a mind that contains a single stream of consciousness, this will not be possible within a dynamically disunified mind. Instead, high-grade integration will be possible only between those states that occur within the same stream of consciousness. Because conscious states that are not co-conscious will have the potential to be co-conscious, in a dynamically disunified mind there are no barriers to co-consciousnes at the level of conscious state types in the way that there are within a statically disunified mind.

It seems to me that the notion of a dynamically disunified mind is consistent with the functional constraints that govern the identity of mental states. True, token conscious states within a dynamically disunified mind would not be available for high-grade integration with each other in the ways in which simultaneously co-mental states ought to be, but this departure from the functional roles of mentality is not, it would seem, grave enough to reduce the notion of a dynamically disunified mind to incoherence. Of course, one might argue that functional constraints on consciousness itself—rather than those that merely concern the identity of particular kinds of mental states—require that co-mental states that are simultaneously conscious must also be co-conscious (or at least potentially so). But even if this claim were to be granted—and I myself would be reluctant to grant it—it is not clear that it couldn't be met by a dynamically disunified mind. After all, in a dynamically disunified mind any two conscious states will be potentially co-conscious even if they are not actually co-conscious. (More carefully, any two conscious state tokens will be tokens of types of mental states that can have co-conscious tokens.)

The upshot of these reflections is this. On the one hand, the functional constraints on the identity of mental states and consciousness itself place important constraints in the ways in which a single mind can exhibit phenomenal disunity. It is no accident that our minds are phenomenally unified, for phenomenal unity stands at the heart of any properly functioning mind. We might think of phenomenal unity as a kind of 'regulative ideal' on minds, such that there would be 'pressure' for a mind with two streams of consciousness to either fragment into two minds or for those two streams of consciousness to merge into a single stream. On the other hand, we have no *a priori* guarantee that simultaneously co-mental states must be co-conscious. Indeed, the model of dynamic disunity that we developed suggests that it might even possible for a single mind to exhibit phenomenal disunity as its normal form of operation.

So much for the question of whether it is possible for a single mind to exhibit phenomenal disunity. Let me now turn to the question of how we ought to assign selves in such contexts. Should we describe a disunified mind as a single self with two streams of consciousness, or should we instead say that we are dealing with two conscious selves?

Let us begin with the question of ownership. There is certainly *something* to be said for ascribing ownership of conscious states to the mind in which they occur. After all, on the functionalist account of mental states within which we have been working a state's identity will be fixed in part by the relations that it bears to those states with which it is co-mental.[5] But there is *also* something to be said for ascribing ownership of such states to the stream of consciousness in which they figure, for the fact that the state is a conscious state will depend on the properties underlying that stream of consciousness. Consider a phenomenally disunified mind in which experience e_1 occurs in one conscious stream and e_2 in the other. In order to explain why the one stream includes e_1 whilst the other stream includes e_2 we will need to appeal to features underlying the evolution of each of these two streams. And that in turn requires thinking of these two streams as playing the kind of explanatory role that selves play. In other words, there is

---

[5] In his early writing on personal identity Shoemaker argued that the psychological account of personal identity falls out of a functionalist analysis of mental states—that psychological continuity is simply the playing out over time of the defining functional roles of mental states. However, in considering the relationship between mental unity and the unity of consciousness Shoemaker later suggested that the psychological continuity that fixes the defining functional roles of mental states may in fact be that which constitutes the identity over time of a stream of consciousness (1996: 192). If this suggestion is right—and there is certainly something to it—then this provides further reason for thinking that selves cannot be prised apart from streams of consciousness.

something to be said for thinking of a situation in which a mind contains more than one stream of consciousness as a situation in which we have multiple conscious selves within a single mind.

What about the self considered as the referent of first-person thought? Could 'I'-thoughts tokened within each stream of a two-stream mind be co-referential, or should we instead take them to refer to different selves? Davis (1997) and Hirsch (1991), among others, have assumed that 'I'-thoughts contained within different streams could be co-referential. In adopting this position they face the same challenge that the animalist faces in explaining how I*-thoughts tokened in each of Cerberus' two minds could be both genuine 'I'-thoughts and also co-referential. The basic argument, you will remember, is that I*-tokened thoughts in distinct streams will not be available for the kinds of high-grade integration that co-referential 'I'-thoughts must be available for. This lack of inferential promiscuity will be most pronounced in the context of the static model, but it also holds in the context of the dynamic model.

What about the perspectival role of the self? How many perspectives should we think of a disunified mind as having? There is no doubt that *a* case can be made for thinking of such a mind as having a single perspective or point of view. For one thing, the intentional stance (Dennett 1987) will be of some use in explaining and predicting its behaviour, although given the lack of high-grade integration resulting from phenomenal disunity we might expect such a mind to exhibit rather less consistency and coherence than is exhibited by a phenomenally unified mind. But there is another—and arguably deeper—sense in which we should think of a phenomenally disunified mind as having *two* experiential perspectives. What it would be like to enjoy the one stream of consciousness would be distinct from what it would be like to enjoy the other stream of consciousness. Or, to put the point more carefully, since we cannot think of a self as *having* multiple perspectives, we should take there to be two perspectives in a disunified mind, each of which is had by a distinct self. A disunified mind would not itself have any conscious perspective.

It is time to recap. Despite the Lockean roots of their view the advocates of the psychological conception of the self have had rather little to say about how the unity of consciousness might be related to the self. Drawing on Shoemaker's work, I have argued that although there are limits to the ways in which phenomenal unity and mental unity might come apart, we have no *a priori* reason to deny that a single mind could support two streams of consciousness. I suggest that were such a situation to obtain, we should think of it as a scenario in which there are two conscious selves within a single mind rather than a single self with two streams of consciousness.

12.4 Selves and streams

We can identify where the biological and psychological approaches to the self go wrong by returning to the unity thesis. The unity thesis, you will recall, claims that any subject of experience will have a single total phenomenal state at any one point in time. This phenomenal state will subsume each of the conscious states that the subject has at the time in question—it will fully capture what it is like to be that subject of experience. In evaluating the unity thesis I stipulated that subjects of experience are to be understood in biological terms—as human beings. Thus understood, the unity thesis is clearly an *a posteriori* claim. Further, if true, it is a contingent truth rather than one that is metaphysically necessary. But there is another way to approach the unity thesis. Rather than start with a fixed conception of the self and ask whether selves thus understood must have a unified consciousness, we might start with the thought that selves must have a unified consciousness and use this claim to *constrain* our conception of the self. In fact, I would suggest that this is precisely the lesson to be learnt from the previous two sections: the biological and psychological accounts of the self fail because neither ensures that simultaneously co-subjective conscious states must be phenomenally unified. We need a notion of the self according to which the relationship between the self and the unity of consciousness is *constitutive*.

In broad outlines the approach required at this point is obvious: we need a *phenomenalist* conception of the self. In other words, we need to construct selves out of streams of consciousness. As we will see, there is more than one way in which the phenomenalist approach to the self can be developed. Perhaps the most flat-footed version of phenomenalism holds that selves are nothing but streams of consciousness. Just as the animalist identifies the self with an animal and the neo-Lockean identifies the self with a mind, this kind of phenomenalist identifies the self with a stream of consciousness. Given the repeated references to consciousness in Locke's own account of personal identity we might describe this view as a kind of neo-Lockean account of the self were that label not already associated with the psychological account. Instead, I will call this position *naïve phenomenalism*.

I will evaluate the prospects of naïve phenomenalism by considering a number of objections to it. A first objection to naïve phenomenalism is that it gets the ontology of selves wrong. Selves, one might be tempted to say, cannot simply *be* streams of consciousness for selves are things 'in their own right' whereas streams of consciousness are not—they are modifications of selves. I have some sympathy with this objection, but it is surely too quick when put this way, for there is surely some sense in which streams of consciousness *are* 'things in their own right'. After all, streams of consciousness have their own principle of unity that binds their parts together. Conscious states are not grouped together into streams of consciousness in an arbitrary or haphazard manner. Instead, they are bound together by relations of synchronic and diachronic phenomenal unity. In fact, it is arguable that the forces that knit together the components of a stream of consciousness are no less robust than those that knit together the parts of a single mind or even those that knit together the parts of a single animal. In each case, we have a genuine entity—a thing in its own right.

A second objection: 'Naïve phenomenalism cannot do justice to the sense in which streams of consciousness are "owned" or "had by" selves. Selves cannot "own" or "have" their experiences if they just are streams of consciousness'. One option for the naïve phenomenalist here is to interpret talk of selves as 'owning' or 'having' their experiences in mereological terms. The idea, in other words, is that experiences belong to selves in the way in which the parts of a whole belong to that whole. Selves have states of consciousness in the way in which pizzas have slices, universities have philosophy departments, and cricket matches have innings. Since a stream of consciousness qualifies as an improper part of itself, this move can even accommodate a (deflationary) sense in which a self can have an entire stream of consciousness.

A third objection: 'Naïve phenomenalism cannot do justice to many of the everyday assertions we make about ourselves. Such claims as "I weigh 64 kilograms" or "I will die" could not be true if the object of first-person reference is nothing but a stream of consciousness'. But although the naïve phenomenalist might not be able to take such claims at face value, finding a plausible reinterpretation of them is not overly difficult. Streams of consciousness don't weigh 64 kg nor are they mortal, but the animal with which a stream of consciousness is associated might well have such properties. In this way, the naïve phenomenalist can provide a plausible interpretation of such sentences.

A fourth objection: 'Naïve phenomenalism cannot account for the modal properties of the self. We believe that we could have had experiences other than those that we've actually had. Indeed, we often *wish* that we were having completely different experiences from those that we actually have. But if phenomenalism were true then such thoughts would be false and such desires incoherent. If I am identical to a stream of consciousness then I couldn't have had any experiences other than those that I have actually had. As Eddy Zemach puts it, 'Propositions such as, "Had I married Jane rather than Sue, my entire life would have been different"; "Had my parents not immigrated to this country when I was a baby, I would have perished in the holocaust" do not seem to be self-contradictory, but if I am the majority of my actual experiences they must be considered logically false' (Zemach 1987: 215).

Why exactly does Zemach think that these propositions must be considered logically false? The thought, I take it, is that streams of consciousness are akin to sets insofar as they have their members essentially. And if that is right, then naïve phenomenalism entails that one couldn't have had any experiences other than those that one has actually had. But the objection can be resisted by denying that streams of consciousness possess their parts essentially. Like any complex event, it is not difficult to conceive of one's stream of consciousness as having had different experiential constituents. We can conceive of an alternative world in which the Second World War started off in much the same way that it did but took a rather different turn at the Battle of Britain. Similarly, we can conceive of a world in which a stream of consciousness began in the same way it did in the actual world but unfolded very differently. Perhaps, as Zemach suggests, one could have married someone other than the person who one did in fact marry, and as a result had a very different set of experiences. We don't need to say that in such a world one would have had a different stream of consciousness—instead, we can say that in such a world one's stream of consciousness would have had different constituents. Alternatively, one can start from one's current experiences, and imagine that a different set of experiences led up to them.

More challenging for the naïve phenomenalist, perhaps, will be cases in which there are no experiences in common between one's actual self and the possible self that one is imagining (Sidelle 2002). Prima facie, it seems to be coherent to suppose that one could have enjoyed a stream of consciousness that had no experience in common with those that one has actually enjoyed. This is a problem for the naïve phenomenalist to the extent that it is unclear what might make the two streams counterparts of each other. The phenomenalist appears to need an anchor for such claims, something in virtue of which we can say that the imagined stream is a counterpart of the actual stream with which it is being compared. We will see that other versions of phenomenalism have the resources to provide such an anchor, but it is not clear that the naïve phenomenalist does. The naïve phenomenalist may need to accept that it is incoherent to suppose that one could have had radically different experiences.

This may be an objection to naïve phenomenalism but it is not a knockout blow, for a good case can be made for thinking that *any* plausible account of the self will need to reject some of the modal intuitions that surround the self. Psychological accounts must reject the apparently plausible claim that one could have had massive brain damage as a baby, since massive brain damage would presumably have led to the formation of a different psychological economy than that to which one is identical (Snowdon 1995). For their part biological theorists must reject the intuition that one could have been a different animal, or perhaps even a non-biological subject of experience—intuitions that are easily elicited by fairy tales and myths. So even if the phenomenalist were required to reject widespread intuitions about the modal properties of the self he or she would not be alone in this regard.

Another objection: 'Suppose that your stream of consciousness were to fission into two streams without loss of phenomenal continuity. Which of the two resulting streams would be yours? The phenomenalist can't say that both streams would be yours, for that would be to flout the claim that selves and streams of consciousness are inseparable. But if the post-fission selves are distinct from one another—as they appear to be—then they cannot both be identical to the pre-fission self. Given this, how could phenomenal continuity secure the continued existence of the self?'

Is phenomenal fission really possible? I think that this is something of an open question (§2.4). Perhaps there is something about the deep nature of consciousness that prevents a single stream of consciousness from splintering into phenomenal fragments. Lockwood attempts to motivate the thought that phenomenal fission is coherent by inviting us to imagine what it would be like to undergo a 'split-brain operation while conscious, where one strand of the corpus callosum is severed at a time' (1989: 87). Lockwood suggests that one would experience one's stream of consciousness gradually splitting into two. Perhaps so. But our ignorance about the physical basis of consciousness suggests that a certain amount of agnosticism may be in order here. Perhaps this procedure would lead instead to the instantaneous creation of two streams of consciousness, neither of which would qualify as a continuant of the earlier stream.

Even if phenomenal fission is possible the challenge that it would pose is not one that the phenomenalist would face alone. As with most of the objections examined in this section, versions of this objection can be levelled against both the biological and psychological conceptions of the self. Indeed, the naïve phenomenalist can appropriate the responses that the biological and psychological theorists have made to fission. According to one response, fission marks the separation of two pre-existing selves whose careers partially overlap (see Lewis 1976; Robinson 1985). According to another response, fission involves a single person dividing into two people who are numerically identical with one another and also with the person who divided into them (Dainton 1992). And according to a third response, phenomenal continuity ensures the continued existence of the self unless it takes a branching form (in which case the self ceases to exist) (Parfit 1971; Shoemaker 1970). Each of these responses incurs some intuitive cost, but fission is such a strange prospect that we shouldn't expect it to sit comfortably with our self-conception.

A final objection to naïve phenomenalism concerns phenomenal gaps—periods during which consciousness is entirely absent. The typical stream of consciousness probably lasts at most sixteen or so hours—roughly, the period between intervals of dreamless sleep. Within such an interval, each total experience is directly unified with its temporal neighbours, for the first experience in the stream will be linked to the last by an unbroken chain of phenomenal continuity. But the experiences that one has on falling asleep at night are not phenomenally unified with the experiences that one has on reawakening the following morning, for periods of unconsciousness intervene between them. How then might the naïve phenomenalist hold that these two streams of consciousness—the evening stream and the morning stream—are components of one and the same overarching stream of consciousness? And if the naïve phenomenalist allows that these streams are not 'co-streamal', then what grounds does she have for thinking that both streams can be assigned to a single subject of experience?

Let me begin by noting and then setting to one side two rather extreme responses to this problem. The first of these two responses involves denying that phenomenal gaps occur—or even that they could occur. Perhaps there is no hiatus in consciousness during the life of a normal individual, but only periods during which consciousness leaves no imprint on memory. But although this view has had notable advocates—Descartes seems to have held it, as did Leibniz and Husserl—evidence in its favour is rather thin on the ground. And even if there are no phenomenal gaps, the crucial point is that we have little hesitation in assuming that we could survive a temporary loss of consciousness. The continuity of consciousness is not essential to our *conception* of the self, and it is really our conception of the self that we are most interested in here.

A second extreme response to the objection is to bite the bullet, and hold that selves do indeed last only as long as unbroken chains of phenomenal continuity allow. This approach might appeal to those who are prepared to hold a radically revisionist conception of the self, but it does not tempt me. My aim here is to understand the role that the self plays within our conceptual scheme, and it is quite clear that we regard ourselves as being able to survive the onset of dreamless sleep.

In order to deal with problem of phenomenal gaps the naïve phenomenalist will need to engage in a project of 'bridge-building' (see Foster 1979, 1991;

Dainton & Bayne 2005). To fix ideas, let us consider what might make a stream of consciousness that occurs in one morning the (or at least 'a') continuation of a stream that occurred in the previous evening. What kind of relation might hold between these two streams such that they qualify as co-streamal (that is, as segments of a single overarching stream of consciousness)? One might be inclined to say that the two streams are co-streamal because they are had by the same subject of experience, but of course this route is not available to us here, for we are attempting to construct the self 'out of' streams of consciousness.

One approach to bridge-building appeals to qualitative similarity between the contents (or phenomenal character more generally) of the two streams (see Foster 1979, 1991). We might say that one stream is co-streamal with another if and only if the latter's content is a 'continuation' of the former's content—that is, if the contents of the two streams ensures that they are 'joinable'. The approach has some surface plausibility, for one does occasionally regain consciousness in a state whose character resembles that which one was in before one lost consciousness. However, the problems with this approach are also immediately apparent, for it is not uncommon to regain consciousness in a phenomenal state that is in no natural sense a continuation of that which one enjoyed when one lost consciousness. There are various stratagems that the advocate of this account might appeal to in order to meet this objection, but I will not rehearse them here, for the following two problems suggest that this approach to bridge-building is fundamentally flawed.[6]

The first problem is that phenomenal continuation clearly does not *suffice* to make successive streams components of a single overarching stream. Suppose that by some quirk of cosmic coincidence *you* wake up in precisely the same experiential state that *I* was in when I lost consciousness on the previous night. Your stream of consciousness would be a perfect continuation of mine, but these two streams would obviously not be co-streamal.

In response, the naïve phenomenalist might be temped to suggest that there are certain phenomenal features that are necessarily unique to particular streams of consciousness, and prevent those streams from being 'duplicated'. These features act as identity markers, 'branding' successive streams of consciousness with the mark of a particular subject of experience and thus binding them together as the components of a single overarching stream. But the idea of such a phenomenal 'brand' is surely implausible. Why should there be a phenomenal quality unique to one's own experience? And even if there is such a thing, what possible evidence could one have of its existence?

---

[6] See Dainton and Bayne (2005) and especially Dainton (2008).

The second problem facing any attempt to construct a phenomenal bridge out of relations of phenomenal similarity is that such joints are not *necessary* for the continuation of the self. This is one of the lessons to be learnt from Bernard Williams' famous paper 'The self and the future'.[7] In this paper Williams describes a scenario in which someone informs him that he is going to be tortured tomorrow. However, he is assured that he shall not remember being told that this will happen to him, since shortly before the torture something else will be done which will ensure that he will have a completely different set of apparent memories. As Williams puts it, none of this is likely to make the prospect of torture any less terrifying. Indeed,

I can at least conceive the possibility, if not the concrete reality, of going completely mad, and thinking perhaps that I am George IV or somebody; and being told that something like that was going to happen to me would have no tendency to reduce the terror of being told authoritatively that I was going to be tortured, but would merely compound the horror. (Williams 1970: 167–8)

In this scenario one knows that one will lack any experiential links between one's current self and the tortured self, and yet one is still inclined—perhaps even very strongly inclined—to project oneself into the phenomenal field of the victim. This, I think, is the final nail in the coffin of naïve phenomenalism.

Naïve phenomenalism turns out to be too naïve, but perhaps the basic approach can be salvaged. Rather than identify the self with the stream of consciousness perhaps we should identify it with the underlying substrate that is responsible for generating the stream of consciousness—the *machinery* in which consciousness is grounded. Mackie seems to have something like this position in mind in suggesting that 'unity of consciousness is, as it were, the nominal essence of personal identity . . . But the real essence of personal identity will be whatever underlies and makes possible the unity of consciousness' (Mackie 1976: 200).[8] Let us call this view *substrate phenomenalism*.

The substrate phenomenalist has a plausible response to the challenge of phenomenal gaps, for she can hold that an evening stream and a morning stream are co-streamal in virtue of the fact that they are produced by a single consciousness generating mechanism. Not only can the substrate phenomenalist accommodate the fact that qualitative identity in the contents of two streams of consciousness is not sufficient to make the two streams of consciousness

---

[7] Williams' paper is commonly taken to show that thought experiments are unreliable when it comes to adjudicating between rival accounts of personal identity (Gendler (1998); Rovane (1998)). As I argue in §12.5, I think the moral of Williams' paper is rather different.

[8] See Dainton & Bayne (2005) and especially Dainton (2008) for developments of this approach.

components of the same stream, it can also accommodate the fact that streams need not have *any* contents in common in order to qualify as components of a single stream of consciousness.

But although the substrate phenomenalist has a plausible response to the challenge of phenomenal gaps this version of phenomenalism is no more tenable than naive phenomenalism. Because there is no *a priori* guarantee that a single consciousness-generating mechanism will produce only one stream of consciousness at a time, the substrate phenomenalist cannot ensure that simultaneous co-subjective experiences will be phenomenally unified. But the entire motivation for adopting the phenomenalist approach was to account for the intuition that simultaneous co-subjective experiences *must* be phenomenally unified.

In response, the substrate phenomenalist might argue that we can rescue the intuition that there is a constitutive relation between the self and the unity of consciousness by distinguishing conceptual possibility from metaphysical possibility. Although it might be conceptually possible that the substrate of consciousness is capable of producing phenomenally disunified experiences it doesn't follow that this is a metaphysical possibility. In order to know whether this is a metaphysical possibility we need to know just what the substrate of consciousness is. And—the substrate phenomenalist might continue—there are accounts of consciousness according to which it is metaphysically impossible for the substrate of consciousness to produce multiple streams of consciousness at once. For example, if the substrate of consciousness turns out to be an immaterial substance then it might simply be impossible for a single consciousness-generating mechanism to generate conscious states that fail to be phenomenally unified with each other. Indeed, this might even turn out to be the case on certain physicalist accounts of the substrate of consciousness.

I'm not persuaded by this line of response. For one thing, I think what we want here really is a conceptual necessity rather than a (merely) metaphysical necessity. Even if it should turn out that the mechanism underlying my stream of consciousness is (metaphysically) incapable of generating two streams of consciousness at once, this fails to secure the kind of constitutive relation between selves and the unity of consciousness that we are after here. We want a relation that holds *a priori*, not one that is dependent on the results of an investigation into the mechanisms underlying the production of consciousness. Secondly, I rather doubt that it *is* metaphysically impossible for the mechanisms underlying our streams of consciousness to generate phenomenally disunified experiences. Whether or not these mechanisms are purely physical or at least partly non-physical, I can see no reason why it shouldn't be metaphysically possible for them to generate more than one stream of consciousness at a time. I conclude that the prospects of substrate phenomenalism are no brighter than those of naïve phenomenalism.

12.5 Virtual phenomenalism

We need to take a step back and reconsider the 'logical space' in which we have operated thus far. The two versions of phenomenalism that I have examined each identify selves with concrete particulars: streams of consciousness in the case of naïve phenomenalism and the mechanisms underlying those streams in the case of substrate phenomenalism. But there is another way in which we might hope to forge a constitutive link between streams of consciousness and selves. Rather than looking for something onto which we might map representations of the self, we might think of selves as merely intentional entities—entities whose identity is determined by the cognitive architecture underlying a stream of consciousness. Appropriating Dennett's (1992) notion of the self as a centre of narrative gravity, I suggest that we should think of the self as a merely virtual centre of 'phenomenal gravity'.[9]

The central notion in this approach to the self is that of *de se* representation (Lewis 1979). In *de se* representation the subject represents themselves as themselves. *De se* representation isn't the exclusive provenance of explicitly self-conscious thought, but permeates consciousness through and through. As Pollock (1988) has argued, the conscious states evoked by the presentations of one's senses are automatically *de se*. In effect, this means that streams of consciousness—at least the kinds of streams of consciousness that we enjoy— are constructed 'around' a single intentional object. The cognitive architecture underlying your stream of consciousness represents that stream as had by a single self—the virtual object that is brought into being by *de se* representation.

This account forges an essential tie between the self and the unity of consciousness, for the cognitive architecture underlying consciousness ensures that any *de se* representations that occur within a single phenomenal field will be co-referential. For phenomenal selves, the rule is one subjective perspective at a time. No self can have more than one experiential perspective at a time, for *de se* thought cannot bridge the gaps between phenomenal fields. The functional role of *de se* representation guarantees that the boundaries of the virtual self are limned by the boundaries of the phenomenal field (at least, at a time).

---

[9] This section draws heavily on the thoughts of many others. I am particularly indebted to conversations with Grant Gillett, Mark Johnston, and John Pollock.

How deep does this link between *de se* thought and the unity of consciousness run? Is *de se* structure an essential feature of consciousness as such, or is it merely a feature of our cognitive architecture—indeed, perhaps not even a particularly deep feature of our cognitive architecture? I'm not convinced that *de se* representation must structure the experiences of any possible subject of experience, but I do think that a case can be made on broadly Kantian grounds for the view that *de se* content must inform the representations of any creature whose experiences purport to represent an objective world. (I won't, however, try to make that case here). Leaving to one side the question of whether there might be a necessary link between consciousness and *de se* representation, it is certainly very plausible to suppose that *de se* structure is an essential feature of our cognitive architecture. A case can be made for thinking that it is retained even in those pathologies of self-consciousness—such as the schizophrenic phenomenon of thought insertion and the dissociative phenomenon of inter-alter access (see chapter 7)—in which individuals experience aspects of their own mental life as alien in some way. I suggest that what has been lost in such conditions is only the subject's ability to keep track of their own thoughts and experiences.

We can now see where other approaches to the self go wrong: they assume that there must be some 'real' entity that plays the role of the self. The only thing that plays the self role—indeed, perhaps the only thing that *could* play the role of the self—is a merely intentional entity. Experiences do indeed have 'owners' or 'bearers', but the owner of an experience is nothing 'over and above' a virtual object—indeed, the very same virtual object around which that experience is structured. 'I'-thoughts do have referents, but the referent of an I-thought is nothing other than an intentional object. And of course selves have experiential perspectives, but such perspectives are nothing more than the perspectives of intentional objects. Both the naïve phenomenalist and the substrate phenomenalist are right to think that selves depend on streams of consciousness, but they conceive of this relationship in overly concrete terms. To identify the self with a stream of consciousness or its underlying substrate is a bit like identifying Hercule Poirot with the novels in which he figures.

Let us examine how virtual phenomenalism might handle the objections that I raised against the phenomenalist approach in §12.4. It is clear that virtual phenomenalism can handle the challenge posed by phenomenal gaps, for the virtual self created by beings with our kind of cognitive architecture is more than capable of reaching across interruptions of phenomenal continuity. How does it do this? Well, how is a novelist able to bridge the gap between works of fiction? What makes it the case that the Belgian detective featured in *The Mysterious Affair at Styles* is one and the same Belgian detective who appears in

Murder on the Orient Express? No doubt the details are highly complicated, but in outline the solution is clear: authors draw on conventions that their readers pick up on. Similarly, the identity of the virtual self also rests on conventions of a kind. However, these 'conventions' are not dependent on social practice—or at least not primarily so—but are built into our cognitive architecture. We simply appropriate to ourselves those experiences that we are aware of 'from the inside'. As James put it in his inimitable way: 'Each of us, when he awakens says, Here's the same old self again, just as he says, Here's the same old bed, the same old room, the same old world' (James 1890/1950: vol I: 317). We assume that the character at the centre of our current stream of consciousness is one and the same as the character at the centre of those streams of consciousness with which we are in direct contact via autobiographical memory. In making such assumptions we are not merely *tracking* our selves but *creating* them.

This virtual identification is not only retrospective but also prospective. We project one and the same virtual self into future phenomenal fields, assuming that we ourselves will reappear as the lead character in particular streams of consciousness. One of the striking things about this practice of prospective identification is just how unstable and easily modified by narrative scaffolding it is. When certain experiences are described in one way we might be inclined to think of them as ours; but when described another way we might be inclined to withdraw this judgement. (This is the lesson to be drawn from Williams' paper 'The self and the future'.) Our uncertainty here mirrors that which can be generated by questions about the identity of fictional entities. Suppose that I were to write a story about a Belgian detective by the name of 'H.P.'. Would the Belgian detective that I refer to by these initials be one and the same as the Belgian detective with those initials who figures in *The Mysterious Affair at Styles* and *Murder on the Orient Express*? Well, it depends on what I say. On the one hand, I could write a story according to which it is clear that H.P. is Hercule Poirot. For example, my story might focus on Monsieur Poirot's early years and lead up to the incidents recounted in Agatha Christie's novels. On the other hand, I could write a story such that H.P. is clearly not identical to his more famous namesake. For example, I might assert that my detective had been called H.P. in honour of Agatha Christie's detective. But I could *also* write a story in which it is simply indeterminate whether or not H.P. is Hercule Poirot. To think that there must be a fact of the matter as to whether or not 'H.P' and 'Hercule Poirot' pick out one and the same person would be to misunderstand the nature of fiction. Similarly, I suggest that it may simply be indeterminate whether or not the self around which one stream of consciousness is structured is one and the same as the self around which another stream of consciousness is structured, for the cognitive architectures underlying these two streams might fail to determine whether or not the *de se* representations internal to them refer to the same intentional entity or not.

We are now in a better position to make sense of the conflicting intuitions that are generated by divisions within the stream of consciousness. Suppose that you are contemplating the prospect of phenomenal fission. The phenomenal continuity between your current states and the future states within each of the two streams that it splits into will encourage you to think of the *de se* thoughts internal to these two streams as referring to your current self, but the fact that the two streams will contain experiences that are not phenomenally unified with each other stands as a barrier to the notion that the *de se* thoughts internal to these two streams might be co-referential. Thus, the scenario contains inconsistent cues about how to assign intentional states. The situation is akin to one in which an author ascribes inconsistent properties to a protagonist—for example, by stating in one chapter that Monsieur Poirot solved the crime only to state elsewhere that the crime went unsolved. Such a situation puts pressure on the claim that we are being 'truly' informed about the protagonist's activities. In a similar way, we struggle to make sense of a narrative in which one's current experiences are continuous with sets of simultaneous experiences that are not themselves phenomenally unified with each other. Our judgements about the survival of the self will be affected by just which aspects of the scenario we attend to: attending to facts about phenomenal continuity will incline us to think that we are dealing with one and the same self, whereas attending to facts about phenomenal disunity will incline us to the view that we are dealing with two new selves.

Virtual phenomenalism can also account for many of the modal intuitions associated with the self. In the same way that we can make sense of the thought that Poirot might have retired after solving his first crime, so too we can make sense of the thought that one could have had experiences that were very different from those that one has actually had. It should also be clear that virtual phenomenalism can meet the initial objection to phenomenalism— namely, that streams of consciousness are not identical to selves but are 'had by' or 'owned' by them. In generating a virtual self the cognitive architecture underlying the stream of consciousness also ensures that the self is represented as the owner or bearer of those experiences that are responsible for its very existence. The intentional structure of the phenomenal field leads us to experience ourselves as entities that stand over and against our experiences— as inhabiting the 'centre' of a phenomenal field.

A final objection is unique to virtual phenomenalism. The worry is this: if the self is a 'merely intentional entity' then doesn't it follow that it is unreal— that selves don't *really* exist. And not only is the denial of the self of dubious coherence—it is certainly not how virtual phenomenalism was advertised. I said I was going to provide an account of the self, not an account that explained the self *away*.

Whether or not this account explains what selves are or whether it instead explains them away depends on just what one is looking for. Although selves are merely intentional there is nonetheless a sense in which self talk is perfectly legitimate. It needn't be rejected (indeed, I doubt whether it could be rejected), nor need it be legitimized by finding something in consciousness or its underlying substrate that might qualify as its referent, for it needs no such referent. It should not be thought that the self is fictional in the way that Hercule Poirot and other creatures of fiction are. Although Hercule Poirot is a Belgian detective, his name would not appear on a list of Belgian detectives. (And if by chance the name 'Hercule Poirot' did appear on such a list it wouldn't refer to the Hercule Poirot that features in the writings of Agatha Christie.) Hercule Poirot is a fictional Belgian detective, and his mode of existence is to be contrasted with that of real (non-fictional, actual, existent) Belgian detectives. But there is no kind of real self with which our kinds of selves could be contrasted, for it is in the very nature of selves to be virtual. The kinds of selves that we possess are as real as selves get. This kind of reality might not be enough for some, but I think it provides all the reality that we might have reasonably hoped for here. Perhaps more importantly, it provides all the reality that we *need*.

12.6 Conclusion

I began the chapter by arguing that neither biological nor psychological approaches to the self do justice to the deep links between the self and the unity of consciousness. This is perhaps most obvious with respect to biological treatments of the self, for—as the case of Cerberus showed—it is clear that a single animal can support (or sustain) multiple selves at one time. Matters are more complicated with respect to the psychological (or 'neo-Lockean') approach to the self, for there are reasons to suppose that there may be constitutive connections between mental unity on the one hand and phenomenal unity on the other. Nonetheless, we saw that a single mind might be able to support two streams of consciousness under certain conditions. I argued that in such cases there is much to be said for assigning the conscious states located in each stream to separate selves.

Having rejected biological and psychological accounts of the self, in the second half of this chapter I turned to the question of what a viable phenomenal treatment of the self might look like. I began with naïve phenomenalism—the view that selves can be identified with streams of consciousness. Although naïve phenomenalism has the resources to respond to a number of objections, it succumbs to the problem of phenomenal gaps. Substrate phenomenalism has the resources to bridge the gaps between successive streams of consciousness, but it fails to ensure that the simultaneous experiences of a single self must be phenomenally unified.

The way forward, I argued, is to conceive of the self as a merely virtual object, an object whose identity is given by the intentional structure of the phenomenal field. Adopting one of Dennett's terms, we should think of the self as a centre of phenomenal gravity: like the creatures of the writer's imagination, there is nothing more to the nature of the self than what we take there to be. But this isn't to say that anything goes, for the self is a non-negotiable feature of our cognitive architecture, and it is no more possible to think away one's own self than it is to think away one's own life.

References

Adcock, R. A., Constable, R. T., Gore, J. C., and Goldman-Rakic, P. S. 2000. Functional Neuroanatomy of Executive Processes Involved in Dual-task Performance. *Proceedings of the National Academy of Sciences*, 97: 3567–72.

Aglioti, S., De Souza, J. F. X., Goodale, M. A. 1995. Size-contrast Illusions Deceive the Eye but not the Hand. *Current Biology*, 5: 679–85.

Ahmed, A., and Ruffman, T. 1998. Why do Infants make A not B Errors in a Search Task, yet show Memory for the Location of Hidden Objects in a Nonsearch Task? *Developmental Psychology*, 34: 441–53.

Aimola Davies, A., Davies, M., Ogden, J. A., Smithson, M., and White, R. C. 2008. Cognitive and Motivational Factors in Anosognosia. In T. Bayne and J. Fernández (eds.), *Delusion and Self-deception: Affective Influences on Belief Formation*. Hove: Psychology Press, pp. 187–225.

Akelaitis, A. 1943. Studies of the corpus callosum VII. Study of Language Functions (Tactile and Visual Lexia and Graphia) Unilaterally Following Section of the Corpus Callosum. *Journal of Neuropathology and Experimental Neurology*, 2: 226–62.

——1944. A Study of Gnosis, Praxis and Language Following Section of the Corpus Callosum and Anterior Commissure. *Journal of Neurosurgery*, 1: 94–102.

Alais, D., and Burr, D. 2004. The Ventriloquist Effect Results from Near-Optimal Bimodal Integration. *Current Biology*, 14: 257–62.

Alkire, M. T., Haier, R. J., and Fallon, J. H. 2000. Toward a Unified Theory of Narcosis: Brain Imaging Evidence for a Thalamocortical Switch as the Neurophysiologic basis of Anesthesia-Induced Unconsciousness. *Consciousness and Cognition*, 9: 370–86.

——and Miller, J. 2005. General Anesthesia and the Neural Correlates of Consciousness. In S. Laureys (ed.), *Progress in Brain Research*, Vol. 150 *The Boundaries of Consciousness*, pp. 445–55.

Allport, A. 1988. What Concept of Consciousness? In A. J. Marcel and E. Bisiach (eds.), *Consciousness in Contemporary Science*. Oxford: Clarendon, pp. 159–82.

American Psychiatric Association 2004. *Diagnostic and Statistical Manual of Mental Disorders* (DSM-IV-TR). Washington, DC: American Psychiatric Association.

Andreasen, N. 1985. Positive vs. Negative Schizophrenia: A Critical Evaluation. *Schizophrenia Bulletin*, 11: 380–9.

——and Carpenter, W. 1993. Diagnosis and Classification of Schizophrenia, *Schizophrenia Bulletin*, 19: 199–213.

Andresen, D. R., and Marsolek, C. J. 2005. Does a Causal Relation Exist Between the Functional Hemispheric Asymmetries of Visual Processing Subsystems? *Brain and Cognition* 59: 135–44.

Anema, H. A., van Zandvoort, M. J., de Haan, E., Kappelle, L. J, de Kort, P. L., Jansen, B. P., Dijkerman, H. C. 2009. A Double Dissociation Between Somatosensory Processing for Perception and Action. *Neuropsychologia*, 47: 1615–20.

Anscombe, R. 1987. The Disorder of Consciousness in Schizophrenia. *Schizophrenia Bulletin*, 13/2: 241–60.

Ansorge, U., Klotz, W., and Neumann, O. 1998. Manual and Verbal Responses to Completely Masked (unreportable) Stimuli: Exploring some Conditions for the Metaconstrast Dissociation. *Perception*, 27: 1177–89.

Anton, G. 1898. Über Herderkrankungen des Gehirnes, Welche vom Patienten Selbst Nicht Wahrgenommen Werden. *Wiener Klinische Wochenschrift*, 11: 227–9.

——1899. Über die Selbstwahrnehmung der Herderkrankungen des Gehirns durch den Kranken bei Rindenblindheit und Rindentaubheit. *Archiv für Psychiatrie und Nervenkrankheiten*, 32: 86–127.

Arguin, M., Lassonde, M., Quattrini, A., del Pesce, M., Foschi, N., Papo, I. 2000. Divided Visuo-Spatial Attention Systems with Total and Anterior Callosotomy, *Neuropsychologia*, 38: 283–91.

Armstrong, D. M. 1962. *Bodily Sensations*. London: Routledge and Kegan Paul.

Arnold, D. H., Clifford, C. W., and Wenderoth, P. 2001. Asynchronous Processing in Vision: Color Leads Motion. *Current Biology*, 11: 596–600.

——and Clifford, C. W. 2002. Determinants of Asynchronous Processing in vision. *Proceedings of the Royal Society of London*, Series B, *Biological Science*, 269: 579–83.

Arzy, S., Overney, L., Landis, T., Blanke, O. 2006. Neural Mechanisms of Embodiment: Asomatognosia due to Premotor Cortex Damage. *Archives of Neurology*, 63: 1022–5.

Atherton, M. 1983. Locke's theory of Personal Identity. In P. A. French, T. E. Uehling, and H. K. Wettstein (eds.), *Midwest Studies in Philosophy*, Vol. viii *Contemporary Perspectives on the History of Philosophy*. Minneapolis, MN: University of Minnesota Press, pp. 273–93.

Atkinson, J., Campbell, F. W., and Francis, M. R. 1976. The Magic Number 4 ± 0: A new look at Visual Numerosity Judgments. *Perception*, 5: 327–34.

Averbach, E., and Sperling, G. 1961. Short Term Storage of Information in Vision. In C. Cherry (ed.), *Information Theory*. Washington, DC: Butterworth and Co, pp. 196–211.

Ayers, M. 1991. *Locke*. New York: Routledge.

Baars, B. 1988. *A Cognitive Theory of Consciousness*. Cambridge: Cambridge University Press.

——1993. How does a Serial, Integrated and very Limited Stream of Consciousness Emerge from a Nervous System that is mostly Unconscious, Distributed, Parallel and of Enormous Capacity? In G. R. Bock and J. Marsh (eds.), *Experimental and Theoretical Studies of Consciousness*. Chichester, England: John Wiley and Sons, pp. 168–79.

Baddeley, A. 2003. Working Memory: Looking Back and Looking Forward. *Nature Reviews Neuroscience*, 4: 829–39.

——2007. *Working Memory, Thought, and Action*. Oxford: Oxford University Press.

Baillargeon, R., and Graber, M. 1988. Evidence of Location Memory in 8-Month-Old Infants in a Non-Search Task. *Developmental Psychology*, 24: 502–11.

Bain, D. 2003. Intentionalism and Pain. *Philosophical Quarterly*, 53: 502–23.

Baker, D., Hunter, E., Lawrence, E., Medford, N., Patel, M., Senior, C., Sierra, M., Lambert, M., Phillips, M., David, A. 2003. Depersonalisation Disorder: Clinical Features of 204 Cases. *British Journal of Psychiatry*, 182: 428–33.

Bancaud, J., Henriksen, O., Rubio-Donnadieu, F., Seino M., Dreifuss, F. E., Penry J. K. 1981. Proposal for a Revised Clinical and Electroencephalographic Classification of Epileptic Seizures. *Epilepsia* 22: 489–501.

Bargh, J. A., Chen, A., Burrows, L. 1996. Automaticity of Social Behavior: Direct Effects of Trait Construct and Stereotype Activation on Action. *Journal of Personality and Social Psychology*, 71: 230–44.

——and Ferguson, M. J. 2000. Beyond Behaviorism: On the Automaticity of Higher Mental Processes. *Psychological Bulletin*, 126: 925–45.

Barresi, J. 1994. Morton Prince and B.C.A.: A Historical Footnote on the Confrontation Between Dissociation Theory and Freudian Psychology in a Case of Multiple Personality. In Raymond M. Klein and Benjamin K. Doane (eds.), *Psychological Concepts and Dissociative Disorders*. Hillsdale, NJ: Lawrence Erlbuam, pp. 85–129.

Bartels, A., and Zeki, S. 1998. The Theory of Multistage Integration in the Visual Brain. *Proceedings of the Royal Society of London*, Series B 265: 2327–32.

————2000. The Architecture of the Colour Center in the Human Visual Brain: New Results and a Review. *European Journal of Neuroscience*, 12: 172–93.

Bayne, T. 2001. Co-consciousness: Review of Barry Dainton's 'Stream of Consciousness'. *Journal of Consciousness Studies*, 8/3: 79–92.

——2005. Divided Brains and Unified Phenomenology: An Essay on Michael Tye's 'Consciousness and Persons'. *Philosophical Psychology*, 18/4: 495–512.

——2007a. Conscious States and Conscious Creatures: Explanation in the Scientific Study of Consciousness. *Philosophical Perspectives 21 (Philosophy of Mind)*: 1–22.

——2007b. Hypnosis and the Unity of Consciousness. In G. Jamieson (ed.) *Hypnosis and Conscious States*. Oxford: Oxford University Press, pp. 93–109.

——2008a. The Phenomenology of Agency. *Philosophy Compass*, 3: 1–21.

——2008b. The Unity of Consciousness and the Split-Brain Syndrome. *The Journal of Philosophy*, 105/6: 277–300.

——2010. The Sense of Agency. In F. Macpherson (ed.) *The Senses*. Oxford: Oxford University Press.

——and Chalmers, D. 2003. What is the Unity of Consciousness? In A. Cleeremans (ed.), *The Unity of Consciousness: Binding, Integration and Dissociation*. Oxford: Oxford University Press, pp. 23–58.

——and Levy, N. 2006. The Feeling of Doing: Deconstructing the Phenomenology of Agency. In W. Prinz and N. Sebanz (eds.), *Disorders of Volition*. Cambridge, MA: MIT Press, pp. 49–68.

Bayne, T., and Montague, M. 2011. *Cognitive Phenomenology*. Oxford: Oxford University Press.

——and Spener, M. 2010. Introspective Humility. In E. Sosa and E. Villanueva (eds.), *Philosophical Issues*, 20: 1–22.

Baynes, K. and Gazzaniga, M. S. 2000. Consciousness, Introspection, and the Split-Brain: The Two Minds/One Body Problem. In M. S. Gazzaniga (ed.), *The New Cognitive Neurosciences* (2nd edn.). Cambridge, MA: MIT Press, 1355–63.

Beaumont, J. G. 1981. Split Brain Studies and the Duality of Consciousness. In G. Underwood and R. Stevens (eds.), *Aspects of Consciousness* Vol 2. *Structural Issues*. London: Academic Press, pp. 189–213.

Bedford, F. L. 2004. Analysis of a Constraint on Perception, Cognition and Development: One Object, One Place, One Time. *Journal of Experimental Psychology: Human Perception and Performance*, 30: 907–12.

Benson, D. F., and Greenberg, J. P. 1969. Visual form Agnosia. *Archives of Neurology*, 20: 82–9.

Bentall, R. (ed.) 1990. *Reconstructing Schizophrenia*. New York: Routledge.

Bermúdez, J. L. 2005. The Phenomenology of Bodily Awareness. In D. W. Smith and A. Thomasson (eds.), *Phenomenology and Philosophy of Mind*. Oxford: Oxford University Press, pp. 295–316.

Bernat, J. L. 2006. Chronic Disorders of Consciousness. *Lancet*, 367: 1181–92.

Berrios, G. E., and Luque, R. 1995a. Cotard's Syndrome: Analysis of 100 Cases. *Acta Psychiatrica Scandinavia*, 91: 185–9.

——————1995b. Cotard's Delusion or Syndrome?: A Conceptual History. *Comprehensive Psychiatry*, 36/3: 218–23.

Bertelson, P. 1999. Ventriloquism: A Case of Cross Modal Perceptual Grouping. In G. Ashersleben, T. Bachmann, J. Müssler (eds.). *Cognitive Contributions to the Perception of Spatial and Temporal Events*. Amsterdam: Elsevier, pp. 347–62.

Berti, A., Làdavas, E., Stracciara, A., Giannarelli, C., and Ossola, A. 1998. Anosognosia for Motor Impairment and Dissociations with Patients' Evaluation of the Disorder: Theoretical Considerations. *Cognitive Neuropsychiatry*, 3/1: 21–44.

Binet, A. 1890/1977a. On Double Consciousness. In Daniel N. Robinson (ed.). *Significant Contributions to the History of Psychology 1750–1920*, Series C, *Medical Psychology*, Vol. v. Washington, DC: University Publications of America.

——1890/1977b. Alterations of Personality. In D. N. Robinson (ed.). *Significant Contributions to the History of Psychology 1750–1920*, Series C, *Medical Psychology*, Vol. v. Washington, DC: University Publications of America.

Bisiach, E. 1988. The (Haunted) Brain and Consciousness. In A. J. Marcel and E. Bisiach (eds.). *Consciousness in Contemporary Science*. Oxford: Oxford University Press, pp. 101–20.

——1992: Understanding Consciousness: Clues from Unilateral Neglect and Related Disorders. In A. D. Milner and M. D. Rugg (eds.) The Neuropsychology of Consciousness, London: Academic Press, pp. 113–39.

——and Berti, A. 1995. Consciousness in Dyschiria. In M. S. Gazzaniga (ed.). *The Cognitive Neurosciences*. Cambridge, MA: MIT Press.

——and Luzzatti, C. 1978. Unilateral Neglect of Representational Space. *Cortex*, 14: 129–33.

——, Vallar, G., and Geminiani, G. 1989. Influence of Response Modality on Perceptual Awareness of Contralateral Visual Stimuli. *Brain*, 112: 1627–36.

——and Geminiani, G. 1991. Anosognosia Related to Hemiplegia and Hemianopia. In G. P. Prigatano and D. L. Schacter (eds.), *Awareness of Deficit After Brain Injury: Clinical and Theoretical Issues*. New York: Oxford University Press, pp. 17–39.

——, Rusconi, M. K., and Vallar, G. 1991. Remision of Somatoparaphrenic Delusion Through Vestibular Stimulation. *Neuropsychologia*, 29: 1029–31.

Blackburn, S. 1997. Has Kant Refuted Parfit? In J. Dancy (ed.) *Reading Parfit*. Oxford: Oxford University Press, pp. 180–201.

Blanke, O., Landis, T., Spinelli L., Seeck M. 2004. Out-of-body Experience and Autoscopy of Neurological Origin. *Brain*, 127: 243–58.

——and Mohr, C. 2005. Out-of-body Experience, Heauoscopy, and Autoscopic Hallucination of Neurological Origin: Implications for Neuroscognitive Mechanisms of Corporeal Awareness and Self-Consciousness. *Brain Research Reviews*, 50: 184–99.

Bliss, E. L., Larson, E. M., Nakashima, S. R. 1983. Auditory Hallucinations and Schizophrenia. *The Journal of Nervous and Mental Disease*, 171/1: 30–3.

Block, N. 1995. On a Confusion About a Function of Consciousness. *Behavioral and Brain Sciences*, 18: 227–87.

——1997. Author's Response: Biology Versus Computation in the Study of Consciousness. *Behavioral and Brain Sciences*, 20/1: 159–66.

——2003. Mental Paint. In M. Hahn and B. Ramberg (eds.) *Reflections on Tyler Burge*. Cambridge, MA: MIT Press, pp. 165–200.

——2005. Two Neural Correlates of Consciousness. *Trends in Cognitive Sciences*, 9/2: 46–52.

——2007. Consciousness, Accessibility and the Mesh between Psychology and Neuroscience. *Behavioral and Brain Sciences*, 30: 481–548.

Blumenfeld, H. 2005. Consciousness and Epilepsy: Why are Patients with Absence Seizures Absent? In S. Laureys (ed.) *The Boundaries of Consciousness: Neurobiology and Neuropathology*. Amsterdam: Elsevier, pp. 271–87.

Bogen, J. E. 1977. Further Discussion on Split-Brains and Hemispheric Capabilities. *The British Journal for the Philosophy of Science*, 28: 281–6.

——1995. Some Historical Aspects of Callosotomy for Epilepsy. In A. G. Reeves and D. W. Roberts (eds.) *Epilepsy and the Corpus Callosum II*. New York: Plenum Press, pp. 107–21.

——1998. Physiological Consequences of Complete or Partial Commissural Section. In *Surgery of the third ventricle* (2nd edn.) M. L. J. Apuzzo (ed.). Baltimore, MD: Williams and Wilkins, pp. 167–86.

——and Vogel, P. J. 1962. Cerebral Commissurotomy in Man: Preliminary Case Report. *Bulletin of the L.A. Neurological Society*, 27: 169–72.

Boly, M., Coleman, M. R., Davis, M. H., Hampshire, A., Bor, D., Moonen, G., Maquet, P. A., Pickard, J. D., Laureys, S., and Owen, A. M. 2007. When Thoughts

Become Action: An fMRI Paradigm to Study Volitional Brain Activity in Noncom-municative Brain Injured Patients. *Neuroimage*, 36: 979–92.

Boring, E. G. 1950. *A History of Experimental Psychology* (2nd edn.). Englewood Cliffs, NJ: Prentice Hall.

Bottini, G., Sterzi, R., Vallar, G. 1992. Directional Hypokinesia in Spatial Hemineglect: A Case Study. *Journal of Neurology, Neurosurgery and Psychiatry*, 55: 562–5.

Bower, G. 1994. Temporary Emotional States Act Like Multiple Personality. In R. M. Klein and B. K. Doane (eds.), *Psychological concepts and dissociative disorders*. Hillsdale NJ: Lawrence Erlbaum Associates, pp. 207–34.

Bowers, K. S. 1990. Unconscious Influences and Hypnosis. In J. L. Singer (ed.), *Repression and dissociation: Implications for personality theory, psychopathology and health*. Chicago: University of Chicago Press, pp. 143–78.

——1991. Dissociation in Hypnosis and Multiple Personality Disorder. *International Journal of Clinical and Experimental Hypnosis*, 39: 155–76.

——and Davidson, T. M. 1991. A Neo-Dissociative Critique of Spanos's Social Psychological Model of Hypnosis. In S. J. Lynn, and J. W. Rhue (eds.), *Theories of Hypnosis: Current Models and Perspectives*. New York: Guildford Press, pp. 105–43.

Bowers, P., Laurence, J. R., and Hart, D. 1988. The Experience of Hypnotic Sugges-tions. *International Journal of Clinical and Experimental Hypnosis*, 36: 336–49.

Boyle, M. 1990. *Schizophrenia: A Scientific Delusion*? London: Routledge.

Braude, S. 1995. *First-Person Plural*. Lanham, MD: Rowman and Littlefield.

Breitmeyer, B. 2007. Visual Masking: Past Accomplishments, Present Status, Future Developments. *Advances in Cognitive Psychology*, 3: 9–20.

——and Ögmen, H. 2006. *Visual masking: Time slices through conscious and unconscious vision*. Oxford: Oxford University Press.

Breuer, J., and Freud, S. 1893. Studies on Hysteria. In *The standard edition of the complete psychological works of Sigmund Freud*, 23: 1955–64.

Bridgeman, B., Lewis, S., Heit, G., and Nagle, M. 1979. Relation between Cognitive and Motor-Oriented Systems of Visual Position Perception. *Journal of Experimental Psychology: Human Perception and Performance*, 5: 692–700.

——, Kirsch, M., and Sperling, G. 1981. Segregation of Cognitive and Motor Aspects of Visual Function using Induced Motion. *Perception and Psychophysics*, 29: 336–42.

Britten, K. H., Shadlen, M. N., Newsome, W. T., and Movshon, J. A. 1992. The Analysis of Visual Motion: A Comparison of Neuronal and Psychophysical Perfor-mance. *Journal of Neuroscience*, 12: 4745–65.

Brook, A. 1994. *Kant and the Mind*. Cambridge. Cambridge University Press.

——and Raymont, P. 2009. The Unity of Consciousness. *Stanford Encyclopedia of Philosophy*, <http://plato.stanford.edu/entries/consciousness-unity>.

Brown, C. 1990. How to Believe the Impossible. *Philosophical Studies*, 58: 271–85.

——1991. Believing the impossible. *Synthese*, 89: 353–64.

Brugger, P., 2006. From Phantom Limb to Phantom Body: Varieties of Autoscopic Awareness. In G. Knoblich, I. M. Thornton, M. Grosjean, and M. Shiffrar (eds.)

Human Body Perception: From the Inside Out. Oxford: Oxford University Press, pp. 171–209.

——, Agosti, R., Regard, M., Wieser, H.-G., Landis, T. 1994. Heautoscopy, Epilepsy, and Suicide. *Journal of Neurology, Neurosurgery and Psychiatry*, 57: 838–9.

Buttelmann, D., Carpenter, M., and Tomasello, M. 2009. Eighteen-Month-Old Infants Show False Belief Understanding in an Active Helping Paradigm. *Cognition*, 112: 337–42.

Butterworth, G. 1977. Object Disappearance and Error in Piaget's Stage IV Task. *Journal of Experimental Child Psychology*, 23: 391–401.

Byrne, A. 2001. Intentionalism Defended. *Philosophical Review*, 110: 199–240.

Calvert, G. A., Stein, B. E., and Spence, C. 2004. *The Handbook of Multisensory Processing*. Cambridge, MA: MIT Press.

Campbell, J. 1999. Schizophrenia, the Space of Reasons, and Thinking as a Motor Process. *The Monist*, 82/4: 609–25.

Cappa, S., Sterzi, R., Vallar, G., Bisiach, E. 1987. Remission of Hemineglect and Anosognosia during Vestibular Stimulation. *Neuropsychologia*, 25: 775–82.

Cappon, D., and Banks, R. 1965. Orientational Perception II. Body Perception in Depersonalization. *Archives of General Psychiatry*, 13: 375–9.

Carey, D. P., Harvey, M., and Milner A. D. 1996. Visuomotor Sensitivity for Shape and Orientation in a Patient with Visual Form Agnosia. *Neuropsychologia*, 34: 329–37.

Carlson, E. 1981. The History of Multiple Personality in the United States. I. The Beginnings. *American Journal of Psychiatry*, 135: 668.

Carlson, S. M., and Moses, L. J. 2001. Individual Differences in Inhibitory Control and Children's Theory of Mind. *Child Development*, 72: 1032–53.

————and Hix, H. R. 1998. The role of Inhibitory Processes in Young Children's Difficulties with Deception and False Belief. *Child Development*, 69/3: 672–91.

Carpenter, K., Berti, A., Oxbury, S., Molyneux, A. J., Bisiach, E., and Oxbury, J. M. 1995. Awareness of and Memory for Arm Weakness During Intracarotid Sodium Amytal Testing. *Brain*, 118: 243–51.

Carpenter, R. H. S. 1988. *Movements of the Eyes*. (2nd edn.). London: Pion.

Carruthers, P. 2005. Conscious Experience Versus Conscious Thought. In *Consciousness: Essays From a Higher-Order Perspective*. Oxford: Oxford University Press, pp. 134–56.

Castiello, U., Paulignan, Y., and Jeannerod, M. 1991. Temporal Dissociation of Motor Responses and Subjective Awareness. *Brain*, 114: 2639–55.

Chalmers, D. 1996. *The Conscious Mind*. Oxford: Oxford University Press.

——2000. What is a Neural Correlate of Consciousness? In T. Metzinger (ed.), *The Neural Correlates of Consciousness*. Cambridge, MA: MIT Press, pp. 17–40.

——2004. The Representational Character of Experience. In B. Leiter (ed.), *The Future for Philosophy*. Oxford: Oxford University Press, pp. 153–81.

Chatterjee, A., and Mennemeier, M. 1996. Anosognosia for Hemiplegia: Patient Retrospections. *Cognitive Neuropsychiatry*, 1: 221–37.

Chen, Y.-C., and Spence, C. 2010. When Hearing the Bark Helps to Identify the Dog: Semantically Congruent Sounds Modulate the Identification of Masked Pictures. *Cognition*, 114: 389–404.

Chiarello, C. 1980. A House Divided? Cognitive Functioning with Callosal Agenesis. *Brain and Language*, 11: 128–58.

Clark, A. 2001. Visual Experience and Motor Action: Are the Bonds too Tight? *Philosophical Review*, 110/4: 495–519.

——2009. Perception, Action, and Experience: Unraveling the Golden Braid. *Neuropsychologia*, 47/6: 1460–8.

Clements, W. A., and Perner, J. 1994. Implicit Understanding of Belief. *Cognitive Development*, 9: 377–95.

Colavita, F. B. 1974. Human Sensory Dominance. *Perception & Psychophysics*, 16: 409–12.

Cole, J., and Paillard, J. 1995. Living without Touch and Peripheral Information about Body Position and Movement: Studies with Deafferented Subjects. In J. L. Bermúdez, A. Marcel, and N. Eilan (eds.), *The Body and the Self*. Cambridge, MA: MIT Press, pp. 245–66.

Comey, G., and Kirsch, I. 1999. Intentional and Spontaneous Imagery in Hypnosis: The Phenomenology of Hypnotic Responding. *International Journal of Clinical and Experimental Hypnosis*, 47: 65–85.

Corballis, M. C. 1994. Split Decisions: Problems in the Interpretation of Results from Commissurotomized Subjects. *Behavioural Brain Research*, 64: 163–72.

——1995. Visual Integration in the Split-Brain. *Neuropsychologia*, 33/8: 937–59.

Cotard, J. 1880. Du Délire Hypocondriaque Dans Une Forme Grave de la Mélancolie Anxieuse. *Annales Médico-Psychologiques*, 38: 168–70.

——1882. Du Délire Des Négations. *Archives de Neurologie*, 4: 152–70, 282–95.

Cowan, N. 2001. The Magical Number 4 in Short-Term Memory: A Reconsideration of Mental Storage Capacity. *Behavioral and Brain Sciences*, 24: 87–114.

Cowey, A. 2009. Achromatopsia. In T. Bayne, A. Cleeremans, and P. Wilken (eds.) *The Oxford Companion to Consciousness*. Oxford: Oxford University Press.

——and Walsh, V. 2000. Magnetically Induced Phosphenes in Sighted, Blind, and Blindsight Subjects. *Neuroreport*, 11: 3269–73.

Crabtree, A. 1985. Mesmerism, Divided Consciousness, and Multiple Personality. In N. M. Schott (ed.), *Franz Anton Mesmer und Die Geschichte Des Mesmerismus*. Stuttgart: Franz Steiner, pp. 133–43.

——1986. Explanations of Dissociation in the First Half of the Twentieth Century. In J. M. Quen (ed.), *Split Minds/ Split Brains*. New York and London: New York University Press, pp. 85–107.

Crane, T. 1988. The Waterfall Illusion. *Analysis*, 48: 142–7.

——2001. *Elements of Mind: An Introduction to the Philosophy of Mind*. Oxford: Oxford University Press.

Crawford, J. H., Macdonald, H., and Hilgard, E. R. 1979. Hypnotic Deafness— Psychophysical Study of Responses to Tone Intensity as Modified by Hypnosis. *American Journal of Psychology*, 92: 193–214.

Crick, F., and Koch, C. 1990a. Some Reflections on Visual Awareness. *Cold Spring Harbor Symposia on Quantitative Biology*, 55: 953–62.

——————1990b. Towards a Neurobiological Theory of Consciousness. *Seminars in the Neurosciences*, 2: 263–75.

Critchley, M. 1953. *The Parietal Lobes*, London: Edward Arnold.

Cronin-Golomb, A. 1986. Sub-Cortical Transfer of Cognitive Information in Subjects with Complete Forebrain Commissurotomy. *Cortex*, 22: 499–519.

Crow, T. J. 1980. Molecular Pathology of Schizophrenia: More than One Disease Process? *British Medical Journal*, 280: 66–8.

Cutting, J. 1985. *The Psychology of Schizophrenia*. Edinburgh: Churchill Livingstone.

Dainton, B. 1992. Time and Division, *Ratio*, 5: 102–28.

——2006. *Stream of Consciousness: Unity and Continuity in Conscious Experience* (2nd ed.). London: Routledge.

——2004. All at Once. *Times Literary Supplement*, 22 Oct., p. 33.

——2008. *The Phenomenal Self*. Oxford: Oxford University Press.

——, and Bayne, T. 2005. Consciousness as a Guide to Personal Persistence. *The Australasian Journal of Philosophy*, 83/4: 549–71.

David, A., Owen, A. M., and Förstl, H. 1993. An Annotated Summary and Translation of 'on the Self-Awareness of Focal Brain Diseases by the Patient in Cortical Blindness and Cortical Deafness', by Gabriel Anton (1899). *Cognitive Neuropsychology*, 10: 263–72.

——, Kemp, R., Smith, L., and Fahy, T. 1996. Split Minds: Multiple Personality and Schizophrenia. In P. W. Halligan and J. C. Marshall (eds.) *Method in Madness: Case Studies in Cognitive Neuropsychiatry*. Hove, E. Sussex: Psychology Press, pp. 123–46.

Davis, L. 1997. Cerebral Hemispheres. *Philosophical Studies*, 87: 207–22.

de Lacoste, M. C., Kirkpatrick, J. B., Ross, E. D. 1985. Topography of the Corpus Callosum. *Journal of Neuropathology and Experimental Neurology*, 44: 578–91.

de Langavant, C. L., Trinkler, I., Cesaro, P., and Bachoud-Lévi, A. C. 2009. Heterotopagnosia: When I Point at Parts of Your Body. *Neuropsychologia*, 47: 1745–55.

de'Sperati, C., and Baud-Bovy, G. 2008. Blind Saccades: An Asynchrony between Seeing and Looking. *The Journal of Neuroscience*, 28/17: 4317–21.

de Vignemont, F. 2007. Habeas Corpus: The Sense of Ownership of One's Own Body. *Mind and Language*, 22/4: 427–49.

——, F., Tsakiris, M., and Haggard, P. 2005. Body Mereology. In G. Knoblich, I. M. Thornton, M. Grosjean, and M. Shiffrar (eds.), *Human Body Perception from the Inside Out*. Oxford: Oxford University Press, pp. 147–70.

——, F., Ehrsson, H. H., and Haggard, P. 2005. Bodily Illusions Modulate Tactile Perception. *Current Biology*, 15: 1286–90.

Dehaene, S., and Naccache, L. 2001. Towards a Cognitive Neuroscience of Consciousness: Basic Evidence and a Workspace Framework. *Cognition*, 79: 1–37.

——and Changeux, J.-P. 2004. Neural Mechanisms for Access to Consciousness. In M. Gazzaniga (ed.) *The Cognitive Neurosciences III*. Cambridge, MA: MIT Press, pp. 1145–58.

Dening, T. R., and Berrios, G. E. 1994. Autoscopic Phenomena. *British Journal of Psychiatry*, 165: 808–17.

Dennett, D., 1971. Intentional systems. *Journal of Philosophy*, 68: 87–106.

——1987. True Believers: The Intentional Strategy and Why it Works. In D. Dennett, *The Intentional Stance*. Cambridge, MA: MIT Press, pp. 13–35.

——1991. *Consciousness Explained*. New York: Little Brown, and Company.

Dennett, D., 1992. The Self as a Center of Narrative Gravity. In F. Kessel, P. Cole and D. Johnson (eds.), *Self and Consciousness: Multiple Perspectives*. Hillsdale, NJ: Erlbaum, pp. 103–18.

——2001. Surprise, Surprise. *Behavioral and Brain Sciences*, 24: 982.

——and Humphrey, N. 1998. Speaking for Ourselves. In D. Dennett *Brain-children*. Cambridge, MA: MIT Press.

——and Kinsbourne, M. 1992. Time and the Observer: The Where and When of Consciousness in the Brain. *Behavioral and Brain Sciences*, 15: 183–247.

Diamond, A. 1985. Development of the Ability to Use Recall to Guide Action, as Indicated by Infants' Performance on AB. *Child Development*, 56/4: 868–83.

——1990. Developmental Time Course in Human Infants and Infant Monkeys, and the Neural Basis of, Inhibitory Control in Reaching. *Annals of the New York Academy of Sciences*, 608: 637–76.

——, Cruttenden, L., and Neiderma, D. 1994. AB with Multiple Wells: 1. Why are Multiple Wells Sometimes Easier than Two Wells? 2. Memory or Memory + Inhibition? *Developmental Psychology*, 30: 192–205.

Dijksterhuis, A., and Bargh J. A. 2001. The Perception-Behavior Expressway: Automatic Effects of Social Perception on Social Behaviour. In M. P. Zanna (ed.), *Advances in Experimental Social Psycology* (Vol. 33). San Diego, CA: Academic Press, pp. 1–40.

Dimond, S. J. 1976. Depletion of Attentional Capacity After Total Commissurotomy in Man. *Brain*, 99: 347–56.

Dorahy, M. J. 2001. Dissociative Identity Disorder and Memory Dysfunction: The Current State of Experimental Research and its Future Directions. *Clinical Psychology Review*, 21/5: 771–95.

Dretske, F. 1995. *Naturalizing the Mind*. Cambridge, MA: MIT Press.

——2004. Change Blindness. *Philosophical Studies*, 120/1–3: 1–18.

——2006. Perception without Awareness. In T. S. Gendler and J. Hawthorne (eds.), *Perceptual Experience*, Oxford: Oxford University Press, pp. 147–80.

Driver, J., and Mattingley, J. B. 1998. Parietal Neglect and Visual Awareness. *Nature Neuroscience*, 1: 17–22.

——and Noesselt, T. 2008. Multisensory Interplay Reveals Crossmodal Influences on 'Sensory-Specific' Brain Regions, Neural Responses, and Judgments. *Neuron*, 57: 11–23.

Duhamel, J.-R., and Brouchon, M. 1990. Sensorimotor Aspects of Unilateral Neglect: A Single Case Analysis. *Cognitive Neuropsychology*, 7/1: 57–74.

Eccles, J. C. 1965. *The brain and the unity of conscious experience*. Cambridge: Cambridge University Press.

Eckhorn, R. 1999. Neural Mechanisms of Visual Feature Binding Investigated with Microelectrodes and Models. *Visual Cognition*, 6: 231–66.

Eimer, M., and Schlaghecken, F. 1998. Effects of Masked Stimulus on Motor Activation: Behavioural and Electrophysiological Evidence. *Journal of Experimental Psychology: Human Perception and Performance*, 24: 1737–47.

Ellenberg, L., and Sperry, R. W. 1980. Lateralized Division of Attention in the Commissurotomized and Intact Brain. *Neuropsychologia*, 18: 411–18.

Ellenberger, H. 1970. *The Discovery of the Unconscious*. New York: Basic Books.

Engel, A. K., Fries, P., König, P., Brecht, M., Singer, W. 1999a. Temporal Binding, Binocular Rivalry, and Consciousness. *Consciousness and Cognition*, 8: 128–51.

——————————1999b. Concluding Commentary. Does Time Help to Understand Consciousness? *Consciousness and Cognition*, 8: 260–8.

——, and Singer, W. 2001. Temporal Binding and the Neural Correlates of Sensory Awareness. *Trends in Cognitive Sciences*, 5: 16–25.

Enoch, M. D., and Trethowan, W. 1991. *Uncommon Psychiatric Syndromes*. Oxford and Boston: Butterworth-Heinemann.

Erikson, C. W., Becker, B. B., Hoffman, J. E. 1970. Safari to Masking Land: A Hunt for the Elusive U. *Perception and Psychophysics*, 8: 245–50.

Ernst, M. O. and Bülthoff, H. H. 2004. Merging the Senses into a Robust Percept. *Trends in Cognitive Sciences*, 8/4: 162–9.

Ettlinger, G., Blakemore, C. B., Milner, A. D., and Wilson, J. 1974. Agenesis of the Corpus Callosum: A Further Behavioral Investigation. *Brain*, 97: 225–34.

Evans, F. J. 1980. Posthypnotic amnesia. In G. D. Burrows and L. Dennerstein (eds.), *Handbook of Hypnosis and Psychosomatic Medicine*. Amsterdam: Elsevier, pp. 85–103.

Fagot, C., and Pashler, H. 1992. Making Two Responses to a Single Object: Exploring the Central Bottleneck. *Journal of Experimental Psychology: Human Perception and Performance*, 18: 1058–79.

Fantl, J., and Howell, R. 2003. Sensations, Swatches, and Specked Hens. *Pacific Philosophical Quarterly*, 84: 371–83.

Farah, M. 1997. Visual Perception and Visual Awareness After Brain Damage: A Tutorial Overview. In N. Block, O. Flanagan, and G. Güzeldere (eds.), *The Nature of Consciousness*, Cambridge, MA: MIT Press, pp. 203–36.

——2004. *Visual Agnosia* (2nd edn). Cambridge, MA: MIT Press.

Farrell, B. 1950. Experience. *Mind*, 49: 170–98.

Fehrer, E., and Biederman, I. 1962. A Comparison of Reaction Time and Verbal Report in the Detection of Masked Stimuli. *Journal of Experimental Psychology*, 64: 126–30.

——and Raab, D. 1962. Reaction Time to Stimuli Masked by Metacontrast. *Journal of Experimental Psychology*, 63: 143–7.

Feinberg, T. E., Haber, L. D., Leeds, N. E. 1990. Verbal Asomatognosia. *Neurology*, 40: 1391–4.

Fendrich, R., and Corballis, P. M. 2001. The Temporal Cross-Capture of Audition and Vision. *Perception and Psychophysics*, 63: 719–25.

Fergusen, S. M., Rayport, M., and Corrie, W. S. 1985. Neuropsychiatric Observation on Behavioral Consequences of Corpus Callosum Section for Seizure Control. In A. G. Reeves (ed.) *Epilepsy and the Corpus Callosum*. New York: Plenum, pp. 501–14.

Ferriss, G. D., and Dorsen, M. M. 1975. Agenesis of the Corpus Callosum: Neuro-Spsychological Studies. *Cortex*, 11: 95–122.

Flanagan, O. 1992. *Consciousness Reconsidered*. Cambridge, MA: MIT Press.

Forde, E. M. F., and Wallesch, C.-W. 2003. 'Mind-Blind for Blindness': A Psychological Review of Anton's Syndrome. In C. Code, C.-W. Wallesch, Y. Joanette, and A. Roch (eds.), *Classic Cases in Neuropsychology*, Vol. ii. Hove, East Sussex: Psychology Press, pp. 199–222.

Forget, J., Lippé, S., and Lassonde, M. 2009. Perceptual Priming does not Transfer Interhemispherically in the Acallosal Brain. *Experimental Brain Research*, 192: 443–54.

Förstl, H., Owen, A. M., David, A. S. 1993. Gabriel Anton and 'Anton's Syndrome': On Focal Diseases of the Brain which are not Perceived by the Patient (1898). *Neuropsychiatry, Neuropsychology, and Behavioral Neurology*, 6/1: 1–8.

Foster, J. 1979. In *Self*-Defence. In G. F. Macdonald (ed.) *Perception and Identity: Essays Presented to A. J. Ayer with His Replies*. London: Macmillan, pp. 161–85.

——1991. *The Immaterial Self*. London: Routledge.

Fourneret, P., and Jeannerod, M. 1998. Limited Conscious Monitoring of Motor Performance in Normal Subjects. *Neuropsychologia*, 36/11: 1133–40.

Franz, E. A., Eliassen, J. C., Ivry, R. B., Gazzaniga, M. S. 1996. Dissociation of Spatial and Temporal Coupling in the Bimanual Movements of Callosotomy Patients. *Psychological Science*, 7/5: 306–10.

Frassinetti, F., Bolognini, N., and Ladavas, E. 2002. Enhancement of Visual Perception by Cross-Modal Visual-Auditory Interaction. *Experimental Brain Research*, 147: 332–43.

Freedman, B. J. 1974. The Subjective Experience of Perceptual Cognitive Disturbance in Schizophrenia: A Review of Autobiographical Accounts. *Archives of General Psychiatry*, 30: 333–40.

Freeman, N. H., Lewis, C., Doherty, M. 1991. Preschoolers' Grasp of a Desire for Knowledge in False Belief Prediction: Practical Intelligence and Verbal Report. *British Journal of Developmental Psychology*, 9: 139–57.

Freud, S. 1910/1955. *The Standard Edition of the Complete Psychological Works of Sigmund Freud*, Vol. xx (1925–6), trans. J. Strachey. London: Hogarth Press.

——1915/1955. *The Standard Edition of the Complete Psychological Works of Sigmund Freud*, Vol. xiv, trans. J. Strachey. London: Hogarth Press.

——1962. *Civilization and its discontents*, trans J. Strachey. Boston: Norton.

Fried, I. 2005. Auras and Experiential Responses Arising in the Temporal Lobe. In S. Salloway, P. Malloy, and J. L. Cummings (eds.), *The Neuropsychiatry of Limbic and Subcortical Disorders*. Washington, DC: American Psychiatric Press, pp. 113–22.

Frisby, J. P. 1979. *Seeing*. Oxford: Oxford University Press.

Frith, C. 1992. *The Cognitive Neuropsychology of Schizophrenia*. Hove: Psychology Press.

——, Perry, R., and Lumer, E. 1999. The Neural Correlates of Conscious Experience: an Experimental Framework. *Trends in Cognitive Sciences*, 3: 105–14.

Frye, D., Zelazo, P. D., and Palfai, T. 1995. Theory of Mind and Rule-Based Reasoning. *Cognitive Development*, 10: 483–527.

Fu, K. M., Shah, A. S., O'Connell, M. N., McGinnis, T., Eckholdt, H., Lakatos, P., Smiley, J., and Schroeder, C. E. 2004. Timing and Laminar Profile of Eye-position Effects on Auditory Responses in Primate Auditory Cortex. *Journal of Neurophysiology*, 92: 3522–31.

Funnell, M. G., Corballis, P. M., and Gazzaniga, M. S. 2000a. Insights into the Functional Specificity of the Human Corpus Callosum. *Brain*, 123: 920–6.

————2000b. Cortical and Subcortical Interhemispheric Interactions following Partial and Complete Callosotomy. *Archives of Neurology*, 57: 185–9.

Gallace, A., Tan, H. Z., and Spence, C. 2006. Numerosity Judgments of Tactile Stimuli Distributed Over the Body Surface. *Perception*, 35: 247–66.

Gallagher, S. 2000 Self-Reference and Schizophrenia: A Cognitive Model of Immunity to Error Through Misidentification. In D. Zahavi (ed.), *Exploring the Self: Philosophical and Psychopathological Perspectives on Self-experience*. Amsterdam and Philadelphia: John Benjamins, pp. 203–42.

Garnham, W. A., and Perner, J. 2001. Actions Really do Speak Louder than Words—but only Implicitly: Young Children's Understanding of False Belief in Action. *British Journal of Developmental Psychology*, 19: 413–32.

——and Ruffman, T. 2001. Doesn't see, Doesn't Know: Is Anticipatory Looking Really Related to Understanding of Belief? *Developmental Science*, 4/1: 94–100.

Gazzaniga, M. S. 1987. Perceptual and Attentional Processes Following Callosal Section in Humans. *Neuropsychologia*, 25/1A: 119–33.

——1995. Consciousness and the Cerebral Hemispheres. In M. S. Gazzaniga (ed.), *The Cognitive Neurosciences*. Cambridge, MA: MIT Press, pp. 1391–1400.

——2005. Forty-Five Years of Split-Brain Research and Still Going Strong. *Nature Reviews Neuroscience*, 6: 653–9.

Gazzaniga, M. S., Bogen, J. E., and Sperry, R. W. 1963. Laterality Effects in Somesthesis following Cerebral Commissurotomy in Man. *Neuropsychologia*, 1: 209–15.

——and Freedman, H. 1973. Observations on Visual Processes After Posterior Callosal Section. *Neurology*, 23: 1126–30.

——and Hillyard, S. A. 1971. Language and Speech Capacity of the Right Hemisphere. *Neuropsychologia*, 9: 273–80.

——and LeDoux, J. 1978. *The Integrated Mind*. New York: Plenum Press.

——and Sperry, R.W. 1966. Simultaneous Double Discrimination Response Following Brain Bisection. *Psychonomic Science*, 4: 261–2.

Gendler, T. S. 1998. Exceptional Persons: On the Limits of Imaginary Cases. *Journal of Consciousness Studies*, 5: 592–610.

Gennaro, R. 2004. (ed.) *Higher-Order Theories of Consciousness: An Anthology*. Amsterdam and Philadelphia: John Benjamins.

Gerrans, P. 2000. Refining the Explanation of Cotard's Delusion. *Mind and Language*, 15/1: 111–22.

Ghazanfar, A. A., Maier, J. X., Hoffman, K. L., and Logothetis, N. K. 2005. Multisensory Integration of Dynamic Faces and Voices in Rhesus Monkey Auditory Cortex. *Journal of Neuroscience*, 25: 5004–12.

Giacino, J. T. 2005. The Minimally Conscious State: Defining the Borders of Consciousness. In S. Laureys (ed.), *The Boundaries of Consciousness: Neurobiology and Neuropathology, Advances in Brain Research* Vol. 150. Amsterdam: Elsevier, pp. 381–96.

Giacino, J. T., Ashwal, S., Childs, N., Cranford, R., Jennett, B., Katz, D. I., Kelly, J. P., Rosenberg, J. H., Whyte, J., Zafonte, R. D., Zasler, N. D. 2002. The Minimally Conscious State: Definition and Diagnostic Criteria. *Neurology*, 58: 349–53.

Gilbert, S. J., Spengler, S., Simons, J. S., Steele, J. D., Lawrie, S. M., Frith, C. D. 2006. Functional Specialization within Rostral Prefrontal Cortex (Area 10): A Meta-Analysis. *Journal of Cognitive Neuroscience*, 18: 932–48.

Gillett, G. 1986. Brain Bisection and Personal Identity. *Mind*, 95: 224–9.

Gloor, P. 1986. Consciousness as a Neurological Concept in Epileptology: A Critical Review. *Epilepsia*, 27 (suppl. 2): S14–S26.

——1990. Experiential Phenomena of Temporal Lobe Epilepsy: Facts and Hypotheses. *Brain*, 113: 1673–94.

——, Olivier, A., and Ives, J. 1980. Loss of Consciousness in Temporal Lobe Seizures: Observations Obtained with Sterotaxic Depth Electrode Recordings and Stimulations. In R. Canger, F. Angeleri, and J. K. Penry (eds.), *Advances in Epileptology: XIth Epilepsy International Symposium*, pp. 349–53.

—— ——, Quesney, L. F., Andermann, F., and Horowitz, S. 1982. The Role of the Limbic System in Experiential Phenomena of Temporal Lobe Epilepsy. *Annals of Neurology*, 12: 129–44.

Glüer, K. 2009. In Defence of a Doxastic Account of Experience. *Mind and Language*, 24: 297–327.

Gold, I. 1999. Does 40-Hz Oscillation Play a Role in Visual Consciousness? *Consciousness and Cognition*, 8: 186–95.

Goldberg, E., and Barr, W. B. 1991. Three Possible Mechanisms of Unawareness of Deficit. In G. P. Prigatano and D. L. Schacter (eds.), *Awareness of Deficit after Brain Injury: Clinical and Theoretical Issues*. New York: Oxford University Press, pp. 152–75.

Goldenberg, G., Müllbacher, W., and Nowak, A. 1995. Imagery without Perception: A Case Study of Anosognosia for Cortical Blindness. *Neuropsychologia*, 33: 1373–82.

Goodale, M., and Milner, A. D. 2003. *Sight Unseen: An Exploration of Conscious and Unconscious Vision*. Oxford: Oxford University Press.

——, Jakobson, L. S., Milner, A. D., Perrett, D. I., Benson, P. J., and Hietanen, J. K. 1994. The Nature and Limits of Orientation and Pattern Processing Supporting Visualmotor Control In a Visual Form Agnosic. *Journal of Cognitive Neuroscience*, 6: 46–56.

Gordon, H. W. and Sperry, R. 1969. Lateralization of Olfactory Perception in the Surgically Separated Hemispheres in Man. *Neuropsychologia*, 7: 111–20.

Gott, P. S. and Saul, R. W. 1978. Agenesis of the Corpus Callosum: Limits of Functional Compensation. *Neurology*, 28: 1271–9.

Graham, G. 2004. Thought Insertion. In J. Radden (ed.), *The Philosophy of Psychiatry: A Companion*. Oxford: Oxford University Press, pp. 89–105.

Gray, J. A., Rawlins, J. N. P., Hemsley, D. R., and Smith, A. D. 1991. The Neuropsychology of Schizophrenia. *Behavioural and Brain Sciences*, 14: 1–84.

Greenwald, A. G. 2003. On Doing Two Things at Once: III. Confirmation of Perfect Timesharing when Simultaneous Tasks are Ideomotor Compatible. *Journal of Experimental Psychology: Human Perception and Performance*, 29: 859–68.

——and Shulman, H. G. 1973. On Doing Two Things at Once: II. Elimination of the Psychological Refractory Period. *Journal of Experimental Psychology*, 101: 70–6.

Greenwood, J. D. 1993. Split-brains and Singular Personhood. *The Southern Journal of Philosophy*, 31/3: 285–306.

Grice, H. P. 1962. Some Remarks about the Senses. In R. J. Butler (ed.) *Analytical Philosophy* (1st ser.). Oxford: Basil Blackwell, pp. 133–53.

Grimes, P. 1996. On the Failure to Detect Changes in Scenes Across Saccades. In K. Akins, *Perception (Vancouver Studies in Cognitive Science), vol. 2*. New York: Oxford University Press, pp. 89–110.

Hacking, I. 1995. *Rewriting the Soul: Multiple Personality and the Sciences of Memory.* Princeton, NJ: Princeton University Press.

Hadjikhani, N., Liu, A. K., Dale, A. M., Cavanagh, P., Tootell, R. B. H. 1998. Retinotopy and Colour Sensitivity in Human Visual Cortical Area V8. *Nature Neuroscience*, 1/3: 235–41.

Haggard, P. 2008. Human Volition: Towards a Neuroscience of Will. *Nature Reviews Neuroscience*, 9/12: 934–46.

Hall, R. 2008. If it Itches, Scratch! *Australasian Journal of Philosophy* 86:525–35.

Halligan, P., and Marshall, J. C. 1989. Laterality of Motor Response in Visuo-Spatial Neglect: A Case Study. *Neuropsychologia*, 27/10: 1301–7.

——, Manning, L., and Marshall, J. C. 1991. Hemispheric Activation vs Spatio-Temporal Motor Cueing in Visual Neglect: A Case Study. *Neuropsychologia*, 29/2: 165–76.

Harman, G. 1990. The Intrinsic Quality of Experience. *Philosophical Perspectives*, 4: 31–52.

Harriman, P. L. 1942. The Experimental Production of Some Phenomena Related to Multiple Personality. *Journal of Abnormal and Social Psychology*, 37: 244–55.

Harrington, A. 1987. *Medicine, Mind, and the Double Brain*. Princeton, NJ: Princeton University Press.

Harris, P. L. 1986. Bringing Order to the A-not-B Error. *Monographs of the Society for Research in Child Development*, 51: 52–61.

Harrison, K. and Fox, R. 1966. Replication of Reaction Time to Stimuli Masked by Metacontrast. *Journal of Experimental Psychology*, 71: 162–3.

Hartmann, J. A., Wolz, W. A., Roeltgen, D. P., and Loverso F. L. 1991. Denial of Visual Perception. *Brain and Cognition*, 16: 29–40.

Hassin, R. R., Uleman, J. A., and Bargh, J. A. 2004. *The New Unconscious*. Oxford: Oxford University Press.

Heeger, D., Boynton, G. M., Demb, J. B., Seidemann, E., and Newsome, W. T. 1999. Motion Opponency in Visual Cortex. *Journal of Neuroscience*, 19/16: 7162–74.

Heil, J. 1994. Going to Pieces. In G. Graham and G. L. Stephens (eds.), *Philosophical Psychopathology*. Cambridge, MA: MIT Press, pp. 111–34.

Heilman, K. M. 1991. Anosognosia: Possible Neuropsychological Mechanisms. In G. P. Prigatano and D. L. Schacter (eds.), *Awareness of Deficit after Brain Injury*. New York: Oxford University Press, 53–62.

——Barrett, A. M., and Adair, J. C. 1998. Possible Mechanisms of Anosognosia: A Defect In Self-Awareness. *Philosophical Transactions of the Royal Society of London*, B 353: 1903–9.

Helbig, H. B. and Ernst, M. O. 2007. Optimal Integration of Shape Information from Vision and Touch. *Experimental Brain Research*, 179/4: 595–606.

Henderson, J. M., and Hollingworth, A. 1999. High Level Scene perception. *Annual Review of Psychology*, 50: 243–71.

————2003. Eye Movements and Visual Memory: Detecting Changes to Saccade Targets in Scenes, *Perception and Psychophysics*, 65/1: 58–71.

Hilgard, E. R. 1973. A Neodissociation Interpretation of Pain Reduction in Hypnosis. *Psychological Review*, 80: 396–411.

——1977. *Divided consciousness: multiple controls in human thought and action*. New York: John Wiley and Sons.

——1992. Divided Consciousness and Dissociation. *Consciousness and Cognition*, 1: 16–31.

——Hilgard, J. R., Macdonald, H., Morgan, A. H., and Johnson, L. S. 1978. Covert Pain in Hypnotic Analgesia: Its Reality as Tested by the Real-Simulator Design. *Journal of Abnormal Psychology*, 87: 655–63.

——, Morgan, A. H., and Macdonald, H. 1975. Pain and Dissociation in the Cold Pressor Test: A Study of Hypnotic Analgesia with 'Hidden Reports' Through Automatic Key Pressing and Automatic Talking. *Journal of Abnormal Psychology*, 84: 280–9.

Hill, C. 1991. *Sensations: A Defense of Type Materialism*. Cambridge: Cambridge University Press.

Hirsch, E. 1991. Divided Minds. *Philosophical Review*, 100/1: 3–30.

Hofstadter, M. C., and Reznick, J. S. 1996. Response Modality Affects Human Infant Delayed-Response Performance. *Child Development*, 67: 646–58.

Hohwy, J. 2007. The search for Neural Correlates of Consciousness, *Philosophy Compass* 2/3: 461–74.

——2009. The Neural Correlates of Consciousness: New Experimental Approaches Needed? *Consciousness and Cognition*, 18/2: 428–38.

Hollingworth, A., Williams, C. C., and Henderson, J. M. 2001. To See and Remember: Visually Specific Information is Retained in Memory from Previously Attended Objects in Natural Scenes. *Psychonomic Bulletin and Review*, 8: 761–8.

Holtzman, J. D. 1984. Interactions between Cortical and Subcortical Visual Areas: Evidence from Human Commissurotomy Patients. *Vision Research*, 24/8: 801–13.

——and Gazzaniga, M. S. 1982. Dual Task Interactions Due Exclusively to Limits in Processing Resources. *Science*, 218: 1325–7.

Holtzman, J. D., Volpe, B. T., and Gazzaniga, M. S. 1984. Spatial Orientation following Commissural Section. In R. Parasuraman and D. R. Davies (eds.), *Varieties of Attention*. Orlando, FL: Academic Press, pp. 375–94.

Hood, B., Cole-Davies, V., and Dias, M. 2003. Looking and Search Measures of Object Knowledge in Preschool Children. *Developmental Psychology*, 39: 61–70.

Horgan, T., and Tienson, J. 2002. The intentionality of Phenomenology and the Phenomenology of Intentionality. In D. Chalmers (ed.), *Philosophy of Mind: Classical and Contemporary Readings*. Oxford: Oxford University Press, pp. 520–33.

————and Graham, G. 2003. The Phenomenology of First-Person Agency. In S. Walter and H. D. Heckmann (eds.), *Physicalism and Mental Causation: The Metaphysics of Mind and Action*. Exeter: Imprint Academic, pp. 323–40.

Howard, I. P., and Templeton, W. B. 1966. *Human Spatial Orientation*. New York: Wiley.

——, Treisman, A., and Pashler, H. 2007. Characterizing the Limits of Human Visual Awareness. *Science*, 317: 823–5.

Hughlings-Jackson, J. 1889. On a Particular Variety of Epilepsy ('intellectual aura') One Case with Symptoms of Organic Brain Disease. *Brain*, 11: 179–207.

Huk, A., Ress D., Heeger D. J. 2001. Neuronal Basis of the Motion Aftereffect Reconsidered. *Neuron*, 32: 161–70.

Humphrey, N. K. 1972. Seeing and Nothingness. *New Scientist*, 53: 682–4.

——1974. Vision in a Monkey without Striate Cortex: A Case Study. *Perception*, 3: 241–55.

——1995. Blocking out the Distinction between Sensation and Perception: Superblindsight and the Case of Helen. *Behavioral and Brain Sciences*, 18: 257–8.

Humphreys, G. W. 1999. Integrative Agnosia. In G. W. Humphreys, (ed.), *Case Studies in the Neuropsychology of Vision*. London: Psychology Press, pp. 41–58.

Hurley, S. L. 1994. Unity and Objectivity. In C. Peacocke (ed.), *Objectivity, Simulation and the Unity of Consciousness: Current Issues in the Philosophy of Mind* (Proceedings of the British Academy, 83), Oxford: Oxford University Press, pp. 49–77.

——1998. *Consciousness in Action*. Cambridge, MA: Harvard University Press.

——2000. Clarifications: Responses to Kobes and Kinsbourne. *Mind and Language*, 15/5: 556–61.

——2003. Action, the Unity of Consciousness, and Vehicle Externalism. In A. Cleeremans (ed.) *The Unity of Consciousness: Binding, Integration and Dissociation*. Oxford: Oxford University Press, pp. 78–91.

——2010. The Varieties of Externalism. In R. Menary (ed). *The Extended Mind*. Cambridge, MA: MIT Press, pp. 101–54.

Iacoboni, M., Woods, R. P., and Mazziotta, J. C. 1996. Brain-Behavior Relationships: Evidence from Practice Effects in Spatial Stimulus-Response Compatibility. *Journal of Neurophysiology*, 76: 321–31.

Irwin, D. E. 1996. Integration and Accummulation of Information Across Saccadic Eye Movements. In J. McClelland and T. Inui (eds.), *Attention and Performance*, Vol. xvi. *Information Integration in Perception and Communication*. Cambridge, MA: MIT Press, pp. 125–56.

Ivry, R., Franz, E. A., Kingstone, A., and Johnston, J. 1998. The Psychological Refractory Period Effect Following Callosotomy: Uncoupling of Lateralized Response Codes. *Journal of Experimental Psychology: Human Perception and Performance*, 24/2: 463–80.

Jackson, F. 1982. Epiphenomenal Qualia. *Philosophical Quarterly*, 32: 127–36.

Jahanshahi, M., and Frith, C. 1998. Willed Action and its Impairments. *Cognitive Neuropsychology*, 15/6–8: 483–533.

James, W. 1890/1950. *Principles of Psychology*, 2 Vols. London: Macmillan.

Janet, P. 1913. *L'Automatisme psychologique* (7th edn.). Paris: Félix Alcan.

Jaspers, K. 1962. *General Psychopathology*. Translated from the German, 7th edn. by J. Hoenig and Marian W. Hamilton. Manchester: Manchester University Press.

Jeeves, M. A. 1979. Some Limits to Interhemispheric Integration in Cases of Callosal Agenesis and Partial Commisurotomy. In I. S. Rusell, M. W. van Hof, and G. Berlucchi (eds.). *Structure and Function of Cerebral Commissures*, Baltimore, MD: University Park Press, pp. 449–74.

Jehkonen, M., Ahonen, J.-P., Dastidar, P., Koivisto, A.-M., Laippala, P., and Vilkki, J. 2000. Unawareness of Deficits After Right Hemisphere Stroke: Double Dissociation of Anosognosias. *Acta Neurologica Scandinavica*, 102: 378–84.

Jennett, B. 2002. *The Vegetative State*. Cambridge: Cambridge University Press.

Jiang, Y., and Kanwisher, N. 2003. Common Neural Mechanisms for Response Selection and Perceptual Processing. *Journal of Cognitive Neuroscience*, 15: 1095–110.

——, Costello, P., Fang, F., Huang, M., and Sheng, H. 2006. A Gender- and Sexual Orientation-Dependent Spatial Attentional Effect of Invisible Images. *Proceedings of the National Academy of Sciences, USA*, 103: 17048–52.

Joanette, Y., Brouchon, M., Gauthier, L., and Samson, M. 1986. Pointing with Left vs. Right Hand in Left Visual Field Neglect. *Neuropsychologia*, 24: 391–6.

Johnson, L. E. 1984a. Vocal Responses to Left Visual Field Stimuli Following Forebrain Commissurotomy Subjects. *Neuropsychologia*, 22: 153–66.

——1984b. Bilateral Visual Cross-Integration by Human Forebrain Commissurotomy Subjects. *Neuropsychologia*, 22: 167–75.

Johnston, M. 1987. Human Beings. *Journal of Philosophy*, 84: 59–83.

Kamitani, Y., and Shimojo, S. 2001. Sound Induced Visual 'Rabbit'. *Journal of Vision*, 1/3: 478a.

Kammer, T. 1999. Phosphenes and Transient Scotomas Induced by Magnetic Stimulation of the Occipital Lobe: Their Topographic Relationship. *Neuropsychologia*, 37: 191–8.

Kampman, R. 1976. Hypnotically Induced Multiple Personality: An Experimental Study. *International Journal of Clinical and Experimental Hypnosis*, 24: 215–27.

Kant, I. 1781/1787/1999. *The Critique of Pure Reason*. P. Guyer and A. W. Wood (trans.) Cambridge: Cambridge University Press.

Kanwisher, N. 2001. Neural Events and Perceptual Awareness. *Cognition*, 79: 89–113.

Kashino, M., and Hirahara, T. 1996. One, Two, Many—Judging the number of Concurrent Talkers. *Journal of the Acoustical Society of America*, 99: 2596–2603.

Kayser, C., and Logothetis, N. K. 2007. Do Early Sensory Cortices Integrate Cross-Modal Information? *Brain Structure and Function*, 212/2: 121–32.

Keller, P. 1998. *Kant and the Demands of Self-Consciousness*. Cambridge: Cambridge University Press.

Kennerley, S. W., Diedrichsen, J., Hazeltine, E., Semjen, A., Ivry, R. B. 2002. Callosotomy Patients Exhibit Temporal Coupling During Continuous Bimanual Movements. *Nature Neuroscience*, 5: 376–81.

Kennett, J., and Matthews, S. 2003. Delusion, Dissociation and Identity. *Philosophical Explorations*, 6/1: 31–49.

Kentridge, R. W., Heywood C. A., and Weiskrantz, L. 1999. Attention without Awareness in Blindsight. *Proceedings of the Royal Society of London*, B, 266: 1805–11.

————————2004. Spatial Attention Speeds Discrimination without Awareness in Blindsight. *Neuropsychologia*, 42: 831–5.

Kihlstrom, J. F. 1985. Hypnosis. *Annual Review of Psychology*, 35: 385–418.

——1987. The Cognitive Unconscious. *Science*, 237/4821: 1445–52.

——and Barnier, A. 2005. The Hidden Observer: A Straw Horse, Undeservedly Flogged. *Contemporary Hypnosis*, 22: 144–51.

Kim, J. 1976. Events as Property Exemplifications. In M. Brand and D. Walton (eds.), *Action Theory*. Doredrecht: D. Reidel, pp. 159–77.

Kind, A. 2003. What's so Transparent about Transparency? *Philosophical Studies*, 115/3: 225–44.

Kingstone, A., and Gazzaniga, M. S. 1995. Subcortical Transfer of Higher Order Information: More Illusory than Real? *Neuropsychologia*, 9: 321–8.

Kinsbourne, M. 1974. Mechanisms of Hemispheric Interaction in Man: Cerebral Control and Mental Evolution. In M. Kinsbourne and W. L. Smith (eds.), *Hemispheric Disconnection and Cerebral Function*. Springfield, IL.: C. C. Thomas, pp. 260–89.

——2000. Consciousness in Action: Antecedents and Origins. *Mind and Language*, 15: 545–55.

Kirchner, H., and Thorpe, S. J. 2006. Ultra-Rapid Object Detection with Saccadic Eye Movements: Visual Processing Speed Revisited. *Vision Research*, 46: 1762–76.

Kirsch, I. and Lynn, S. J. 1998. Social-Cognitive Alternatives to Dissociation Theories of Hypnotic Involuntariness. *Review of General Psychology*, 2/1: 66–80.

Klein, C. 2007. An Imperative Theory of Pain. *The Journal of Philosophy*, 104: 517–32.

Klotz, W., and Neurmann, O. 1999. Motor Activation without Conscious Discrimination in Metacontrast Masking. *Journal of Experimental Psychology: Human Perception and Performance*, 25/4: 976–92.

Kluft, R. P. 1987. First-Rank Symptoms as a Diagnostic Clue to Multiple Personality Disorder. *American Journal of Psychiatry*, 144: 293–8.

Knox, V. J., Morgan, A. H., and Hilgard, E. R. 1974. Pain and Suffering in Ischemia: The Paradox of Hypnotically Suggested Anesthesia as Contradicted by Reports from the Hidden Observer. *Archives of General Psychiatry*, 30: 840–7.

Koch, C. 2004. *The Quest for Consciousness*. Englewood, CO: Roberts and Co.

——and Crick, F. 2001. On the Zombie Within. *Nature*, 411: 893.

Kohler, I., 1951/1964. Formation and Transformation of the Perceptual World, Trans. H. Fiss. *Psychological Issues*, 3/4: 1–173.

Kolb, F. C., and Braun, J. 1995. Blindsight in Normal Observers. *Nature*, 377: 336–8.

Kolers, P. A., and von Grünau, M. 1976. Shape and Color in Apparent Motion. *Vision Research*, 16: 329–35.

Kölmel, H. 1985. Complex Visual Hallucinations in the Hemianopic Field. *Journal of Neurology, Neurosurgery, and Psychiatry*, 48: 29–38.

Kornblum, S., Hasbroucq, T., and Osman, A. 1990. Dimensional Overlap: Cognitive Basis for Stimulus-Response Compatibility—a Model and Taxonomy. *Psychological Review*, 97: 253–70.

Kourtzi, Z. and Kanwisher, N. 2000. Activation in Human MT/MST by Static Images with Implied Motion. *Journal of Cognitive Neuroscience*, 12: 48–55.

Kraepelin, E. 1896. *Psychiatrie* (4th edn.). Leipzig, J. A. Barth.

Kreuter, C., Kinsbourne, M., Trevarthen, C., 1972. Are Deconnected Cerebral Hemispheres Independent Channels? A Preliminary Study of the Effect of Unilateral Loading on Bilateral Finger Tapping. *Neuropsychologia*, 10: 453–61.

Kriegel, U. 2007. Intentional Inexistence and Phenomenal Intentionality. *Philosophical Perspectives*, 21: 307–40.

——and Williford, K. (eds.), 2006. *Self-Representational Approaches to Consciousness*. Cambridge, MA: MIT Press.

Kulvicki, J. 2007. What is what it's Like? Introducing Perceptual Modes of Presentation. *Synthese*, 156: 205–29.

Lachter, J., and Durgin, F. 1999. Metacontrast Masking Functions: A Question of Speed? *Journal of Experimental Psychology: Human Perception and Performance*, 25/4: 936–47.

————and Washington, T. 2000. Disappearing Percepts: Evidence for Retention Failure in Metacontrast Masking. *Visual Cognition*, 7: 269–79.

Ladavas, E., Paladini, R., and Cubelli, R. 1993. Implicit Associative Priming in a Patient with Left Unilateral Neglect. *Neuropsychologia*, 31: 1307–20.

Lakatos, P., Chen, C. M., O'Connell, M. N, Mills, A., and Schroeder, C. E. 2007. Neuronal Oscillations and Multisensory Interaction in Primary Auditory Cortex, *Neuron*, 53: 279–92.

Lalanne, C., and Lorenceau, J. 2004. Crossmodal Integration for Perception and Action. *Journal of Physiology* (Paris), 98: 265–79.

Lambert, A. 1991. Interhemispheric Interaction in the Split-Brain. *Neuropsychologia*, 29/10: 941–7.

——1993. Attentional Interaction in the Split-Brain: Evidence from Negative Priming. *Neuropsychologia*, 31/4: 313–24.

Lamme, V. A. F. 2006. Towards a True Neural Stance on Consciousness. *Trends in Cognitive Sciences*, 10/11: 494–501.

——and Roelfsema, P. R. 2000. The Distinct Modes of Vision Offered by Feedforward and Recurrent Processing. *Trends in Neuroscience*, 23: 571–9.

Landis, T., Assal, G., and Perret, E. 1979. Opposite Cerebral Hemispheric Superiorities for Visual Associative Processing of Emotional Facial Expressions and Objects. *Nature*, 278: 739–40.

——, Graves, R., and Goodglass, H. 1981. Dissociated Awareness of Manual Performance on Two Different Visual Associative Tasks: A 'Split-Brain' Phenomenon in Normal Subjects? *Cortex*, 17: 435–40.

Lassonde, M., Sauerwein, H., McCabe, N., Laurencelle, L., and Geoffrey, G. 1988. Extent of the Limits of Cerebral Adjustment to Early Section or Congenital Absence of the Corpus Callosum. *Behavioral Brain Research*, 30: 165–81.

——, Sauerwein, H., Chicoine, A., and Geoffrey, G. 1991. Absence of Disconnexion Syndrome in Callosal Agenesis and Early Callosotomy: Brain Reorganization or Lack of Structural Specificity During Ontogeny? *Neuropsychologia*, 29: 481–95.

——— and Lepore, F. 1995. Extent and Limits of Callosal Plasticity: Presence of Disconnection Symptoms in Callosal Agenesis. *Neuropsychologia*, 33: 989–1007.

Lau, H. C., and Passingham, R. E. 2006. Relative Blindsight in Normal Observers and the Neural Correlate of Visual Consciousness. *Proceedings of the National Academy of Sciences*, 103/49: 18763–8.

———2007. Unconscious Activation of the Cognitive Control System in the Human Prefrontal Cortex. *The Journal of Neuroscience*, 27: 5805–11.

Laurence, J.-R. and Perry, C. 1981. The 'Hidden Observer' Phenomenon in Hypnosis: Some Additional Findings. *Journal of Abnormal Psychology*, 90/4: 334–44.

——— and Kihlstrom, J. F. 1983. 'Hidden Observer' Phenomena in Hypnosis: an Experimental Creation. *Journal of Personality and Social Psychology*, 44: 163–9.

Laureys, S., Faymonville, M. E., Luxen, A., Lamy, M., Franck, G., and Maquet, P. 2000. Restoration of Thalamocortical Connectivity after Recovery from Persistent Vegetative State. *Lancet*, 355: 1790–1.

LeDoux, J. E., Wilson, D. H., and Gazzaniga, M. S. 1977. A Divided Mind: Observations on the Conscious Properties of the Separated Hemispheres. *Annals of Neurology*, 2: 417–21.

Lengfelder, A., and Gollwitzer, P. M. 2001. Reflective and Reflexive Action Control in Patients with Frontal Brain Lesions. *Neuropsychology*, 15/1: 80–100.

Leuthold, H., and Kopp, B. 1998. Mechanisms of Priming by Masked Stimuli: Inferences from Event-Related Brain Potentials. *Psychological Science*, 9: 263–9.

Levine, D. N. 1990. Unawareness of Visual and Sensorimotor Defects: A Hypothesis. *Brain and Cognition*, 13: 233–81.

Levine, J. 1983. Materialism and Qualia: The Explanatory Gap. *Pacific Philosophical Quarterly*, 64: 354–61.

Levy, J. 1977. Manifestations and Implications of Shifting Hemi-Inattention in Commissurotomy Patients. *Advances in Neurology*, 18: 83–92.

——1990. Regulation and Generation of Perception in the Asymmetric Brain. In C. Trevarthen (ed.), *Brain Circuits and Functions of the Mind: Essays in Honour of Roger W. Sperry*. Cambridge: Cambridge University Press, pp. 231–48.

——and Trevarthen, C. 1976. Metacontrol of Hemispheric Function in Human Splitbrain Patients. *Journal of Experimental Psychology: Human Perception and Performance*, 2: 299–312.

Levy, J., Nebes, R. D., and Sperry, R. W. 1971. Expressive Language in the Surgically Separated Minor Hemisphere. *Cortex*, 7: 49–58.

——, Trevarthen, C., and Sperry, R. W. 1972. Perception of Bilateral Chimeric Figures Following Hemispheric Deconnexion. *Brain*, 95: 61–78.

Levy, N. 2008. Self-deception Without Thought Experiments. In T. Bayne and J. Fernández (eds.), *Delusion and Self-Deception: Affective and Motivational Influences on Belief Formation*. Hove: Psychology Press, pp. 227–42.

Levy, R., and Goldman-Rakic, P. 2000. Segregation of Working Memory Functions within the Dorsolateral Prefrontal Cortex. *Experimental Brain Research*, 133: 23–32.

Lewis, D. 1976. Survival and Identity. In A. O. Rorty (ed.), *The Identities of Persons*. Berkeley and Los Angeles, University of California Press, pp. 17–40.

——1979. Attitudes de Dicto and De Se. *Philosophical Review*, 87: 513–43.

——1986. *On the Plurality of Worlds*. Oxford: Blackwell.

——1994. Reduction of Mind. In S. Guttenplan (ed.), *A Companion to the Philosophy of Mind*. Oxford: Blackwell, pp. 412–30.

Liddle, P. F. 1987. The Symptoms of Chronic Schizophrenia: A Re-Examination of the Positive-Negative Dichotomy. *British Journal of Psychiatry*, 151: 145–51.

Linden, D. E. J., Kallenbach, U., Heinecke, A., Singer, W., and Goebel, R. 1999. The Myth of Upright Vision: A Psychophysical and Functional Imaging Study of Adaptation to Inverting Spectacles. *Perception*, 28: 469–81.

Livermore, A., and Laing, D. G. 1996. The Influence of Training and Professional Experience on the Perception of Odor Mixtures. *Journal of Experimental Psychology: Human Perception and Performance*, 22: 267–77.

————1998. The Influence of Chemical Complexity on the Perception of Multi-component Odor Mixtures. *Perception and Psychophysics*, 60: 650–61.

Locke, J. 1690/1975. *An Essay Concerning Human Understanding*. (ed.) P. Nidditch, Oxford: Clarendon.

Lockwood, M. 1989. *Mind, Brain and the Quantum*. Oxford: Basil Blackwell.

——1994. Issues of Unity and Objectivity. In C. Peacocke (ed.), *Objectivity, Simulation, and the Unity of Consciousness: Current Issues in the Philosophy of Mind* (Proceedings of the British Academy, 83), Oxford: Oxford University Press, 89–95.

Loewenstein, R. J., Hamilton, J., Alagna, S., Reid, N., and deVries, M. 1987. Experiential Sampling in the Study of MPD. *American Journal of Psychiatry*, 144: 19–24.

Logothetis, N. 1998. Object Vision and Visual Awareness. *Current Opinion in Neurobiology*, 8: 536–44.

Logothetis, N. K., Leopold, D. A., and Sheinberg, D. L. 2003. Neural Mechanisms of Perceptual Organization. In N. Osaka (ed.), *Neural basis of consciousness: Advances in Consciousness Research*, vol. 49. Amsterdam: John Benjamins, pp. 87–103.

Lormand, E. 1996. Nonphenomenal Consciousness. *Noûs*, 30: 242–61.

Lovelace, C. T., Stein, B. E., and Wallace, M. T. 2003. An Irrelevant Light Enhances Auditory Detection in Humans: A Psychophysical Analysis of Multisensory Integration in Stimulus Detection. *Cognitive Brain Research*, 17: 447–53.

Luck, S. J., Hillyard, S. A., Mangun, G. R., Gazzaniga, M. S. 1989. Independent Hemispheric Attentional Systems Mediate Visual Search in Split-Brain Patients. *Nature*, 342/6249: 543–5.

———————1994. Independent Attentional Scanning in the Separated Hemispheres of Split-Brain Patients. *Journal of Cognitive Neuroscience*, 6: 84–91.

——and Vogel, E. K. 1997. The Capacity of Visual Working Memory for Features and Conjunctions. *Nature*, 390/6657: 279–81.

Lunn, V. 1970. Autoscopic Phenomena, *Acta Psychiatrica Scandinavia*, 46: 118–25 (suppl. 219).

Lyamin, O. I., Manger, P. R., Mukhametov, L. M., Siegel, J. M., and Shpak, O. V. 2000. Rest and Activity States in a Gray Whale. *Journal of Sleep Research*, 9: 261–7.

——, Mukhametov, L. M., Siegel, J. M., Nazarenko, E. A., Polyakova, I. G., and Shpak, O. V. 2002a. Unihemispheric Slow Wave Sleep and the State of the Eyes in a White Whale. *Behavioural Brain Research*, 129: 125–9.

—— ——, Chetyrbok, I. S., and Vassiliev, A. V. 2002b. Sleep and Wakefulness in the Southern Sea Lion. *Behavioural Brain Research*, 128: 129–38.

Lycan, W. 2001. A Simple Argument for a Higher-Order Representational Theory of Consciousness. *Analysis*, 61: 3–4.

Lyons, W. E. 1986. *The Disappearance of Introspection*. Cambridge, MA: MIT Press.

Macaluso, E., 2006. Multisensory Processing in Sensory-Specific Cortical Areas. *The Neuroscientist*, 12: 327–38.

——and Driver, J. 2005. Multisensory Spatial Interactions: a Window onto Functional Integration in the Human Brain. *Trends in Neuroscience*, 28: 264–71.

McConkie, G. W., and Rayner, K. 1975. The Span of the Effective Stimulus During a Fixation in Reading. *Perception and Psychophysics*, 17: 578–86.

—— and Zola, D. 1979. Is Visual Information Integrated Across Successive Fixations in Reading? *Perception and Psychophysics*, 25: 221–4.

McDaniel, K. D., and McDaniel, L. D. 1991. Anton's Syndrome in a Patient with Posttraumatic Optic Neuropathy and Bifrontal Contusions. *Archives of Neurology*, 48/1: 101–5.

McDonald, J. J., Teder-Salejarvi, W. A., and Hillyard, S. A. 2000. Involuntary Orienting to Sound Improves Visual Perception. *Nature*, 407: 906–8.

—— ——, Di Russo, F., and Hillyard, S. A. 2005. Neural Basis of Auditory-Induced Shifts in Visual Time-Order Perception. *Nature Neuroscience*, 8: 1197–1202.

MacDonald, N. 1960. The Other Side: Living with Schizophrenia. *Canadian Medical Association Journal*, 82: 218–21.

McGhie, A., and Chapman, J. 1961. Disorders of Attention and Perception in Early Schizophrenia. *British Journal of Medical Psychology*, 34: 103–16.

McGinn, C. 1982. *The Character of Mind*. Oxford: Oxford University Press.

——1989. *Mental Content*. Oxford: Blackwell.

——1993. Consciousness and Cosmology: Hyperdualism Ventilated. In M. Davies and G. W. Humphreys (eds.), *Consciousness*. Oxford: Blackwell, pp. 155–77.

McGlynn, S. M., and Schacter, D. L. 1989. Unawareness of Deficits in Neuropsychological Syndromes. *Journal of Clinical and Experimental Neuropsychology*, 11: 143–205.

McGurk, H., and McDonald, J. 1976. Hearing Lips and Seeing Voices. *Nature*, 264: 746–8.

McIntosh, R. D., McClements, K. I., Schindler, I., Cassidy, T. P., Birchall, D., and Milner, A. D. 2004a. Avoidance of Obstacles in the Absence of Visual Awareness. *Proceedings of the Royal Society of London Series B Biological Sciences*, 271: 15–20.

——, Dijkerman, R. C., Mon-Williams, M., and Milner, A. D. 2004b. Grasping what is Graspable: Evidence from Visual form Agnosia. *Cortex*, 40: 695–702.

McKay, A. P., McKenna, P. J., and Laws, K. 1996. Severe Schizophrenia: What is it Like? In P. W. Halligan and J. C. Marshall (eds.) *Method in Madness: Case Studies in Cognitive Neuropsychiatry*. Hove: Psychology Press, pp. 95–122.

McKenna, P. J. 1994. *Schizophrenia and Related Syndromes*. Oxford: Oxford University Press.

MacKay, D. M. 1966. Cerebral Organization and the Conscious Control of Action. In J. C. Eccles (ed.), *Brain and Conscious Experience*. Heidelberg: Springer-Verlag, pp. 422–45.

——and MacKay, V. 1982. Explicit Dialogue between Left and Right Half-Systems of Split Brains. *Nature*, 295: 690–1.

Mackie, J. L. 1976. *Problems from Locke*. Oxford: Oxford University Press.

Mangun, G. R, Hillyard, S. A., Luck S. J, Handy, T., Plager, R., Clark, V. P., Loftus, W., and Gazzaniga, M. S. 1994. Monitoring the Visual World: Hemispheric Asymmetries and Subcortical Processes in Attention. *Journal of Cognitive Neuroscience*, 6: 267–75.

Maravita, A., Spence, C., and Driver, J. 2003. Multisensory Integration and the Body Schema: Close to Hand and Within Reach. *Current Biology*, 13: R531–R539.

Marcel, A. J. 1983. Conscious and Unconscious Perception: Experiments on Visual Masking and Word Recognition. *Cognitive Psychology*, 15: 197–237.

——1993. Slippage in the Unity of Consciousness. In G. R. Bock and J. Marsh (eds.), *Experimental and Theoretical Studies of Consciousness*. Chichester, England: John Wiley and Sons, pp. 168–79.

——1994. What is Relevant to the Unity of Consciousness? In C. Peacocke (ed.), *Objectivity, Simulation, and the Unity of Consciousness: Current Issues in the Philosophy of Mind* (Proceedings of the British Academy, 83), Oxford: Oxford University Press, pp. 79–88.

Marcel, A., Tegnér, R., and Nimmo-Smith, I. 2004. Anosognosia for Plegia: Specificity, Extension, Partiality and Disunity of Bodily Awareness. *Cortex*, 40: 19–40.

Mark, V. 1996. Conflicting Communicative Behavior in a Split-Brain Patient: Support for Dual Consciousness. In S. R. Hammeroff, A. W. Kasniak, and A. C. Scott (eds.), *Toward a Science of Consciousness*. Cambridge, MA: MIT Press.

Marks, C. 1981. *Commissurotomy, Consciousness and Unity of Mind*. Cambridge, MA: MIT Press.

Marsolek, C., Nicholas, C. D., and Andresen, D. R. 2002. Interhemispheric Communication of Abstract and Specific Visual-form Information. *Neuropsychologia*, 40: 1983–99.

Mattingly, J. B., Driver, J., Beschin, N., and Robertson, I. H. 1997. Attentional Competition between Modalities: Extinction between Touch and Vision After Right Hemisphere Damage. *Neuropsychologia*, 35: 867–80.

Meador, K. J., Loring, D. W., Feinberg, T. E., Lee, G. P., and Nichols, M. E. 2000. Anosognosia and Asomatognosia During Intracarotid Amobarbital Inactivation. *Neurology*, 55: 816–20.

Mellor, C. H. 1970. First Rank Symptoms of Schizophrenia. *British Journal of Psychiatry*, 117: 15–23.

Mellor, D. H. 1988. Crane's Waterfall Illusion. *Analysis*, 48: 147–50.

Melzack, R. 1992. Phantom Limbs. *Scientific American*, 4: 90–6.

——Israel, R., Lacroix, R., and Schultz, G. 1997. Phantom Limbs in People with Congenital Limb Deficiency or Amputation in Early Childhood. *Brain*, 120: 1603–20.

Merleau-Ponty, M. 1962. *Phenomenology of Perception*, trans Colin Smith. New York: The Humanities Press.

Merskey, H. 1992. The Manufacture of Personalities: The Production of Multiple Personality Disorder. *British Journal of Psychiatry*, 157: 327–40.

Meyer, D. E., and Kieras, D. E. 1997. A Computational Theory of Executive Cognitive Processes and Multiple-Task Performance: Part 1. Basic Mechanisms. *Psychological Review*, 104: 3–65.

Miller, J., Riehle, A., and Requin, J. 1992. Effects of Preliminary Perceptual Output on Neuronal Activity of the Primary Motor Cortex. *Journal of Experimental Psychology: Human Perception and Performance*, 18: 1121–38.

Miller, M. E., and Bowers, K. S. 1993. Hypnotic Analgesia: Dissociated Experience or Dissociated Control? *Journal of Abnormal Psychology*, 102: 29–38.

Miller, M., and Kingstone, A. 2005. Taking the High Road on Subcortical Transfer. *Brain and Cognition*, 57: 162–4.

Milner, A. D., and Dunne, J. J. 1977. Lateralized Perception of Bilateral Chimaeric Faces by Normal Subjects. *Nature*, 268/5616: 175–6.

——and Goodale, M. A. 2006. *The Visual Brain in Action*. New York: Oxford University Press.

————2008. Two Visual Systems Reviewed. *Neuropsychologia*, 46: 774–85.

Milner, B. 1963. Effects of Different Brain Lesions on Card Sorting. *Archives of Neurology*, 9: 90–100.

——Taylor, L., and Sperry, R. W. 1968. Lateralized Suppression of Dichotically Presented Digits after Commissural Section in Man. *Science*, 161: 184–6.

Milner, B., Taylor, L., and Jones-Gotman, M. 1990. Lessons from Cerebral Commissurotomy: Auditory Attention, Haptic Memory, and Visual Images in Verbal Associative-Learning. In C. Trevarthen (ed.), *Brain Circuits and Functions of the Mind*. Cambridge: Cambridge University Press, pp. 293–303.

Milner, P. 1974. A Model for Visual Shape Recognition. *Psychological Review*, 8/6: 521–35.

Molholm, S., Ritter, W., Murray, M. M., Javitt, D. C., Schroeder, C. E., and Foxe, J. J. 2002. Multisensory Auditory-Visual Interactions During Sensory Early Sensory Processing in Humans: A High-Density Electrical Mapping Study. *Cognitive Brain Research*, 14: 115–28.

Montague, M. 2007. Against Propositionalism. *Noûs*, 41/3: 503–18.

Moor, J. 1982. Split-Brains and Atomic Persons. *Philosophy of Science*, 49: 91–106.

Morein-Zamir, S., Soto-Faraco, S., and Kingstone, A. 2003. Auditory Capture of Vision: Examining Temporal Ventriloquism. *Cognitive Brain Research*, 17/1: 154–63.

Moro, V., Zampini, M., and Aglioti, S. M. 2004. Changes in Spatial Position of Hands Modify Tactile Extinction but not Disownership of Contralesional Hand in Two Right Brain-Damaged Patients. *Neurocase*, 10: 437–43.

Morsella, E. 2005. The Function of Phenomenal States: Supramodular Interaction Theory. *Psychological Review*, 112/4: 1000–21.

Mukhametov, L. M., Supin, A. Y., and Polyakova, I. G. 1977. Interhemispheric Asymmetry of the Electroencephalographic Sleep Patterns in Dolphins. *Brain Research*, 134: 581–4.

——Lyamin, O. I., and Polyakova, I. G., 1985. Interhemispheric Asynchrony of the Sleep EEG in Northern Fur Seals. *Cellular and Molecular Life Sciences*, 41: 1034–5.

Mullins, S., and Spence, S. 2003. Re-Examining Thought Insertion. *British Journal of Psychiatry*, 182: 293–8.

Munakata, Y., McClelland, J. L., Johnson, M. H., and Siegler, R. 1997. Rethinking Infant Knowledge: Toward an Adaptive Process Account of Successes and Failures in Object Permanence Tasks. *Psychological Review*, 104: 686–713.

——and Yerys, B. E. 2001. All Together Now: When Dissociations between Knowledge and Action Disappear. *Psychological Science*, 12/4: 335–7.

Naccache, L. 2006. Is She Conscious? *Science*, 313: 1395–6.

Nagel, T. 1971. Brain Bisection and the Unity of Consciousness. *Synthese*, 22: 396–413.

——1974. What is it Like to be a Bat? *Philosophical Review*, 83: 435–50.

Naikar, N. 1996. Perception of Apparent Motion of Colored Stimuli after Commissurotomy. *Neuropsychologia*, 34/11: 1041–9.

——and Corballis, M. 1996. Perception of Apparent Motion Across the Retinal Midline following Commissurotomy. *Neuropsychologia*, 34/4: 297–309.

Nakayama, K. 1990. The Iconic Bottleneck and the Tenuous Link between Early Visual Processing and Perception. In C. Blakemore (ed.), *Vision: Coding and Efficiency*. Cambridge: Cambridge University Press, pp. 411–22.

Nathanson, M., Bergman, P., and Gordon, G. 1952. Denial of Illness: Its Occurrence in One Hundred Consecutive Cases of Hemiplegia. *Archives of Neurology and Psychiatry*, 68: 380–7.

Nebes, R. D., and Sperry, R. 1971. Hemispheric Deconnection Syndrome with Cerebral Birth Injury in the Dominant Arm Area. *Neuropsychologia*, 9: 247–59.

Nelkin, N. 1989. Propositional Attitudes and Consciousness. *Philosophy and Phenomenological Research*, 49/3: 413–30.

Neumann, O., and Klotz, W. 1994. Motor Responses to Non-Reportable, Masked Stimuli: Where is the Limit of the Direct Parameter Specification? In C. Umiltà and M. Moscovitch (eds.), *Attention and Performance XV: Conscious and Unconscious Information Processing*, Cambridge, MA: MIT Press, pp. 123–50.

——and Müsseler, J. 1990. 'Judgment' vs 'Response': A General Problem and some Experimental Illustrations. In H.-G. Geißler, M. H. Müller, and W. Prinz (eds.), *Psychophysical Explorations of Mental Structures*. Göttingen: Hogrefe, pp. 445–55.

Nikolinakos, D. D. 2004. Anosognosia and the Unity of Consciousness. *Philosophical Studies*, 119: 315–42.

Nogrady, H., McConkey, K. M., Laurence, J.-R., and Perry, C. 1983. Dissociation, Duality, and Demand Characteristics in Hypnosis. *Journal of Abnormal Psychology*, 92: 223–35.

Noirhomme, Q., Schnakers, C., and Laureys, S. 2008. A Twitch of Consciousness: Defining the Boundaries of Vegetative and Minimally Conscious States. *Journal of Neurology, Neurosurgery and Psychiatry*, 79/7: 741–2.

Noonan, H. 1989. *Personal Identity*. New York: Routledge.

Nozick, R. 1981. *Philosophical Explanations*. Cambridge, MA: Harvard University Press.

O'Brien, G., and Opie, J. 1998. The Disunity of Consciousness. *Australasian Journal of Philosophy*, 76/3: 378–95.

————2000. Disunity Defended. *Australasian Journal of Philosophy*, 78/2: 255–63.

O'Callaghan, C. 2008. Seeing What You Hear: Cross-Modal Illusions and Perception. *Philosophical Issues 18: Interdisciplinary Core Philosophy*, 316–38.

——forthcoming. Perception and Multimodality. In E. Margolis, R. Samuels, and S. Stich (eds.) *Oxford Handbook of Philosophy and Cognitive Science*. Oxford: Oxford University Press.

O'Dea, J. 2008. Transparency and the Unity of Experience. In E. Wright (ed.), *The Case for Qualia*. Cambridge, MA: MIT Press, pp. 299–308.

——2010. A Proprioceptive Account of the Sensory Modalities. In F. Macpherson (ed.), *The Senses*. Oxford: Oxford University Press.

O'Regan, J. K. 1992. Solving the 'Real' Mysteries of Perception: The World as an Outside Memory. *Canadian Journal of Psychology*, 46/3: 461–88.

O'Reilly, R. C., Busby, R. S., and Soto, R. 2003. Three Forms of Binding and their Neural Substrates: Alternatives to Synchrony. In A. Cleeremans (ed.), *The Unity of Consciousness: Binding, Integration, and Dissociation*. Oxford: Oxford University Press, pp. 168–90.

O'Shaughnessy, B. 1980. *The Will* (2 Vols.). Cambridge: Cambridge University Press.

——2003. The Epistemology of Physical Action. In J. Roessler and N. Eilan (eds.), *Agency and Self-Awareness*. Oxford: Clarendon Press, pp. 345–57.

Oliva, A. 2005. Gist of the Scene. In L. Itti, G. Reiss, and J. K. Tsotsos (eds.), *Neurobiology of Attention*. San Diego, CA: Elsevier, pp. 251–6.

Olson, E. 1997. *The Human Animal*. Oxford: Oxford University Press.

Onishi, K. H., and Baillargeon, R. 2005. Do 15-month-old Infants Understand False Beliefs? *Science*, 308/5719: 255–8.

Orne, M. T. 1959. The Nature of Hypnosis: Artifact and Essence. *Journal of Abnormal Psychology*, 58: 277–99.

Owen, A. M., and Coleman, M. R. 2008. Detecting Awareness in the Vegetative State. *Annals of the New York Academy of Sciences*, 1129: 130–8.

————Boly, M., Davis, M. H., Laureys, S., and Pickard, J. D. 2006. Detecting Awareness in the Vegetative State. *Science*, 313: 1402.

Owen, A. M., Stern, C. E., Look, R. B., Tracey, I., Rosen, R. B., Petrides, M. 1998. Functional Organization of Spatial and Nonspatial Working Memory Processing within the Human Lateral Frontal Cortex. *Proceedings of the National Academy of Sciences*, 95: 7721–6.

——, Herrod, N. J., Menon, D. K., Clark, J. C., Downey, S. P., Carpenter, T. A., Minhas, P. S., Turkheimer, F. E., Williams, E. J., Robbins, T. K., Sahakian, B. J., Petrides, M., and Pickard, J. D. 1999. Redefining the Functional Organization of Working Memory Processes within Human Lateral Prefrontal Cortex. *European Journal of Neuroscience*, 11: 567–74.

Papagno, C., and Vallar, G. 2003. Anosognosia for Left Hemiplegia: Babinski's (1914) Cases. In C. Code, C.-W. Wallesch, Y. Joanette, and A. R. Lecours (eds.). *Classic Cases in Neuropsychology* (Vol. 2), Hove, East Sussex: Psychology Press, pp. 171–89.

Papineau, D. 2002. *Thinking about Consciousness*. Oxford: Oxford University Press.

Parfit, D. 1971. Personal identity. *Philosophical Review*, 80: 3–27.

——1984. *Reasons and Persons*. Oxford: Clarendon Press.

Pashler, H. 1992. Attentional Limitations in Doing Two Tasks at the Same Time. *Current Directions in Psychological Science*, 1: 44–8.

——1994. Dual Task Interference in Simple Tasks—Data and Theory. *Psychological Bulletin*, 116: 220–44.

——1998. *The Psychology of Attention*. Cambridge, MA: MIT Press.

——, Luck, S. J., Hillyard, S. A., Mangun, G. R., O'Brien, S., and Gazzaniga, M. S. 1994. Sequential Operation of Disconnected Cerebral Hemispheres in Split-Brain Patients. *Neuroreport*, 5: 2381–4.

Pasupathy, A., and Connor, C. E. 1999. Responses to Contour Features in Macaque Area V4. *Journal of Neurophysiology*, 82: 2490–502.

————2001. Shape Representation in Area v4: Position-Specific Tuning for Boundary Conformation. *Journal of Neurophysiology*, 86: 2505–19.

Pavani, F., Spence, C., and Driver, J. 2000. Visual Capture of Touch: out-of-the-body Experiences with Rubber Gloves. *Psychological Science*, 11/5: 353–9.

Peacocke, C. 1983. *Sense and Content*. Oxford: Oxford University Press.

——1994. The Issues and Their Further Development. In C. Peacocke (ed.), *Objectivity, Simulation and the Unity of Consciousness: Current Issues in the Philosophy of Mind* (Proceedings of the British Academy, 83), Oxford: Oxford University Press, pp. xi–xxvi.

Perner, J., and Ruffman, T. 2005. Infants' Insights into the Mind: How Deep? *Science*, 308: 214–16.

Perry, C. and Walsh, B. 1978. Inconsistencies and Anomalies of Response as a Defining Characteristic of Hypnosis. *Journal of Abnormal Psychology*, 87: 547–77.

Perry, J. 1979. The Problem of the Essential Indexical. *Noûs*, 13: 3–22.

Petrides, M. 1995. Impairments on Nonspatial Self-Ordered and Externally Ordered Wording Memory Tasks After Lesions of the Mid-Dorsal Part of the Lateral Frontal Cortex in the Monkey. *Journal of Neuroscience*, 15: 359–75.

Phillips, I. (Forthcoming). Perception and Iconic Memory. Mind and Language.

Piaget, J. 1954. *The Construction of Reality in the Child*, trans. M. Cook. New York: Basic Books.

Pitcher, G. 1970. The Awfulness of Pain. *Journal of Philosophy*, 67: 481–91.

Pitt, D. 2004. The Phenomenology of Cognition Or What is it Like to Think That P? *Philosophy and Phenomenological Research*, 69: 1–36.

Poland, J. 2007. How to Move Beyond the Concept of Schizophrenia. In M. Chung, K. W. Fulford, and G. Graham (eds.), *Reconceiving Schizophrenia*. Oxford: Oxford University Press, pp. 167–91.

Pollock, J. 1988. My Brother the Machine. *Noûs*, 22/2: 173–212.

Potter, M. 1976. Short-term Conceptual Memory for Pictures. *Journal of Experimental Psychology: Human Learning and Memory*, 2: 509–22.

Powell, T. 1990. *Kant's Theory of Self-Consciousness*. Oxford: Oxford University Press.

Preilowski, B. 1972. Possible Contribution of the Anterior Forebrain Commissures to Bilateral Motor Coordination. *Neuropsychologia*, 10: 267–77.

Priest, G. 1999. Perceiving Contradictions. *Australasian Journal of Philosophy*, 77/4: 439–46.

Prigatano, G. P. and Schachter, D. L. (eds.) 1991. *Awareness of Deficit after Brain Injury: Clinical and Theoretical Issues*. New York: Oxford University Press.

Prince, M. 1905/1978. *The Dissociation of a Personality*. New York: Oxford University Press.

——1907a. A Symposium on the Subconscious: Prefatory Note. *Journal of Abnormal Psychology*, 2: 22–5.

——1907b. A Symposium on the Subconscious. *Journal of Abnormal Psychology*, 2: 67–80.

Prince, W. F. 1915/16. The Doris Case of Multiple Personality. *Proceedings of the American Society for Psychical Research*, 9: 1–700; 10: 701–1419.

Prinz, J. 2004. *Gut Reactions: A Perceptual Theory of Emotion*. Oxford: Oxford University Press.

——2007. All Consciousness is Perceptual. In B. McLaughlin and J. Cohen (eds.), *Contemporary Debates in Philosophy of Mind*. Oxford: Blackwell, pp. 335–57.

——2011. The Sensory Basis of Cognitive Phenomenology. In T. Bayne and M. Montague (eds.), *Cognitive Phenomenology*. Oxford: Oxford University Press.

Prochazka, A., Clarac, F., Loeb, G. E., Rothwell, J. C., and Wolpaw, J. R. 2000. What do *Reflex* and *Voluntary* Mean? Modern Views on an Ancient Debate. *Experimental Brain Research*, 130: 417–32.

Puccetti, R. 1981. The Case for Mental Duality: Evidence from Split-Brain Data and Other Considerations. *Behavioral and Brain Sciences*, 4: 93–123.

Putnam, F. 1986. The Scientific Investigation of Multiple Personality Disorder. In J. M. Quen (ed.), *Split Minds/Split Brains: Historical and Current Perspectives*. New York: NYU Press, pp. 109–25.

Putnam, F. W., Guroff, J. J., Silberman, E. K., Barban, L., and Post, R. M. 1986. The Clinical Phenomenology of Multiple Personality Disorder: Review of 100 Recent Cases. *Journal of Clinical Psychiatry*, 47: 285–93.

Pylyshyn, Z., and Storm, R. 1988. Tracking Multiple Independent Targets: Evidence for a Parallel Tracking Mechanism. *Spatial Vision*, 3/3: 1–19.

Ramachandran, V. S. 1995. Anosognosia in Parietal Lobe Syndrome. *Consciousness and Cognition*, 4: 22–51.

——Cronin-Golomb, A., and Myers, J. J. 1986. Perception of Apparent Motion by Commissurotomy Patients. *Nature*, 320: 358–9.

——and Blakeslee, S. 1998. *Phantoms in the Brain: Probing the Mysteries of the Human Mind*. New York: William Morrow.

——and Hirstein, W. 1998. The Perception of Phantom Limbs. *Brain*, 121: 1603–30.

Rattenborg, N. C., Amlaner, C. J., Lima, S. L. 2001. Unilateral Closure and Interhemispheric EEG Asymmetry During Sleep in the Pigeon (Columba livia). *Brain, Behavior and Evolution*, 58/6: 323–32.

Raymont, P., and Brook, A. 2009. Unity of Consciousness. In B. McLaughlin, A. Beckermann, and S. Walter (eds.), *The Oxford Handbook of Philosophy of Mind*. Oxford: Clarendon Press, pp. 565–77.

Reason, J. T. 1979. Actions not as Planned: The Price of Automatization. In G. Underwood and R. Stevens (eds.), *Aspects of consciousness*, Vol. 1. *Psychological Issues*. New York: Academic Press, pp. 67–89.

Recanzone, G. H. 2003. Auditory Influences on Visual Temporal Rate Perception. *Journal of Neurophysiology*, 89: 1078–93.

Redlich, E., and Dorsey, J. F. 1945. Denial of Blindness by Patients with Cerebral Disease. *Archives of Neurology and Psychiatry*, 53: 407–17.

Rees, G. 2001. Neuroimaging of Visual Awareness in Patients and Normal Subjects. *Current Opinion in Neurobiology*, 11/2: 150–6.

——Wojciulik, E., Clarke, K., Husain, M., Frith, C., and Driver, J. 2002. Neural Correlates of Conscious and Unconscious Vision in Parietal Extinction. *Neurocase*, 8/5: 387–93.

Rensink, R., O'Regan, J. K., and Clark, J. J. 1997. To See or not to See: The Need for Attention to Perceive Changes in Scenes. *Psychological Science*, 8: 368–73.

Reuter-Lorenz, P. A. 2003. Parallel Processing in the Bisected Brain: Implications for Callosal Function. In E. Zaidel and M. Iacoboni (eds.), *The Parallel Brain: The Cognitive Neuroscience of the Corpus Callosum*. Cambridge, MA: MIT Press, pp. 341–53.

Revonsuo, A. 1999. Binding and the Phenomenal Unity of Consciousness. *Consciousness and Cognition*, 8: 173–85.

Reynolds, D., and Jeeves, M. A. 1977. Further Studies of Tactile Perception and Motor Coordination in Agenesis of the Corpus Callosum. *Cortex*, 13: 257–72.

Ribot, T. 1891. *The Diseases of Personality*. Chicago, IL: Open Court Publishing.

Ricci, R., and Chatterjee, A. 2004. Sensory and Response Contributions to Visual Awareness in Extinction. *Experimental Brain Research*, 157: 85–93.

Riddoch, M. J., and Humphreys, G. W. 1987. A Case of Integrative Visual Agnosia. *Brain*, 110: 1431–62.

Robertson, L. C. 2003. Binding, Spatial Attention, and Perceptual Awareness. *Nature Reviews Neuroscience*, 4/2: 93–102.

Robinson, D. 1985. Can Amoeba Divide without Multiplying? *Australasian Journal of Philosophy*, 63: 299–319.

Robinson, E. J., and Mitchell, P. 1995. Masking of Children's Early Understanding of the Representational Mind: Backwards Explanation Versus Prediction. *Child Development*, 66: 1022–39.

Robinson, W. S. 2005. Thoughts without Distinctive Non-Imagistic Phenomenology. *Philosophy and Phenomenological Research*, 70: 534–61.

Rock, I., and Victor, J. 1964. Vision and Touch: An Experimentally Created Conflict between the Two Senses. *Science*, 143: 594–6.

Rode, G., Charles, N., Perenin, M. T., Vighetto, A., Trillet, M., and Aimard, G. 1992. Partial Remission of Hemiplegia and Somatoparaphrenia Through Vestibular Stimulation in a Case of Unilateral Neglect. *Cortex*, 28: 203–8.

Roeflsema, P. R., Engel, A. K., Konig, P., and Singer, W. 1997. Visuomotor Integration is Associated with Zero Time-Lag Synchronization Among Cortical Areas. *Nature*, 385: 157–61.

Rolls, E. T. 2004. A Higher Order Syntactic Thought (HOST) Theory of Consciousness. In R. Gennaro (ed.), *Higher-Order Theories of Consciousness: An Anthology*, Amsterdam and Philadelphia, John Benjamins pp. 137–72.

——2008. Emotion, Higher Order Syntactic Thoughts and Consciousness. In L. Weiskrantz and M. Davies (eds.), *Frontiers of Consciousness*. Oxford: Oxford University Press, pp. 131–68.

Rosenthal, D. 2003. Unity of Consciousness and the Self. *Proceedings of the Aristotelian Society*, 103: 325–52.

Roser, M., and Gazzaniga, M. S. 2004. Automatic Brains-Interpretive Minds. *Current Directions in Psychological Science*, 13/2: 56–9.

Roskies, A. L. 1999. The Binding Problem. *Neuron*, 24: 7–9.

Ross, C. A., Miller, S. D., Reagor, P., Bjornson, L., Fraser, G. A., Anderson, G. 1990. Schneiderian Symptoms of Multiple Personality Disorder and Schizophrenia. *Comprehensive Psychiatry*, 31/2: 111–18.

Rousselet, G. A., Fabre-Thorpe, M. and Thorpe, S. J. 2002. Parallel Processing in High-Level Categorization of Natural Images, *Nature Neuroscience*, 5/7: 629–30.

Rovane, C. 1998. *The Bounds of Agency*. Princeton, NJ: Princeton University Press.

Rubens, A. B. 1985. Caloric Stimulation and Unilateral Visual Neglect. *Neurology*, 35: 1019–24.

Ruffman, T., Garnham, W., Import, A., and Connolly, D. 2001. Does Eye Gaze Indicate Implicit Knowledge of False Belief? Charting Transition in Knowledge. *Journal of Experimental Child Psychology*, 80: 201–24.

Sarri, M., Blakenberg, F., and Driver, J. 2006. Neural Correlates of Crossmodal Visual-tactile Extinction and of Tactile Awareness Revealed by fMRI in a Right-Hemisphere Stroke Patient. *Neuropsychologia*, 44: 2398–410.

Saul, R., and Sperry, R. W. 1968. Absence of Commissurotomy Symptoms with Callosal Agenesis of the Corpus Callosum. *Neurology*, 18: 307.

Sauvé, K. 1999. Gamma-band Synchronous Oscillations: Recent Evidence Regarding their Functional Significance. *Consciousness and Cognition*, 8/2: 213–24.

Schacter, D. L., McAndrews, M. P., Moscovitch, M. 1988. Access to Consciousness: Dissociations between Implicit and Explicit Knowledge in Neuropsychological Syndromes. In L. Weiskrantz (ed.), *Thought Without Language*. Oxford: Clarendon Press, pp. 242–78.

Schechter, E. 2010. Individuating Mental Tokens: The Split-Brain Case. *Philosophia*, 38: 195–216.

Schenk, T., and McIntosh, R. D. 2010. Do we have Independent Visual Streams for Perception and Action? *Cognitive Neuroscience*, 1: 52–78.

Schiff, N. D. 2004. The Neurology of Impaired Consciousness: Challenges for Cognitive Neuroscience. In M. S. Gazzaniga (ed.) *The Cognitive Neurosciences* (3rd edn.). Cambridge, MA: MIT Press, pp. 1121–32.

Schiffer, F., Zaidel, E., Bogen, J., and Chasan-Taber, S. 1998. Different Psychological Status in the Two Hemispheres of Two Split-Brain Patients. *Neuropsychiatry, Neuropsychology, and Behavioral Neurology*, 11: 151–6.

Schilder, P. 1953. *Medical Psychology*. New York: John Wiley and Sons.

Schiller, P. H. and Smith, M. C. 1966. Detection in Metacontrast. *Journal of Experimental Psychology*, 71: 32–9.

Schlaghecken, F., and Eimer, M. 1997. The Influence of Subliminally Presented Primes on Response Preparation. *Sprache und Kognition*, 16: 166–75.

Schnakers, C., Perrin, F., Schabus, M., Majerus, S., Ledoux, D., Damas, P., Boly, M., Vanhaudenhuyse, A., Bruno, M.-A., Moonen, G., and Laureys, S. 2008. Voluntary Brain Processing in Disorders of Consciousness. *Neurology*, 71: 1614–20.

Schooler, J. W. 2002. Re-representing Consciousness: Dissociations between Experience and Meta-consciousness. *Trends in Cognitive Sciences*, 6/8: 339–44.

——and Fiore, S. M. 1997. Consciousness and the Limits of Language: You Can't Always Say What You Think of Think What You Say. In J. D. Cohen and J. W. Schooler (eds.), *Scientific Approaches to Consciousness*. Hillsdale, NJ: Lawrence Erlbaum, pp. 241–57.

Schroeder, C. E., and Foxe, J. 2005. Multisensory Contributions to Low-level, 'Unisensory' Processing. *Current Opinion in Neurobiology*, 15: 454–8.

Schumacher, E. H., Seymour, T. L., Glass, J. M., Fencsik, D. E., Lauber, E. J., Kieras, D. E., and Meyer, D. E. 2001. Virtually Perfect Time Sharing in Dual Task Performance: Uncorking the Central Cognitive Bottleneck. *Psychological Science*, 12: 101–8.

——, Elston, P. A., and D'Esposito, M. 2003. Neural Evidence for Representation-specific Response Selection. *Journal of Cognitive Neuroscience*, 15: 1111–21.

Schwitzgebel, E. 2007. Do you have Constant Tactile Experience of your Feet in your Shoes? Or is Experience Limited to What's in Attention? *Journal of Consciousness Studies*, 14/3: 5–35.

——2008. The Unreliability of Naïve Introspection. *Philosophical Review*, 117: 245–73.

Searle, J. 1983. *Intentionality*. Cambridge: Cambridge University Press.

——1992. *The Rediscovery of the Mind*. Cambridge, MA: MIT Press.

——2000. Consciousness. *Annual Review of Neuroscience*, 23: 557–78.

Sears, C. R., and Pylyshyn, Z. 2000. Multiple Object Tracking and Attentional Processing. *Canadian Journal of Psychology*, 54/1: 1–14.

Sellal, F., Renaseau-Leclerc, C., and Labreceque, R. 1996. L'Hommme a Six Bras. *Revue Neurologique*, 152: 190–5.

Senkowski, D., Talsma, D., Hermann C. S., and Woldorff, M. H. 2005. Multisensory Processing and Oscillatory Gamma Responses: Effects of Spatial Selective Attention. *Experimental Brain Research*, 166: 411–26.

Seymour, S. E., Reuter-Lorenz, P. A., and Gazzaniga, M. S. 1994. The Disconnection Syndrome: Basic Findings Reaffirmed. *Brain*, 117: 105–15.

Shadlen, M. N., and Movshon, J. A. 1999. Synchrony Unbound: a Critical Evaluation of the Temporal Binding Hypothesis. *Neuron*, 24: 67–77.

Shams, L., Kamitani, Y., and Shimojo, S. 2000. What You See is What You Hear. *Nature*, 408: 788.

Sheinberg, D. L., and Logothetis, N. K. 1997. The Role of Temporal Cortical Areas in Perceptual Organization. *Proceedings of the National Academy of Sciences USA*, 94: 3408–13.

Shepard, R. N. 1964. Circularity in Judgements of Relative Pitch. *The Journal of the Acoustical Society of America*, 36/12: 2346–53.

Shimojo, S., and Shams, L. 2001. Sensory Modalities are not Separate Modalities: Plasticity and Interactions. *Current Opinion in Neurobiology*, 11: 505–9.

Shoemaker, S. 1970. Persons and Their Pasts. *American Philosophical Quarterly*, 7: 269–85

——1984. Personal Identity: A Materialist's Account. In S. Shoemaker and R. Swinburne, *Personal Identity*. Oxford: Basil Blackwell, pp. 67–132.

——1996. Unity of Consciousness and Consciousness of Unity. In *The First-Person Perspective and Other Essays*. Cambridge: Cambridge University Press, pp. 176–97.

——2003. Consciousness and Co-consciousness. In A. Cleeremans (ed.), *The Unity of Consciousness: Binding, Integration and Dissociation*. Oxford: Oxford University Press, pp. 59–71.

Shorvon, H. J. 1946. The Depersonalization Syndrome. *Proceedings of the Royal Society of Medicine*, 39: 779–92.

Sidelle, A. 2002. Some Episodes in the Sameness of Consciousness. *Philosophical Topics*, 30/1: 269–93.

Sidtis, J. J. 1986. Can Neurological Disconnection Account for Psychiatric Dissociation? In J. M. Quen (ed.), *Split Minds/Split Brains: Historical and Current Perspectives*. New York: New York University Press, pp. 127–48.

Sierra, M., and Berrios, G. E. 1997. Depersonalization: A Conceptual History. *History of Psychiatry*, 8: 213–29.

————2001. The Phenomenological Stability of Depersonalization: Comparing the Old With the New. *The Journal of Nervous and Mental Diseases*, 189/9: 629–36.

Siewert, C. 1998. *The Significance of Consciousness*. Princeton, NJ: Princeton University Press.

——2001. Self-knowledge and Phenomenal Unity. *Noûs*, 35/4: 542–68.

Silberpfennig, J. 1949. Contributions to the Problem of Eye Movements: III. Disturbances of Ocular Movements with Pseudo Hemianopsia in Frontal Tumors. *Confinia Neurologica*, 4: 1–13.

Silberman, E. K., Putnam, F. W., Weingartner, H., Braun, B. G., Post, R. M. 1985. Dissociative States in Multiple Personality Disorder. *Psychiatry Research*, 15: 253–60.

Simons, D. J., and Levin, D. T. 1997. Change Blindness. *Trends in Cognitive Sciences*, 1: 261–7.

——, Chabris, C. F., Schnur, T. 2002. Evidence for Preserved Representations of Change Blindness. *Consciousness and Cognition*, 11/1: 78–97.

Singer, W. 2009. Consciousness and Neuronal Synchronization. In S. Laureys and G. Tononi (eds.). *The Neurology of Consciousness*. Amsterdam: Elsevier, pp. 43–52.

——and Gray, C. M. 1995. Visual Feature Integration and the Temporal Correlation Hypothesis. *Annual Review of Neuroscience*, 18: 555–86.

Sinnett, S., Soto-Faraco, S., and Spence, C. 2008. The Co-occurrence of Multisensory Competition and Facilitation. *Acta Psychologica*, 128: 153–61.

Slachevsky, A., Pillon, B., Fourneret, P., Pradat-Diehl, P., Jeannerod, M., and Dubois, B. 2001. Preserved Adjustment but Impaired Awareness in a Sensory-motor Conflict Following Prefrontal Lesions. *Journal of Cognitive Neuroscience*, 13: 332–40.

Smania, N., Martini, M. C., Prior, M., Marzi, C. 1996. Input and Response Determinants of Visual Extinction: A Case Study. *Cortex*, 32: 567–91.

Smeets, J., and Brenner, E. 2001. Action Beyond our Grasp. *Trends in Cognitive Sciences*, 5/7: 287.

————2008. Why we Don't Mind to be Inconsistent. In P. Calvo and T. Gomila (eds.), *Handbook of Cognitive Science: An Embodied Approach*. Amsterdam: Elsevier, pp. 207–17.

Smid, H. G. O. M., Mulder, G., Mulder, L. J. M. 1990. Selective Response Activation can begin before Stimulus Recognition is Complete: A Psychophysiological and Error Analysis of Continuous Flow. *Acta Psychologica*, 74: 169–201.

Snowdon, P. 1990. Persons, Animals and Ourselves. In C. Gill (ed.), *The Person and the Human Mind*. Oxford: Clarendon Press, pp. 83–107.

——1995. Persons, Animals, and Bodies. In J. L. Bermúdez, A. Marcel, and N. Eilan (eds.), *The Body and the Self*. Cambridge, MA: MIT Press, pp. 71–86.

Sober, E. 2000. Evolution and the Problem of Other Minds. *Journal of Philosophy*, 97: 365–87.

Sorensen, R. 1996. Modal Bloopers: Why Believable Impossibilities are Necessary. *American Philosophical Quarterly*, 33/1: 247–61.

Soto-Faraco, S., Spence, C., and Kingstone, A. 2004. Cross Modal Dynamic Capture: Congruency Effects in the Perception of Motion Across Sensory Modalities. *Journal of Experimental Psychology: Human Perception and Performance*, 30: 330–45.

Southgate, V., Senju, A., and Csibra, G. 2007. Action Anticipation Through Attribution of False Belief by 2-year-olds. *Psychological Science*, 18/7: 587–92.

Spanos, N. P. 1983. The Hidden Observer as an Experimental Creation. *Journal of Personality and Social Psychology*, 44/1: 170–6.

——and Barber, T. X. 1972. Cognitive Activity During 'Hypnotic' Suggestibility: Goal-directed Fantasy and the Experience of Nonvolition. *Journal of Personality*, 40: 510–24.

Spanos, N. P., and Hewitt, E. C. 1980. The Hidden Observer in Hypnotic Analgesia: Discovery or Experimental Creation? *Journal of Personality and Social Psychology*, 39: 1201–14.

——Gwynn, M. I., and Stam, H. J. 1983. Instructional Demands and Ratings of Overt and Hidden Pain During Hypnotic Analgesia. *Journal of Abnormal Psychology*, 92: 479–88.

——Radtke, H. L., and Bertrand, L. D. 1985. Hypnotic Amnesia as a Strategic Enactment: Breaching Amnesia in Highly Susceptible Subjects. *Journal of Personality and Social Psychology*, 47/5: 1155–69.

Spence, C. 2008. Cognitive Neuroscience: Searching for the Bottleneck in the Brain. *Current Biology*, 18: R965–R968.

——2009. Explaining the Colavita Visual Dominance Effect. *Progress in Brain Research*, 176: 245–58.

——and Driver, J. 2004. *Crossmodal Space and Crossmodal Attention*. Oxford: Oxford University Press.

——and Squire, S. 2003. Multisensory Integration: Maintaining the Perception of Synchrony. *Current Biology*, 13: R519–R521.

——Parise, C., and Chen, Y-C. (Forthcoming). The Colavita Visual Dominance Effect, In M. Murray and M. Wallace (eds.), *Frontiers in the Neural Bases of Multisensory Processes*.

——Pavani, F., and Driver, J. 1998. What Crossing the Hands can Reveal about Visuotactile Links in Spatial Attention. *Abstracts of the Psychonomic Society*, 3: 13.

—— ——, Maravita, A., and Holmes, N. P. 2008. Multi-sensory Interactions. In M. C. Lin and M. A. Otaduy (eds.), *Haptic Rendering: Foundations, Algorithms, and Applications*. Wellesley, MA: AK Reters, pp. 21–52.

Spencer, S. S., Gates, J. R., Reeves, A. R., Spencer, D. D., Maxwell, R. E., and Roberts, D. 1987. Corpus Callosum Section. In J. Engel, Jr (ed.), *Surgical Treatment of the Epilepsies*. New York: Arven Press, pp. 425–44.

——, Spencer, D. D., Williamson, P. D., Sass, K. J., Novelly, R. A., and Mattson, R. H. 1988. Corpus Callosotomy for Epilepsy, II. Neuropsychological Outcome. *Neurology*, 38: 24–8.

Sperling, G. 1960. The Information Available in Brief Visual Presentations. *Psychological Monographs*, 74/11.

Sperry, R. W. 1974. Lateral Specialization in the Surgically Separated Hemispheres. In F. O. Schmitt and F. G. Worden (eds.), *Neuroscience, 3rd Study Programme*. Cambridge, MA: MIT Press, pp. 5–19.

——1976. Mental Phenomena as Causal Determinants in Brain Function. In G. Globus, G. Maxwell, and I. Savodnik (eds.), *Consciousness and the Brain: A Scientific and Philosophical Inquiry*. New York: Plenum Press, pp. 163–77.

——1977. Forebrain Commissurotomy and Conscious Awareness. *The Journal of Medicine and Philosophy*, 2/2: 101–26.

Sperry, R. W. 1984. Consciousness, Personal Identity, and the Divided Brain. *Neuropsychologia*, 22/6: 661–73.

——, Zaidel, E., and Zaidel, D. 1979. Self-recognition and Social Awareness in the Deconnected Minor Hemisphere. *Neuropsychologia*, 17: 153–66.

Stalnaker, R. 1984. *Inquiry*. Cambridge, MA: MIT Press.

Stein, B. E., and Meredith M. A. 1993. *The Merging of the Senses*. Cambridge, MA: MIT Press.

——, Stanford, T. R., Ramachandran, R., Perrault, T. J. Jr., Rowland, B. A. 2009. Challenges in Quantifying Multisensory Integration: Alternative Criteria, Models, and Inverse Effectiveness. *Experimental Brain Research*, 198: 113–26.

Steinberg, M., Cicchetti, D., Buchanan, J., Rakfeldt, J., Rounsaville, B. 1994. Distinguishing between Multiple Personality Disorder (Dissociative Identity Disorder) and Schizophrenia using the Structured Clinical Interview for DSM-IV Dissociative Disorders. *Journal of Nervous and Mental Diseases*, 182/9: 495–502.

Stephens, G. L., and Graham, G. 2000. *When Self-Consciousness Breaks*. Cambridge, MA: MIT Press.

————2007. Philosophical Psychopathology and Self-consciousness. In M. Velmans and S. Schneider (eds.), *The Blackwell Companion to Consciousness*. Oxford: Blackwell, pp. 194–208.

Strawson, G. 1994. *Mental Reality*. Cambridge, MA: MIT Press.

——1997. The 'Self'. *Journal of Consciousness Studies*, 4/5–6: 405–28.

Stoljar, D. 2004. The Argument from Diaphanousness. In M. Ezcurdia, R. Stainton, and C. Viger (eds) *New Essays in the Philosophy of Language and Mind*, suppl. vol. of the *Canadian Journal of Philosophy*. Calgary: University of Calgary Press, pp. 341–90.

——2007. The Consequences of Intentionalism. *Erkenntnis*, 66: 247–70.

Sugita, Y., and Suzuki, Y. 2003. Audiovisual Perception: Implicit Estimation of Sound-arrival Time. *Nature*, 421: 911.

Surian, L., Caldi, S., and Sperber, D. 2007. Attribution of Beliefs by 13-month Old Infants. *Psychological Science*, 18/7: 580–6.

Swartz, B. E., and Brust, J. C. M. 1984. Anton's Syndrome Accompanying Withdrawal Hallucinosis in a Blind Alcoholic. *Neurology*, 34: 969–73.

Taylor, J. G. 1962. *The Behavioural Basis of Perception*. New Haven, CT: Yale University Press.

Taylor, J. L., and McCloskey, D. I. 1990. Triggering of Preprogrammed Movements as Reactions to Masked Stimuli. *Journal of Neurophysiology*, 63/3: 439–46.

————1996. Selection of Motor Responses on the Basis of Unperceived Stimuli. *Experimental Brain Research*, 110: 62–6.

Tegnér, R., and Levander, B. 1991. Through a Looking Glass: A New Technique to Demonstrate Directional Hypokinesia in Unilateral Neglect. *Brain*, 114/4: 1943–51.

Teng, E. L., and Sperry, R. W. 1973. Interhemispheric Interaction During Simultaneous Bilateral Presentation of Letters or Digits in Commissurotomized Patients. *Neuropsychologia*, 11: 131–40.

———— 1974. Interhemispheric Rivalry During Simultaneous Bilateral Task Presentation in Commissurotomized Patients. *Cortex*, 10: 111–20.

Théoret, H., Kobayashi, M., Ganis, G., Di Capua, P., and Pascual-Leone, A. 2002. Repetitive Transcranial Magnetic Stimulation of Human Area MT/V5 Disrupts Perception and Storage of the Motion Aftereffect. *Neuropsychologia*, 40: 2280–7.

Thigpen, C. H., and Cleckley, H. 1954. A Case of Multiple Personality. *Journal of Abnormal and Social Psychology*, 49: 135–51.

Thompson, B. 2009. Senses for Senses. *The Australasian Journal of Philosophy*, 87/1: 99–117.

Thompson, E. 2008. Representationalism and the Phenomenology of Mental Imagery. *Synthese*, 160: 397–415.

Tong, F., Nakayama, K., Vaughan, J. T., and Kanwisher, N. 1998. Binocular Rivalry and Visual Awareness in Human Extrastriate Cortex. *Neuron*, 21: 753–9.

Tononi, G. 2004. An Information Integration Theory of Consciousness. *BMC Neuroscience*, 5: 42.

——2007. The information Integration Theory of Consciousness. In M. Velmans and S. Schneider (eds.), *The Blackwell Companion to Consciousness*. Oxford: Blackwell, pp. 287–99.

——and Edelman, G. M. 1998. Consciousness and Complexity. *Science*, 282/5395: 1846–51.

Tootell, R. B., Reppas, J. B., Dale, A. M., Look, R. B., Sereno, M. A., Malach, R., Brady, T. J., and Rosen, B. R. 1995. Visual Motion Aftereffect in Human Cortical Area MT Revealed by Functional Magnetic Resonance Imaging. *Nature*, 375: 139–41.

————, Kwong, K. K., Malach, R., Brady, T. J., Rosen, B. R., and Belliveau, J. 1995. Functional Analysis of Human MT/V5 and Related Visual Cortical Areas using Magnetic Resonance Imaging. *Journal of Neuroscience*, 15/4: 3215–30.

Treisman A. 1996. The Binding Problem. *Current Opinion in Neurobiology*, 6: 171–8.

——2003. Consciousness and Perceptual Binding. In A. Cleeremans (ed.), *The Unity of Consciousness: Binding, Integration and Dissociation*. Oxford: Oxford University Press, pp. 95–113.

Trevarthen, C. 1970. Experimental Evidence for a Brainstem Contribution to Visual Perception in Man. *Brain Behavior and Evolution*, 3: 338–52.

——1974a. Analysis of Cerebral Activities that Generate and Regulate Consciousness in Commissurotomy Patients. In S. J. Diamond and J. Graham (eds.), *Hemisphere Function in the Human Brain*. London: Elek Science, pp. 235–63.

——1974b. Functional Relations of Disconnected Hemispheres with the Brain Stem, and with Each Other: Monkey and Man. In M. Kinsbourne and W. L. Smith (eds.), *Hemispheric Disconnection and Cerebral Function*. Springfield, IL: Charles C. Thomas, pp. 187–207.

——and Sperry, R. W. 1973. Perceptual Unity of the Ambient Visual Field in Human Commissurotomy Patients. *Brain*, 96: 547–70.

Tuller, B., and Kelso, J. A. S. 1989. Environmentally-specified Patterns of Movement Coordination in Normal and Split-brain Patients. *Experimental Brain Research*, 75: 306–16.

Tye, M. 1995. *Ten Problems of Consciousness*. Cambridge, MA: MIT Press.

——2003. *Consciousness and Persons*. Cambridge, MA: MIT Press.

——2009. A New Look at the Speckled Hen. *Analysis*, 69/2: 258–63.

Tye, M. and Wright, B. 2011. Is there a Phenomenology of Thought? In. T. Bayne and M. Montague (eds.) *Cognitive Phenomenology*, Oxford: Oxford University Press.

Vallar, G., Sterzi, R., Bottini, G., Cappa, S., and Rucsoni, M. L. 1990. Temporary Remission of Left Hemianesthesia after Vestibular Stimulation: A Sensory Neglect Phenomenon. *Cortex*, 26: 123–31.

Vallar, G., Rusconi, M. K., and Bisiach, E. 1994. Awareness of Contralesional Information in Unilateral Neglect: Effects of Verbal Cueing, Tracing, and Vestibular Stimulation. In M. Moscovitch and C. Umiltà (eds.), *Attention and Performance*, XV. Cambridge, MA: MIT Press, pp. 377–91.

van Cleve, J. 1983. Conceivability and the Cartesian Argument for Dualism. *Pacific Philosophical Quarterly*, 64: 35–45.

——1999. *Problems from Kant*. New York: Oxford University Press.

van Gulick, R. 1994. Deficit Studies and the Function of Phenomenal Consciousness. In G. Graham and G. L. Stephens (eds.), *Philosophical Psychopathology*. Cambridge, MA: MIT Press, pp. 25–50.

——2004. Higher-Order Global States (HOGS): An Alternative Higher-order Model of Consciousness. In R. J. Gennaro (ed.), *Higher-Order Theories of Consciousness: An Anthology*. Amsterdam and Philadelphia: John Benjamins, pp. 67–92.

van Inwagen, P. 1990. *Material Beings*. Ithaca, NY: Cornell University Press.

Velleman, J. D. 2006. The Self as Narrator. In *Self to Self*. Cambridge: Cambridge University Press, pp. 203–23.

Venneri, A., and Shanks, M. F. 2004. Belief and Awareness: Reflections on a Case of Persistent Anosognosia. *Neuropsychologia*, 42: 230–8.

von der Malsburg 1995. Binding in Models of Perception and Brain Function. *Current Opinion in Neurobiology*, 5: 520–6.

Vuilleumier, P. 2000. Anosognosia. In J. Bogousslavsky and J. L. Cummings (eds.), *Behavior and Mood Disorders in Focal Brain Lesions*. Cambridge, Cambridge University Press, pp. 465–519.

——2004. Anosognosia: The Neurology of Beliefs and Uncertainties. *Cortex*, 40: 9–17.

——Reverdin, A., and Landis, T. 1997. Illusory Reduplication of the Lower Limbs after Bilateral Parietal Lobe Damage. *Archives of Neurology*, 54: 1543–7.

——and Rafal, R. D. 2004. A Systematic Study of Visual Extinction: Between- and within-field Deficits of Attention in Hemispatial Neglect. *Brain*, 123: 1263–79.

Wade, N. 2009. Beyond Body Experiences: Phantom Limbs, Pain and the Locus of Sensation, *Cortex*, 45: 243–55.

Warrington, E. K. 1986. Visual Deficits Associated with Occipital Lobe Lesions in Man. *Experimental Brain Research Supplement*, 11: 247–61.

Watkins, S., Shams, L., Tanaka, S., Haynes, J. D., and Rees, G. 2006. Sound Alters Activity in Human V1 in Association will Illusory Visual Perception. *Neuroimage*, 31: 1247–56.

Weinstein, E. A., and Kahn, R. L. 1950. The Syndrome of Anosognosia. *Archives of Neurology and Psychiatry*, 64: 772–91.

——— 1955. *Denial of illness: Symbolic and physiological aspects*. Springfield, IL: Thomas.

Weiskrantz, L. 2009. *Blindsight* (2nd edn.). Oxford: Oxford University Press.

—— 1997. *Consciousness Lost and Found*. Oxford: Oxford University Press.

—— Warrington, E. L., Saunders, M. D., and Marshall J. 1974. Visual Capacity in the Heminopic Field Following a Restricted Occipital Ablation. *Brain*, 97: 709–28.

Weisstein, N., and Wong, E. 1986. Figure-ground Organization and the Spatial and Temporal Responses of the Visual System. In E. G. Schwab and H. C. Nusbaum (eds.), *Pattern Recognition by Humans and Machines*, 2. *Visual Perception*. New York: Academic Press, pp. 31–64.

Wellman, H. M., Cross, D., and Bartsch, K. 1986. Infant Search and Object Permanence: A Meta-analysis of the A-not-B Error. *Monographs of the Society for Research in Child Development*, 51: 1–51, 62–7.

——— and Watson, J. 2001. Meta-analysis of Theory-of-mind Development: The Truth About False Belief. *Child Development*, 72: 655–84.

Werner-Reiss, U., Kelly, K. A., Trause, A. S., Underhill, A. M., and Groh, J. M. 2003. Eye Position Affects Activity in Primary Auditory Cortex in Primates. *Current Biology*, 13: 554–62.

White, N. S., and Alkire, M. T. 2003. Impaired Thalamortical Connectivity in Humans During General-anesthetic-induced Unconsciousness. *Neuroimage*, 19: 402–11.

White, S. 1987. What is it Like to be a Homunculus? *Pacific Philosophical Quarterly*, 68: 148–74.

Wilkes, K. 1988. *Real People*. Oxford: Clarendon.

Williams, B. 1970. The Self and the Future. *The Philosophical Review*, 79: 161–80.

Wilson, D. H., Reeves, A. G., Gazzaniga, M. S., and Culver, C. 1977. Cerebral Commissurotomy for Control of Intractable Seizures. *Neurology*, 27: 708–15.

—— 1982. Central Commissurotomy for Intractable Generalized Epilepsy, Series Two. *Neurology*, 32: 687–97.

Wimmer, H., and Perner, J. 1983. Beliefs about Beliefs: Representation and Constraining Function of Wrong Beliefs in Young Children's Understanding of Deception. *Cognition*, 13: 103–28.

Wittgenstein, L. 1965. *The Blue and Brown Books*. New York: Harper.

Wolford, G., Miller, M. B., and Gazzaniga, M. S. 2004. Split Decisions. In M. S. Gazzaniga (ed.), *The Cognitive Neurosciences III*. Cambridge, MA: MIT Press, pp. 1189–2000.

Yantis, S. 1992. Multielement Visual Tracking: Attention and Perceptual Organization. *Cognitive Psychology*, 24: 419–33.

Young, A., and Leafhead, K. M. 1996. Betwixt Life and Death: Case Studies of the Cotard Delusion. In P. Halligan and J. Marshall (eds.), *Method in Madness: Case Studies in Cognitive Neuropsychiatry*. Hove, E. Sussex: Psychology Press, pp. 147–71.

Zaidel, D. 1994. A View of the World from a Split-brain Perspective. In E. M. R. Critchley (ed.), *The Neurological Boundaries of Reality*. London: Farrand Press, pp. 161–74.

Zaidel, E. 1995. Interhemispheric Transfer in The Split-brain: Long-term Status Following Complete Cerebral Commissurotomy. In R. J. Davidson and K. Hugdahl (eds.), *Brain Asymmetry*. Cambridge, MA: MIT Press, pp. 491–532.

——and Sperry, R. W. 1973. Performance on the Raven's Colored Progressive Matrices Test by Subjects with Cerebral Commisurotomy. *Cortex*, 9: 34–9.

————1977. Some Long-term Motor Effects of Cerebral Commissurotomy in Man. *Neuropsychologia*, 15: 193–204.

——Zaidel, D. W., and Bogen, J. E. 1990. Testing the Commissurotomy Patient. In A. A. Boulton, G. B. Baker, and M. Hiscock (eds.), *Neuromethods*, 17. *Neuropsychology*. Clifton, NJ: Humana Press, pp. 147–201.

——and Iacoboni, M. 2003. Sensorimotor Integration in the Split Brain. In E. Zaidel and M. Iacoboni (eds.), *The Parallel Brain*. Cambridge, MA: MIT Press, pp. 319–36.

——Iacoboni, M., Zaidel, D. W., Bogen, J. E. 2003. The Callosal Syndromes. In K. H. Heilman and E. Valenstein (eds.), *Clinical Neuropsychology* (4th edn.) Oxford: Oxford University Press, pp. 347–403.

Zamansky, H. S. and Ruehle, B. L. 1995. Making Hypnosis Happen: The Involuntariness of the Hypnotic Experience. *International Journal of Clinical and Experimental Hypnosis*, 43: 386–98.

Zapparoli, G. C., and Reatto, L. L. 1969. The Apparent Movement between Visual and Acoustic Stimulus and the Problem of Intermodal Relations. *Acta Psychologica*, 29: 256–67.

Zeki, S. 2001. Localization and Globalization in Conscious Vision. *Annual Review of Neuroscience*, 24: 57–86.

——and Bartels, A. 1998a. The Asynchrony of Consciousness. *Proceedings of the Royal Society of London B*, 265: 1583–5.

————1998b. The Autonomy of the Visual Systems and the Modularity of Conscious Vision. *Philosophical Transactions of the Royal Society of London B*, 353: 1911–14.

————1999. Towards a Theory of Visual Consciousness. *Consciousness and Cognition*, 8: 225–59.

Zelazo, P. D., Frye, D., and Rapus, T. 1996. An Age-related Dissociation between Knowing Rules and Using Them. *Cognitive Development*, 11: 37–63.

——and Reznick, J. 1991. Age-related Asynchrony of Knowledge and Action. *Child Development*, 62: 719–35.

Zemach, E. 1986. Unconscious Mind or Conscious Minds? In P. French, T. Uehling, and W. Wettstein (eds.), *Studies in the Philosophy of Mind: Midwest Studies in Philosophy 10*. Minneapolis: University of Minnesota Press, pp. 101–20.

——1987. Looking out for Number One. *Philosophy and Phenomenological Research*, 98/ 2: 209–33.

Zeman, A. 2002. The Persistent Vegetative State: Conscious of Nothing? *Practical Neurology*, 2: 214–17.

Zihl, J., and von Cramon, D. 1980. Registration of Light Stimuli in the Cortically Blind Hemifield and its Effect on Localization. *Behavioural Brain Research*, 1: 287–98.

—— ——and Mai, N. 1983. Selective Disturbance of Movement Vision After Bilateral Brain Damage. *Brain*, 106: 313–40.

Index